GPU Pro³

GPU Pro³

Advanced Rendering Techniques

Edited by Wolfgang Engel

CRC Press
Taylor & Francis Group
Boca Raton London New York

CRC Press is an imprint of the
Taylor & Francis Group, an **informa** business

AN A K PETERS BOOK

Cover images courtesy of Crytek GmbH.

CRC Press
Taylor & Francis Group
6000 Broken Sound Parkway NW, Suite 300
Boca Raton, FL 33487-2742

First issued in hardback 2019

ISBN-13: 978-1-4398-8782-0 (hbk)

Library of Congress Cataloging-in-Publication Data

GPU Pro 3 : advanced rendering techniques / edited by Wolfgang Engel.
   p. cm.
   Summary: "This book explores the latest developments in advanced rendering techniques in interactive media and games that run on the DirectX or OpenGL run-times or any other run-time with any language available. It covers geometry manipulation, handheld devices programming, effects in image space, shadows, 3D engine design, and environmental effects. A dedicated section on general purpose GPU programming focuses on CUDA, DirectCompute, and OpenCL examples. The book also provides tips on how to render real-time special effects and visualize data on common consumer software platforms"-- Provided by publisher.
   Includes bibliographical references.
   ISBN 978-1-4398-8782-0 (hardback)
   1. Rendering (Computer graphics) 2. Graphics processing units--Programming. 3. Computer graphics. 4. Real-time data processing. I. Engel, Wolfgang F.

T385.G6886 2011
006.6'8--dc23

2011043868

Visit the Taylor & Francis Web site at
http://www.taylorandfrancis.com

and the CRC Press Web site at
http://www.crcpress.com

Contents

VI   GPGPU   321
Sebastien St-Laurent, editor

Acknowledgments

The *GPU Pro: Advanced Rendering Techniques* book series covers ready-to-use ideas and procedures that can solve many of your daily graphics-programming challenges.

The third book in the series wouldn't have been possible without the help of many people. First, I would like to thank the section editors for the fantastic job they did. The work of Wessam Bahnassi, Sebastien St-Laurent, Carsten Dachsbacher, and Christopher Oat ensured that the quality of the series meets the expectations of our readers.

The great cover screenshots have been provided courtesy of Crytek, GmbH. You can find the article on CryENGINE 3 on page 133.

The team at A K Peters made the whole project happen. I want to thank Alice and Klaus Peters, Sarah Chow, and the entire production team, who took the articles and made them into a book. Special thanks go out to our families and friends, who spent many evenings and weekends without us during the long book production cycle.

I hope you have as much fun reading the book as we had creating it.

—Wolfgang Engel

P.S. Plans for an upcoming *GPU Pro 4* are already in progress. Any comments, proposals, and suggestions are highly welcome (wolfgang.engel@gmail.com).

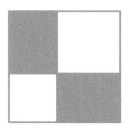

Web Materials

Example programs and source code to accompany some of the chapters are available at http://www.akpeters.com/gpupro. The directory structure closely follows the book structure by using the chapter number as the name of the subdirectory. You will need to download the DirectX August 2009 SDK or the DirectX June 2010 SDK.

General System Requirements

To use all of the files, you will need:

- The DirectX August 2009 SDK

- OpenGL 1.5-compatible graphics card

- A DirectX 9.0 or 10-compatible graphics card

- Windows XP with the latest service pack; some require VISTA or Windows 7

- Visual C++ .NET 2008

- 2048 MB RAM

- The latest graphics card drivers

Updates

Updates of the example programs will be periodically posted.

Comments and Suggestions

Please send any comments or suggestions to wolf@shaderx.com.

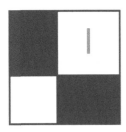

Geometry Manipulation

This part on geometry manipulation focuses on the ability of graphics processing units (GPUs) to process and generate geometry in exciting ways.

The first chapter in this section, "Vertex Shader Tessellation" by Holger Gruen presents a method to implement tessellation using only the vertex shader. It requires DirectX 10 and above to work. This method does not require any data in addition to the already available vertex data, in contrast to older techniques that were called "Instanced Tessellation." It relies solely on the delivery of `SV_VertexID` and uses the original vertex and index buffers as input shader resources.

The next chapter, "Real-Time Deformable Terrain Rendering with DirectX 11" by Egor Yusov, describes a high-quality real-time terrain visualization of large data sets, which dynamically controls the triangulation complexity. This terrain system combines efficient compression schemes for the height map with the GPU-accelerated triangulation construction, while at the same time supports dynamic modifications.

In "Optimized Stadium Crowd Rendering," Alan Chambers describes in detail the design and methods used to reproduce a 80,000-seat stadium. This method was used in the game *Rugby Challenge* on XBOX 360, PS3, and PC. Chambers reveals several tricks used to achieve colored "writing" in the stands, ambient occlusion that darkens the upper echelons, and variable crowd density that can be controlled live in-game.

The last article in the section, "Geometric Antialiasing Methods" is about replacing hardware multisample antialiasing (MSAA) with a software method that works in the postprocessing pipeline, which has been very popular since a multisample antialiasing (MLAA) solution on the GPU was presented in *GPU Pro*[2]. Persson discusses two antialiasing methods that are driven by additional geometric data generated in the geometry shader or stored upfront in a dedicated geometry buffer that might be part of the G-Buffer.

—Wolfgang Engel

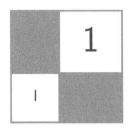

Vertex Shader Tessellation

Holger Gruen

1.1 Overview

This chapter presents a method to implement tessellation using vertex shaders only. It only works on DX10 class hardware and above. The technique itself doesn't need any data in addition to the already available vertex data in contrast to instanced tessellation techniques like those given in [Gruen 05, Tatarinov 08]. It solely relies on the delivery of `SV_VertexID` and the usage of the original vertex and index buffers as input shader resources to the vertex shader that performs the tessellation. Furthering the work in [Gruen 05, Tatarinov 08], we present here a way to support edge-based fractional tessellation.

This method not only enables a new tessellation technique on DX10 class hardware, but it also can be used in combination with the DX11 tessellation pipeline to reach overall tessellation factors that are higher than 64. This is important as often triangles in typical game scenes are too large to apply techniques like tessellated displacement mapping to them with a maximum tessellation factor of "only" 64. Although the approach described here is used in the context of tessellation, the same basic ideas can be used to do any sort of geometry amplification. In theory, using these insights, the geometry shader stage introduced with DirectX 10 can be made largely redundant.

1.2 Introduction

Having a low polygon-count (low poly) object representation that can later on be refined and smoothed on-the-fly has always been a very desirable goal.

The downside of a low poly mesh is obvious; it simply does not look as good as a high polygon-count (high poly) object. Some aspects of this low poly look can be improved by using normal maps to display fine details using per-pixel lighting. Still, the silhouettes of objects rendered using normal mapping look crude.

Tessellation is a refinement technique that can be used to generate a high number of output triangles per input triangle; it can thus smooth silhouettes to generate an organic look. Relatively low poly objects can then be used to save precious video memory, something that is especially relevant on game consoles.

One approach to generate nice silhouettes for low poly objects is to replace triangles of the object with curved surface patches. Alternatively, one can represent the object completely by the control points necessary to define these patches.

Ideally, one wants to evaluate curved surfaces over objects completely on-the-fly on the GPU, and this is where tessellation comes into play. With the introduction of DX11 class hardware, tessellation has become a mainstream hardware feature. This article tries to simplify the use of tessellation on DX10 class hardware and to make it a "first-class citizen" for all game-development efforts.

1.3   The Basic Vertex Shader Tessellation Algorithm

In order to understand the basic algorithm, please consider the following steps:

1. Set up an empty vertex input layout. As a consequence, no data will be delivered to the vertex shader from any vertex buffer.

2. Unbind all index and vertex buffers from the device.

3. Define `SV_VertexID` (or the appropriate OpenGL identifier) as the only input to the vertex shader. Only a vertex-ID will be delivered to the vertex shader.

4. Issue a draw call that delivers enough vertices (however, only `SV_VertexID` will be delivered) to the vertex shader to create a tessellation.

5. Bind all vertex and index buffers necessary to draw the current mesh as shader resources for the vertex stage.

A tessellation with a tessellation factor of N generates $N^2 - 1$ subtriangles as shown in Figure 1.1. In order to generate such a tessellation, it is now necessary to issue a draw call that delivers enough vertex-IDs to the vertex shader to output $N^2 - 1$ triangles. As each triangle in the tessellation needs three vertices, the overall number of vertex IDs to be issued is $3 \times (N^2 - 1)$.

So how does one then use the delivered vertex-IDs in the vertex shader to output a tessellation as shown in Figure 1.1? The answer lies in assigning an ID to each subtriangle of the tessellation. Figure 1.1 shows how to assign these IDs.

The vertex shader now needs to perform the following steps:

1. Compute the ID of the current subtriangle from `SV_VertexID`.

2. From the subtriangle-ID, compute an initial barycentric coordinate for the output vertex of the current subtriangle.

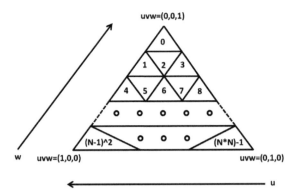

Figure 1.1. Assigning IDs to every subtriangle of a tessellation with tessellation factor N.

3. Compute the index of the current mesh triangle from `SV_VertexID`.

4. Fetch the three indices for the current mesh triangle from the index buffer using Load().

5. Fetch the vertex data for all three vertices of the current mesh triangle from the vertex buffers using the indices from Step 4.

6. Modify the barycentric coordinates from Step 2 to move to the right vertex of the subtriangle based on `SV_VertexID`.

7. Use the barycentric coordinates from Step 7 to compute the output vertex from three sets of vertex attributes from mesh vertices fetched in Step 5.

Listing 1.1 shows a real-world implementation of Steps 1–7.

```
// original vertex input structure
struct VS_RenderSceneInput
{
    float3 f3Position    : POSITION;
    float3 f3Normal      : NORMAL;
    float2 f2TexCoord    : TEXCOORD;
};

// ib and vb bound as shader resource by the vertex shader
Buffer<uint>         g_bufIndices                 : register( t0  );
Buffer<float4>       g_bufVertices                : register( t1  );

Vs_to_ps VS_Tessellate( uint in_vertexID : SV_VertexID )
{
    Vs_to_ps O;

    // g_uSubTriangles holds the number of subtriangles for the
    // current tessellation factor e.g., (N*N)-1
```

```
// compute what subtriangle we're in at the moment
uint subTriID = ( in_vertexID / 3 ) % g_uSubTriangles;

// subTriID to float
float fSubTriID = float(subTriID );

// compute barycentric coords u, v, and w
float fRow  = floor( sqrt( fSubTriID ) );  // how far we are along u
float incuv = 1.0f / g_fTessFactor;
float u     = ( 1.0f + fRow ) / g_fTessFactor;

// compute how far along the row we are
float fCol  = fSubTriID - ( fRow * fRow );
uint  uCol  = uint( fCol );
float v     = incuv * floor( fCol * 0.5f );

// correct u
u -= v;

// setup w
float w = 1.0f - u - v;

// compute the vertex index in the current mesh
uint vertexID = ( ( in_vertexID / 3 ) / g_uSubTriangles ) * 3
                + ( in_vertexID % 3 );

// compute offsets for fetching indices from index buffer
uint  uOffset1 = ( vertexID / uint(3) ) * 3;
uint3 uOffset3 = uint3( uOffset1, uOffset1 + 1, uOffset1 + 2 )
                + g_StartIndexLocation.xxx; // start offset for idxs

// fetch indices
uint3 indices;

indices.x = g_bufIndices.Load( uOffset3.x ).x;
indices.y = g_bufIndices.Load( uOffset3.y ).x;
indices.z = g_bufIndices.Load( uOffset3.z ).x;

// add base vertex location from constant buffer
indices += g_BaseVertexLocation.xxx;

// compute offset for vertices into the vertex buffer
uint3 voffset3 = indices * g_VertexStride.xxx + g_VertexStart.xxx;

// load vertex data for u=1.0 - vertex 0 of the mesh triangle
float4 dataU0  = g_bufVertices.Load( voffset3.x );
float4 dataU1  = g_bufVertices.Load( voffset3.x + 1 );
float3 f3PosU  = dataU0.xyz;
float3 f3NormU = float3( dataU0.w, dataU1.xy );
float2 f2TexU  = dataU1.zw;

// load vertex data for v=1.0 - vertex 1 of the mesh triangle
float4 dataV0  = g_bufVertices.Load( voffset3.y );
float4 dataV1  = g_bufVertices.Load( voffset3.y + 1 );
float3 f3PosV  = dataV0.xyz;
float3 f3NormV = float3( dataV0.w, dataV1.xy );
float2 f2TexV  = dataV1.zw;

// load vertex data for w=1.0 - vertex 2 of the mesh triangle
float4 dataW0  = g_bufVertices.Load( voffset3.z );
float4 dataW1  = g_bufVertices.Load( voffset3.z + 1 );
float3 f3PosW  = dataW0.xyz;
float3 f3NormW = float3( dataW0.w, dataW1.xy );
float2 f2TexW  = dataW1.zw;
```

```
// compute output vertex based on vertexID
// shift uvw based on this
uint uVI = vertexID % uint( 3 );

[flatten] if( uVI == uint( 0 ) ) // vertex at u==1
{
    [flatten] if( ( uCol & uint(1) ) != 0 )
        v += incuv, u -= incuv; // constant w line
}
else [flatten] if( uVI == uint( 1 ) ) // vertex at v == 1
{
    [flatten] if( ( uCol & uint(1) ) == 0 )
        v += incuv, u -= incuv; // constant w line
    else
    {
        v += incuv, u -= incuv; // constant w line
        w += incuv, u -= incuv; // constant v line
    }
}
else // vertex at w ==1
{
    [flatten] if( ( uCol & uint(1) ) == 0 )
        u -= incuv, w += incuv; // constant v line
    else
        w += incuv, u -= incuv; // constant v line
}

// Pass through world space position
O.f3Position = ( mul( float4( u * f3PosU + v * f3PosV
                    + w * f3PosW, 1.0f ), g_f4x4World ) ).xyz;

O.f3Normal = u * f3NormU + v * f3NormV + w * f3NormW;
O.f3TexC   = u * f3TexU + v * f3TexV + w * f3TexW;

return O;
}
```

Listing 1.1. A tessellation vertex shader.

We have described how to tessellate in the triangular domain. In a similar way, we can implement tessellation for quadrangular domains. In the following section, we present a technique to implement fractional tessellation factors for a quadrangular tessellation.

1.4 Per-Edge Fractional Tessellation Factors

The only way to implement per-edge fractional tessellation factors is to send enough vertices to the vertex-shader stage to support the maximum-per-edge tessellation factor. Actually, one even needs to send two additional vertices to allow for the phasing in of the new fractional vertices on the left- and right-hand sides of the edge center to make sure that a fully symmetrical tessellation is created. Such a symmetrical tessellation is necessary to make sure that there are no gaps between meeting edges from adjacent triangles.

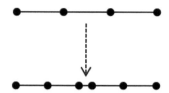

Figure 1.2. Fractional transitioning between a tessellation factor 3.0 and a tessellation factor 5.0 of an edge.

Figure 1.2 shows the tessellation that a fractional tessellation factor of roughly 3.5 would create.

For edges of the tessellated triangles and for interior vertices that need a lower than maximum fractional tessellation factor, the vertex shader must ensure that a number of zero-area triangles get created.

This is not the most efficient way of creating a tessellation, especially when there are big differences between the tessellation factors on the three edges of a triangle or the four edges of a quad. Nevertheless, it is the only way to deal with this problem on DX10-class hardware.

In general, however, this does not pose a severe problem, since one can, for example, use one fractional tessellation factor for an object or a mesh. This will work nicely as long as the objects or meshes that get tessellated are not too large.

If objects or meshes get large, for example, when the mesh represents a large terrain, then one tessellation factor is not enough. In such a case, it makes sense to break up the mesh into a number of patches that have similar maximum-per-edge fractional tessellation factors. Each set of patches can then be sent to the vertex shader for tessellation in one draw call.

Listing 1.2 shows an implementation of a vertex shader that supports per-edge fractional tessellation factors for quadrangular terrain patches. For the quad domain, one needs to issue six vertices per subquad (generated by the tessellation) since the vertex shader needs to output two triangles per quad.

Please note that the vertex shader in Listing 1.2 relies on the use of instanced draw calls to kick off the tessellating vertex shader. The instanced draw calls issue six vertices per subquad and one instance per quad of the untessellated terrain.

```
static const float2 uv_shift[4] = {
                                    float2( 0.0f, 0.0f ),
                                    float2( 1.0f, 0.0f ),
                                    float2( 1.0f, 1.0f ),
                                    float2( 0.0f, 1.0f ),
                                  };

VS_OUTPUT VSTessellateEdges( uint in_vertId : SV_VertexID,
                             uint in_instID : SV_InstanceID )
```

```
{
    VS_OUTPUT O;

    int i;

    // get the four tess factors for the four edges of the quad
    float4 f4EdgeFactor = g_f4EdgeFactor;

    // get the maximum tess factor (needs to be 2 + max edge factor)
    float   tf          = float( g_uVSTessFactor.x );

    // use vertex id to compute the id of the subquad
    // and to compute the row/col in the quad tessellation
    uint  uSubQuadID    = in_vertId / 6;
    float fSubQuadID    = float( uSubQuadID );
    float inv_tf        = 1.0f / tf;
    float fRow          = float( uSubQuadID / g_uVSTessFactor.x );
    float fCol          = floor( fSubQuadID - fRow * tf );

    // now compute u and v
    float v     = fRow * inv_tf;
    float u     = fCol * inv_tf;

    // compute offset into vertex buffer that holds
    // the vertices of the terrain
    uint offset = ( in_instID ) * 4;

    // fetch data for the 4 corners of the quad
    float4 data0 = g_bufVertices.Load( offset );
    float4 data1 = g_bufVertices.Load( offset + 1 );
    float4 data2 = g_bufVertices.Load( offset + 2 );
    float4 data3 = g_bufVertices.Load( offset + 3 );

    float3 f3Pos[4];

    // use data to init the corner positions in f3Pos[4]
    . . .
    . . .

    // update u, v based on what vertex of the 6 vertices
    // that are used to output the 2 triangles that make
    // up a subquad (==quad created by the tessellation)
    uint vID = in_vertId % 6;
    vID = vID < 3 ? ( vID == 2 ? 3 : vID ) :
                    ( vID > 4 ? 3 : ( vID - 2 ) );

    float2 uv_off = inv_tf * uv_shift[ vID ];

    u += uv_off.x;
    v += uv_off.y;

    // compute screen space adjusted tessellation factors for each
    // edge of the original input quad
    // please note that on the CPU the same tessefactors
    // get computed in order to bin terrain quads into bins
    // with comparable maximum tessellation factors
    f4EdgeFactor = computeEdgeTessFactors( f3Pos[0], f3Pos[1],
                                           f3Pos[2], f3Pos[3] );

    // combine tessellation factors to a single one that depends
    // on the current uv position in the highest res tessellation
    float4 f4EdgeFlag = ( float4( 1.0f - v, 1.0f - u , v, u ) +
                        ( 1.0f/128.0f ).xxxx ) >= (1.0f).xxxx ?
                        (1.0f).xxxx : (0.0f).xxxx;
```

```
float  fDotEf     = dot( f4EdgeFlag, (1.0f).xxxx );
float  fInterpTF  = max( max( f4EdgeFactor.x, f4EdgeFactor.y ),
                         max( f4EdgeFactor.z, f4EdgeFactor.w ) );

[flatten]if( fDotEf != 0.0f )
{
    fInterpTF = f4EdgeFlag.x != 0.0f ? f4EdgeFactor.x : fInterpTF;
    fInterpTF = f4EdgeFlag.y != 0.0f ? f4EdgeFactor.y : fInterpTF;
    fInterpTF = f4EdgeFlag.z != 0.0f ? f4EdgeFactor.z : fInterpTF;
    fInterpTF = f4EdgeFlag.w != 0.0f ? f4EdgeFactor.w : fInterpTF;
}

// now we need to compute the closest uv position in the next
// closest (lower but even) tessfactor
float fLowTF  = float( ( uint( floor( fInterpTF +
                          ( 1.0f / 128.0f ) ) ) ) >> 1 ) ) * 2.0f;
float fHighTF = fLowTF + 2.0f;
float fHighU  = 0.5f + ( u > 0.5f ?
                    floor( ( u - 0.5f ) * fHighTF +( 1.0f/ 128.0f ) ) :
                    - floor( ( 0.5f - u ) * fHighTF +( 1.0f / 128.0f ) ) )
                    / fHighTF ;
float fHighV  = 0.5f + ( v > 0.5f ?
                    floor( ( v - 0.5f ) * fHighTF +( 1.0f / 128.0f ) ) :
                    - floor( ( 0.5f - v ) * fHighTF +( 1.0f / 128.0f ) ) )
                    / fHighTF ;
float fLowU   = 0.5f + ( fHighU > 0.5f ?
                    floor((fHighU - 0.5f) * fLowTF + (1.0f / 128.0f) ) :
                    - floor((0.5f - fHighU) * fLowTF + (1.0f / 128.0f) ) )
                    / fLowTF ;
float fLowV   = 0.5f + ( fHighV > 0.5f ?
                    floor((fHighV - 0.5f) * fLowTF  + (1.0f / 128.0f)) :
                    - floor((0.5f - fHighV) * fLowTF  + (1.0f / 128.0f)))
                    / fLowTF ;

// now we need to update the real uv morphing between low tess and
// high tess UV
float fLerp = 1.0f - ( ( fHighTF - fInterpTF ) / 2.0f );

// lerp uv - this will generate zero area triangles for
// triangles that are not needed
u = ( 1.0f - fLerp ) * fLowU + fLerp * fHighU;
v = ( 1.0f - fLerp ) * fLowV + fLerp * fHighV;

// compute bilinear lerp of corners
O.vPosition.xyz = ( 1.0f - u ) * ( ( 1.0f - v ) * f3Pos[0] +
                                        v    * f3Pos[1] ) +
                        u    * ( ( 1.0f - v ) * f3Pos[3] +
                                        v    * f3Pos[2] );
O.vPosition.w   = 0.0f;

// do whatever you need to do to make the terrain look
// interesting
. . .
. . .

// transform position
O.vPosition = mul( float4( O.vPosition.xyz, 1.0f ),
                g_mWorldViewProjection );

return 0;
```

Listing 1.2. A vertex shader that implements quad domain.

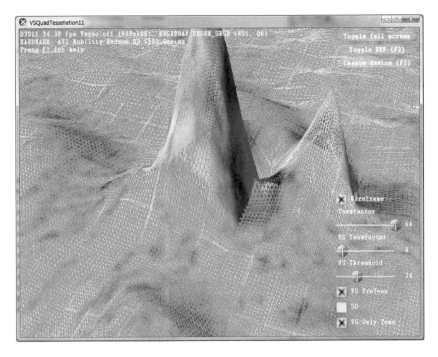

Figure 1.3. Wireframe view showing fractional tessellation factors implemented in a vertex shader.

Figure 1.3 shows the vertex shader in action. Although the sample application that was used to generate the screenshot is a genuine DX11 application, the shot shown uses the vertex shader only to generate the tessellation shown. The fractional tessellation factors can clearly be observed as seams between patches.

1.5 Conclusion

This chapter has presented a simplified way to implement tessellation in a vertex shader. The method is simplified in that it does not need any data other than what is already present in the vertex and index buffers. In addition, we present a way to implement fractional tessellation factors.

The concepts shown in this chapter can easily be used to get around using a geometry shader under many circumstances. As geometry shader performance relies on the sizing of internal buffers, using the concepts presented here may lead to faster and parallel performance.

Bibliography

[Gruen 05] H. Gruen. "Efficient Tessellation on the GPU through Instancing." *Journal of Game Development* 1:3 (2005), pp. 5–21.

[Tatarinov 08] A. Tatarinov. "Instanced Tessellation in DirectX 10." Available at http://developer.download.nvidia.com/presentations/2008/GDC/Inst_Tess_Compatible.pdf, 2008.

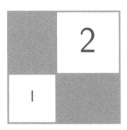

2

Real-Time Deformable Terrain Rendering with DirectX 11
Egor Yusov

2.1 Introduction

High geometric fidelity real-time terrain visualization is a critical part of many applications such as flight simulators and computer games. For a large data set, a brute-force approach cannot be exploited even on the highest-end graphics platforms due to memory and computational-power limitations. Thus, it is essential to dynamically control the triangulation complexity and reduce the height-map size to fit the hardware limitations and meet real-time constraints.

Figure 2.1. Puget Sound elevation data set rendered with the proposed method.

To effectively render large terrains, many dynamic multiresolution approaches have been developed in the past years. These algorithms typically adapt the terrain tessellation using local surface-roughness criteria together with the view parameters. This allows dramatic reduction of the model complexity without significant loss of visual accuracy. New capabilities of DX11-class graphics hardware enable a new approach, when adaptive terrain tessellation is built entirely on the GPU using the dedicated hardware unit. This increases the triangle throughput and reduces the memory-storage requirements together with the CPU load. It also reduces the amount of data to be transferred from the main memory to the GPU that improves rendering performance as well.

To reduce the storage requirements, several recent approaches exploit compression schemes. Examples of such methods are geometry clipmaps [Losasso and Hoppe 04] and C-BDAM [Gobbetti et al. 06]. Though these methods are optimized for maximum GPU efficiency, they completely ignore local terrain surface features, significantly increasing the GPU load, and do not support real-time deformations.

Dynamic terrain modifications are an important feature for a number of applications such as games, where the action changes the terrain, landscape editors, and other elements. It poses a number of problems such as the need to construct new triangulation and update internal data structures, which are especially complex when compressed representation is exploited. As a result, real-time terrain deformations are usually not considered.

The new terrain-rendering technique presented in this chapter combines an efficient compression scheme with the GPU-accelerated triangulation construction method and, at the same time, supports dynamic modifications. The technique has the following advantages:

- The proposed multiresolution compressed height-map representation substantially reduces the storage requirements and enables direct control of a reconstruction precision.

- Height-map decompression is accelerated by the GPU, which reduces expensive CPU-GPU data-transfer overhead and eliminates data duplication in main and GPU memory.

- Triangulation construction is completely done by the tessellation unit of recent graphics hardware:

  ○ Topology is not encoded and completely generated by the GPU for each camera position.

  ○ Strict screen space error bound of the rendered surface is provided.

  ○ The topology is updated automatically as the terrain is modified.

- The technique is efficiently implemented using hardware-supported features such as texture arrays and instancing.

- The terrain is fully dynamic; all modifications are permanent and all affected regions are updated in the compressed representation.

2.2 Algorithm Overview

At the preprocess step, the initial height map is converted to a quadtree data structure. To reduce the storage requirements, the hierarchy is encoded using a simple and efficient compression algorithm described in Section 2.3.

At run time, an unbalanced patch quadtree is maintained in decompressed form. It defines the coarse block-based terrain approximation. Each patch in this approximation is precisely triangulated using the hardware, such that the simplified triangulation tolerates the given screen space error bound. For this purpose, each patch is subdivided into equal-sized small blocks that are independently triangulated by the GPU-supported tessellation unit, as described in Section 2.4.

Procedural terrain texturing presented in Section 2.5 provides high-quality terrain surface texture with minimal memory requirements. Dynamic terrain modifications described in Section 2.6 consists of two parts. The first part is instant and is done on the GPU. The second part is asynchronous and is performed by the CPU: each modified terrain region is read back to the main memory and re-encoded. To achieve high rendering performance, a number of technical tricks described in Section 2.7 are exploited. Performance results are given in Section 2.8 and Section 2.9 concludes the paper.

2.3 Compressed Multiresolution Terrain Representation

2.3.1 The Patch Quadtree

Our multiresolution terrain model is based on a quadtree of equal-sized square blocks (hereinafter referred to as *patches*), a widely used structure in real-time terrain rendering (Figure 2.2). Each patch is $(2^n + 1) \times (2^n + 1)$ in size (65×65, 129×129, 257×257 etc.) and shares a one-sample boundary with its neighbors to eliminate cracks. We denote the patch located in level l ($0 \le l \le l_0$) at node (i, j) ($0 \le i, j < 2^l$) by $H_{i,j}^{(l)}$. The sample located at column c and row r of the patch $H_{i,j}^{(l)}$ is denoted by $h_{c,r}^{(l)}$:

$$H_{i,j}^{(l)} = (h_{c,r}^{(l)}), 0 \le c, r \le 2^n.$$

Note that $h_{c,r}^{(l)}$ notation will always refer to the sample of the patch $H_{i,j}^{(l)}$ so indices i, j are implied, but not included in the notation to simplify it. Quadtree construction is performed in a bottom-up order starting from level $l = l_0$ as follows:

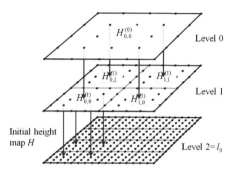

Figure 2.2. A three-level patch quadtree over the 17×17 input height map. The patch size is 5×5 ($n = 2$). (Courtesy of WSCG.)

1. Initial height map H is subdivided into $(2^n + 1) \times (2^n + 1)$ overlapping square blocks, which constitute patches $H_{i,j}^{(l_0)}$ at the finest resolution level $l = l_0$: $h_{c,r}^{(l_0)} = h_{2^n i + c, 2^n j + r}$, $0 \le c, r \le 2^n$, where $h_{c,r}$ denotes the input height-map sample located at column c and row r.

2. Patches $H_{i,j}^{(l)}$ at coarse levels $l < l_0$ are derived from their children with the following steps:

   (a) Patch offspring are combined into a single $(2 \cdot 2^n + 1) \times (2 \cdot 2^n + 1)$ matrix $O_{i,j}^{(l)} = (o_{c,r}^{(l)})$, $0 \le c, r \le 2 \times 2^n$:

   $$O_{i,j}^{(l)} = H_{2i,2j}^{(l+1)} \cup H_{2i+1,2j}^{(l+1)} \cup H_{2i,2j+1}^{(l+1)} \cup H_{2i+1,2j+1}^{(l+1)};$$

   (b) The matrix $O_{i,j}^{(l)}$ is decreased by rejecting every odd column and row as shown in Figure 2.3: $h_{c,r}^{(l)} = o_{2c,2r}^{(l)}$, $0 \le c, r \le 2^n$. We denote this operation by $\downarrow_{2,2}$ (): $H_{i,j}^{(l)} = \downarrow_{2,2} (O_{i,j}^{(l)})$.

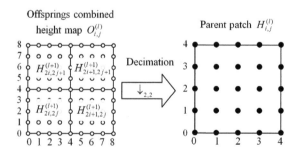

Figure 2.3. Deriving the parent patch height map from its offspring.

Quadtree construction stops at the coarsest resolution level ($l=0$) represented by the single patch $H_{0,0}^{(0)}$ covering the entire terrain.

2.3.2   The Compression Algorithm

To reduce memory overhead, the multiresolution hierarchy is maintained in a compressed form. The compression is done directly during the quadtree construction process. We exploit a simple yet quite efficient compression scheme that is derived from our previous work [Yusov and Shevtsov 11]. The proposed technique has the following key properties:

1. Reconstruction error is precisely bounded by the specified error tolerance.

2. Decompression is accelerated by the GPU.

3. A single pass bottom-up compression order enables dynamic height-map deformations. After the patch at the finest resolution level is modified, all updates can be propagated to coarser levels.

4. Patches from different terrain regions are processed independently and can be compressed/decompressed in parallel.

Quantization. During the compression, we input 16-bit height-map samples (which constitute patches $H_{i,j}^{(l_0)}$ at the finest resolution level $l = l_0$) to be quantized. Given a user-defined maximum reconstruction-error threshold $\delta \geq 0$, the following uniform quantizer with a dead zone is applied to each sample:

$$\tilde{h}_{c,r}^{(l_0)} = \left\lfloor (h_{c,r}^{(l_0)} + \delta)/(2\delta + 1) \right\rfloor \cdot (2\delta + 1), \quad 0 \leq i,j < 2^{l_0}, 0 \leq c,r \leq 2^n,$$

where $\lfloor x \rfloor$ rounds to the largest integer that is less than or equal to x; $h_{c,r}^{(l_0)}$ and $\tilde{h}_{c,r}^{(l_0)}$ are exact and quantized samples, respectively.

Quantized patches will be further denoted by $\tilde{H}_{i,j}^{(l)}$. Each quantized height $\tilde{h}$ is identified by an integer value $q = Q(h)$ where $Q(h) = \lfloor (h + \delta)/(2\delta + 1) \rfloor$. Knowing q, the decoder reconstructs $\tilde{h}$ as follows:

$$\tilde{h} = (2\delta + 1) \cdot q.$$

This quantization rule assures that the maximum reconstruction error is bounded by δ:

$$\max_{0 \leq c,r \leq 2^n} |\tilde{h}_{c,r}^{(l_0)} - h_{c,r}^{(l_0)}| \leq \delta, \quad 0 \leq i,j < 2^{l_0}.$$

Quantized patches $\tilde{H}_{i,j}^{(l)}$ at coarse levels $l < l_0$ are derived from their offspring in the same way as described in Section 2.3.1.

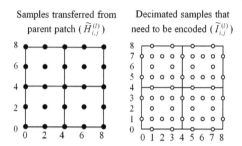

Figure 2.4. (a) Parent patch $\tilde{H}_{i,j}^{(l)}$ samples that are transferred to $\tilde{O}_{i,j}^{(l)}$. (b) Samples missing in $\tilde{O}_{i,j}^{(l)}$ that need to be encoded.

Encoding. Let us consider a patch's quantized height map $\tilde{H}_{i,j}^{(l)}$ and its offsprings' quantized combined height map $\tilde{O}_{i,j}^{(l)}$. Since decompression is performed in a top-down order, we can assume that $\tilde{H}_{i,j}^{(l)}$ is already decoded. Thus, samples located at even columns and rows in $\tilde{O}_{i,j}^{(l)}$ (Figure 2.4(a)) can be simply copied from $\tilde{H}_{i,j}^{(l)}$. The remaining samples (Figure 2.4(b)) were removed during the decimation and constitute refinement data that is required to completely reconstruct $\tilde{O}_{i,j}^{(l)}$. We denote these samples by $\tilde{I}_{i,j}^{(l)}$: $\tilde{I}_{i,j}^{(l)} = \tilde{O}_{i,j}^{(l)} / \tilde{H}_{i,j}^{(l)}$.

Encoding samples from $\tilde{I}_{i,j}^{(l)}$ consists of the following steps:

1. The sample value is predicted from the neighboring parent patch samples;

2. The predicted value is quantized;

3. The prediction error is calculated as the difference between exact quantized and predicted quantized values;

4. The error is encoded using arithmetic coding.

The prediction error is calculated for each $\tilde{h}_{c,r}^{(l)} \in \tilde{I}_{i,j}^{(l)}$ according to the following expression:

$$d_{c,r}^{(l)} = Q[\, P(\tilde{h}_{c,r}^{(l)})\,] - q_{c,r}^{(l)},$$

where $d_{c,r}^{(l)}$ is the prediction error for the sample $\tilde{h}_{c,r}^{(l)} \in \tilde{I}_{i,j}^{(l)}$, $P(\tilde{h}_{c,r}^{(l)})$ is the prediction operator for the sample, and $q_{c,r}^{(l)} = Q(\tilde{h}_{c,r}^{(l)})$ is the exact quantized value. We denote the prediction-error matrix for patch $\tilde{H}_{i,j}^{(l)}$ by $D_{i,j}^{(l)}$.

For the sake of GPU acceleration, we exploit the bilinear predictor $P_{BiL}(\tilde{h}_{c,r}^{(l)})$ that calculates a predicted value of $\tilde{h}_{c,r}^{(l)} \in \tilde{I}_{i,j}^{(l)}$ as a weighted sum of four nearest samples from $\tilde{H}_{i,j}^{(l)}$. A 1D illustration for this predictor is given in Figure 2.5.

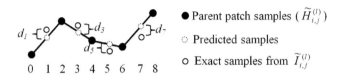

Figure 2.5. Linear prediction of missing samples and prediction errors (quantization of predicted values is not shown).

The magnitudes $|d_{c,r}^{(l)}|$ and signs $\text{sign}(d_{c,r}^{(l)})$ of the resulting prediction errors $d_{c,r}^{(l)}$ are encoded separately using adaptive arithmetic coding [Witten et al. 87] and output to the final encoded bit stream. We use an adaptive approach that learns the statistical properties of the input symbol stream on the fly. This is implemented as a histogram that counts corresponding symbol frequencies (see [Witten et al. 87] for details).

Compressed data structure. The operations described above are done for all patches in the hierarchy. After the preprocessing, the resulting encoded multiresolution hierarchy is represented by

- The coarsest level patch $\tilde{H}_{0,0}^{(0)}$ at level 0, which covers the entire terrain;

- Refinement data (prediction errors) for all patches in the hierarchy, excepting those at the finest resolution.

An encoded representation of the quadtree shown in Figure 2.2 is illustrated in Figure 2.6. Note that nodes at level $l = l_0$ do not contain data.

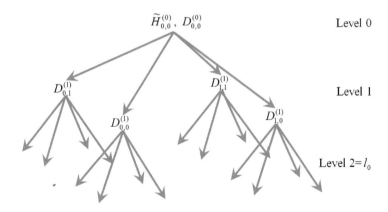

Figure 2.6. Compressed hierarchy structure.

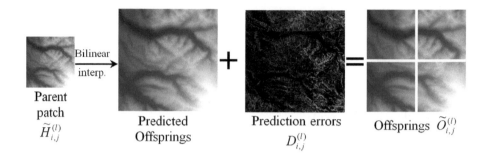

Parent patch $\tilde{H}_{i,j}^{(l)}$ Predicted Offsprings   Prediction errors $D_{i,j}^{(l)}$ Offsprings $\tilde{O}_{i,j}^{(l)}$

Figure 2.7. Offspring reconstruction diagram.

The matrix $D_{i,j}^{(l)}$ contains all the information that is required to reconstruct the offspring of patch $\tilde{H}_{i,j}^{(l)}$ (Figure 2.7). Repeating the decompression process starting from the root, the entire original height map can be progressively reconstructed.

In contrast to our original approach [Yusov and Shevtsov 11], in the compression scheme presented here, a single error threshold is used for each level of the hierarchy. This has the following benefits:

- Compression and decompression can be performed in one step (the original approach consists of two steps);

- A higher compression ratio;

- A simpler error control.

2.3.3   GPU-Based Decompression

In our system, the decompression is done in three steps:

1. At the first step, the CPU reads an arithmetically-encoded bit stream and uploads decoded prediction errors $D_{i,j}^{(l)}$ to the temporary $(2 \cdot 2^n + 1)$ $\times(2 \cdot 2^n + 1)$ 8-bit texture T_D.

2. At the second step, child patch height maps $\tilde{O}_{i,j}^{(l)}$ are reconstructed by the GPU and stored as a temporary $(2 \cdot 2^n + 1) \times (2 \cdot 2^n + 1)$ 16-bit texture T_O.

3. At the third step, appropriate regions of T_O are copied to four offspring $(2^n + 1) \times (2^n + 1)$ height-map textures.

At the second step, a full-screen quad covering the entire T_O texture is rendered; the required operations are done by the pixel shader. During the rasterization, the parent patch height-map is interpolated using hardware-supported bilinear filtering; interpolation errors are loaded from T_D and added to the predicted values. The corresponding code is presented in Listing 2.1.

```
#define HEIGHT_MAP_SAMPLING_SCALE 65535.f
float DecompressOffspringsPS(VS_OUTPUT In) : SV_TARGET
{
   // Clamp parent patch height map UV coordinates to the
   // decoded area
   float2 ParentPatchUV = clamp( In.m_ParentPatchUV,
         g_ParentPatchUVClampArea.xy,
         g_ParentPatchUVClampArea.zw );
   // Filter parent patch height map and get the predicted value
   int PredictedElev = g_tex2DParentHeightMap.SampleLevel(
                              samLinearClamp, ParentPatchUV, 0)
                                  *HEIGHT_MAP_SAMPLING_SCALE;
   // Load residual
   int iQuantizedResidual =
     g_tex2DResiduals.Load( int3(In.m_ResidualIJ.xy, 0) );
   // Quantize predicted height
   int iQuantizedPredictedElev =
           QuantizeValue( PredictedElev, g_uiReconstrPrecision );
   // Add refinement label and dequantize
   int ReconstructedChildElev = DequantizeValue(
      iQuantizedPredictedElev + iQuantizedResidual,
      g_uiReconstrPrecision );
   // Scale to [0,1]. Note that 0.f corresponds to 0u and 1.f
   // corresponds to 65535u
   return (float)ReconstructedChildElev / HEIGHT_MAP_SAMPLING_SCALE;
}
```

Listing 2.1. GPU-part of the decompression.

Important point. UNORM textures are filtered differently on Nvidia and ATI GPUs. On ATI hardware, the texture sampler returns an exact weighted result, while on Nvidia hardware, the filtering result is always in the form of f/N where f and N are integers and N is the normalization constant ($N = 65535$ for 16-bit UNORM texture). In the latter case, it is necessary to filter the texture manually to get a precise filtering result. The demo determines if texture filtering is done precisely by the GPU and uses a hardware-supported filtering unit or performs filtering manually, if it is not.

GPU-based decompression has the following benefits:

- It reduces the data-transfer overhead: instead of uploading 16-bit decompressed height maps to the GPU memory, only 8-bit prediction errors are uploaded.

- It eliminates the need to duplicate the data in main and GPU memory.

- It improves decompression performance.

Note that in practice, a number of coarse levels (three, for instance) are kept in main memory as well to perform collision detection.

2.3.4   Extending Height Maps to Guarantee Seamless Normal Maps

Normal maps required to perform lighting calculations are generated at run time
when the corresponding patch is decompressed. This is done on the GPU using
discrete gradient approximation. While $(2^n + 1) \times (2^n + 1)$ patches provide geometric continuity, normals located on the boundaries of neighboring patches are
not calculated equally, which leads to noticeable seams. To guarantee consistent
normal map calculation at the patch boundaries, the finest resolution patches
contain one additional contour around the patch perimeter and, thus, have a size
of $(2^n + 3) \times (2^n + 3)$. To encode these additional contours, parent patch boundary
samples are extended as if filtering with a clamp mode were used. This is what
the first operator of the `DecompressOffspringsPS()` shader does:

```
float2 ParentPatchUV = clamp( In.m_ParentPatchUV,
                              g_ParentPatchUVClampArea.xy,
                              g_ParentPatchUVClampArea.zw );
```

All patches are stored as $(2^n + 4) \times (2^n + 4)$ textures. Patches at coarser
resolution levels do not contain additional contour and have an encoded area of
$(2 \cdot 2^n + 1) \times (2 \cdot 2^n + 1)$. The remaining samples of the patch height maps are
obtained through linear extrapolation of the boundary samples.

2.3.5   Guaranteed Patch Error Bound

During the quadtree construction, each patch in the hierarchy is assigned a world-
space approximation error, which conservatively estimates the maximum geometric deviation of the patch's reconstructed height map from the underlying original
full-detail height map. This value is required at runtime to estimate the screen-
space error and to construct the patch-based adaptive model, which approximates
the terrain with the specified screen-space error (Section 2.4).

Let's denote the upper error bound of patch $\tilde{H}_{i,j}^{(l)}$ by $\mathrm{Err}(\tilde{H}_{i,j}^{(l)})$. To calculate
$\mathrm{Err}(\tilde{H}_{i,j}^{(l)})$, we first calculate the *approximation error* $\mathrm{Err}_{\mathrm{Appr}}(H_{i,j}^{(l)})$, which is the
upper bound of the maximum distance from the patch's *precise* height map to
the samples of the underlying full-detail (level l_0) height map. It is recursively
calculated using the same method as that used in ROAM [Duchaineau et al. 97]
to calculate the thickness of the nested bounding volumes (called wedges):

$$\mathrm{Err}_{\mathrm{Appr}}(H_{i,j}^{(l_0)}) = 0,$$

$$\mathrm{Err}_{\mathrm{Appr}}(H_{i,j}^{(l)}) = \mathrm{Err}_{\mathrm{Int}}(H_{i,j}^{(l)}) + \max_{s,t=\pm 1}\big\{\,\mathrm{Err}_{\mathrm{Appr}}(H_{2i+s,2j+t}^{(l+1)})\,\big\}, l = l_0 - 1, ...0,$$

where $\mathrm{Err}_{\mathrm{Int}}(H_{i,j}^{(l)})$ is the maximum geometric deviation of the linearly interpolated patch's height map from its offspring. A 1D illustration for determining
$\mathrm{Err}_{\mathrm{Int}}(H_{i,j}^{(l)})$ is given in Figure 2.8.

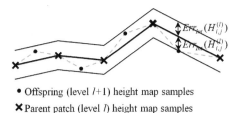

• Offspring (level $l+1$) height map samples

✗ Parent patch (level l) height map samples

Figure 2.8. 1D illustration for the patch interpolation error. (Courtesy of WSCG.)

Since the reconstructed height map for the patch $\tilde{H}_{i,j}^{(l)}$ deviates from the exact height map by at most δ, the final patch's upper error bound is given by

$$\text{Err}(\tilde{H}_{i,j}^{(l)}) = \text{Err}_{\text{Appr}}(H_{i,j}^{(l)}) + \delta.$$

2.4   Hardware-Accelerated Terrain Tessellation

At run time, an unbalanced patch quadtree (Figure 2.9(a)) is maintained in de-compressed form. It defines the block-based terrain approximation (Figure 2.9(b)), in which each patch satisfies the given screen-space error tolerance for the current camera position and view parameters.

The unbalanced quadtree is cached in GPU memory and is updated as the camera moves. Since we already have the maximum geometric error $\text{Err}(\tilde{H}_{i,j}^{(l)})$

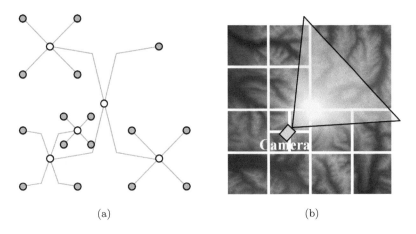

(a)   (b)

Figure 2.9. (a) Unbalanced quadtree maintained in decompressed form. (b) Corresponding approximation of the terrain.

for the vertices within each patch, we can conservatively estimate the maximum screen-space vertex error $\mathrm{Err}_{\mathrm{Scr}}(\tilde{H}_{i,j}^{(l)})$ for that patch using the standard LOD formula (see [Ulrich 00, Levenberg 02]):

$$\mathrm{Err}_{\mathrm{Scr}}(\tilde{H}_{i,j}^{(l)}) = \gamma \frac{\mathrm{Err}(\tilde{H}_{i,j}^{(l)})}{\rho(c, V_{i,j}^{(l)})},$$

where $\gamma = \frac{1}{2}\max(R_h \cdot \mathrm{cotan}(\varphi_h/2),\ R_v \cdot \mathrm{cotan}(\varphi_v/2))$, R_h, and R_v are horizontal and vertical resolutions of the view port, φ_h and φ_v are the horizontal and vertical camera fields of view, and $\rho(c, V_{i,j}^{(l)})$ is the distance from the camera position c to the closest point on the patch's bounding box $V_{i,j}^{(l)}$.

Screen-space error estimation $\mathrm{Err}_{\mathrm{Scr}}(\tilde{H}_{i,j}^{(l)})$ is compared to the user-defined error threshold ε for each patch in the current model. Depending on the results of the comparison, new patches are extracted from the compressed representation for these regions where additional accuracy is required; on the other hand, patches that represent the surface with the exceeded precision are destroyed and replaced with their parents.

Each patch in the current unbalanced quadtree is triangulated using the hardware tessellation unit as described below. Section 2.4.1 gives a brief overview of the new stages of the Direct3D 11 pipeline that are used in the proposed method.

2.4.1 Tessellation Stages in Direct3D 11

The Direct3D 11 pipeline contains new stages that drive tessellation entirely on the GPU (see Figure 2.10):

- *Hull Shader (programmable stage).* Transforms a set of input control points (from a vertex shader) into a set of output control points.

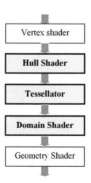

Figure 2.10. Tessellation stages in the Direct3D 11 pipeline.

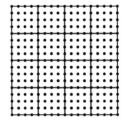

Figure 2.11. Subdividing a 17×17 patch into 5×5 ($d_0 = 2$) tessellation blocks.

- *The Tessellator (fixed stage).* Subdivides a domain (quad, tri, or line) into many smaller objects (triangles, points, or lines).

- *Domain Shader (programmable stage).* Calculates the vertex position of a subdivided point in the output patch.

2.4.2 Tessellation Blocks

To construct an adaptive view-dependent triangulation, each patch in the decompressed model is subdivided into the small equal-sized blocks ($(2^{d_0}+1) \times (2^{d_0}+1)$ in size) that we call *tessellation blocks* (Figure 2.11). For instance, a 65×65 patch can be subdivided into the 4×4 grid of 17×17 tessellation blocks or into the 8×8 grid of 9×9 blocks, and so on.

Each tessellation block can be rendered at the resolution 2^d, $d = 1, 2, ..., d_0$ (Figure 2.12). Optimal resolution for each block is determined by the hull shader.

To precisely determine the degree of simplification for each block, a series of block errors is calculated when the patch is created. These errors represent the maximum geometric approximation error of the terrain region covered by the tessellation block rendered at a particular resolution d.

Let's denote the error of the tessellation block located at the (r, s) position in the patch $H_{i,j}^{(l)}$ rendered at resolution 2^d by $\lambda_{r,s}^{(d)}$. Then, $\lambda_{r,s}^{(d)}$ can be computed as a sum of two components: the patch error bound and the maximum deviation of the patch samples to the simplified triangulation of the tessellation block:

$$\lambda_{r,s}^{(d)} = \max_{v \notin T_{r,s}^{(d)}} \rho(v, T_{r,s}^{(d)}) + \mathrm{Err}(\tilde{H}_{i,j}^{(l)}), \quad d = 1, 2, \ldots,$$

where $T_{r,s}^{(d)}$ is the tessellation block (r, s) triangulation at resolution 2^d and $\rho(v, T_{r,s}^{(d)})$ is the vertical distance from the vertex v to the triangulation $T_{r,s}^{(d)}$. Two- and four-times simplified triangulations as well as these samples (dotted circles) of the patch height map that are used to calculate $\lambda_{r,s}^{(2)}$ and $\lambda_{r,s}^{(1)}$ are shown in Figure 2.12 (center and right images, respectively).

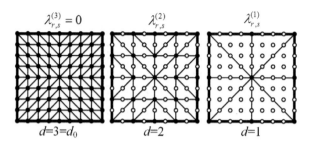

$$\lambda_{r,s}^{(3)} = 0 \qquad \lambda_{r,s}^{(2)} \qquad \lambda_{r,s}^{(1)}$$

$$d=3=d_0 \qquad d=2 \qquad d=1$$

Figure 2.12. Different resolution levels of a 9×9 ($d_0 = 3$) tessellation block. (Courtesy of WSCG.)

In our implementation, we calculate errors for four simplification levels such that a tessellation block triangulation can be simplified by a maximum factor of $(2^4)^2 = 256$ (if the tessellation block is large enough). This enables us to store the tessellation block errors as a four-component vector. The corresponding code is presented in Listing 2.2.

```
float4 CalculateTessBlockErrors(float2 ElevationMapUV,
                                float fPatchApproxErrorBound,
                                float fElevDataTexArrayIndex)
{
#define MAX_ERR 1.7e+34f
  float TessBlockErrors[4] =
    { MAX_ERR, MAX_ERR, MAX_ERR, MAX_ERR };

#define GET_ELEV(Col, Row) \
    g_tex2DElevationMap.SampleLevel(samPointClamp, \
      ElevationMapUV.xy + float2(Col,Row)*g_ElevDataTexelSize, \
      ) * HEIGHT_MAP_SAMPLING_SCALE

  for(int iCoarseLevel = 1; iCoarseLevel <= 4; iCoarseLevel++)
  {
      float fTessBlockCurrLevelError = 0.f;
      int iStep = 1 << iCoarseLevel;
      // Minimum tessellation factor for the tessellation
      // block is 2, which corresponds to the step
      // g_iTessBlockSize/2. There is no point in considering
      // larger steps
      if( iStep > g_iTessBlockSize/2 )
        break;

      // Tessellation block covers height map samples in the
      // range [-g_iTessBlockSize/2, g_iTessBlockSize/2]
      for(int iRow = -(g_iTessBlockSize>>1);
              iRow <= (g_iTessBlockSize>>1); iRow++)
        for(int iCol = -(g_iTessBlockSize>>1);
                iCol <= (g_iTessBlockSize>>1); iCol++)
        {
            int iCol0 = iCol & (-iStep);
            int iRow0 = iRow & (-iStep);
            int iCol1 = iCol0 + iStep;
```

```
            int iRow1 = iRow0 + iStep;

            float fHorzWeight =
              ((float)iCol - (float)iCol0) / (float)iStep;
            float fVertWeight =
              ((float)iRow - (float)iRow0) / (float)iStep;

            float fElev00 = GET_ELEV(iCol0, iRow0);
            float fElev10 = GET_ELEV(iCol1, iRow0);
            float fElev01 = GET_ELEV(iCol0, iRow1);
            float fElev11 = GET_ELEV(iCol1, iRow1);
            float fInterpolatedElev =
              lerp( lerp(fElev00, fElev10, fHorzWeight ),
                    lerp(fElev01, fElev11, fHorzWeight ),
                    fVertWeight );

            float fCurrElev = GET_ELEV(iCol, iRow);
            float fCurrElevError =
              abs(fCurrElev - fInterpolatedElev);
            fTessBlockCurrLevelError =
              max(fTessBlockCurrLevelError, fCurrElevError);
        }

      TessBlockErrors[iCoarseLevel-1] =
          fTessBlockCurrLevelError;
    }

    return float4(TessBlockErrors[0], TessBlockErrors[1],
              TessBlockErrors[2], TessBlockErrors[3]) +
          fPatchApproxErrorBound;
}
```

Listing 2.2. Calculating tessellation block errors.

One may ask why we don't use a compute shader to calculate tessellation block errors. The primary reason is that we do not need special features of the compute shader, such as random memory access, shared memory, or thread synchronization, to calculate the errors. Besides, we will be required to select such parameters as thread group size, which can affect performance. With a pixel shader-based approach, all these tasks are done by the driver; thus this approach is more universal and efficient. Another problem is that currently it is not possible to bind a 16-bit UNORM or UINT resource as an unordered access view.

2.4.3   Selecting Tessellation Factors for the Tessellation Blocks

When the patch is to be rendered, it is necessary to estimate how much its tessellation blocks' triangulations can be simplified without introducing unacceptable error. This is done using the current frame's world-view projection matrix. Each tessellation block is processed independently, and for each block's edge, a tessellation factor is determined. To eliminate cracks, tessellation factors for shared edges of neighboring blocks must be computed in the same way. The tessellation factors are then passed to the tessellation stage of the graphics pipeline, which generates the final triangulation.

Tessellation factors for all edges are determined identically. Let's consider some edge and denote its center by e_c. Let's define edge errors $\Lambda_{e_c}^{(d)}$ as the maximum error of the tessellation blocks sharing this edge. For example, block (r, s) left edge's errors are calculated as follows:

$$\Lambda_{e_c}^{(d)} = \max\left(\lambda_{r-1,s}^{(d)}, \lambda_{r,s}^{(d)}\right), \quad d = 1, 2, \ldots.$$

Next let's define a series of segments in a world space specified by the end points $e_c^{(d),-}$ and $e_c^{(d),+}$ determined as follows:

$$e_c^{(d),-} = e_c - \Lambda_{e_c}^{(d)}/2 \cdot e_z,$$
$$e_c^{(d),+} = e_c + \Lambda_{e_c}^{(d)}/2 \cdot e_z,$$

where e_z is the world space z-axis unit vector. Thus $e_c^{(d),-}$ and $e_c^{(d),+}$ define a segment of length $\Lambda_{e_c}^{(d)}$ directed along the z-axis such that the edge center e_c is located in the segment's middle.

If we project this segment onto the viewing plane using the world-view projection matrix, we will get the edge screen-space error estimation (Figure 2.13) given that the neighboring tessellation blocks have detail level 2^d. We can then select the minimum tessellation factor d for the edge that does not lead to unacceptable error as follows:

$$d = \arg\min_d \mathrm{proj}(\overline{e_c^{(d),-}, e_c^{(d),+}}) < \varepsilon.$$

The code that calculates the edge tessellation factor is presented in Listing 2.3.

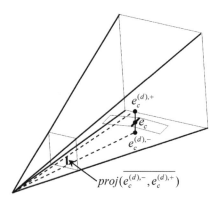

Figure 2.13. Calculating edge screen-space error. (Courtesy of WSCG.)

```
float GetScrSpaceError(float EdgeError, float3 EdgeCenter)
{
   float3 ShftdPoint1 = EdgeCenter - float3(0, 0, EdgeError/2.f);
   float3 ShftdPoint2 = EdgeCenter + float3(0, 0, EdgeError/2.f);
   float4 ShftdPoint1_PS =
     mul( float4(ShftdPoint1, 1), g_mWorldViewProj );
   float4 ShftdPoint2_PS =
     mul( float4(ShftdPoint2, 1), g_mWorldViewProj );

   ShftdPoint1_PS /= ShftdPoint1_PS.w;
   ShftdPoint1_PS /= ShftdPoint2_PS.w;
   ShftdPoint1_PS.xy *= g_ViewPortSize.xy/2;
   ShftdPoint2_PS.xy *= g_ViewPortSize.xy/2;
   return length(ShftdPoint1_PS.xy - ShftdPoint2_PS.xy);
}
#define MIN_EDGE_TESS_FACTOR 2
float CalculateEdgeTessFactor(float4 Errors,
                              float3 EdgeCenter)
{
   float EdgeTessFactor = BLOCK_SIZE;
   float4 ScrSpaceErrors;
   ScrSpaceErrors.x = GetScrSpaceError(Errors.x, EdgeCenter);
   ScrSpaceErrors.y = GetScrSpaceError(Errors.y, EdgeCenter);
   ScrSpaceErrors.z = GetScrSpaceError(Errors.z, EdgeCenter);
   ScrSpaceErrors.w = GetScrSpaceError(Errors.w, EdgeCenter);

   // Compare screen-space errors with the threshold
   float4 Cmp =
       (ScrSpaceErrors.xyzw < g_fScrSpaceErrorThreshold.xxxx);
   // Calculate number of errors less than the threshold
   float SimplPower = dot( Cmp, float4(1,1,1,1) );
   // Compute simplification factor
   float SimplFactor = exp2( SimplPower );
   // Calculate edge tessellation factor
   EdgeTessFactor /= SimplFactor;
   return max(EdgeTessFactor, MIN_EDGE_TESS_FACTOR);
}
```

Listing 2.3. Calculating tessellation factors.

The same selection process is used for each edge. The tessellation factor for the block interior is then defined as the minimum of its edge tessellation factors. This method assures that tessellation factors for shared edges of neighboring blocks are computed consistently and guarantees seamless patch triangulation. An example of tessellation factors assigned to tessellation block edges and the final patch triangulation is given in Figure 2.14.

To hide gaps between neighboring patches, we construct "vertical skirts" around the perimeter of each patch as proposed by T. Ulrich [Ulrich 00]. The top of the skirt matches the patch's edge and the skirt height is selected such that it hides all possible cracks. The skirts are rendered as additional tessellation blocks surrounding the patch, which have a special triangulation (see Figure 2.15).

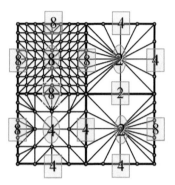

Figure 2.14. Tessellation factors assigned to block edges and the final patch triangulation.

The method can be summarized as follows:

- `D3D11_PRIMITIVE_TOPOLOGY_1_CONTROL_POINT_PATCH_LIST` primitive topology with fractional even partitioning is set.

- The vertex shader simply passes the data to the hull shader.

- The hull shader constant function calculates the tessellation factor for each edge (Figure 2.16 (left)) and passes the data to the tessellator.

- The tessellator generates topology and domain coordinates (Figure 2.16 (middle)) that are passed to the domain shader.

- The domain shader fetches the height-map value from the appropriate texture and calculates world-space position for each vertex (Figure 2.16 (right)).

- The resulting triangles then pass in a conventional way via the rasterizer.

Since our method enables using a small screen-space error threshold (two pixels or less) with high frame rates (more than 300 fps in a typical setup), we

Figure 2.15. Vertical skirts around the patch perimeter.

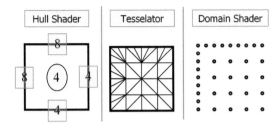

Figure 2.16. Tessellation stages.

did not observe any popping artifacts during our experiments even though there is no morph between successive LODs in our current implementation. In addition, on large thresholds, we noticed that it is much more important to perform a morph of the diffuse texture and the normal map rather than a geometry morph; these are implemented in the demo.

The proposed technique has the following benefits:

- Triangulation is fully constructed by the hardware, which saves CPU time and eliminates data transfer necessary to upload adaptive triangulation topology.

- The triangulation is computed using the current frame world-view projection matrix, it is adaptive to each camera position, and it tolerates the user-defined screen-space error bound.

- After updating the tessellation block errors, the triangulation is updated automatically.

2.5 Texturing

Terrain texture is generated procedurally based on the local terrain height and slope. The proposed method is based on the technique presented in [Dachsbacher and Stamminger 06]. The texturing method is driven by the list of materials. Each material is characterized by the unique texture that is tiled across the surface and the allowable ranges of height and slope. All material textures are stored in single texture array objects that enable selecting materials in the pixel shader.

Each patch has its unique 8-bit material index map that stores an index of the material that is the most appropriate for each patch region. In contrast to a traditional alpha texture that stores weights for four materials in its r, g, b, and a channels, the material index map stores only one 8-bit index. The material index map is calculated on the GPU by selecting the material with the best matching height and slope.

Terrain texturing is performed in the pixel shader. The shader reads the material index map and samples the appropriate texture-array element. To implement smooth transitions between materials, the shader reads the four nearest materials and blends them with appropriate weights. The shader code snippet is presented in Listing 2.4.

```
float2 TexUVSclaed =
  In.DiffuseTexUV.xy*g_MtrlIdxTexSize.xy - float2(0.5, 0.5);
float2 TexIJ = floor(TexUVSclaed);
float2 BilinearWeights = TexUVSclaed - TexIJ;
TexIJ = (TexIJ + float2(0.5, 0.5)) / g_MtrlIdxTexSize.xy;

float2 Noise = g_tex2DNoiseMap.Sample(samLinearWrap,
                    In.DiffuseTexUV.xy * 50).xy;
BilinearWeights =
  saturate(BilinearWeights + 0.5*(Noise - 0.5));

float4 Colors[2][2];
for(int i=0; i<2; i++)
 for(int j=0; j<2; j++)
 {
    float MtrIdx = g_tex2DMtrlIdx.Sample( samPointClamp,
                    TexIJ.xy, int2(i,j) )*255;
    Colors[i][j] = g_tex2DSrfMtrlArr.Sample(samAnisotropicWrap,
                    float3(In.TileTexUV.xy, MtrIdx) );
 }

SurfaceColor = lerp(
  lerp(Colors[0][0], Colors[1][0], BilinearWeights.x),
  lerp(Colors[0][1], Colors[1][1], BilinearWeights.x),
  BilinearWeights.y );
```

Listing 2.4. Calculating procedural surface color in a pixel shader.

The advantages of the proposed texturing technique are the following:

- There is a high-detailed surface. Material textures are tiled across the terrain and provide high-quality details.

- The number of materials is practically unlimited; the performance does not depend on the number of materials used.

- Each patch has an 8-bit material index texture instead of a 32-bit alpha texture storing blend weights in r, g, b, and a channels.

- After the material index map is regenerated, the terrain texture is updated automatically.

2.6   Dynamic Modifications

2.6.1   Asynchronous Tasks

All time-consuming tasks in the system are done asynchronously. Each node of the current unbalanced quadtree can be assigned one of the following asynchronous tasks:

- *Increase LOD.* This task is assigned to the quadtree node when its level of detail is about to increase.

- *Decrease LOD.* This task is assigned to the quadtree node when its level of detail is about to decrease.

- *Recompress.* This task is assigned to the coarse-level node when its offspring need to be recompressed.

The tasks are scheduled for execution and asynchronously processed by the system. Before any new task can be assigned to the node, the previous one must be completed.

2.6.2   Modifications

Terrain modifications are represented by the displacement map (which can be negative or positive). The modification object contains texture storing the displacement values.

Modifying the terrain consists of two parts. The first part is instant modification that is applied to each patch in the current unbalanced quadtree affected by the modification. Instant modification is performed by rendering to the appropriate regions of the affected patches. Since rendering to texture is done very efficiently, instant modifications are very inexpensive and cause almost no performance drop. When a patch is modified, its tessellation block errors, normal map, and material-index textures are marked as invalid. These textures are regenerated just before the patch is rendered. Since the triangulation topology is constructed entirely on the GPU, it will be updated automatically as the new tessellation block errors are calculated.

The second part is an asynchronous task that re-encodes the modified height map into the compressed representation. There are two possible cases that are processed differently:

1. The modified patch is located in the finest resolution level.

2. The modified patch is located in the coarse level.

Modifying patches in the finest resolution level. In this case, affected patches simply accumulate modifications and are marked as "modified." No data compression is performed at this stage. The height map is compressed asynchronously by the "Decrease LOD" task when affected patches are about to be destroyed. The "Decrease LOD" task checks if patches are modified and performs data recompression if necessary. Since the height map is kept in GPU memory only, it is necessary to read the data back to the main memory. This is done using a number of staging resources. The modified height map is copied to the unused staging resource, which is then mapped with the flag `D3D11_MAP_FLAG_DO_NOT_WAIT` in order to not stall the system. If data is not ready, the attempt to map the texture is repeated on the next frame. After the data is read back, the steps described in Section 2.3.2 are repeated and new prediction errors are stored in the data base. The parent patch is then marked as "modified" as well. It will be re-encoded in the same manner just before it is destroyed.

Modifying patches in coarse resolution levels. The second case is more complex since we cannot apply modification to the coarse patch only, because we will lose some data. In fact, if patch is located at a very coarse level, the whole modification can be lost. Thus, to correctly apply modification, we need to perform the following steps:

1. Decompress patches at the finest resolution level affected by the modification;

2. Apply modification;

3. Re-encode the modified regions in bottom-up order and update the data base.

All these tasks are done on the CPU in a separate thread asynchronously to the rendering thread. As in the previous case, the data is first read back to the CPU memory before starting data recompression.

It is possible that a coarse level patch is modified before the pior recompressing task is finished. In this case, all modifications are added to the list attached to the modified quadtree node. After the recompression task is completed, a new task is started that applies all modifications in the list at the same time.

2.7   Implementation Details

Two different GPU resource management strategies are implemented in the demo app. The first one is the conventional GPU resource cache. The cache stores unused textures released when patches are destroyed. When a new patch is created, appropriate resources are extracted from the cache. This eliminates expensive resource creation.

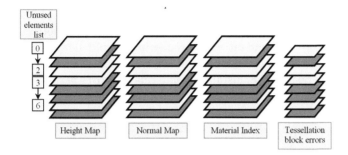

Figure 2.17. Texture arrays storing patch data.

The second strategy exploits the texture-array object introduced in DX10. The texture array contains a collection of identical textures that are interpreted by DirectX as a single object. The texture array can be indexed in the shader such that each individual array element can be accessed. Implementation with the texture arrays has the following advantages that improve performance:

- Texture arrays function as a GPU resource cache.

- The whole terrain can be rendered using a single instanced draw call.

- Multiple textures (normal map, tessellation block errors, and material-index map) can be updated in a single draw call.

The following four texture arrays are naturally maintained in our system (see Figure 2.17): height map, normal map, material index, and tessellation block errors. As it was noted earlier, height, normal, and material index maps are $(2^n+4) \times (2^n+4)$ in size with additional samples required to guarantee consistent surface shading at patch boundaries.

To implement resource cache functionality, a list of unused subresources is supported. When a patch is created, an unused subresource is found in the list. When the patch is destroyed, corresponding texture array elements are marked as free and become available for new patches.

Since all patches in the model share the same topology D3D11_PRIMITIVE _TOPOLOGY_1_CONTROL_POINT_PATCH_LIST, the whole terrain can be rendered using a single instanced draw call. The per-instance data buffer is populated with the patch location, level in the hierarchy, and the texture index. Patch-rendering shaders then access appropriate texture array elements using the index and fetch the required data.

As discussed in previous sections, tessellation block errors, normal maps, and material indices are computed on the GPU for each new or modified patch. Texture arrays enable updating multiple textures during one draw call. For this purpose, a list of texture indices to update is uploaded to the GPU memory and a single instanced draw call is invoked. The geometry shader selects the texture array element on which rendering should be performed using the SV_RenderTargetArrayIndex semantic.

As shown in Section 2.8, instanced rendering improves performance by a factor of more than two.

2.8   Performance

For our tests we used the Puget Sound elevation data set,[1] which is a common benchmark for terrain-rendering systems. The height-map size is 16385×16385 at 10 m spacing, which results in a terrain size of 160×160 km. The patch and tessellation block sizes in our experiments were chosen to be 129×129 and 17×17, respectively. The initial data set (512 MB) was compressed to 48.4 MB with 0.5 m error tolerance and 2.9 MB of auxiliary data (tessellation block errors, min/max elevations, etc.). Performance was measured on the following machine: single Intel Core i7 @2.67; 6.0 GB RAM; Nvidia GeForce GTX480.

Average performance during the recorded fly mode as well as minimal fps (in brackets) are presented in Table 2.1 (with procedural texturing disabled) and in Table 2.2 (with procedural texturing enabled).

Results presented in Table 2.1 demonstrate the efficiency of the proposed GPU-accelerated decompression and hardware-supported adaptive tessellation. Even at 1920×1200 resolution with 1 pixel tolerance, the performance never dropped below 244 fps with an average at 414 fps. With 2 pixel error threshold the visual quality is almost similar, but average frame rate increases to 818 fps. At lower quality settings the performance is even higher.

Tolerance (pixels)	Screen Resolution		
	1920×1200	1600×1200	1280×1024
1	411 (244)	477 (275)	612 (349)
2	818 (543)	944 (605)	1169 (776)
3	1130 (774)	1261 (858)	1462 (1080)

Table 2.1. Average (minimal) frame rates (procedural texturing disabled).

Table 2.2 shows that even with the high-quality procedural texturing, the performance is still very high (243 fps on average at 1920×1200 with 1 pixel screen-space error tolerance).

Table 2.3 shows that using texture arrays improves performance by a factor of more than 2. Table 2.4 reveals how performance depends on the tessellation block size for different error thresholds.

---

[1]Puget Sound elevation data set is available at http://www.cc.gatech.edu/projects/large_models/ps.html

Tolerance (pixels)	Screen Resolution		
	1920×1200	1600×1200	1280×1024
1	243 (177)	287 (208)	390 (270)
2	375 (276)	444 (324)	609 (449)
3	443 (313)	524 (370)	721 (513)

Table 2.2. Average (minimal) frame rates (procedural texturing enabled).

Tolerance (pixels)	Screen Resolution		
	1920×1200	1600×1200	1280×1024
1	411 / 172 (2.39 x)	477 / 201 (2.37 x)	612 / 248 (2.47 x)
2	818 / 372 (2.2 x)	944 / 425 (2.22 x)	1169 / 506 (2.31 x)

Table 2.3. Comparison of average frame rates for rendering with texture arrays and conventional GPU resource cache (procedural texturing disabled).

As can be seen from Table 2.4, the optimal tessellation block size is 17×17. It provides the best trade-off between adaptability and the maximum possible simplification ratio. With a larger tessellation block size (33×33), the triangulation became less adaptive since a single singularity may result in a maximum triangulation density for the whole block. With smaller sizes (9×9 and 5×5), the maximum triangulation simplification ratio is limited to 16 and 4, respectively, which are most often insufficient.

Dynamic terrain modifications affect performance insignificantly. For instance, with procedural texturing enabled and constantly modifying terrain, the performance dropped by less than 6% from 375 to 354 fps.

For a typical flyover (1920×1200, 2 pixel threshold), no more than 512 patches were required for rendering. Thus, expected GPU memory requirements are the following: $132 \times 132 \times$ (2 bytes for height + 2 bytes for normal + 1 byte for material index) $\times 512 + 16 \times 16 \times$ (2 bytes for tess block errors) $\times 512 =$ 42.8 MB.

Tolerance (pixels)	Tessellation block size			
	5×5	9×9	**17 ×17**	33×33
1	200 (103)	**415 (242)**	411 (244)	256 (139)
2	376 (198)	748 (445)	**818 (543)**	575 (350)
3	529 (269)	969 (587)	**1130 (774)**	847 (558)

Table 2.4. Comparison of average (minimal) frame rates for different tessellation block sizes (procedural texturing disabled).

2.9   Conclusion

The technique presented in this paper has a number of benefits. It exploits height-map compression to substantially reduce the storage requirements and uses a hardware-supported tessellation unit to construct adaptive triangulation. The decompression is accelerated by the GPU, which improves performance. Procedural terrain texturing provides a high-quality surface texture with minimal memory requirements. The technique supports dynamic terrain modifications making the terrain fully deformable. It exploits a number of technical tricks such as the use of a texture array and instanced draw calls to improve performance. As a result, it provides high frame rates even in HD resolution, which is not negatively affected by the real-time deformations.

2.10   Acknowledgments

The author would like to thank Andrey Aristarkhov and Artem Brizitsky whose valuable input helped implement the presented technique.

Bibliography

[Dachsbacher and Stamminger 06] Carsten Dachsbacher and Marc Stamminger. "Cached Procedural Textures for Terrain Rendering" In *Shader X4 Advanced Rendering Techniques*, edited by W. Engel, pp. 457–466. Hingham, MA: Charles River Media, 2006.

[Duchaineau et al. 97] M. Duchaineau, M. Wolinsky, D. E. Sigeti, M. C. Miller, C. Aldrich, and M. B. Mineev-Weinstein. "ROAMing terrain: Real-Time Optimally Adapting Meshes." In *Proceedings of IEEE Visualization*, pp. 81–88. Los Alamitos, CA: IEEE Computer Society, 1997.

[Gobbetti et al. 06] E. Gobbetti, F. Marton, P. Cignoni, M. Di Benedetto, and F. Ganovelli. "C-BDAM–Compressed Batched Dynamic Adaptive Meshes for Terrain Rendering." *Computer Graphics Forum* 25:3 (2006), 333–342.

[Levenberg 02] J. Levenberg. "Fast View-Dependent Level-of-Detail Rendering Using Cached Geometry." In *Proceedings of IEEE Visualization*, pp. 259–265. Los Alamitos, CA: IEEE Computer Society, 2002.

[Losasso and Hoppe 04] Frank Losasso and Hugues Hoppe. "Geometry Clipmaps: Terrain Rendering Using Nested Regular Grids." In *Proc. ACM SIGGRAPH*, pp. 769–776. New York: ACM, 2004.

[Ulrich 00] Thatcher Ulrich. "Rendering Massive Terrains Using Chunked Level of Detail." In ACM SIGGRAPH Course *Super-Size It! Scaling up to Massive Virtual Worlds*. New York: ACM, 2000.

[Witten et al. 87] Ian Witten, Radford Neal, and J. Cleary. "Arithmetic Coding for Data Compression." *Comm. ACM* 30:6 (1987), 520–540.

[Yusov and Shevtsov 11] Egor Yusov and Maxim Shevtsov. "High-Performance Terrain Rendering Using Hardware Tessellation." *Journal of WSCG* 19:3 (2011), 85–82.

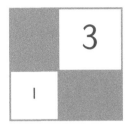

Optimized Stadium Crowd Rendering

Alan Chambers

The video games industry has benefited immensely from the wealth of information on instanced rendering and crowd simulation to have emerged in recent years [Dudash 07]. It has allowed developers to create a much more immersive gaming experience with hoards of visible characters that render at interactive frame rates. However, while these techniques form the basis of efficient crowd rendering within a stadium environment, they often fail to realize the unique set of problems and optimization opportunities that exist within this field. This chapter aims to extend on previous work in the field of crowd rendering, focusing predominantly on the math, techniques, and optimizations that can be made for stadium crowds.

3.1 Introduction

Many sports titles feature stadia that require some degree of crowd rendering technology. The geometric detail required for both the seats and the crowd characters is a problem on current commercial consoles, especially when trying to reproduce an 80,000-seat stadium. This is made more difficult by the fact that stadium crowds are a peripheral feature that we want to spend as little time on as possible. Indeed, many video games end up having to go with a simple solution, prerendered flip book animations. These generally suffer from inconsistent lighting and a flat overall appearance. Instanced crowd simulation provides the basis for a system that is not only visually much better but is also able to react to in-game events, which can greatly enhance the game play experience. However, even some of the latest games that use this technique suffer from perspective issues and completeness problems. This can lead to whole sections of the crowd being incorrectly oriented at times or undesirable gaps appearing when viewing them from certain angles, both of which can detract from the realism of the experience.

The system presented in this chapter tried to address many of these problems in *Rugby Challenge* on PlayStation® 3, Xbox 360, and PC. It begins with a tour of the data pipeline that explains how we can accurately place seats around the stadium and populate them with characters at runtime. A discussion of the real-time rendering process and its problems are then laid out together with performance evaluations that highlight the bottlenecks and potential areas for improvement. In addition to this, we also reveal the tricks for achieving colored "writing" in the stands, ambient occlusion that darkens the upper echelons, and crowd density that can be controlled live in-game. Following this, we are able to focus some discussion on the optimizations that can reduce the cost of the system even further. The symmetrical nature of stadium architectures and their fixed seating structure allow us to make specific optimizations that we could not do for a generic crowd system. Essentially, a complete pipeline for a fast and flexible stadium crowd simulation is presented, together with a discussion of the problems you can expect to face when implementing this type of system.

3.2   Overview

This chapter explores the use of instancing technology, deferred rendering [Policarpo 05], and imposters [Schaufler 95] in reducing the cost of rendering huge crowds on the GPU without compromising the color consistency in the scene.

The system is split into two content pipelines and three rendering phases. Each content pipeline produces data offline that is then loaded at runtime and fed into a specific rendering phase. The results of these two renders are then used in the final phase to shade and light the crowd area of the scene (see Figure 3.1).

The Model Content Pipeline is responsible for creating the character and seat geometry that will be featured in the stadium. It uses our existing model conditioner tools and exports data in an optimal format for the target platform.

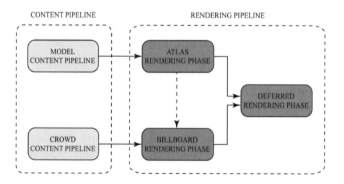

Figure 3.1. Overview of the crowd rendering pipeline.

The Crowd Content Pipeline produces a mesh that ultimately determines where our seats and characters will be instanced in the scene. Each vertex in the crowd mesh represents a real-world seat position from which we will instantiate our imposters.

The Atlas Rendering Phase takes the model set produced in the Model Content Pipeline and generates a texture atlas at runtime using our normal model rendering pipeline. Each model is rendered into the atlas from a specific viewpoint to create an imposter image that we can use multiple times.

The Billboard Rendering Phase instances each position in the crowd mesh to produce a view plane-aligned quadrilateral [Möller et al. 08] that contains one of the imposter images we generated in the Atlas Rendering Phase. It is an intermediate step in producing the final shaded crowd scene.

The Deferred Rendering Phase is the final stage in the pipeline. It uses the buffers produced in the Atlas and Billboard Rendering Phases to shade the crowd in a manner that is consistent with the rest of the scene. These colors are then written into the framebuffer to display our final crowd image.

3.3 Content Pipeline

Accurate seat and character placement is vital for creating a convincing stadium crowd representation. In this section we discuss the model data that we use to generate our imposters and the platform for accurately placing each one around the scene.

3.3.1 Model Content Pipeline

The first content pipeline produces the character and seat data for the Atlas Rendering Phase. Each model we produce needs to be performance friendly, i.e., have a fairly low polygon count with per-pixel lighting disabled. Note that we still require surface normal information to perform our per-pixel lighting calculations later in the pipeline.

The pipeline produces a list of character models, some female and some male, that we can dynamically load at runtime, usually before the start of a match. The geometry is skinned so we can control their gestures at runtime and make them respond to in-game events in a fluid and dynamic manner. If we use an atlas to map a variety of standard clothes for each character, we can swap it out at load time for a dedicated team color strip to introduce home and away supporters. This contributes to the general color in the stands and immediately relates the crowd to the teams on the playing surface.

The seat can be a static piece of geometry that is tailored to each particular stadium. However, this item is a special case since it is not colored directly. Instead, we use a grayscale texture that will act as a mask and a light map. The mask information is contained in the alpha channel so we can identify seat pixels

Figure 3.2. The source models used to create imposters.

and swap out the gray color for a stadium-specific one. Normally this procedure would leave us with a flat color, but if we apply the original grayscale value as a light map, then we will be able to create authentic seats and colorize them on an individual basis (see Figure 3.2).

3.3.2   Crowd Content Pipeline

The second content pipeline provides the data for accurately positioning our seat and character imposters around the stadium. Since the seats have a fixed position in the stadium and the crowd characters occupy the same space, we can use each vertex in a standard mesh to specify the position of both elements. These vertices can then be instanced into a quadrilateral at runtime to map a desired imposter image. Furthermore, we can encode elements of data into an associated color stream to influence the work done in the shader. This makes the rendering pipeline very different than that of a normal mesh. For this reason, we chose to decouple the crowd mesh from the stadium mesh and have it exist as a separate entity, despite the obvious position and orientation dependencies. This decoupling gave us the freedom to make optimizations that would have been awkward to integrate into a generic model rendering pipeline (see Figure 3.3).

The crowd mesh contains four data streams: vertex, billboard UVs, ambient occlusion UVs, and color. Note that since all the vertices are unique and we are instancing each one in our draw calls, we can actually omit the index buffer in our setup to save memory. Each data stream has a special role to play in the system. The vertex stream contains the seat positions that we extrapolate into billboards in the shader to create our imposters. In order to do this, the billboard

Figure 3.3. The crowd mesh is separate from the stadium. Each blue dot is a vertex in the mesh that specifies a real-world seat position.

UV stream needs to be populated with the four unit corners of a quadrilateral so we can map each instanced vertex to a specific corner from within the shader. The ambient occlusion UV stream is used to map each vertex into a texture that describes the ambient light information for the stadium. Finally, we have a four-component color stream for smuggling vertex attributes into the shader. We use this to connect some important values to the vertex data:

- X - density,

- Y - seat ID,

- Z - dude ID,

- W - shirt ID [optional].

The *density* value refers to the probability of someone actually sitting in that seat. It is used by the vertex shader to determine whether the seat is occupied. If the value at that vertex is higher than the required crowd density, then we will draw an empty seat. The *seat ID* is simply an index into a 256×1 color palette that will define the final color for the seat. We use the *dude ID* to index into a specific slot of the atlas so we can specify exactly which person is seated in a particular seat. Finally, we can choose to set up a *shirt ID* to control the appearance of our characters in the same way as the seat ID [Maïm 08]. All of these values are generated offline with the exception of the dude ID, which we create randomly at runtime to avoid patterns in the crowd from appearing. This is not strictly necessary, since the inclusion of various stadia with different crowd

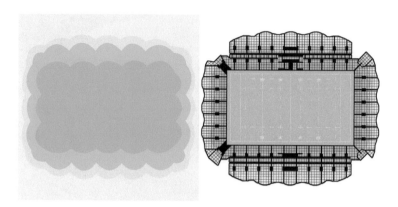

Figure 3.4. Example map that generates our seat color palette and crowd mesh color indices.

meshes, densities, and team colors can be enough to make them seem different every time.

Manually setting density and color indices for individual seats can be a very mundane process, so to help the artists we created a script that allowed them to take hand-painted maps and apply them directly to a crowd mesh, as shown in Figure 3.4. The color range can then be extracted from the texture and stored in a separate palette to determine individual seat colors at runtime.

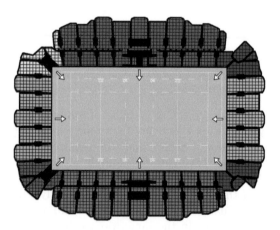

Figure 3.5. Dividing our crowd mesh into eight sections is enough to cover every aspect of the stadium.

The crowd mesh needs to be divided up into sections so we can control the view direction of the characters. To do this, we have each section contain a world-space transform that influences the orientation of our models at render time. Each section will trigger a render of the entire model set to ensure our characters oriented correctly, so we must keep these to a minimum if we are to remain fast at runtime. Most stadia naturally divide up into eight distinct sections, whose spectators coarsely share the same view direction as shown in Figure 3.5. Of course, this simple approach does mean there will be slight discrepancies in the viewing angle for some subsections of the crowd. However, these are almost always unnoticeable. Overall, we found this level of granularity worked well in creating a seamless camera panning experience around the whole arena, even for circular stadia.

Note that each section is set to look at the center of the stadium along the ground plane so each character faces the on-field action.

3.4   Rendering

The problems associated with drawing a large number of characters in a stadium environment can be solved efficiently with three separate draw phases. The first phase renders each of the models into a texture atlas to effectively cache the results and avoid the expense of repeated triangulation setups, transforms, and rasters that we would have to endure with fully fledged models. In this form we can reduce the complexity of the data to one quadrilateral per crowd member and not lose any fidelity. The primary drawback with the process is that rendering large amounts of billboards in such close proximity can, from certain camera angles, create huge amounts of overdraw. This means we are going to compute a lot of pixels that end up being discarded. To minimize the impact of overdraw we can defer the color and lighting to a later stage and use a simple fragment shader to cut down the cost of the actual pixel work. Each phase plays an important part in creating our crowd at an interactive frame rate, and this section describes them in detail.

3.4.1   Atlas Rendering Phase

We need to generate a texture atlas at runtime that contains all the viewpoint renders of our characters and seats so our billboards can reference various imposter images. Essentially, the data produced in the Model Content Pipeline is rendered out to two buffers containing color and normal information. With this data we can apply lighting and bump mapping techniques at a later stage to give our imposters a dynamic appearance. Each of the models needs to be rendered from a specific viewpoint that compensates for the flat 2D billboard projection of the imposters. To do this we have to set up a separate scene that contains the target model at the origin and an offscreen camera that orbits the model at a set distance, as shown in Figure 3.6.

Figure 3.6. The offscreen camera orbit around our models.

The position and orientation of the offscreen camera is fundamental to creating the imposter effect. We need to make the camera orbit the character in a way that reflects the orientation of both the world camera and the crowd section if our imposter is to be displayed correctly. To do this we have three control parameters that can influence the final camera position: pitch, relative angle, and distance.

The *pitch* of the main scene camera can be mapped directly to the offscreen camera to ensure that it shares the same view incline. The *relative angle* refers to the angle between the main scene camera and the crowd section forward vectors. It is a key element to rendering from the correct perspective, essentially providing the orbiting influence around the y-axis. These two parameters allow us to construct a unit vector that defines the ideal line on which to position our camera. A scalar *distance* value can then be applied to determine the final position of our offscreen camera and ensure we orbit an arbitrary focus point at a set distance (see Figure 3.7).

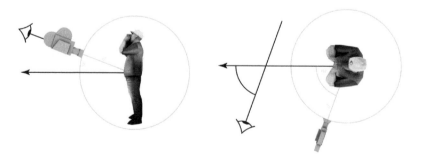

Figure 3.7. The control parameters that influence the orbit.

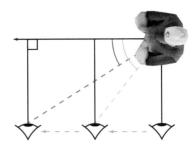

Figure 3.8. The translational influence of the world camera.

However, there is also a relationship between the world-camera position and the crowd section that we must account for if our models are to be correctly oriented within the billboards at all times. Consider the case in Figure 3.8, where the world-camera view direction is perpendicular to that of the crowd section. Here we can clearly see that the offscreen camera view direction needs to change as we translate away from the crowd section.

To compensate for this, we deploy a function to scale the relative angle according to the world-camera position (p_{wc}), the crowd section position (p_{cs}), and the crowd section forward vector (v_{cs}):

$$f(x) = \frac{0.5}{x+1} + 0.5,$$

where $x = (p_{wc} - p_{cs}) \cdot \hat{v}_{cs}$.

If we retrieve the vector between the world camera and the crowd section, we can calculate the scalar product along the crowd vector and feed it into our function to retrieve the amount of compensation required. Note, we made p_{cs} a point on the front edge of the bound of the crowd section so our relative-angle scalar was tuned to the first row of the section. This is important since the game is usually rendered from a position on the pitch, so we need to ensure crowd members closest to the on-field action are rendered with minimal discrepancies.

Finally, we calculate a look-at matrix for the camera with our newly computed orbit position, as shown in Listing 3.1. Generally, this should be focused on a fixed point in the scene so that all the models are framed correctly and consistently.

Since texture size has a direct impact on performance, we need to carefully consider the dimensions of our atlas to ensure it is never a bottleneck. To do this reliably we divide the atlas up into slots that have equal dimensions. Each slot contains a different model render and is mapped through a section ID and a model ID. These values identify the row and column indices that we use to access the character data from a specific slot within the atlas. This setup makes it easy to control the final texture size through the slot resolution while also enabling us to automatically adjust the atlas size when our model set changes.

```
void Section::computeCameraPosition( const Camera& world_camera )
const
{
    Vector3 camera_zaxis( -world_camera.getForwardAxis() );
    Vector3 crowd_xaxis = crowd_matrix.getRightAxis();
    Vector3 crowd_zaxis = crowd_matrix.getForwardAxis();

    camera_zaxis.setY( 0.0f );
    camera_zaxis = normalize( camera_zaxis );

    float x_dot = dot( camera_zaxis, crowd_xaxis );
    float z_dot = dot( camera_zaxis, crowd_zaxis );

    float angle = fast_acos( z_dot );

    angle = x_dot >= 0 ? angle : angle * -1;

    Vector3 crowd_edge_pos = Vector3( 0.0f, 0.0f,
        crowd_bounds.getZ() ) * crowd_matrix;
    Vector3 camera_wpos = world_camera.getPosition();
    camera_wpos.setY( 0.0f );
    Vector3 scale_vector = camera_wpos - crowd_edge_pos;
    float scalar = dot( scale_vector, crowd_zaxis );
    angle *= ( 0.5f / ( abs( scalar ) + 1.0f ) ) + 0.5f;
    float pitch = world_camera.getPitch();

    Vector3 camera_fwd = Matrix3::rotationX( -pitch ).
        getForwardAxis();
    Vector3 camera_dir = Matrix3::rotationY( angle ) * camera_fwd;
    Vector3 camera_pos = camera_dir * MIN_CAMERA_DIST;

    return camera_pos;
}
```

Listing 3.1. Computes an offscreen camera position.

The best resolution to use depends on the number of models and sections in your scene. We found a slot size of 64×128 in an RGBA format gave us a good detail to performance ratio on PlayStation® 3 for eight sections and ten models. Increasing this in powers of two saw significant performance hits as shown in Table 3.1.

Slot Width × Height	PlayStation® 3
64×128	0.16 ms
128×256	0.38 ms
256×512	1.31 ms

Table 3.1. The costs associated with rendering one section containing ten models into the atlas. Each section occupies a separate row of the atlas and each model occupies a separate column.

Figure 3.9. Base and associated normal map atlas.

Since we will be deferring all the color and lighting calculations until later in the pipeline, we need to set the pass up to take advantage of multiple render targets and have the fragment shader output two components: a flat color and a surface normal.

We can now render the model set into the atlas for each visible section. The first model we draw is the seat and it is always rendered into the first slot of the appropriate row in the atlas. This marks out the seat area with our alpha mask value as well as storing its light map information. Since the seat is the same for all the characters, we can copy this image across to the other slots in the row. Each character is then set in a specific pose and rendered over the top from the same viewpoint, as shown in Figure 3.9. Now we only have to perform one texture lookup in the shader to get both the seat and character information. Note that we must take care to ensure the character image is never clipped because of wild cheering animations that exceed the viewport scissor rectangle.

When rendering our texture atlas, care must be given to the use of bilinear filtering as it can cause problems for us in the later parts of the rendering pipeline. The alpha mask values along the edges of our characters will become polluted when they are sampled since the edge texels will be averaged with untouched texels. This can cause visible fringes to appear since our seat texels cannot be detected and swapped out for the correct color. To solve this we can implement a region map that stores the alpha information in a separate A8 texture. We can

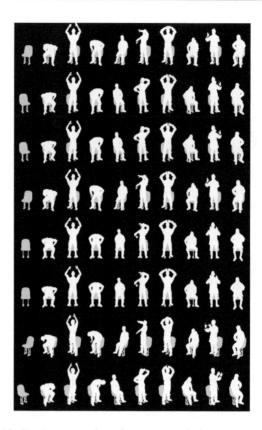

Figure 3.10. Region map identifies seat pixels from character pixels.

then use nearest filtering to sample the region map and safely identify our actual crowd pixels while using bilinear filtering to retrieve our color values from the atlas (see Figure 3.10).

One of the most important techniques we need to deploy as a postprocess over the texture atlas is real-time mip-mapping. Both the Billboard Rendering Phase and the Deferred Rendering Phase require fast texture lookups to reach maximum efficiency. The use of mip-maps improves texture cache performance and essentially speeds up texture fetching, which is vital to make the system run fast. The actual solution we adopted was straightforward. We simply loop through and downsample each level into the next by rendering a quad with the current level as the source texture. Note that the use of bilinear filtering in this step can again be problematic. The alpha value pollution leads to a reduction in the alpha test coverage, i.e., the proportion of pixels that pass the alpha test decreases with each level [Castaño 10]. This causes each level to become progressively more transparent and so the image appears to thin out with distance.

Slot Width × Height	PlayStation® 3
64 × 128	0.17 ms
128 × 256	0.67 ms
256 × 512	3.01 ms

Table 3.2. The costs associated with mip-mapping one row of ten slots in the atlas.

The use of mip-mapping at runtime has an associated cost. Usually the decrease in texture-fetching latency when reading from the atlas makes the process worthwhile. However, the size of the atlas once again becomes a vital consideration. As the resolution of the atlas increases, the cost of performing the mip-mapping in real time increases dramatically as shown in Table 3.2. This further illustrates the importance of selecting the right atlas resolution for your application.

3.4.2 Billboard Rendering Phase

The objective of this phase is to instance each of our crowd quadrilaterals and stencil out the crowd region in the scene. The primary bottleneck is overdraw. To minimize its effect, we render out each visible section of the crowd mesh into several intermediate buffers, as shown in Figure 3.11.

We defer as much computation as possible to the later stages in the pipeline to avoid heavy pixel-processing work that will never end up in the final image. This is done over several steps. First, we set up three fullscreen 2 × 16-bit floating-point render targets together with the main scene depth-stencil buffer. These

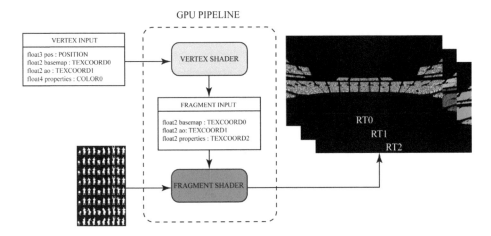

Figure 3.11. An overview of the billboard shader pipeline.

render targets will store information relating to the following:

- RT0 - interpolated base map UVs,

- RT1 - ambient occlusion UVs,

- RT2 - seat ID and section ID.

The stencil buffer provides an easy and efficient means of marking out our crowd region. If we set it up to always pass on write and replace its contents with a custom reference value, we only have to draw into our offscreen render targets to start marking out the area that will be covered by our crowd. The binding of the main scene depth-stencil buffer is important. Despite rendering into an offscreen buffer, we are still able to populate the main scene with depth information and stencil out the region of crowd for further pixel processing (see Figure 3.12).

The crowd mesh is submitted as quad data for rendering. We bind each of the four data streams in the crowd mesh, modulating the billboard UV stream and dividing the others by a factor of four to instance each corner of our quadrilaterals. Each repeated position can then be mapped onto an appropriate corner using the billboard UV information that comes into the vertex shader. This leaves us needing to determine which image in the atlas we will map on to the quadrilateral. The outcome depends on whether we want to render a character or an empty seat at that position. If we have a target density value for a particular match, we can do a step in the shader to see if this is greater than the density value in the color stream and select an appropriate UV set. Dynamically adjusting population levels live in-game then becomes only a matter of changing the target density value that gets sent to the shader. In this way, we can progressively empty the stadium near the end of a match if the home team is losing or populate it with more people over the course of a season if the team is doing well (see Figure 3.13).

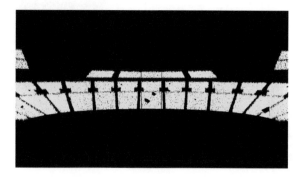

Figure 3.12. The stenciled region of the crowd.

Figure 3.13. Crowd density can change in-game.

The fragment shader for this phase needs to be as cheap as possible. The vast amount of layered quad data can create huge amounts of overdraw, which eats up GPU time when we are trying to render large crowds. To reduce this, we must have the shader perform a minimal number of texture lookups and defer as much of the pixel processing as possible. Texture lookups have an unpredictable cost and since the atlas is rendered in real time, it cannot benefit from swizzling optimizations to speed up neighboring memory accesses. This means we want to avoid them as much as possible to prevent overdraw becoming prohibitively expensive. Note that the application of per-pixel lighting is costly at this stage and can cause explosions in render time when viewing the crowd from certain camera angles. Indeed, any situation that causes the imposters to stack up on top of each other will generate huge layers of work over the same pixel, most of which will end up being discarded (see Figure 3.14).

The performance problems associated with overdraw are highlighted in Figure 3.15. In typical scenes, the crowd occupies between 0 and 25% of our total screen-space area. In these cases, each crowd character usually covers only a

Figure 3.14. The overdraw associated with crowd imposters.

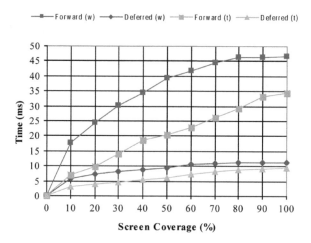

Figure 3.15. Metrics for a section of stadium crowd with 18,600 characters. The (w) timings are worst case. These were taken with a camera that looked down the whole length of the section to maximize overdraw. The (t) timings are typical case. These were taken from a typical in-game perspective that suffers less overdraw.

few pixels, which makes overdraw much less expensive. However, there are times when the crowd can occupy as much 40% or more of the framebuffer. If the camera is zoomed in on the crowd, the pixel space each character occupies will increase and this will drive up the cost of overdraw.

The fact that overdraw is camera dependent means we can control it to a certain extent. However, performance can swing wildly if we are not careful. Figure 3.15 shows us that by deferring the majority of our pixel processing in this phase, we become much less susceptible to swings in performance. The constant nature of the results means we can afford to give our in-game cameras greater freedom without fear of an unforeseen impact on frame rate.

To simplify our fragment shader, we perform just one lookup from the region map. This will determine if we have a crowd texel or a dead space texel. If the alpha value is zero we have a dead space texel and execute a pixel kill in the shader to prevent us from writing into the stencil buffer. However, if the alpha value is nonzero we have a crowd texel and immediately write out the three values that were passed into the shader. This forces a stencil write to the main depth-stencil buffer, which marks out the crowd region while deferring as much computation as possible. Note that because of the simplicity of the shader, we do not submit this phase to our Z-Pre Pass system since it will actually duplicate work and increase the load on the GPU.

3.4.3 Deferred Rendering Phase

The final phase of the rendering pipeline generates a final output color using the outputs from the previous stages (see Figure 3.16). We submit a fullscreen quadrilateral so our code is executed over all the framebuffer pixels and we can draw into our previously stenciled crowd region. Note that the trivial vertex processing in this phase means we are always going to be fragment-shader bound, so changing the GPR allocation accordingly can help speed up the pass on hardware with unified memory architectures. The work is split into three components: color, lighting, and shadows. However, other stages such as a fog and tone mapping [Hable 10] can be added to keep the look and feel completely congruous with the rest of the scene.

The base color contribution is determined from the maps we produced in the previous two phases. The UVs that enter the shader are used to perform a lookup into each of the maps rendered out from the Billboard Rendering Phase. This gives us the RT0, RT1, and RT2 data for a particular fragment. The RT0 value contains our base map UVs and is used to fetch a color value from the texture atlas and an alpha value from the region map. This is going to yield one of three things: a seat texel, a character texel, or a dead space texel. We don't care about dead space texels since they will end up being eliminated by the stencil test in the ROP. However, we do need to determine if we have a seat texel so we can apply the color in the palette associated with the current stadium. We can do this by testing our region map texel for the mask value we used on the seat model. If the seat value is present, we use the index in the RT2 data to fetch a color texel from the palette before applying the light map value in the RGB atlas texel. This gives us a final base-color contribution for the seat and allows us to create convincing effects such as writing in the stands or wave-like patterns as shown in Figure 3.17. If the mask value is not present then we can assume we have a character pixel and simply use the texel value directly as our base-color contribution.

The lighting solution heavily dictates the performance of this phase. We need it to be fast while also reflecting the light setup in the main scene to prevent

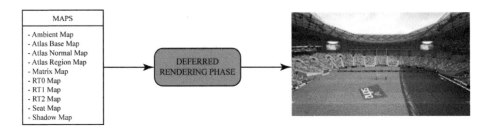

Figure 3.16. The shader pipeline for the final phase.

Figure 3.17. Individual seats can be assigned specific colors to create effects such as writing in the stands.

the crowd looking out of place. Although it would be nice to implement specular lighting using BRDF models [Kelemen et al. 01] and skin shading with subsurface scattering [Green 03], the computation across the whole crowd would be enormous. The main aim here is to produce a system that is fast and efficient while also giving the appearance of high fidelity and consistency with the main scene. To do this we need to cut down the amount of work in the fragment shader by using a small set of lights and cheaper equations that approximate the main scene conditions. We found that supporting one ambient light and one directional light was sufficient for illuminating the entire crowd in a manner that was consistent with the rest of the scene:

$$L_0(v) = (c_{\text{amb}}(c_{\text{ao}})) + (c_{\text{shdw}}(c_{\text{dir}}(n \cdot l_{\text{dir}})),$$

where c_{amb} is the ambient color, c_{ao} is the ambient occlusion contribution, c_{shdw} is the shadow contribution, c_{dir} is the directional light color, n is the surface normal, and l is the directional light vector.

The ambient light is traditionally thought of as a base-color constant that represents light coming from all directions. However, spherical harmonics have enabled us to take into account the color emission from surrounding surfaces as well [Sloan et al. 02]. This can be an expensive runtime process that often requires the computation of multiple coefficients in several directions. However, we can approximate this at load time by computing the light from the stadium in two or three directions and taking an average before it is supplied to the shader. This allows us to coarsely match the ambient light of the scene without impeding performance in the fragment shader.

Furthermore, we know that some areas of the stadium will also be occluded from the main light sources in the scene because of their architectural design.

Figure 3.18. Ambient occlusion that darkens the upper echelons of the stands.

In these cases, the amount of ambient light received will reduce as the field of incoming light decreases. This leads to the far, upper areas of stadia becoming progressively darker as the roof and surrounding walls shield more of the light source. To account for this, we can apply a cheap ambient occlusion solution [Christensen 03] using a map that describes the ambient light levels in the stadium. This allows us to retrieve the proportion of ambient light we need to apply at any point in the scene. The UVs stored in the RT1 buffer can then be used to sample the ambient map for a value that modulates the ambient light color component for the crowd pixel (see Figure 3.18).

The directional light information is used to compute the diffuse component of our lighting equation. However, the values in the normal map are in model local space so we need some way of getting them into the same space as our crowd section before we can evaluate the equation. Ideally we would fetch the transform directly from the crowd section using the section ID but since we cannot access elements of a constant buffer as an array from inside the shader, we have to use a different solution. We created a small RGBA texture and packed the upper 3×3 matrix of all our section transforms into a separate row during an initialize step. Each pixel then contains one vector from the 3×3 matrix in a compressed form, which means all eight sections can be stored in a 3×8 texture. The shader then only has to do three texel lookups to construct a matrix that can transform the values in our normal map into the correct space for a particular section. Note that the size of the texture makes this a cache-friendly operation that can be performed in parallel with ALU operations. Each normal we extract from the map is then transformed and fed into the standard n dot l lighting equation [Shirley et al. 05] to modulate our directional light color and produce an initial diffuse value.

The lighting model also contains a shadow component that needs to be applied to the diffuse. Since the computation of real-time shadows [Diamond 10] is often

Figure 3.19. A well approximated dynamic lighting solution will keep the crowd looking consistent with the rest of the scene.

expensive, we have to aggressively reduce the complexity for the crowd to ensure it runs fast. We decided upon two things:

1. The crowd would not cast shadows.

2. The crowd would receive shadows through an existing shadow map.

Calculating the shadow component now becomes only a case of looking up the shadow map value for the pixel. This is cheap to perform and effectively controls our diffuse input, ensuring no crowd pixels are lit from an obscured directional light source. The result is a convincing shadowing effect that is consistent with the main scene (see Figure 3.19).

A final color is then computed by adding the ambient and diffuse components to produce the lighting value, $L_0(v)$, that modulates our base color contribution. Note that the cost of this phase was fixed to 3.03 ms for a 720 p render target on PlayStation® 3, but this can be easily reduced using early rejection features such as stencil cull, as described in Section 3.5.2.

3.5 Further Optimizations

The technique presented in this chapter outlines an efficient model for real-time generation of stadium crowds. However, it can be optimized even further. This section focuses on areas that can be improved and offers solutions to help boost performance.

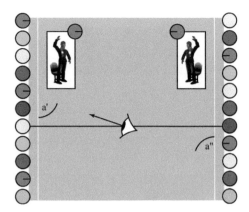

Figure 3.20. Each dot represents a vertex in the crowd mesh; the color corresponds to a particular crowd member to use in the atlas. The symmetry of the scene allows us to eliminate viewpoint renders but it does not mean we have to use the same configuration of crowd members in the opposing section.

3.5.1 Symmetry

The nature of stadium architectures presents us with a unique way in which we can reduce render time. The symmetry that exists between opposing stands allows us to effectively share the images produced in the Atlas Rendering Phase. Since each crowd member has a fixed world position and view direction, we are guaranteed to have congruent camera angles while we remain in the confines of the pitch (see Figure 3.20).

This relationship allows us to render with respect to one section and merely mirror the result for the opposing section in the Billboard Rendering Phase. We can see in Figure 3.9 that there is a mirror image of the models in each row elsewhere in the atlas. By sharing the appropriate row we can effectively halve the number of crowd section renders required for the simulation in the Atlas Rendering Phase. As a result, we only need to render each model from four viewpoints to populate an entire stadium full of people. This reduced the cost of the phase on PlayStation® 3 to a consistent and affordable time of around 1 ms as seen in Table 3.3.

	PlayStation® 3
8 sections	2.87 ms
4 sections	1.20 ms

Table 3.3. The performance benefits of symmetry optimizations. Timings were taken with each section rendering ten models.

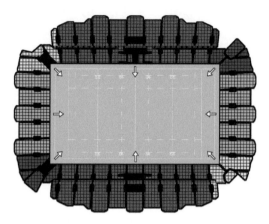

Figure 3.21. The group allocation of opposing sections.

The reduction in size of the atlas is significant for performance. Since we are only rendering half the number of sections we can save both memory and render time. This is significant for two reasons:

1. Sampling is less likely to suffer cache misses.

2. There is less data to mip-map in real time.

To implement the system we need to assign each section in the crowd mesh to one of four groups as shown in Figure 3.21. Each group contains only the sections that are diametrically opposed so we can track the symmetrical relationship and easily share their imposter images. Of course, not every stadium will have opposing stands, or even corner sections. In these cases, we can simply populate the symmetrical group with only one section or remove the group completely to avoid drawing them altogether.

To take advantage of the symmetry between opposing stands we need to modify the code in Listing 3.1. If we use the absolute on the scalar product before calculating the relative angle, we will always get a positive input value that mirrors the angle of the opposing crowd section. We then only have to flip the atlas UVs in the vertex shader to be able to use the image with mirrored crowd sections. Note that opposing crowd sections are still free to have a completely different character and seat configuration since only the atlas itself is mirrored and not the crowd section geometry.

The integration of mirrored rendering has an important consequence for the lighting calculations we do in the Deferred Rendering Phase. Although the image is horizontally flipped for mirrored sections, the actual normal values will remain

Figure 3.22. The need to flip the normals for mirrored sections.

in the same relative space as the original section. If we do not account for this, the lighting equation will not be solved correctly for the mirrored sections. This is easily resolved by adapting some of the matrices we pack into the 3×8 texture. Since these matrices are only used for lighting calculations, we can simply flip the x-axis for the mirrored sections when we pack in the data. The shader will then automatically flip the normal when it applies the lighting transform with no extra overhead incurred (see Figure 3.22).

To be able to detect mirrored sections we need to identify in which half of the stadium the crowd section lies. Fortunately, this can be easily computed, as shown in Listing 3.2.

```
void Section::isMirror() const
{
    Vector3 xAxis( 1.0f, 0.0f, 0.0f );
    Vector3 zAxis( 0.0f, 0.0f, 1.0f );
    Vector3 dir = m_worldTransform.getForwardAxis();

    dir.setY( 0.0f );
    dir = normalize( dir );
    float dp = dot( dir, zAxis ) + dot( dir, xAxis );
    m_isMirror = ( dp >= 0.0f );
};
```

Listing 3.2. Computes the symmetry state for a section

If we take the dot product between the crowd-section forward axis and each unit x- and z-axis, we can add the two results together to determine the side of the stadium the crowd section lies in (see Figure 3.23). Any section that lies in the second half of the arena is then identified as a mirror. Furthermore, we can integrate this functionality into our content build to automatically detect mirrored sections and set up the correct lighting transform to use at runtime.

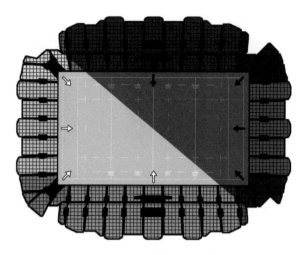

Figure 3.23. Detecting mirrored sections with the dot product.

3.5.2 Stencil Cull

The use of the stencil buffer presented so far only ensures that our crowd system draws to the parts of the framebuffer that we need it to; it does very little for performance. This is because the hardware only rejects pixels based on the stencil test during the ROP stage of the GPU pipeline, which occurs after our main bottleneck, fragment processing, has been executed. Essentially, work will still be carried out for pixels that are never actually displayed unless we take advantage of the stencil cull features in modern hardware. Stencil culling hardware can reject whole pixel quads before they reach the fragment shader provided all the pixels in the quad are set to CULL. However, it can only do this if the results of the stencil buffer are flushed into the stencil cull system. This means we must populate the stencil buffer before we can utilize the early rejection hardware to cull pixel data. Since the Billboard Rendering Phase is already populating the stencil buffer, we can easily instruct the hardware to set the corresponding stencil cull bit to PASS when we stencil out our crowd area. With a properly populated stencil cull region we can set up the Deferred Rendering Phase to recycle the results and early reject all the pixel quads that are still set to CULL. This can avoid the cost of pixel processing for large areas of the framebuffer since our crowd rarely occupies a significant portion of the final image. We found this to provide a very necessary win on both PlayStation® 3 and Xbox 360, as shown in Table 3.4.

	PlayStation® 3
STENCIL CULL OFF	3.03 ms
STENCIL CULL ON	0.57 ms

Table 3.4. The performance benefits of stencil cull on the scene shown in Figure 3.12 at 720 p.

3.5.3 Variation

The technique can be made even cheaper if we minimize the number of model renders in each crowd section. Currently each crowd section triggers a redraw of the entire model set in its associated row of the atlas. While this maximizes the dispersion of models throughout the crowd, it also maximizes the cost of the Atlas Rendering Phase since we have to accommodate all of the available models. The large atlas size increases the cost of the real-time mip-mapping and the chance of enduring texture cache misses. To make it run fast, we need to keep the model set at a minimum without destroying the illusion that there are lots of different people in the crowd.

The optimization is simple; each section renders a subset of the available models. Although this cuts down on the variety within each section itself, it still allows for every model to be used across the whole stadium. Provided there is an overlap of models across neighboring sections, the dispersion can appear seamless to the point where the reduced model set goes unnoticed. This can be taken even further if we assume the corner sections are going to contain less people than the main stands. In this case, we can render half the amount of models for those sections and pack the results into one row of the atlas. Combining this with the mirrored rendering approach means we can effectively drop the number of rows in the atlas to just three with little noticeable reduction in character variety. The performance gains from this are evident in Table 3.5.

Sections × Models	PlayStation® 3
8 × 10	2.87 ms
8 × 6	1.6 ms
3 × 6	0.62 ms

Table 3.5. Minimizing the number of models we render in each crowd section keeps the cost low without adversely affecting perceived variety.

3.5.4 Nighttime Lighting

At night the lighting characteristics are very different from daytime. During the day there is a strong directional light source from the sun but at night, large flood

Figure 3.24. A nighttime scene with pure ambient lighting on the crowd closely resembles real-world conditions.

lights tend to produce a more ambient distribution, with light coming from all directions. If we use a specialized shader for night games, we can take advantage of the conditions and make our crowd run even faster. We can do this by completely removing the computation for the directional light contribution. By performing fewer texture lookups and ALU calculations in the Deferred Rendering Phase, we can save up to 1 ms on PlayStation® 3 and have the final result still closely resemble the conditions of a live match (see Figure 3.24).

3.5.5   Multicore CPUs

The CPU essentially controls the amount of work done by the GPU. The more work the CPU sends to the GPU, the more of its time we will consume. If we are smart, we will avoid sending the GPU work wherever we can, especially if it will never end up being displayed. Modern multicore CPUs present some interesting opportunities for offloading work from the GPU. In some cases, postprocessing techniques such as MLAA [Reshetov 09] have been completely lifted off the GPU and put onto a multicore configuration [De Pereyra 11]. These types of postprocessing techniques usually mean that the GPU has to stall at the end of a frame until the work has finished and it can flip the buffers. However, instead of letting the GPU stay idle for this time, we can give it some work to get on with for the next frame. By hiding work behind some other processing, we effectively get it done for free.

The Atlas Rendering Phase is an ideal candidate. It has to be refreshed every frame and re–mip-mapped. If we can do this while the GPU is normally idle then we can save the cost of the whole phase. Of course, this will lead to the atlas being rendered one frame behind as the results are based on a previous camera configuration. Ordinarily this is not a problem because the discrepancy in viewing angle is so small, it is unnoticeable. However, it can prove to be a problem when the camera suddenly switches direction or position. In this case, the atlas will need a total refresh to avoid a one frame "pop" caused from using stale data. As long as we can detect this camera change, we can re-render the geometry on demand for the affected frame and ensure we never use stale data. A one frame spike every time the camera cuts to a different area is usually more desirable than a permanent slice of GPU-time being lost every frame.

Another area in which we can use the CPU is vertex culling. If we farm a job out to another thread, we can have the CPU point-test every vertex in the crowd mesh against our camera frustum and build up a command buffer of visible vertices to send to the GPU. This can help reduce the cost of triangulation setup and vertex processing since we are essentially rejecting redundant data that will only end up being clipped.

3.6 Limitations

Although the technique is fast and flexible, it is not without limitation. It has been optimized for use within the confines of the stadium and, as such, if the camera is put in obscure places, the illusion can be broken. Often this can be easily rectified by adding new methods for calculating the offscreen camera position that better suit the individual needs of the title. Indeed, the system can be made much more flexible in this respect if we have a selection of specialized routines that each camera can hook into. With the ability to tailor each viewpoint calculation, we can resolve almost any camera complication.

3.7 Conclusion

Realistic stadium crowds are becoming increasingly important for selling a convincing sports arena in video games. However, creating a fast and efficient system to solve this is a complex problem that touches on a wide range of graphical areas.

This article has presented a complete pipeline for implementing realistic crowds on current commercial consoles. It has drawn attention to the main bottleneck of the process—overdraw—and offered a solution that minimizes the GPU workload. This was strengthened with several suggestions to optimize the system even further with symmetry, early-rejection hardware, and multicore CPUs.

Despite the ground made in the article, there is still plenty of room for improvement. In particular, the technique does not consider close-quarters rendering of the crowd. If the camera frustum includes a section of crowd at close range, then implementing a LOD system that can generate higher-resolution renders would be advantageous.

In summary, the technique has several benefits. It provides a way to create crowds that look and move in a fluid manner while also maintaining the color consistency in the scene. The system is fast and having been broken down into several phases, there is scope to hide the processing of whole sections behind other work on the CPU or GPU. This leads us to conclude that rendering large crowds in a stadium environment is even more viable on today's commercial consoles than those in an open air environment where there are less optimization opportunities.

3.8 Acknowledgments

I would like to extend an extra special thanks to Kester Maddock for being such a brilliant source of graphical knowledge on the project and always making himself available to discuss ideas. I also want to thank Wolfgang Engel, Robert Higgs, and Stuart Sharpe for giving me some great feedback on the article. I'm also grateful to Duncan Withers for producing some of the art that you see in the paper. Finally, I'd like to thank Mario Wynands and Tyrone McAuley at Sidhe for supporting my work and allowing me to publish the material.

Bibliography

[Castaño 10] Ignacio Castaño. "Computing Alpha Mipmaps." Available at http://the-witness.net/news/2010/09/computing-alpha-mipmaps, 2010.

[Christensen 03] Per H. Christensen. "Global Illumination and All That." In *ACM SIGGRAPH Course 9 (RenderMan, Theory and Practice)*. New York: ACM, 2003.

[De Pereyra 11] Alexandre De Pereyra. "MLAA: Efficiently Moving Antialiasing from the GPU to the CPU." Intel Labs, 2011.

[Diamand 10] Ben Diamand. "Shadows in God of War III" Paper presented at the Game Developer's Conference, San Francisco, March 9–13, 2010.

[Dudash 07] Bryan Dudash. "Animated Crowd Rendering." In *GPU Gems 3*, edited by Hubert Nguyen, pp. 39–52. Reading, MA: Addison Wesley, 2007.

[Green 03] Simon Green. "Real-Time Approximations to Subsurface Scattering." In *GPU Gems*, edited by Randima Fernando, pp. 263–278. Reading, MA: Addison Wesley, 2003.

[Hable 10] John Hable. "Uncharted 2—HDR Lighting." Paper presented at the Game Developer's Conference, San Francisco, March 9–13, 2010.

[Kelemen et al. 01] Csaba Kelemen and Lázló Szirmay-Kalos "A Microfacet Based Coupled Specular-Matte BRDF Model with Importance Sampling." In *Proceedings Eurographics*, pp. 25–34. Aire-la-Ville, Switzerland: Eurographics Association, 2001.

[Maïm 08] Jonathan Maïm and Daniel Thalman. "Improved Appearance Variety for Geometry Instancing." In *ShaderX*^{6}, edited by Wolfgang Engel, pp. 17–28. Hingham, MA: Charles River Media, 2008.

[Möller et al. 08] Thomas Akenine-Möller, Eric Haines, and Naty Hoffman. *Real-Time Rendering.* Wellesley, MA: A K Peters, 2008.

[Policarpo 05] Fabio Policarpo and Francisco Fonseca. "Deferred Shading Tutorial." http://bat710.univ_Tyon1.fr/~jciehl/Public/educ/GAMA/2007/Deferred_Shading_Tutorial_SBGAMES2005.pdf, 2005.

[Reshetov 09] Alexander Reshetov. "Morphological Antialiasing." Intel Labs, 2009.

[Schaufler 95] Gernot Schaufler. "Dynamically Generated Imposters." In *Modeling Virtual Worlds—Distributed Graphics, MVD Workshop*, pp. 129–135. Infix Verlag, GOP, Austria, 1995.

[Shirley et al. 05] Peter Shirley, Michael Ashikhmin, Michael Gleicher, Stephen R. Marschner, Erik Reinhard, Kelvin Sung, William B. Thompson, and Peter Willemsen. *Fundamentals of Computer Graphics*, Second Edition. Wellesley, MA: A K Peters, 2005.

[Sloan et al. 02] Peter-Pike Sloan, Jan Kautz, and John Snyder. "Precomputed Radiance Transfer for Real-Time Rendering in Dynamic, Low-Frequency Lighting Environments." *Proc. SIGGRAPH '02, Transactions on Graphics* 21:3 (2002), 527–536.

Geometric Antialiasing Methods

Emil Persson

4.1 Introduction and Previous Work

Recently a number of techniques have been introduced for performing antialiasing as a postprocessing step, such as morphological antialiasing (MLAA) [Reshetov09, Jimenez et al. 11], fast approximate antialiasing (FXAA) [Lottes 11], and subpixel reconstruction antialiasing (SRAA) [McGuire and Luebke 11]. These techniques operate on the color buffer and/or depth buffer and in the case of SRAA on super-resolution buffers. Another approach is to use the actual geometry information to accomplish the task [Malan 10]. This method relies on shifting vertices to cover gaps caused by rasterization rules and approximates the edge distances using gradients.

In this chapter, we discuss geometric postprocess antialiasing (GPAA) [Persson 11a], which is an alternative approach that operates on an aliased image and applies the antialiasing post-step using geometry information provided directly by the rendering engine. This results in a very accurate smoothing that has none of the temporal aliasing problems seen in MLAA or the super-resolution buffers needed for SRAA or the traditional MSAA. Additionally, we will discuss geometry buffer antialiasing (GBAA) [Persson 11b], which is based on a similar idea, but is implemented by storing geometry information to an additional buffer. This technique is expected to scale better with dense geometry and provides additional benefits, such as the ability to antialias alpha-tested edges.

4.2 Algorithm

Two geometric antialiasing methods will be discussed here. The first method operates entirely in a postprocess step and is called geometric postprocessing antialiasing (GPAA). This method draws lines over the edges in the scene and applies the proper smoothing. The second method is more similar to traditional MSAA in that it lays down the required information during main scene rendering and does the smoothing in a final resolve pass. This has scalability advantages over GPAA with dense geometry and provides additional opportunities for smoothing alpha-tested edges, geometric intersection edges, etc. On the down side, it requires another screen-sized buffer to hold the geometric information. Hence, it is called geometry buffer antialiasing (GBAA).

4.2.1 Geometric Postprocessing Antialiasing

Overview. Provided there is an aliased image and geometric information available in the game engine, it is possible to antialias the geometric edges in the scene. The algorithm can be summarized as follows:

1. Render the scene.

2. Copy the backbuffer to a texture.

3. Overdraw aliased geometric edges in a second geometry pass and blend with a neighbor pixel to produce a smoothed edge.

Steps 1 and 2 are straightforward and require no further explanation. Step 3 is where the GPAA technique is applied. For each edge in the source geometry a line is drawn to the scene overdrawing that edge in the framebuffer. Depth testing is enabled to make sure only visible edges are considered for antialiasing. A small depth-bias will be needed to make sure lines are drawn on top of the regular triangle-rasterized geometry. For best results, it is better to bias the scene geometry backwards instead of pushing the GPAA lines forward since you can apply slope depth-bias for triangles. However, if the edges are constructed from a geometry shader, it is possible to compute the slope for the primitive there, as well as for the adjacent primitives across the edge.

The antialiasing process is illustrated in Figure 4.1. Here, a geometric edge is shown between two primitives. It may be adjacent triangles sharing an edge or a foreground triangle somewhere over the middle of a background surface.

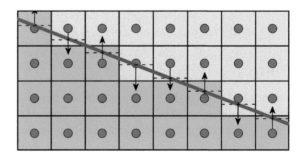

Figure 4.1. GPAA sample direction and coverage computation.

The first step in smoothing an edge is determining the major direction of its line in screen space, i.e., if it is more horizontal than vertical or vice versa. In Figure 4.1 the line is considered to be mostly horizontal, in which case we will choose neighbors vertically. Whether to go up or down depends on which side of the pixel center the edge is. If the edge is below the pixel center, we sample down, otherwise up. The same logic applies for the vertical case, except we choose between left and right.

Vertex shader. In processing an edge, the vertex shader first transforms the vertices to clipspace and then converts to screen-space positions in pixel units. A direction vector from first to second vertex is computed. If the absolute value of the x-component is larger than the absolute value of the y-component, then the major direction is horizontal, otherwise vertical. The line equation for the edge as well as a flag indicating the major direction is passed down to the pixel shader. Listing 4.1 shows the vertex shader.

```
struct VsIn {
    float3 Position0 : Position0;
    float3 Position1 : Position1;
};

struct PsIn {
    float4 Position : SV_Position;

    // The parameters are constant across the line, so
    // use the nointerpolation attribute. This way the
    // vertex shader can be slightly shorter.
    nointerpolation float4 KMF : KMF;
};

float4x4 ViewProj;
float4 ScaleBias;

PsIn main(VsIn In) {
    PsIn Out;

    float4 pos0 = mul(ViewProj, float4(In.Position0, 1.0));
    float4 pos1 = mul(ViewProj, float4(In.Position1, 1.0));

    Out.Position = pos0;

    // Compute screen-space position and direction of line
    float2 pos = (pos0.xy / pos0.w) * ScaleBias.xy
                + ScaleBias.zw;
    float2 dir = (pos1.xy / pos1.w) * ScaleBias.xy
                + ScaleBias.zw - pos;

    // Select between mostly horizontal or vertical
    bool x_gt_y = (abs(dir.x) > abs(dir.y));

    // Pass down the screen-space line equation
    if (x_gt_y) {
        float k = dir.y / dir.x;
        Out.KMF.xy = float2(k, -1);
    } else {
```

```
        float k = dir.x / dir.y;
        Out.KMF.xy = float2(-1, k);
    }
    Out.KMF.z = -dot(pos.xy, Out.KMF.xy);
    Out.KMF.w = asfloat(x_gt_y);

    return Out;
}
```

Listing 4.1. The GPAA vertex shader.

We are passing down a line equation of the form $y = k \cdot x + m$, or $x = k \cdot y + m$ in the vertical case. Depending on the major direction, we pass the slope factor k in the x- or y-component of the KMF output. In the pixel shader, we compute the signed distance from the pixel center to the line, so we want to subtract the pixel's y in the horizontal case and x in the vertical case. Thus we pass down -1 in the other component so that a simple dot product can be used regardless of the major direction of the line. The m parameter is computed to the z-component KMF output and the w gets the direction flag.

Pixel shader. Provided the line equation and a copy of the backbuffer, the antialiasing can be done with a fairly simple pixel shader (see Listing 4.2).

```
Texture2D BackBuffer;
SamplerState Filter;
float2 PixelSize;

float4 main(PsIn In) : SV_Target {
    // Compute the distance from pixel to the line
    float diff = dot(In.KMF.xy, In.Position.xy) + In.KMF.z;

    // Compute the coverage of the neighboring surface
    float coverage = 0.5f - abs(diff);
    float2 offset = 0;

    if (coverage > 0) {
        // Select direction to sample a neighbor pixel
        float off = (diff >= 0)? 1 : -1;
        if (asuint(In.KMF.w))
            offset.y = off;
        else
            offset.x = off;
    }

    // Blend with neighbor pixel using texture filtering.
    return BackBuffer.Sample(Filter,
        (In.Position.xy + coverage * offset.xy) * PixelSize);
}
```

Listing 4.2. The GPAA pixel shader.

First, we evaluate the distance to the line and use that to compute the coverage. Note that the coverage computed here is that of the other surface from which we sample a neighboring pixel, not the pixel's own coverage. If the edge cuts through the pixel center, the distance will be zero and consequently the coverage 0.5, i.e., the pixel is split evenly between the current pixel and the neighbor. If the edge touches the edge of the pixel, the distance is -0.5 or 0.5 depending on if it is the top or bottom edge, and the coverage consequently goes to zero, meaning the neighbor pixel does not contribute to the final antialiased value of this pixel. The observant reader notes that the neighbor coverage never goes above 0.5. One might initially think that it should range from 0 to 1, but a quick look at Figure 4.1 illustrates why this is not the case. Had the coverage been over 0.5 the neighboring surface would have covered the pixel center, and consequently no longer have been a "neighbor surface" but the pixel's own surface. In other words, push the line in Figure 4.1 up and across a pixel center and that pixel goes from belonging to the green surface to the orange surface.

Results. Given that we operate on the backbuffer with the actual geometry at hand, the antialiasing results are very accurate in terms of coverage calculation. Ideally the pixel should blend with the background surface sampled at the same pixel center. That information is not available in the backbuffer; however, a neighbor pixel is in most practical circumstances sufficiently close. It should be noted, however, that recent development using DirectX 11 hardware has made order-independent translucency somewhat practical [Thibieroz 11]. Using such a method, it is possible to have the underlying surface available and sample down

Figure 4.2. Aliased scene before applying GPAA.

Figure 4.3. Scene antialiased with GPAA.

in the depth order instead of a neighbor pixel for slightly more accurate results (see Figures 4.2 and 4.3).

One notable property of GPAA is that it performs really well in all edge angles. Interestingly, it is the most accurate in the near horizontal and near vertical case, unlike MSAA and most other antialiasing methods where this is the worst case. GPAA has its worst case at diagonal edges, where other methods tend to work the best. But it is worth noting that even in this case, the quality is good.

Figures 4.4(a) and 4.4(b) show a standard pixel-zoomed antialiasing comparison. Before applying GPAA we have the regular stair-stepped edge. After applying GPAA the edge is very smooth.

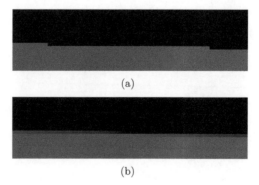

Figure 4.4. (a) Zoomed pixels before GPAA. (b) Zoomed pixels after GPAA.

While the GPAA approach works and produces high-quality output, it has some notable drawbacks. There is a scalability problem. The demo application for this method shows great performance for GPAA, but on the other hand it has a quite low polygon count. With increasingly dense geometry the cost will increase, especially since we rely on line rasterization, something for which regular consumer-level GPUs are not particularly optimized. Once a triangle is sufficiently small it is faster just to fill it than render the wireframe. Also, the overhead of having a second geometry pass for antialiasing may prove costly with a high vertex count.

4.2.2 Geometry Buffer Antialiasing

Overview. This method is similar in spirit to GPAA, but with the key difference being that the geometry information is stored to an additional render target during main scene rendering. Hence, no second geometry pass is required. A geometry shader is used to extract the geometric information on the fly and pass to the pixel shader. In the end, a fullscreen resolve pass is applied to the buffer to apply antialiasing.

Geometry shader. Given an existing vertex shader and pixel shader combination in the main scene, a geometry shader is inserted that adds another interpolator to pass down to the pixel shader. This interpolator contains three floats indicating the signed distance to each edge of the triangle. The fourth component contains flags indicating the major direction in screen space for the three edges. Using an interpolator instead of passing line equations is done so that only one interpolator is needed instead of three, and so that we can move the majority of the work to the geometry shader instead of the pixel shader. The geometry shader is presented in Listing 4.3.

```
struct PsIn {
    // Original pixel shader inputs go here
    // ...

    // Interpolator added for GBAA
    noperspective float4 Diff : Diff;
};

float ComputeDiff(const float2 pos0, const float2 pos1,
                  const float2 pos2, out uint major_dir)
{
    float2 dir = normalize(pos1 - pos0);
    float2 normal = float2(-dir.y, dir.x);
    float dist = dot(pos0, normal) - dot(pos2, normal);

    // Check major direction
    bool x_gt_y = (abs(normal.x) > abs(normal.y));

    major_dir = x_gt_y;
    return dist / (x_gt_y? normal.x : normal.y);
```

```
}

[maxvertexcount(3)]
void main(in triangle GsIn In[3], inout TriangleStream<PsIn> TS)
{
    float2 pos0 = (In[0].Position.xy / In[0].Position.w)
        * ScaleBias.xy + ScaleBias.zw;
    float2 pos1 = (In[1].Position.xy / In[1].Position.w)
        * ScaleBias.xy + ScaleBias.zw;
    float2 pos2 = (In[2].Position.xy / In[2].Position.w)
        * ScaleBias.xy + ScaleBias.zw;

    uint3 major_dirs;
    float diff0 = ComputeDiff(pos0, pos1, pos2, major_dirs.x);
    float diff1 = ComputeDiff(pos1, pos2, pos0, major_dirs.y);
    float diff2 = ComputeDiff(pos2, pos0, pos1, major_dirs.z);

    // Pass flags in last component. Add 1.0f (0x3F800000)
    // and put something in LSB bits to give the interpolator
    // some slack for precision.
    float major_dir = asfloat((major_dirs.x << 4) |
        (major_dirs.y << 5) | (major_dirs.z << 6) | 0x3F800008);

    TS.Append( Vertex(In[0], float4(0, diff1, 0, major_dir)) );
    TS.Append( Vertex(In[1], float4(0, 0, diff2, major_dir)) );
    TS.Append( Vertex(In[2], float4(diff0, 0, 0, major_dir)) );
}
```

Listing 4.3. The GBAA geometry shader.

First, we compute the screen-space position of the input vertices. To set up an interpolator for the line between pos0 and pos1 we first compute the signed distance of pos2 to this line. However, what we are really interested in is the distance along the major direction axis. This is just different by a scale factor, which is the reciprocal of the line normal's magnitude in that direction. Figure 4.5 illustrates how an interpolator is set up for a particular edge.

In Figure 4.5 the distance from the top vertex to the bottom edge of the triangle is computed as d. Given that the edge's major direction is horizontal we

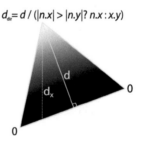

$$d_{dir} = d / (|n.x| > |n.y| ? n.x : x.y)$$

Figure 4.5. Setting up an interpolator to return the distance to the edge along the major direction.

are computing d_x, i.e., the vertical distance from the vertex to the edge, which is done using the equation for d_{dir} in Figure 4.5. This distance, which is returned from ComputeDiff() in the code, is set to that vertex, whereas the two vertices on the line naturally get a distance of exactly zero. So for the first line, the first two vertices get their x-component set to zero and the third vertex gets the edge distance. The same logic is applied to the other two edges and passed down in the y- and z-components, respectively. Note that the interpolator has to be declared with the noperspective attribute to make sure interpolation is done in screen space.

Given that the interpolator is a float4 the w-component will be a floating point, whereas we really want to submit a bit-field. We accomplish this by encoding the bits into the mantissa of the float. To be friendly with the interpolator we have to give it a valid float; just throwing a smallish integer into the bottom bits will give us a denormalized float and all bets are off. In our tests we just got all zeros. Using 1.0f as the base is a reasonable choice, although any other valid float with enough zero bits in it will get the task done. The bitwise representation of 1.0f is 0x3F800000. We could throw our bits in the bottom of that number, and this appears to work in practice on the hardware we tried it on; however, it could be wise to not rely on the interpolator being precise to the last bits, even if all inputs are identical. So, we rather arbitrarily use bits 4 to 6, and enable bit 3 to make sure the lowest four bits can be imprecise in both directions without affecting the bits we use. So the bits we finally add in addition to our flags are 0x3F800008.

Pixel shader. In Listing 4.4 we take a look at the work we add to the pixel shader. In addition to whatever the shader was doing before, we add a snippet to take the input edge distances as provided by the interpolator and select the edge that is closest to the pixel. Using the major direction of the closest edge, we output a two-component distance value indicating horizontal or vertical distance to the edge.

```
PsOut main(PsIn In)
{
    // Other outputs of the shader go here
    // ...

    // Select the smallest distance
    float diff = In.Diff.x;
    int major_dir = asuint(In.Diff.w) & (1 << 4);

    if (abs(In.Diff.y) < abs(diff))
    {
        diff = In.Diff.y;
        major_dir = asuint(In.Diff.w) & (1 << 5);
    }
    if (abs(In.Diff.z) < abs(diff))
    {
```

```
        diff = In.Diff.z;
        major_dir = asuint(In.Diff.w) & (1 << 6);
    }

    float2 offset = 0;

    // Select direction to sample a neighbor pixel
    if (major_dir)
        offset.x = diff;
    else
        offset.y = diff;

    Out.Diff = offset;
}
```

Listing 4.4. The GBAA pixel shader.

Selecting the closest edge is merely a matter of selecting the component with the smallest absolute value. The corresponding direction flag is also extracted and the difference is supplied in either x or y. Note that we only ever shift along one axis, so we could easily pack the information into one component and just put a flag in the low-order bit indicating the direction, but keeping it as two values makes the shader output and the final resolve shader a bit simpler. Depending on the balance between ALU, bandwidth, memory, and buffer layout, however, it may sometimes be beneficial to squeeze it into one component.

Resolve. Once the scene has been rendered and we have a geometry buffer filled with edge distance information, we are ready to apply GBAA to antialias the image. The resolve pass is rendered as a fullscreen pass where we sample from a copy of the backbuffer and from the geometry buffer. Initially, we sample the

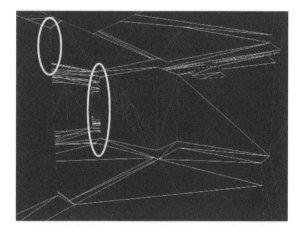

Figure 4.6. Gaps occurring in the geometry buffer along silhouette edges.

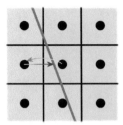

Figure 4.7. Patching the geometry buffer by considering neighbors' geometry information.

geometry buffer at the pixel location. Using the edge information, if any, we compute a texture-coordinate offset to sample the backbuffer texture using the texture filter to blend with a neighbor pixel. This will work for all edges where geometry information is present on both sides of the edge, i.e., for shared edges within a mesh. It will not work for silhouette edges of geometry in front of a background surface. In this case, only one side of the edge holds the relevant edge information. The background surface knows nothing about the geometry covering it. The problem is illustrated in Figure 4.6.

When visualizing the distance information there are noticeable gaps. The circled areas in Figure 4.6 show a couple of places where silhouette edges lack relevant geometry information on one side of the edge because those pixels were shaded by the background surface. To cover up the holes, we need to consider geometry information in neighboring pixels. If the pixel's own geometry information does not indicate that it is crossed by a geometric edge, we search the immediate neighborhood for pixels that might indicate otherwise. Figure 4.7 illustrates this process.

Here the green center pixel belongs to a background surface. It does not know that the cyan foreground surface is crossing over its territory. By checking its left neighbor, it can find that indeed there is an edge and it is indeed crossing over this pixel. The neighbor's information is then converted to the range of the pixel and used. Note that in Figure 4.7 there is also valid geometry information available in the pixel below it. Given that this edge is mostly vertical, it will point horizontally to the right, however, and will not be useful for the center pixel and

Neighbor	Range	Converted offset
Left	offset.x in $[0.5 \ldots 1.0]$	offset.x $- 1.0$
Right	offset.x in $[-1.0 \ldots -0.5]$	offset.x $+1.0$
Up	offset.y in $[0.5 \ldots 1.0]$	offset.y -1.0
Down	offset.y in $[-1.0 \ldots -0.5]$	offset.y $+1.0$

Table 4.1. Detecting and converting neighbors' geometry information.

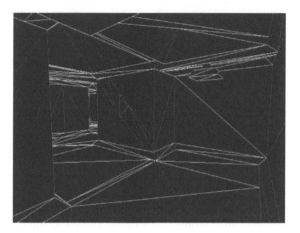

Figure 4.8. Patched geometry buffer with all gaps filled.

thus not used. The bottom-right pixel might look at it, but in this case it will
be rejected because the distance is out of range, i.e., the edge does not cross that
pixel. For patching up the geometry buffer we only need to check neighbors left,
right, up, and down. Table 4.1 shows the offset ranges to look for in neighboring
pixels and how to convert them. Figure 4.8 shows the final visualization of the
geometry buffer after filling up the gaps.

Once we have patched the missing information from the geometry buffer, we
can now blend with a neighbor pixel. As with GPAA, we use the texture filter to
accomplish the blending. The final edge-distance information is thus converted to
a sampling offset, and a single sample is taken from the backbuffer to get the final
antialiased pixel. The complete GBAA resolve shader is presented in Listing 4.5.

```
Texture2D BackBuffer;
Texture2D <float2> GeometryBuffer;
SamplerState Linear, Point;
float2 PixelSize;

float4 main(PsIn In) : SV_Target
{
    float2 offset = GeometryBuffer.Sample(Point, In.TexCoord);

    // Check geometry buffer for an edge cutting through
    // the pixel, otherwise search neighbors
    [flatten]
    if (min(abs(offset.x), abs(offset.y)) >= 0.5f) {
        offset = 0.5f;

        float2 offset0 = GeometryBuffer.Sample(Point,
            In.TexCoord, int2(-1, 0));
        float2 offset1 = GeometryBuffer.Sample(Point,
            In.TexCoord, int2(+1, 0));
```

```
        float2 offset2 = GeometryBuffer.Sample(Point,
            In.TexCoord, int2(0, -1));
        float2 offset3 = GeometryBuffer.Sample(Point,
            In.TexCoord, int2(0, +1));

        if (abs(offset0.x - 0.75f) < 0.25f)
            offset = offset0 + float2(-1, 0.5f);

        if (abs(offset1.x + 0.75f) < 0.25f)
            offset = offset1 + float2(1, 0.5f);

        if (abs(offset2.y - 0.75f) < 0.25f)
            offset = offset2 + float2(0.5f, -1);

        if (abs(offset3.y + 0.75f) < 0.25f)
            offset = offset3 + float2(0.5f, 1);
    }

    // Convert distance to texture coordinate shift
    float2 off = (offset >= float2(0, 0))?
                  float2(0.5f, 0.5f) : float2(-0.5f, -0.5f);
    offset = off - offset;

    // Blend with neighbor pixel using texture filter
    return BackBuffer.Sample(Linear,
        In.TexCoord + offset * PixelSize);
}
```

Listing 4.5. The GBAA resolve shader.

Antialiasing alpha-tested edges. An important advantage of GBAA over GPAA is that the former is not strictly tied to geometric edges. Any form of edges that can be encoded in the geometry buffer will be properly antialiased. This means we can also antialias alpha-tested edges. All we need to do in the alpha-tested pass is to compute the distance to the edge, i.e., the cross-over point where the alpha value falls below the threshold value, in the same fashion as for geometric edges. A pretty straightforward way to accomplish this is presented in Listing 4.6. Essentially, we get the slope of alpha in x and y in screen space using gradient instructions and simply compute how far we need to go in either direction to get down to the alpha-reference value, and then we select the shortest direction.

```
float dx = ddx(alpha);
float dy = ddy(alpha);

float2 alpha_dist = 0.0f;

if (abs(dx) > abs(dy))
  alpha_dist.x = (alpha_ref - alpha) / dx;
else
  alpha_dist.y = (alpha_ref - alpha) / dy;
```

Listing 4.6. Alpha-tested edge distance.

Figure 4.9. Alpha-tested edges before applying GBAA.

Other types of edges for which it might be interesting to use GBAA are bump edges internal to the surface when using parallax occlusion mapping [Brawley and Tatarchuk 04].

Results. Other than the ability to antialias alpha-tested edges, GBAA is for all practical purposes identical to GPAA in terms of image quality. Figures 4.2–4.4 are thus representative of the GBAA quality as well. For alpha-tested edges Figures 4.9 and 4.10 illustrate the quality of alpha-tested edge with and without antialiasing.

Figure 4.10. Alpha-tested edges antialiased with GBAA.

4.2.3   Performance and Optimizations

The main difference between GPAA and GBAA lies in performance characteristics
and engine integration. With a small amount of geometry, such as in the provided
demo applications, GPAA wins the performance race, although GBAA is not
particularly slow in this case either. As geometry gets denser, GBAA gets more
favorable, depending on hardware, resolution, and other factors.

For GBAA, where we have a fullscreen resolve pass, we can simply render
the scene to a temporary buffer and then resolve to the backbuffer. GPAA, on
the other hand, requires a copy of the backbuffer to be sampled as a texture.
While this is a relatively small cost for a modern GPU, it is probably still worth
optimizing when possible. Depending on what the engine is doing, it may already
have a copy of the backbuffer at hand, for example, for refraction effects or post-
effect purposes. In that case all is fine and the available copy can be used at
no extra cost. In other cases, it should be noted that strictly speaking there
is nothing in the technique that requires the use of a copy of the backbuffer
rather than modifying it in place directly. However, reading from and writing
to the same surface at the same time causes a read-after-write hazard and is
generally considered a bad idea. Given the long pipelines of GPUs, as well as
caching on the render backend, values tend to be written to memory long after a
shader invocation produced its final outputs, and even if it is written to memory
already, new shader invocations are not guaranteed to receive the updated value
when sampling the texture since old values may still hang around in the texture
cache.

For this reason, APIs generally declare this case as undefined. Some APIs,
such as DirectX 10 and 11, actively prevent you from entering such a state.
While undefined certainly gives you no guarantees of anything, in practice it
generally means that you receive either the old or the new value. For these
two techniques, these values are either the same, or both acceptable. So if you
feel a bit adventurous, and your API does not prevent you, you may want to
experiment with in-place modification. For fixed hardware platforms, such as
consoles, where you don't have to worry about things breaking on a particular
driver or hardware revision, it basically boils down to trying it out, and if it works
it works. Unfortunately, in the case of the Xbox 360 the renderable memory
(EDRAM) is separate from texture-sampleable memory (regular video memory),
so on this platform it is impossible to do in-place modification for hardware
reasons. In OpenGL there is the `GL_NV_texture_barrier` extension [Bolz 09],
which relaxes the rules for read-after-write cases and thus allows for in-place
modification. At the time of this writing, it is supported by both Nvidia and
AMD. Strictly speaking, we do not fully comply with the conditions of that
extension since we are sampling a neighbor pixel, but in practice it will almost
certainly work. It is the closest we get to a defined behavior today. The important
thing is that this extension also tells us that the driver will not actively prevent

us from entering this "dangerous" state since it is now valid on the API level to have the same texture bound on both input and output.

An optimization for GPAA is to prefilter the mesh geometry and only draw lines for edges that are deemed necessary to antialias. For instance, shared edges between coplanar polygons can be excluded. It is also possible to store the polygon normals for each edge and only draw silhouette edges, i.e., where one normal points towards the camera and one points away. Using a geometry shader and adjacency, it is also possible to accomplish the same. In this case no additional memory is required for storing the vertices or indices.

4.3   Conclusion and Future Work

Two techniques have been presented that produce very high-quality antialiasing. However, there are several open opportunities for improvements and additional research. This includes efficient ways to remove internal edges from antialiasing when using a geometry shader, such as for GBAA. Currently these edges are needlessly antialiased. Typically this does not cause any problems, but ideally it should not be done.

Currently only one edge is considered per pixel. This could cause small artifacts in corners. Sometimes single pixels along an edge are off, because the method went by a different edge from the background. It may be possible to include several edges and blend with multiple neighbors, or alternatively, to prioritize edges based on depth or other heuristics.

Both techniques have been implemented on a PC using DirectX 10. It would be interesting to see how well these techniques would fit on current generation consoles. The consoles do not support a geometry shader, for instance, but there are ways around this limitation, although possibly at the cost of additional memory.

The current implementations of these techniques do not catch edges between intersecting meshes, such as for example, buildings placed on terrain where some parts of the buildings are bound to go some distance into the ground. For static geometry there is nothing preventing such edges from being detected in a preprocess step and stored, albeit this is not necessarily a small undertaking. For dynamic objects, it may not be very practical to attempt to detect such edges in real time. Theoretically, it ought to be possible to detect such edges by looking for creases in the depth buffer. Promising experiments have been done in this area.

Finally, it would be interesting to see what effect on quality blending with a background layer (OIT style) would have compared to blending with a neighbor pixel.

Bibliography

[Bolz 09] Jeff Bolz. "NV_texture_barrier." Available at http://www.opengl.org/registry/specs/NV/texture_barrier.txt

[Brawley and Tatarchuk 04] Zoe Brawley and Natalya Tatarchuk. "Parallax Occlusion Mapping: Self-Shadowing, Perspective-Correct Bump Mapping Using Reverse Height Map Tracing." In *ShaderX*^{3}, edited by Wolfgang Engel, pp. 135–154. Hingham, MA: Charles River Media, 2004.

[Jimenez et al. 11] Jorge Jimenez, Belen Masia, Jose I. Echevarria, Fernando Navarro, and Diego Gutierrez. "Practical Morphological Anti-Aliasing." In *GPU Pro*^{2}, edited by Wolfgang Engel, pp. 95–114. Natick, MA: A K Peters, 2011.

[Lottes 11] Timothy Lottes. *NVIDIA FXAA*. Available at http://timothylottes.blogspot.com/2011/03/nvidia-fxaa.html

[McGuire and Luebke 11] Morgan McGuire and David Luebke. "Subpixel Reconstruction Antialiasing." Available at http://research.nvidia.com/publication/subpixel-reconstruction-antialiasing, 2011.

[Malan 10] Hugh Malan. "Edge Anti-Aliasing by Post-Processing." In *GPU Pro*, edited by Wolfgang Engel, pp. 265–289. Natick, MA: A K Peters, 2010.

[Persson 11a] Emil Persson. "Geometric Post-process Anti-Aliasing." Available at http://www.humus.name/index.php?page=3D&ID=86, 2011.

[Persson 11b] Emil Persson. "Geometry Buffer Anti-Aliasing." Available at http://www.humus.name/index.php?page=3D&ID=87, 2011.

[Reshetov09] Alexander Reshetov. "Morphological Antialiasing." Available at http://visual-computing.intel-research.net/publications/papers/2009/mlaa/mlaa.pdf, 2009.

[Thibieroz 11] Nicolas Thibieroz. "Order-Independent Transparency using Per-Pixel Linked Lists." In *GPU Pro*^{2}, edited by Wolfgang Engel, pp. 409–432. Natick, MA: A K Peters, 2011.

Rendering

The field of real-time rendering is constantly evolving and it can be challenging to keep up-to-date with the latest tricks and techniques. The goal of the rendering section is to introduce beginners as well as seasoned graphics programmers to some of the latest advancements in real-time rendering. These techniques are all very practical and many can be found in the latest games on the market.

The first article in this section is "Practical Elliptical Texture Filtering on the GPU," by Pavlos Mavridis and Georgios Papaioannou. This article presents a useful technique for achieving high quality, shader-based texture filtering on the GPU. The authors provide a reference implementation that can easily be integrated into an existing renderer.

The next article is "An Approximation to the Chapman Grazing-Incidence Function for Atmospheric Scattering," by Christian Schüler. This article describes an inexpensive approximation to atmospheric scattering and will be of particular interest to those interested in physically based, fully dynamic, virtual environments in which both visual realism and computational efficiency are of high importance.

The third article in the rendering section is "Volumetric Real-Time Water and Foam Rendering," by Daniel Scherzer, Florian Bagar, and Oliver Mattausch. This article presents a dynamic, multilayered approach for rendering fluids and foam. This technique is presented in the context of a GPU-based fluid simulation but is compatible with other forms of fluid simulation as well.

The fourth article in this section is "CryENGINE 3: Three Years of Work in Review," by Tiago Sousa, Nick Kasyan, and Nicolas Schulz. This article covers some of the latest features of a production-proven, highly successful real-time rendering engine. The authors discuss many cutting-edge topics with an eye on efficiency and scalability. Some of the many techniques they cover include screen-space methods for reflections, character self-shadowing, and efficient stereoscopic image-pair generation.

The last article in this section, "Inexpensive Antialiasing of Simple Objects," by Mikkel Gjøl and Mark Gjøl, explores the use of discontinuity edge overdraw for antialiasing simple objects on mobile phones. The essence of this technique is to render a "smooth" line on top of aliasing primitive edges to cover the aliasing edge.

The ideas and techniques presented in this section represent some of the latest developments in the realm of computer graphics. I would like to thank our authors for sharing their exciting new work with the graphics community and I hope that these ideas inspire readers to further extend the state of the art in real-time rendering.

—Christopher Oat

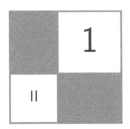

Practical Elliptical Texture Filtering on the GPU

Pavlos Mavridis and Georgios Papaioannou

1.1 Introduction

Hardware texture filtering, even on state-of-the-art graphics hardware, suffers from several aliasing artifacts, in both the spatial and temporal domain. These artifacts are mostly evident in extreme conditions, such as grazing viewing angles, highly warped texture coordinates, or extreme perspective, and become especially annoying when animation is involved. Poor texture filtering is evident as excessive blurring or moiré patterns in the spatial domain and as pixel flickering in the temporal domain, as can be seen in Figure 1.1 and the accompanying demo application.

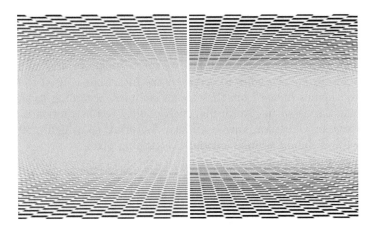

Figure 1.1. A benchmark scene consisting of two infinite planes demonstrating the improvement of elliptical filtering over the native hardware texture filtering.

In this chapter, we present a series of simple and effective methods to perform high quality texture filtering on modern GPUs. We base our methods on the theory behind the elliptical weighted average (EWA) filter [Greene and Heckbert 86]. EWA is regarded as one of the highest quality texture filtering algorithms and is used as a benchmark to test the quality of other algorithms. It is often used in offline rendering to eliminate texture aliasing in the extreme conditions mentioned above, but due to the high computational cost it is not widely adopted in real-time graphics.

We first present an exact implementation of the EWA filter that smartly uses the underlying bilinear filtering hardware to gain a significant speedup. We then proceed with an approximation of the EWA filter that uses the underlying anisotropic filtering hardware of the GPU to construct a filter that closely matches the shape and the properties of the EWA filter, offering vast improvements in the quality of the texture mapping. To further accelerate the method, we also introduce a spatial and temporal sample distribution scheme that reduces the number of required texture fetches and the memory bandwidth consumption, without reducing the perceived image quality. We believe that those characteristics make our method practical for use in games and other interactive applications, as well as applications that require increased fidelity in texture mapping, like GPU renderers and image manipulation programs. We first described these methods at the 2011 Symposium on Interactive 3D Graphics and Games [Mavridis and Papaioannou 11]. This chapter reviews the main ideas of that paper with an emphasis on small, yet important implementation details.

1.2   Elliptical Filtering

This section provides an overview of the theory behind texture filtering and the elliptical weighted average (EWA) filter.

In computer graphics the pixels are point samples. The pixels do not have an actual shape, since they are points, but we often assign an area to them. This area is the footprint (the nonzero areas) of the filter that is used to reconstruct the final continuous image from these point samples, according to the sampling theorem. As discussed in [Smith 95], high quality reconstruction filters, like a truncated sinc or Gaussian, have a circular footprint, so a high quality texture filtering method should assume circular overlapping pixels.

The projection of a pixel with circular footprint to texture space is an ellipse with arbitrary orientation, as illustrated in Figure 1.2. In degenerate cases, like extreme grazing viewing angles, the projection is actually an arbitrary conic section, but for our purposes an elliptical approximation suffices, since, for these cases, any visible surface detail is lost anyway. A texture filtering algorithm should return a convolution of the texels (texture point samples) inside the projected area S of the pixel with the projection of the reconstruction filter H in

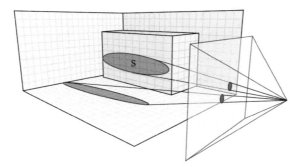

Figure 1.2. The projection of a pixel with circular footprint on a surface covers an elliptical region.

texture space. In particular, it should compute the following equation:

$$C_f(s,t) = \sum_{u,v \in S} H(u,v)C(u,v),$$

where $C(u,v)$ is the color of the texel at the (u,v) texture coordinates and $C_f(s,t)$ is the filtered texture color. In the above equation H is normalized.

The EWA algorithm approximates the projected pixel footprint with an elliptical region, defined by the following equation [Heckbert 89]:

$$d^2(u,v) = Au^2 + Buv + Cv^2,$$

where the center of the pixel is assumed to be at $(0,0)$ in texture space and

$$A = A_{nn}/F,$$
$$B = B_{nn}/F,$$
$$C = C_{nn}/F,$$
$$F = A_{nn}C_{nn} - B_{nn}^2/4,$$
$$A_{nn} = (\partial v/\partial x)^2 + (\partial v/\partial y)^2,$$
$$B_{nn} = -2 * (\partial u/\partial x * \partial v/\partial x + \partial u/\partial y * \partial v/\partial y),$$
$$C_{nn} = (\partial u/\partial x)^2 + (\partial u/\partial y)^2.$$

The partial derivatives $(\partial u/\partial x, \partial u/\partial y, \partial v/\partial x, \partial v/\partial y)$ represent the rate of change of the texture coordinates relative to changes in screen space. The quantity d^2 denotes the squared distance of the texel (u,v) from the pixel center when projected back into screen space. The algorithm scans the bounding box of the elliptical region in texture space and determines which texels reside inside the ellipse $(d^2 \leq 1)$. These samples contribute to the convolution sum, with weights

```
// Computes the Elliptical Weighted Average filter
// p are the sampling coordinates
// du/dv are the derivatives of the texture coordinates
vec4 ewaFilter(sampler2D tex, vec2 p, vec2 du, vec2 dv)
{
    // compute ellipse coefficients A, B, C, F:
    float A,B,C,F;
    A = du.t*du.t+dv.t*dv.t+1;
    ...

    // Compute the ellipse's bounding box in texture space
    int u_min, u_max, v_min, v_max;
    u_min = int(floor(p.s - 2. / (-B*B+4.0*C*A)*
            sqrt((-B*B+4.0*C*A)*C*F)));
    ...

    // Iterate over the ellipse's bounding box and
    // calculate Ax^2+Bxy*Cy^2; when this value
    // is less than F, we're inside the ellipse.
    vec4 color = 0;
    float den = 0;
    for (int v = v_min; v <= v_max; ++v)
    {
        float q = A*u*u+B*u*v*C*v*v;
        for (int u = u_min; u <= u_max; ++u)
            if (q < F)
            {
                float d = q / F;
                float weight = Filter(d);
                color += weight* texture2D(tex, vec2(u+0.5,v+0.5)/size);
                den += weight;
            }
    }

    return color*(1./den);
}
```

Listing 1.1. Pseudocode implementation of the EWA filter.

proportional to the distance d. Listing 1.1 outlines this idea. `Filter(d)` denotes the reconstruction filter. [Greene and Heckbert 86] propose the usage of a Gaussian filter, but in practice any reconstruction filter can be used.

1.2.1 Bounding the Runtime Cost

The runtime of the brute-force algorithm is directly proportional to the area of the ellipse in texture space and the number of texels it includes. To reduce the number of the texture samples in this area, a mip-map pyramid is used and sampling is performed from the mip-map level in which the minor ellipse radius is between one and three pixels, depending on the required quality and performance. Even when using mip-maps, the area of a highly eccentric ellipse can be arbitrarily

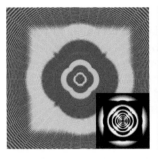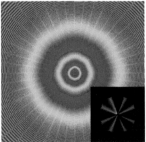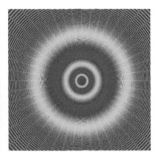

Figure 1.3. Comparison of the lod calculation of an Nvidia Fermi card when using the lowest quality settings in the drivers (left), the highest possible quality settings (middle), and the optimal lod calculations (right).

high, resulting in unacceptably long running times. To avoid this, the maximum eccentricity of the ellipse is clamped to a predefined maximum. Taking these two measures ensures a bounded runtime for the algorithm.

Computing the mip-map level (lod) and clamping ellipses with high eccentricity requires the computation of the minor (R_{minor}) and major (R_{major}) radius of the ellipse

$$r = \sqrt{(A - C)^2 + B^2},$$
$$R_{\mathrm{major}} = \sqrt{2/(A + C - r)},$$
$$R_{\mathrm{minor}} = \sqrt{2/(A + C + r)},$$
$$\mathrm{lod} = \log_2(R_{\mathrm{minor}}/\text{texels-per-pixel.}) \tag{1.1}$$

Instead of computing the lod level based on the minor ellipse radius, we have investigated the option to use the lod values calculated explicitly by the hardware. On newer hardware this can be done using the appropriate shading language function (`textureQueryLOD()` in GLSL), or in older hardware by fetching a texel from a texture with color-coded lod levels. Figure 1.3 visualizes the lod selection on the latest Nvidia graphics cards and compares it with the ideal lod selection based on the ellipse minor radius. We observe that Nvidia's hardware, at the highest quality settings, performs a piecewise approximation of the optimal calculations, resulting in suboptimal lod selection on pixels depending on their angle and that the measured deviation (shown in the insets of Figure 1.3) peaks at intervals of 45 degrees. An overestimation of the lod level will result in excessive blurriness, while underestimation will result in longer runtimes. In practice, we have observed that using the hardware lod calculations does not result in visible quality degradation, while the performance of the method is increased.

Hardware trilinear filtering interpolates between the closest two lod levels, in order to avoid discontinuities. We have found that it is much more preferable to perform better filtering in the high detail lod level (by using more samples), than to compute two inferior estimates and interpolate between them. In that case, discontinuities from the lod selection can only be observed in very extreme cases, and even then can be dealt with using more projected texels in each pixel (Equation (1.1)).

1.2.2 Filtering sRGB Textures

A very important implementation detail that is often omitted, is that all the texture filtering and antialiasing operations should be done in linear color space. On the other hand, 8 bits-per-component textures are usually stored in sRGB color space, in order to better take advantage of the available precision, by taking into account the characteristics of human vision. Therefore, the texture data should be first converted to a linear color space before the filtering operations. And, after the shading operations, colors should be converted back to sRGB for display in the output device. Fortunately, the latest graphics hardware can do this conversion using specialized fixed-function hardware, without any additional overhead. In OpenGL in particular, this can be done by using the `GL_EXT_texture_sRGB` and `GL_EXT_framebuffer_sRGB` extensions, while Direct3D provides similar mechanisms. Furthermore, all the prefiltered mip-maps should also be computed in linear color space. The importance of filtering in the proper color space is demonstrated in Figure 1.4. (All the images in this chapter were produced with filtering in linear color space.)

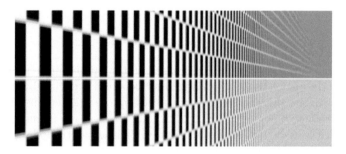

Figure 1.4. Texture filtering using mip-maps computed in sRGB color space (top). Proper filtering in linear color space (bottom). Filtering in nonlinear color space leads to incorrect darkening when the lowest mip-map levels are used.

1.2.3 GPU Optimizations

A naïve direct implementation of the EWA filter on the GPU would read every texel in the bounding box of the elliptical region, and if it were located inside the ellipse, it would be weighted and accumulated. A much better approach is to

use the linear filtering of the graphics hardware to reduce the number of fetches
to one half, by smartly fetching two texels at a time using one bilinear fetch.
For two neighboring texels C_i and C_{i+1}, with weights w_i and w_{i+1}, respectively,
the following weighted sum can be replaced by a single bilinear texture fetch
operation at position x between the two texel centers:

$$w_i C_i + w_{i+1} C_{i+1} = C_x(w_i + w_{i+1}),$$

$$x = i + \frac{w_{i+1}}{w_i + w_{i+1}},$$

$$0 \leq \frac{w_{i+1}}{w_i + w_{i+1}} \leq 1.$$

The last inequality is always true for reconstruction filters with positive weights,
like the Gaussian one. In our case, the texel weight w_i is derived from the
reconstruction filter (`Filter(d)` in Listing 1.1) and the distance d of the texel to
the filter center, as explained in Section 1.2. The for loop in Listing 1.1 should be
adjusted to process two texels at a time. An important implementation detail is
that when using this technique, we should take into account the exact coordinates
of the texel centers. In the case of OpenGL, texel centers are assumed to be at
the centers of a grid (meaning that texels are located at coordinates integer $+0.5$).

This technique assumes that the cost of one texture fetch with bilinear filtering
is less than the cost of two fetches with point sampling plus the time to combine
them. Our experiments confirm that this assumption is true. The results from
this method should be identical with the ones from the reference implementation,
but slight deviations may occur due to the difference in the precision in which
operations are performed by the shader units and by the fixed-function bilinear
filtering units.

Extending the same principle in two dimensions, we can replace four weighted
texture fetches with a single fetch from the appropriate position. While it is trivial
to find this position in the case of a box filter, in the case of a Gaussian filter the
weights can only be approximated. In other words, we can calculate the position
that best approximates the Gaussian weights and perform a single texture fetch
from that position. In practice we did not observe any significant performance
gain from this method, while on the other hand it imposes significant constraints
on the nature of the reconstruction filters that can be used.

1.3   Elliptical Footprint Approximation

In the same spirit as the Feline algorithm [McCormack et al. 99], we present a
method that uses simpler shapes to closely match the shape of the ideal elliptical
filter. Instead of using simple trilinear probes like in the Feline algorithm, we
propose the usage of the anisotropic probes provided by the graphics hardware.

We place the probes on a line along the major axis of the ellipse, as shown in
Figure 1.5. The length of the line L and the number of probes N_{probes} are given

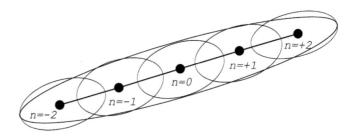

Figure 1.5. The basic idea of our method: approximating a highly eccentric ellipse with many ellipses of low eccentricity. This way we can overcome the limits imposed by the hardware and better filter elliptical footprints with high degrees of anisotropy.

by the following equations

$$N_{\text{probes}} = 2 * (R_{\text{major}}/(\alpha * R_{\text{minor}})) - 1,$$
$$L = 2 * (R_{\text{major}} - \alpha * R_{\text{minor}}), \tag{1.2}$$

where α is the degree of anisotropy of the underlying hardware probes. For $\alpha = 1$ our algorithm is equivalent to Feline. For simplicity, an odd number of probes is considered. Similar to Feline, probes are placed around the midpoint (u_m, v_m) of the filter, as follows:

$$\theta = \operatorname{atan}(B/(A - C))/2,$$
$$du = \cos(\theta) * L/(N_{\text{probes}} - 1),$$
$$dv = \sin(\theta) * L/(N_{\text{probes}} - 1),$$
$$(u_n, v_n) = (u_m, v_m) + n/2 * (du, dv), \quad n = 0, \pm 2, \pm 4 \ldots, \tag{1.3}$$

where (u_n, v_n) is the position of n-th probe. To better match the shape of the EWA filter, the probes are weighted proportionally to their distance from the center of the footprint, according to a Gaussian function. The shape of the filter in texture space compared to an exact EWA filter is shown in Figure 1.6.

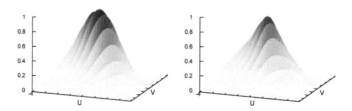

Figure 1.6. Comparison of the exact EWA filter (left) with our approximation using three elliptical probes (right).

We don't have any strong guarantees about the quality or the shape of those probes, since the OpenGL specification does not explicitly enforce any particular method for anisotropic filtering. The only hint given by the hardware implementation is that the probes approximate an anisotropic area with maximum anisotropy of N. In the above analysis, we have assumed that the hardware anisotropic probes are elliptical, but in practice, to compensate for their potential imperfections in shape and to better cover the area of the elliptical filter, we just increase the number of probes depending on the desired quality. Using an adaptive number of probes creates an irregular workload per pixel for the graphics hardware scheduler, which should be avoided. In practice, setting the number of probes to a constant number gives better performance. In our tests, using five probes eliminated all the visible artifacts on the Nvidia hardware (with high quality texture filtering enabled). For more than five probes, no significant improvement in image quality could be measured.

If the probes fail to cover the ellipse, then aliasing will occur. On the other hand, if the probes exceed the extents of the ellipse (e.g., by placing them beyond half the length of the central line in each direction) then blurring will occur. Our method always avoids the second case, but the first case can still happen in extreme cases, since we have clamped the maximum number of probes. Still, our method always provides an improvement over hardware texture filtering.

1.3.1 Spatial Filter

After some investigation of the benchmark scenes, we have observed that the regions where the hardware filtering fails are limited. For the majority of a scene, the quality of the image is free of any aliasing artifacts. As expected, the problematic regions are regions with high anisotropy, and, in particular, on the

Figure 1.7. Regions in red denote areas with anisotropy greater than 16, the limit in current hardware implementations. An infinite tunnel benchmark scene (left). A typical game scene (right).

Nvidia hardware, regions with anisotropy greater than 16, which is the advertised maximum anisotropy of the hardware unit. Figure 1.7 highlights the problematic regions on the benchmark scene and one typical game scene.

After this observation, we perform high-quality filtering only in the regions highlighted with red, and for the rest of the scene we use hardware filtering. The anisotropy of a pixel is accurately measured using Equations (1.1). To eliminate any visible seams between the two regions, areas close to the threshold level use a blend of hardware and software filtering. This approach creates exactly two different workloads for the hardware, one high and one low. In the majority of cases, the two different sampling methods are used in spatially coherent pixel clusters within a frame. Therefore, compared to a completely adaptive sample selection, our tests indicate that this case is handled more efficiently by the GPU hardware scheduler and results in a sizable performance gain.

1.3.2 Temporal Sample Distribution

In order to further improve the runtime performance of our filtering algorithm in games and other real-time applications that display many rendered images at high frame rates, we present a temporal sample distribution scheme, where texture filtering samples are distributed among successive frames.

In particular, the n anisotropic samples (probes) of Equation (1.3) are distributed in two successive frames. The first frame uses samples $0, \pm 4, \pm 8 \ldots$ and the next one $0, \pm 2, \pm 6 \ldots$. The sample at the center of the filter (sample 0) is included in both frames to minimize the variance between the two. When the frames are displayed in quick succession, the human eye perceives the average of the two frames.

For this technique to work, the application should maintain a stable and vertical sync-locked frame rate of 60 Hz or more. The usage of vertical sync is mandatory; otherwise the rate of the rendered frames will not match the rate at which they are displayed and are perceived by the human eye, and the method naturally fails. This is a shortcoming, but we should note that in the era of high-performing graphics hardware, rendering without vertical sync makes little sense, since it introduces visible tearing. Obviously the method can be extended to distribute samples in more than two frames when the refresh rate of the application and the output device is high enough.

Using this method, the quality of texture filtering is enhanced considerably for static or distant objects, but fast-moving objects receive fewer samples. This is hardly objectionable, since in that case potential aliasing artifacts are difficult to notice. In our tests, the usage of temporal sample distribution always improved the perceived image quality for a given number of samples.

Overall, this temporal method is very simple to implement, does not require additional memory, and always provides a constant speedup. The obvious shortcoming is that the application should maintain a high frame rate. The success of the method is also highly dependent on the ability of the output device to be synchronized with the graphics hardware. We had great success when using PC monitors, but some projection equipment might fail in the synchronization with the graphics hardware.

1.4 Results

Figure 1.8 demonstrates the improvement our method produces in a benchmark scene consisting of an infinite tunnel with a checkerboard texture. To better assess the extent of the improvement, the reader is highly encouraged to run the accompanying demo application, since the aliasing artifacts are highly objectionable in motion. The same figure also shows the resulting filtering from all the filtering methods we have presented in this chapter.

Figure 1.9 demonstrates the improvement from increasing the maximum degrees of anisotropy. A higher maximum degree of anisotropy offers more detail at grazing angles. We observe that direct convolution filtering with an anisotropic ratio of 64:1 preserves more detail at the center of the tunnel. An ideal filtering algorithm would show the lines to converge at the center of the left image,

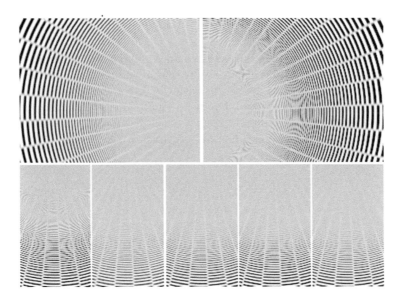

Figure 1.8. Top: A benchmark scene consisting of an infinite tunnel demonstrating the improvement of elliptical filtering (left) over the native hardware texture filtering (right). Close-up comparisons of the various texture filtering methods (bottom). From left to right: hardware filtering, elliptical, approximated filter, spatial filter, temporal filter (average of two frames).

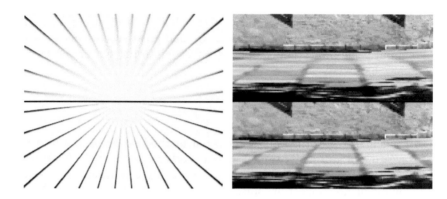

Figure 1.9. Close-ups demonstrating the improved clarity when increasing the maximum degrees of anisotropy from 16 (up) to 64 (down).

but in practice this is very difficult because an infinite anisotropy level would be required. Apart from the increased clarity, in practice we also observe that the elliptical filtering eliminates the occasional pixel flickering (temporal aliasing) of the hardware implementation.

1.4.1 Performance Measurements

Figure 1.10 presents comprehensive performance and quality measurements for all the methods presented in this chapter. The spatial and temporal sample distribution schemes can be used to accelerate both the direct convolution methods and the ellipse approximation method, but since we are interested in the highest possible performance, we only present results when distributing the samples of the ellipse approximation method. The performance of the method was measured

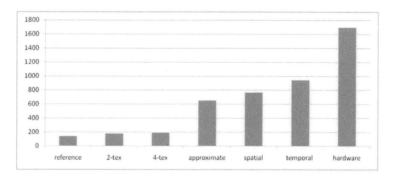

Figure 1.10. The performance of the methods presented in this chapter measured in Mtexes/sec on an Nvidia GTX460.

on the tunnel scene of the accompanying demo application on a middle range graphics card. We observe that the direct convolution methods (reference, 2-tex, 4-tex) are an order of magnitude slower than the approximating ones, making their applicability for real-time applications rather limited.

1.4.2   Integration with Game Engines

The proposed texture filtering algorithms can be implemented as a direct replacement to the built-in texture lookup functions, making the integration with game engines trivial. In the accompanying material of this book, we provide our proof-of-concept implementation in GLSL. In the case of temporal filtering, the current frame number should be exposed inside the shaders. One integration option is to globally replace all the texturing function calls with the enhanced ones, but this method is probably an overkill. Alternatively, at content-creation time, the enhanced texture filtering could selectively be applied only on certain problematic surfaces. The second option can lead to better runtime performance, but at the cost of increased authoring time.

1.5   Conclusions

We have shown that high-quality elliptical filtering is practical on today's GPUs, by employing several methods to speed up the reference algorithm. Texture filtering quality is one issue that separates the offline production rendering from the real-time one, and this work can provide a viable texture filtering improvement for hardware-accelerated rendering applications.

1.6   Acknowledgments

The authors would like to thank Matt Pharr for providing a sample CPU implementation of the EWA filter on his website, which was a starting point for this project, and Inigo Quilez for providing the GLSL code to ray-trace the infinite plane and tunnel test scenes, as part of Shader Toy.

Bibliography

[Greene and Heckbert 86] Ned Greene and Paul S. Heckbert. "Creating Raster Omnimax Images from Multiple Perspective Views Using the Elliptical Weighted Average Filter." *IEEE Comput. Graph. Appl.* 6:6 (1986), 21–27.

[Heckbert 89] Paul S. Heckbert. "Fundamentals of texture mapping and image warping." Technical Report UCB/CSD-89-516, EECS Department, University of California, Berkeley, 1989.

[Mavridis and Papaioannou 11] Pavlos Mavridis and Georgios Papaioannou. "High Quality Elliptical Texture Filtering on GPU." In *Symposium on Interactive 3D Graphics and Games, I3D '11*, pp. 23–30. New York: ACM Press, 2011.

[McCormack et al. 99] Joel McCormack, Ronald Perry, Keith I. Farkas, and Norman P. Jouppi. "Feline: Fast Elliptical Lines for Anisotropic Texture Mapping." In *Proceedings of SIGGRAPH '99, Proceedings, Annual Conference Series*, edited by Alyn Rockwood, pp. 243–250. Reading, MA: ACM Press/Addison-Wesley Publishing, 1999.

[Smith 95] Alvy Ray Smith. "A pixel is not a little square, a pixel is not a little square, a pixel is not a little square! (And a voxel is not a little cube)." Technical report, Technical Memo 6, Microsoft Research, 1995.

An Approximation to the Chapman Grazing-Incidence Function for Atmospheric Scattering

Christian Schüler

2.1 Introduction

Atmospheric scattering for computer graphics is the treatment of the atmosphere as a participating medium, essentially "calculating the color of the sky." This is interesting for any application where the time of day, the season, or the properties of the atmosphere are not known in advance, or the viewpoint may not be restricted to a point on the earth's surface. It is a historically difficult effect to render, especially at planetary scale.

Early attempts at atmospheric scattering can be found in [Klassen 87] and [Nishita et al. 93]. Recent implementations with an emphasis on real time are [Hoffmann and Preetham 02], [O'Neil 05], and [Bruneton and Neyret 08]. A common theme of all these approaches is finding ways to efficiently evaluate or precompute the Chapman function, $Ch(x, \chi)$. This is the density integral for a ray in a spherically symmetric, exponentially decreasing atmosphere.

The Chapman function has been subject to extensive treatment in the physics literature. Approximations and tabulations have been published, most of it with a focus on precision. This article explores a different direction for its evaluation: an approximation so cheap that $Ch(x, \chi)$ can be considered a commodity, while still being accurate enough for our graphics needs.

2.2 Atmospheric Scattering

This section is a brief review of atmospheric scattering and a definition of terms.

When light travels through air, it will be partly absorbed and partly scattered into other directions. This gives rise to the phenomenon of *aerial perspective*. The

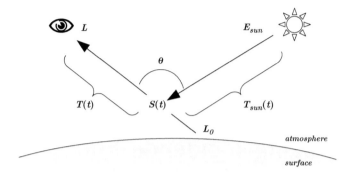

Figure 2.1. Atmospheric scattering 101. See the text for an explanation of the symbols.

fraction of light that is unimpeded along a path is the transmittance T, and the amount that is added into the path due to scattering is the in-scatter S (see Figure 2.1). Thus, the aerial perspective of a distant source of radiance L_0 is seen by an observer as the radiance L:

$$L \;=\; L_0\,T + S.$$

To arrive at the total in-scatter S, in general one would have to integrate it along the path. Then, the in-scatter at a particular point $S(t)$ would have to be calculated from the local irradiance field E over the entire sphere of directions Ω with an atmosphere-dependent phase function $f(\theta)$:

$$S \;=\; \int S(t)\,T(t)\,dt,$$

$$S(t) \;=\; \int_{\Omega} E(t)\,f(\theta)\,d\Omega.$$

The irradiance is usually discretized as a sum of individual contributions. Especially during the day, the single most important contributor is the sun, which can be simplified to a directional point source E_{sun}, for the irradiance arriving at the outer atmosphere boundary; E_{sun} is attenuated by the transmittance T_{sun} for the path from the atmosphere boundary towards point $S(t)$:

$$S(t) \;=\; E_{\text{sun}}\,T_{\text{sun}}(t)\,f(\theta).$$

The transmittance itself is an exponentially decreasing function of the airmass m times an extinction coefficient β. The latter is a property of the scattering medium, possibly wavelength dependent. The airmass is an integral of the air density $\rho(t)$ along the path:

$$T = \exp(-\beta m),$$
$$m = \int \rho(t)dt.$$

To complete the calculation, we need a physical model for β and f. There exists Rayleigh theory and Mie theory, which have been discussed in depth in previous publications, e.g., [Nishita et al. 93] and [Hoffmann and Preetham 02]. It is beyond the scope of this article to provide more detail here.

2.3 The Chapman Function

In order to reduce the algorithmic complexity, it would be nice to have an efficient way to calculate transmittances along rays. It turns out that this reduces to an evaluation of the Chapman function.

Without loss of generality, let's start a ray at an observer inside the atmosphere and extend it to infinity (see Figure 2.2). The ray can be traced back to a point of lowest altitude r_0. We take the liberty to call this point the *periapsis* even though the path is not an orbit. Here we define $t = 0$, and the altitude for any point along the ray as follows:

$$r(t) = \sqrt{r_0^2 + t^2}.$$

Let's further assume a spherically symmetric atmosphere with an exponentially decreasing density, characterized by a scale height H. We normalize the

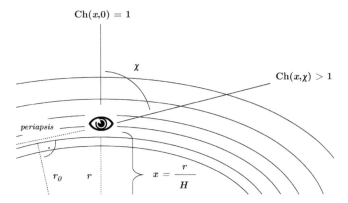

Figure 2.2. The Chapman function. Relative airmass in an exponentially decreasing atmosphere with scale height H, normalized observer altitude x and incidence angle χ. The lowest altitude is at r_0.

density to a reference density ρ_0 at reference altitude R. The density at any altitude is then

$$\rho(r) \;=\; \rho_0 \, \exp\left(\frac{R - r}{H}\right).$$

Combining these expressions yields an integral for the airmass along the entire ray. The integration boundary is trigonometrically related to the observer altitude r and the incidence angle χ:

$$m \;=\; \rho_0 \int\limits_{r\cos\chi}^{\infty} \exp\left(\frac{R - \sqrt{r_0^2 + t^2}}{H}\right) dt,$$
$$r_0 \;=\; r \sin\chi.$$

This integral does not have a simple solution, except when looking straight upwards into the zenith ($\chi = 0$). In this case, the mass along the ray is just the mass of the air column above the observer. This is, by the definition of the density distribution, one scale height times the density at the observer. Let's call that mass $m_\perp$:

$$m_\perp \;=\; \rho_0 \, H \exp\left(\frac{R - r}{H}\right).$$

Can we possibly have a function that relates $m_\perp$ to m? We can, for this is the Chapman function $\mathrm{Ch}(x, \chi)$, named after the physicist who was the first to formulate this problem [Chapman 31]. We write the Chapman function as follows:

$$m \;=\; m_\perp \, \mathrm{Ch}(x, \chi),$$
$$\text{with}$$
$$x \;=\; \frac{r}{H}.$$

The arguments are historically named x for normalized altitude and the Greek letter chi for incidence angle (don't blame me for that). The function is independent of scale and is usually tabulated or approximated numerically. For convenience, an analytic expression is given below. This has been stripped down from a more general solution found in [Kocifaj 96]:

$$\mathrm{Ch}(x, \chi) = \frac{1}{2}\left[\cos(\chi) + \right.$$
$$\left. + \exp\left(\frac{x\cos^2\chi}{2}\right) \mathrm{erfc}\left(\sqrt{\frac{x\cos^2\chi}{2}}\right)\left(\frac{1}{x} + 2 - \cos^2\chi\right)\sqrt{\frac{\pi x}{2}}\right].$$

The above expression is not practical for real-time evaluation, for several reasons: it contains the complementary error function, erfc, which needs a numerical approximation for itself. It has bad numerical behavior for large x and small χ, where the exp-term becomes very large and the erfc-term virtually zero. We use this expression, however, as our ground-truth standard, evaluated with arbitrary precision math software.

2.4 Towards a Real-Time Approximation

To better understand the Chapman function, we will plot a graph of it (see Figure 2.3) and observe a number of important properties:

$$\text{The function is even wrt. } \chi; \qquad \text{Ch}(x, \chi) = \text{Ch}(x, -\chi).$$
$$\text{There is unity at } \chi = 0; \qquad \text{Ch}(x, 0) = 1.$$
$$\text{There is a limit for large } x; \qquad \lim_{x \to \infty} \text{Ch}(x, \chi) = \frac{1}{\cos \chi}.$$

These properties are easily explained. The even symmetry follows from the problem specification. Only the cosine of the incidence angle appears in the expression. This allows us to reduce the covered range to $0 < \chi < 180°$. Second, since $\text{Ch}(x, \chi)$ relates $m_\perp$ to m, its value must approach unity for small incidence angles. And finally, in the limit of a flat earth, the Chapman function must approach the secant function.

These properties can be used to engineer our approximation, Ch'. The limit for large x suggests a rational approximation, as we are going to cope with a pole. Runtime efficiency demands the lowest possible order. So we are going to

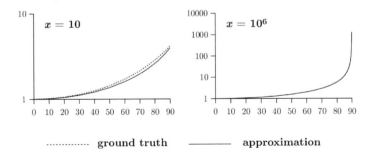

Figure 2.3. Graph of the Chapman function. $\text{Ch}(x, \chi)$ is plotted on a logarithmic scale as a function of incidence angle χ, for two extreme cases of x. An observer on the earth's surface with an atmosphere scale height of 8.4 km would correspond to an x of $r_\oplus/8.4 \simeq 760$.

look for a first-order rational function of $\cos \chi$, approaching unity on the left and the value of $\mathrm{Ch}_\|(x)$ on the right, where $\mathrm{Ch}_\|(x)$ is used as a shorthand for the Chapman function evaluated at $\chi = 90°$. There is only one possibility for such a rational function:

$$\mathrm{Ch}'(c, \chi) \quad = \quad \frac{c}{(c-1)\cos(\chi)+1} \quad \bigg| \; |\chi| < 90°,$$

$$\text{with}$$

$$c \quad = \quad \mathrm{Ch}_\|(x).$$

As it turns out, this low-order function is a pretty good approximation. The useful range for χ is, however, limited to below $90°$. Beyond that angle, the approximation grows hyperbolically to a pole at infinity, while the exact Chapman function grows exponentially, and always stays finite. We will look for ways to handle $\chi > 90°$, but we must first turn our attention to the coefficient c.

2.4.1   At the Horizon

If the observer altitude is fixed, we could precalculate a value for c. However, for a moving observer, and in the absence of a Chapman function to fall back on, we need an approximation for c itself. Let's take a look at $\mathrm{Ch}_\|(x)$:

$$\mathrm{Ch}_\|(x) \quad = \quad \left(\frac{1}{2x}+1\right)\sqrt{\frac{\pi x}{2}}.$$

This is already a lot simpler than the full Chapman function, but still requires a square root and a division. To simplify it further, we assume that x is usually large and neglect the term $1/2x$ to get a function that is purely proportional to $\sqrt{x}$. Using the value $\sqrt{\pi/2} \simeq 1.2533$ as a coefficient results in

$$\mathrm{Ch}_\|(x) \quad \simeq \quad 1.2533\sqrt{x} \quad \big| \, x > 10.$$

2.4.2   Beyond the Horizon

Consider Figure 2.4. The airmass m_L along an entire line is the airmass along the forward ray plus the airmass along the backward ray:

$$m_L \quad = \quad \rho\Big[\mathrm{Ch}(x, \chi) + \mathrm{Ch}(x, 180° - \chi)\Big].$$

The above equation must be true for any point along the line. We can move the observer to the periapsis, where both the forward and the backward ray are horizontal. Using trigonometry, the altitude at the periapsis is $x_0 = x\sin\chi$ and density follows as $\rho\exp(x - x_0)$. Another way of expressing m_L is therefore

$$m_L \quad = \quad 2\,\rho\exp(x - x_0)\,\mathrm{Ch}_\|(x_0).$$

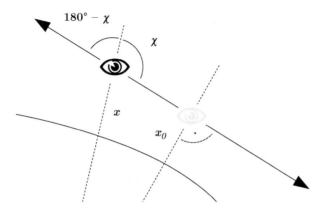

Figure 2.4. Airmass along an entire line. A virtual observer is placed at the periapsis.

Combining the above equations, it is possible to arrive at an identity that expresses the Chapman function in terms of itself with a reflected incidence angle:

$$\mathrm{Ch}(x, \chi) \;=\; 2 \exp(x - x \sin \chi) \, \mathrm{Ch}_{\|}(x \sin \chi) - \mathrm{Ch}(x, 180^\circ - \chi).$$

If the Chapman function is known for $0 < \chi < 90^\circ$, it is therefore known for all χ.

2.5 Implementation

See Listing 2.1 for an implementation of the approximate Chapman function in C. It consists of a branch on the value of χ, either applying the identity or not. The code differs from the mathematical formulae in three aspects, which are discussed in Sections 2.5.1–2.5.3.

2.5.1 Numeric Range

First, a numeric range problem must be resolved, which happens when x is large and x_0 is small. The identity formula contains the exponential $\exp(x - x_0)$, which overflows. To remedy this situation, we introduce a modified function $\mathrm{Ch}_{\mathrm{h}}(X, h, \chi)$:

$$\mathrm{Ch}_{\mathrm{h}}(X, h, \chi) \;=\; \mathrm{Ch}(X + h, \chi) \exp(-h).$$

This function takes a reference altitude X and the corresponding observer height h, and includes the factor $\exp(-h)$. This factor would have to be applied anyway to calculate the airmass. By including it in the function, the range problem cancels out, since $\exp(x - x_0) \exp(-h) = \exp(X - x_0)$.

```
float chapman_h( float X, float h, float coschi )
{
    // The approximate Chapman function
    // Ch(X+h,chi) times exp2(-h)
    // X - altitude of unit density
    // h - observer altitude relative to X
    // coschi - cosine of incidence angle chi
    // X and h are given units of the 50%-height

    float c = sqrt( X + h );
    if( coschi >= 0. )
    {
        // chi above horizon
        return c / ( c * coschi + 1. ) * exp2( -h );
    }
    else
    {
        // chi below horizon, must use identity
        float x0 = sqrt( 1. - coschi * coschi ) * ( X + h );
        float c0 = sqrt( x0 );
        return
            2. * c0 * exp2( X - x0 ) -
            c / ( 1. - c * coschi ) * exp2( -h );
    }
}
```

Listing 2.1. The approximate Chapman function in C, with modifications discussed in the text.

2.5.2 Distance Differences

The second modification relates to the ability of the approximation to stay faithful to sums and differences of path lengths. Special attention is drawn to the case of an observer who is close above a reflective surface. Consider Figure 2.5. Assuming near-horizontal angles, the airmasses m_A, m_B, and m_C for the three segments can be simplified to

$$
\begin{aligned}
m_A &\sim \mathrm{Ch}(x, \chi), \\
m_B &\sim \mathrm{Ch}(x, 180° - \chi) - \mathrm{Ch}(x', 180° - \chi), \\
m_C &\sim \mathrm{Ch}(x', \chi).
\end{aligned}
$$

The question is now, does the approximation satisfy $m_A = m_B + m_C$? This would be required for an exact color match at the horizon above a water surface. The short answer is that the original approximation does not hold for this property. The form of the denominator in the rational function, as well as the factor 1.2533, stand in the way. The approximation must be rigged to enable this

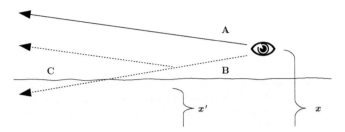

Figure 2.5. The Chapman function on a reflected ray. Is the approximation going to stay true to sums and differences of path lengths?

property; this new approximation is even simpler:

$$\mathrm{Ch}'(c, \chi) \;=\; \frac{c}{c \cos(\chi) + 1},$$

with

$$c \;=\; \sqrt{x}.$$

Dropping the factor of 1.2533 hardly makes a difference in the visual result. The change in the denominator is more severe, causing the approximation to fall below unity for small incidence angles. However, for typical uses with x well in the hundreds, the visual impact is again negligible. If needed, the loss can be compensated by an increase of the β-coefficients.

2.5.3 Using exp2

The code will make exclusive use of the dual exponential 2^x instead of the natural exponential e^x. We will therefore need all scales converted to the dual logarithm. We need a 50%-height H_{50} instead of the scale height H; we need 50%-extinction coefficients, and so on:

$$H_{50} \;=\; H \ln 2,$$
$$\beta_{50} \;=\; \beta \ln 2,$$

$$\cdots$$

The reason for this change is that exp2 is usually the more efficient function to compute. To optimize even more, an implementation can employ a fast exp2 function for all scattering calculations. An example of such a fast exp2 function is presented in the appendix (Section 2.8). It is a definitive win when the calculation is CPU-based, especially if it is vectorized with SIMD, calculating four values at once. On the GPU, there have been assembly instructions for a fast version (called exp2pp for "partial precision") or the shader compiler takes it as a hint if a call to exp2 has both a low-precision argument and a low-precision result.

```
vec3 transmittance( vec3 r, vec3 viewdir )
{
    // calculate the transmittance along a ray
    // from point r towards infinity

    float rsq = dot(r,r);
    float invrl = inversesqrt( rsq );
    float len = rsq * invrl;
    float x = len * invH50;
    float h = x - X50;
    float coschi = dot( r, viewdir ) * invrl;
    return exp2( -beta50 * H50 * chapman_h( X50, h, coschi ) );
}
```

Listing 2.2. Function for the transmittance along a ray.

2.6 Putting the Chapman Function to Use

Finally, in this section we are going to explore the ways in which we can use our shiny new tool. You should consult the example code on the website since not all listings are shown here.

2.6.1 Airmass and Transmittance

The airmass is calculated easily with the modified Chapman function. You need to know the observer height against some reference altitude (conveniently, this is the planet radius, or mean sea level), and the scale height of the atmosphere:

$$m \quad = \quad H\, Ch_h(X, h, \chi).$$

It is a small step from the airmass to the transmittance, since $T = \exp(-\beta m)$. See Listing 2.2 for a function to calculate the transmittance along a straight line through the atmosphere. The scale height and the extinction coefficients must be available globally. In the complete fragment program, this function is used to calculate the local sun color for surface shading.

2.6.2 Aerial Perspective

The full aerial perspective function has two colors as a result: the transmittance and the in-scatter. The function is too long to be listed here, but is included in the fragment program on the website. The signature is as follows:

```
void aerial_perspective( out vec3 T, out vec3 S,
    in vec3 r0, in vec3 r1, in bool infinite );
```

The function calculates the aerial perspective from point r0 to point r1, or alternatively, from point r0 along the ray through r1 to infinity. The resulting transmittance is written to argument T and the in-scatter is written to argument S.

Here is a short explanation of the algorithm: In a first step, the function intersects the ray with the atmosphere boundary to get the integration interval, which is subdivided into a fixed number of segments. It then iterates over all segments in reverse order (back to front). For each segment, the Chapman function is called to calculate airmass, transmittance, and in-scatter. The in-scatter is then propagated along the ray in a way similar to alpha-blending.

2.6.3   The Example Raytracer

The accompanying online material for this article contains a shader (fragment- and vertex program) that implements a fully ray-traced, atmospheric single-scattering solution in real time. See the color images in Figure 2.6. You should be able to load the shader into a shader authoring tool (RenderMonkey, FX-Composer) and apply it on a unit sphere. If you are on the Mac, there is a ShaderBuilder project that you can simply double click.

The code assumes a planet centered at the origin of variable radius, with a Rayleigh atmosphere. For each pixel that hits the atmosphere, aerial_perspective is called once to get the in-scatter against the black background of space. The transmittance is not needed. For each pixel that hits the surface, the aerial_perspective function is called twice, one time for the view ray, and a second time for the ocean reflection.

To give a realistic appearance, the β-values were calculated for a situation similar to Earth. A little bit of orange absorption was added to account for the effect of atmospheric ozone, which is significant at twilight (see [Nielsen 03]). The landmass is shaded according to the Lommel-Seeliger law, which is a good model for rough surfaces, avoiding the typical Lambertian limb darkening. The specular reflection of the sun in the ocean is shaded with an approximate microfacet model (see [Schüler 09]). The final color is then tone mapped with an exponential soft saturation and 2.2 display gamma.

2.7   Conclusion

This article shows a way to accelerate atmospheric scattering calculations, by making the Chapman function an efficient commodity. This allows a strength reduction of the numerical integration, up to the point where the full single-scattering solution can be run in real time in a shader program.

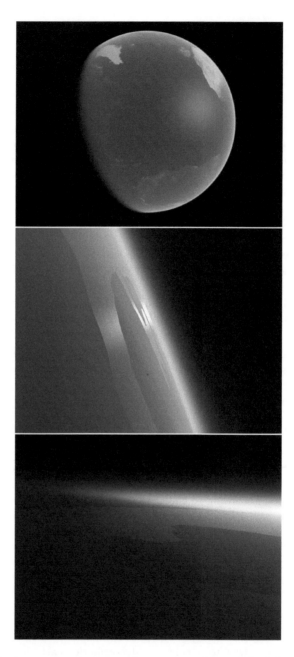

Figure 2.6. Color images from the example ray tracer. View of the Atlantic Ocean (top). Sun reflection, which is yellow due to transmittance (middle). Earth shadow, which is implicit in the solution (bottom).

```
float exp2pp( float x )
{
    // partial precision exp2, accurate to 12 bits

    const float c[3] = { 5.79525, 12.52461, -2.88611 };
    int e = round(x);
    float t = x - e;
    float m = ( t*t + c[0]*t + c[1] ) / ( c[2]*t + c[1] );
    return ldexp( m, e );
}
```

Listing 2.3. An example of a fast **exp2** function.

2.8 Appendix

2.8.1 A fast exp2 function

Listing 2.3 shows an example for a fast **exp2** function for use in atmospheric-scattering calculations. It is a low-order rational function in the range $-1/2$ to $+1/2$ together with the usual range reduction and scaling. Although it is an approximation, it does preserve the property that $1 - \exp(-x)$ is strictly positive if $x > 0$, which is important for the scattering calculations. The function is dependent on an efficient way to assemble a floating point number from a mantissa and an exponent. For the sake of brevity, this part is expressed here in terms of the standard C-function **ldexp**. The optimal method would be a direct bit-manipulation, using language-specific constructs.

Bibliography

[Bruneton and Neyret 08] Éric Bruneton and Fabrice Neyret. "Precomputed Atmospheric Scattering." *Comput. Graph. Forum. Proceedings of the 19th Eurographics Symposium on Rendering 2008* 27:4 (2008), 1079–1086. Special Issue.

[Chapman 31] Sydney Chapman. "The Absorption and Dissociative or Ionizing Effect of Monochromatic Radiation in an Atmosphere on a Rotating Earth." *Proceedings of the Physical Society* 43:1 (1931), 26. Available online (http://stacks.iop.org/0959-5309/43/i=1/a=305).

[Hoffmann and Preetham 02] Naty Hoffmann and Arcot J. Preetham. "Rendering outdoor light scattering in real time." Technical report, ATI Technologies, Inc., 2002. Available online (http://www.ati.com/developer).

[Klassen 87] R. Victor Klassen. "Modeling the Effect of the Atmosphere on Light." *ACM Trans. Graph.* 6 (1987), 215–237. Available online (http://doi.acm.org/10.1145/35068.35071).

[Kocifaj 96] M. Kocifaj. "Optical Air Mass and Refraction in a Rayleigh Atmosphere."
            Contributions of the Astronomical Observatory Skalnate Pleso 26:1 (1996), 23–
            30. Available online (http://www.ta3.sk/caosp/Eedition/Abstracts/1996/Vol_26/
            No_1/pp23-30_abstract.html).

[Nielsen 03] R. S. Nielsen. "Real Time Rendering of Atmospheric Scattering Effects
            for Flight Simulators." Master's thesis, Informatics and Mathematical Modelling,
            Technical University of Denmark, 2003. Available online (http://www2.imm.dtu.
            dk/pubdb/p.php?2554).

[Nishita et al. 93] Tomoyuki Nishita, Takao Sirai, Katsumi Tadamura, and Eihachiro
            Nakamae. "Display of the Earth Taking into Account Atmospheric Scattering."
            In *Proceedings of SIGGRAPH '93, Proceedings, Annual Conference Series*, edited
            by James T. Kajiya, pp. 175–182. New York: ACM Press, 1993. Available online
            (http://doi.acm.org/10.1145/166117.166140).

[O'Neil 05] Sean O'Neil. "Accurate Atmospheric Scattering." In *GPU Gems 2*, edited by
            Matt Pharr and Randima Fernando, pp. 253–268. Reading, MA: Addison-Wesley,
            2005.

[Schüler 09] Christian Schüler. "An Efficient and Physically Plausible Real-Time Shad-
            ing Model." In *ShaderX^7: Advanced Rendering Techniques*, edited by Wolfgang
            Engel, Chapter 2.5, pp. 175–187. Hingham, MA: Charles River Media, 2009.

Volumetric Real-Time Water and Foam Rendering

Daniel Scherzer, Florian Bagar, and
Oliver Mattausch

3.1 Introduction

Over the last decade, simulation and rendering of complex natural phenomena such as fire, smoke, clouds, and fluids have been an active and most diverse research area in computer graphics. Among these phenomena, water may be the most fascinating and challenging problem, due to the familiarity that even a

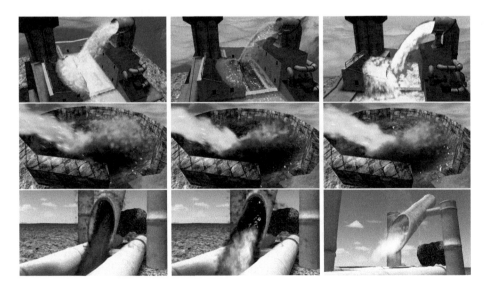

Figure 3.1. The proposed algorithm allows water to be rendered in many ways.

casual observer has with the phenomenon. Although the visual quality of water rendering is continually improving, we are still a long way from capturing all the physical properties of real water, like the forming of foam and droplets and their interaction with the environment.

In this chapter we present a method for creating a fully dynamic multilayered real-time water rendering approach. This approach can represent the volumetric properties of water and the physical formation of volumetric foam, thereby creating much higher visual fidelity than previous real-time approaches. It is based on a very fast particle-based fluid simulation that is fully hardware-accelerated using Nvidia PhysX and rendering in OpenGL, and therefore easily runs at real-time frame rates. The algorithm has a small memory footprint and is simple to implement and integrate into existing rendering engines. Additionally, our method is highly configurable from an artistic point of view, and thus can produce a multiplicity of visual appearances to help to create the desired atmosphere for a scene (see Figure 3.1).

3.2 Simulation

In order to render believable water, we first have to simulate its behavior. The dynamics of water as an incompressible fluid can be described by a version of the Navier–Stokes equations, which apply Newton's second law (conservation of momentum) and conservation of mass to fluid motion. These equations relate the body forces (gravity) and the contact forces (pressure and stress) that act on a fluid. This results in nonlinear partial differential equations that are very hard to solve (assuming that an exact solution for a given case even exists). As we do not need an exact solution, but are mainly concerned with speed, we are fine with an approximate numerical solution. Approximations in this problem domain mainly use Euler integration. (There are more accurate methods, such as Runge-Kutta or midpoint, but these take more time to evaluate.)

3.2.1 Smoothed-Particle Hydrodynamics

Smoothed-particle hydrodynamics (SPH) is a robust and fast way for simulating the behavior of water [Desbrun and Gascuel 96]. The main idea here is to approximate a fluid by a particle system (a division of the fluid into discrete elements) to calculate its dynamic behavior. Each particle has a mass and additional properties, such as position, density, velocity, and lifetime. In classic particle systems, each particle is updated based only on its properties, disregarding particle-particle interaction for the sake of speed. For the simulation of fluids this will not suffice because of the contact forces. Each particle can potentially affect all other particles, which results in a computational complexity in the order of $O(n^2)$—too slow for practical purposes if we use tens of thousands of particles.

```
struct FluidParticle
{
    Vector3         position;
    float           density;
    Vector3         velocity;
    float           lifetime;
    unsigned int    id;        // unique number identifying the particle
    float           foam;
};
```

Listing 3.1. Structure representing the properties of a single particle.

In practice, particles influence each other depending on the distance between them. So it makes sense to define an interaction cut-off distance, inside which a kernel function is applied to weight the influence of the individual particles on each other. This effectively reduces calculation complexity to $O(n)$. Note that this cut-off distance is also called the *smoothing length* because it gives the volume over which properties are "smoothed" by the kernel function (hence the name smoothed-particle hydrodynamics).

All major physics engines already include a solver for SPH. We have used PhysX [Nvidia 11] because of its hardware acceleration, but any other physics engine would do as well.

The fluid simulation is created by passing a fluid description structure to the physics engine, which defines the behavior of the SPH simulation. The simulation data is a nonsorted 3D point cloud and each of the particles has the properties as shown in Listing 3.1. Note that for our use the particle structure also includes a foam parameter that is updated as described in Section 3.2.2. The physics engine updates and returns this point cloud by applying the SPH simulation.

3.2.2 Foam

We want to be able to simulate not only water particles, but also foam. Foam is a substance that is formed by trapping air bubbles inside a liquid (see Figure 3.4). Note that this can be as spray or bubbles above the surface of the fluid, but also deep inside a fluid, as in the case of a waterfall. The formation of foam can be described by the Weber number. It is defined as the ratio of the kinetic energy to the surface energy:

$$We = \frac{\rho v^2 l}{\sigma},$$

where ρ is the density, v is the relative velocity between the liquid and the surrounding gas, l is the droplet diameter, and σ is the surface tension. If We is large, the kinetic energy is greater than the surface energy, which causes water to mix with the surrounding gas (air), and the result is foam. For our purposes, we use the particle size as the droplet diameter and use a constant value for the surface tension. We also assume that the air is not moving, and that therefore the relative velocity is equal to the velocity of the liquid at this point.

The Weber number for each particle can now be calculated by using each particle's ρ and v from the physics engine. This number is then compared to a user-defined threshold that describes how easily this fluid forms foam. Thus, particles can be separated into water particles and foam particles. Thus, foam (from the viewpoint of the simulation) is not a totally different phenomenon, but is just a state of water particles [Bagar et al. 10].

With all these simulation parts in place we now have to tackle the problem of how to render the water.

3.3   Rendering

Rendering water with a scanline renderer in an efficient manner is a twofold problem: first, a water surface has to be extracted from the simulation data and second, the shading of this surface has to take into account the volumetric properties of water. Due to the fact that real-time physics engines are often limited to 64 K particles, while offline systems, as used in movies, often use hundreds of millions of particles, our particle sizes will be much larger; we therefore must take extra care to render believable water surfaces.

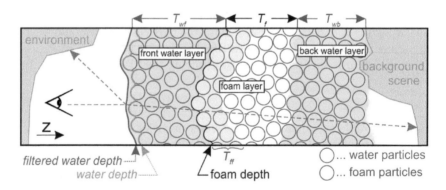

Figure 3.2. A cross section of our layered water model: the volumetric appearance of the result is achieved by accounting for water thickness T_{wb}, foam thickness T_f, and the thickness of water in front of the foam T_{wf} at each pixel. We also partition foam into two differently colored layers (T_{ff}) to achieve more interesting foam. See also Figure 3.5 for renderings of the individual layers.

3.3.1 Splatting

One method for extracting surfaces from particles is to use a marching cubes method. This has a number of disadvantages: First, as the surface of the water is expected to change continually, the surface may exhibit temporal aliasing. Second, marching cubes is very computationally expensive, and third, the resulting geometry will likely be very complex, especially when incorporating foam effects.

A method that avoids these disadvantages and works well on current hardware is splatting: the idea is to splat each particle by using a certain kernel shape (for instance, a sphere) into a depth (and thickness) buffer (see Figures 3.2 and 3.6). By using a 3D kernel, we create volumetric particles. Splatting particles into a depth buffer (with depth test on) results in a screen-space approximation of the water surface (see Listing 3.2). While additively splatting (adding up sphere radii, see Listing 3.3) into a thickness buffer creates an approximation of the water thickness for each pixel (which we will later use for shading the surface). Accumulating water thickness this way is an acceptable approximation because the particles from the physics simulation can be assumed to be largely nonoverlapping.

```
1  FragShaderOutput FluidSplattingFP(  float2 texCoord : TEXCOORD0,
2                                        float4 eyeSpace : TEXCOORD1)
3  {
4      FragShaderOutput OUT;
5      // calculate eye-space normal from texture coordinates
6      float3 n;
7      n.xy = texCoord.xy * float2(2.0f, -2.0f) + float2(-1.0f, 1.0f);
8      float r2 = dot(n.xy, n.xy);
9      // kill pixels outside circle
10     if (r2 > 1.0f) discard;
11     //calculate radius
12     n.z = sqrt(1.0f - r2);
13     // position of this pixel on sphere in eye space
14     float4 eyeSpacePos = float4(eyeSpace.xyz + n*eyeSpace.w, 1.0f);
15     float4 clipSpacePos = mul(glstate.matrix.projection, eyeSpacePos);
16     // output eye-space depth
17     OUT.color = float4(eyeSpacePos.z, 0.0f, 0.0f, 0.0f);
18     OUT.depth = (clipSpacePos.z / clipSpacePos.w) * 0.5f + 0.5f;
19     return OUT;
20 }
```

Listing 3.2. Pixel shader for splatting the particle data as spheres into the depth texture.

```
       // calculate thickness with exponential falloff based on radius
       float thickness = n.z * particleSize * 2.0f * exp(-r2 * 2.0f);
       OUT.color = float4(thickness, 0.0f, 0.0f, 0.0f);
```

Listing 3.3. Splatting the particle data into the thickness texture. (Note: This shader is based on the shader shown in Listing 3.2 and replaces lines 13–18.)

3.3.2 Adaptive Screen-Space Curvature Flow Filtering

If we use a sphere-shaped kernel to splat the particles, the result of directly
rendering is often unconvincing (see Figure 3.3, upper-left image). The sphere
geometry of the individual particles is clearly visible due to the large particle
size. Making particles smaller and thereby requiring more particles for adequate
simulation of these scenes is not an option because we already operate near the
maximum of 64 K particles, and more particles also make the simulation and the
rendering slower. Another solution is to smooth the depth buffer that contains
the splatted particles in a way that avoids high curvature. This is the idea behind
curvature flow filtering [van der Laan et al. 09]. Here, a surface is shifted along
its normal vector depending on the mean curvature of the surface:

$$\frac{\partial z}{\partial t} = H,$$

where z is the depth (as found in the depth buffer), t is a smoothing time step,
and H is the mean curvature. For a surface in 3D space, the mean curvature is
defined as follows:

$$2H = \nabla \cdot \hat{n}, \qquad\qquad (3.1)$$

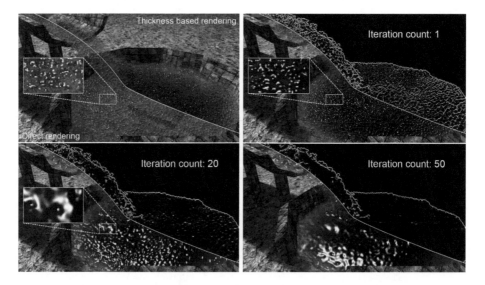

Figure 3.3. Directly rendering the particles from the simulation as spheres results in
jelly-like water. Shading of the water can be improved by using the thickness of the
water to attenuate the water color (upper-left). Iteratively smoothing the depth buffer
by applying screen-space curvature flow filtering reduces the curvature of the water and
leads to more convincing results.

where $\hat{n}$ is the unit normal of the surface. The normal is calculated by taking the cross product between the derivatives of the viewspace position P in x- and y-directions, resulting in a representation of the unit normal [van der Laan et al. 09]:

$$\hat{n}(x,y) = \frac{n(x,y)}{|n(x,y)|} = \frac{(-C_y\frac{\partial z}{\partial x}, -C_x\frac{\partial z}{\partial y}, C_y z)^T}{\sqrt{D}}, \qquad (3.2)$$

where

$$D = C_y^2\left(\frac{\partial z}{\partial x}\right)^2 + C_x^2\left(\frac{\partial z}{\partial y}\right)^2 + C_x^2 C_y^2 z^2.$$

Finite differencing is used to calculate the spatial derivatives, and C_x and C_y are the viewpoint parameters in the x- and y-directions, respectively. They are computed from the field of view and the size of the viewport V_x and V_y, as shown in Equations (3.3) and (3.4):

$$C_x = \frac{2}{V_x \tan\left(\frac{FOV}{2}\right)}, \qquad (3.3)$$

$$C_y = \frac{2}{V_y \tan\left(\frac{FOV}{2}\right)}. \qquad (3.4)$$

The unit normal $\hat{n}$ from Equation (3.2) is substituted into Equation (3.1), which enables the derivation of H, leading to

$$2H = \frac{\partial \hat{n}_x}{\partial x} + \frac{\partial \hat{n}_y}{\partial y} = \frac{C_y E_x + C_x E_y}{D^{\frac{3}{2}}},$$

in which

$$E_x = \frac{1}{2}\frac{\partial z}{\partial x}\frac{\partial D}{\partial x} - \frac{\partial^2 z}{\partial x^2}D,$$

$$E_y = \frac{1}{2}\frac{\partial z}{\partial y}\frac{\partial D}{\partial y} - \frac{\partial^2 z}{\partial y^2}D.$$

The GLSL shader in Listing 3.4 performs this operation in screen space.

The effect of applying this filter repeatedly is shown in Figure 3.3. Iterative filtering leads to a greater smoothing effect. If we want to maintain a certain level of smoothness for water that is at the same time near and distant to the viewer, the number of iterations has to be adjusted adaptively for each pixel. We found that the number of iterations is indirectly proportional to the eye-space distance—water nearby needs more iterations—far-away water needs fewer iterations. Details regarding this derivation can be found in our paper [Bagar et al. 10].

```
// samples for finite differencing (vsp = view space position)
float depth = texRECT(depthMap, vsp.xy).x;
float depth_d = texRECT(depthMap, vsp.xy + float2( 0.0f,-1.0f)).x;
float depth_l = texRECT(depthMap, vsp.xy + float2(-1.0f, 0.0f)).x;
float depth_r = texRECT(depthMap, vsp.xy + float2( 1.0f, 0.0f)).x;
float depth_u = texRECT(depthMap, vsp.xy + float2( 0.0f, 1.0f)).x;
// derivatives (finite differencing)
float dx = (0.5f * (depth_r - depth_l));
float dy = (0.5f * (depth_u - depth_d));
// second derivatives
float dxx = (depth_l - 2.0f * depth + depth_r);
float dyy = (depth_d - 2.0f * depth + depth_u);
// constants
const float dx2 = dx*dx; const float dy2 = dy*dy;
const float Cx2 = Cx*Cx; const float Cy2 = Cy*Cy;
// calculate curvature
float D = Cy2*dx2 + Cx2*dy2 + Cx2*Cy2*depth*depth;
float H =  Cy*dxx*D - Cy*dx*(Cy2*dx*dxx + Cx2*Cy2*depth*dx)
    + Cx*dyy*D - Cx*dy*(Cx2*dy*dyy + Cx2*Cy2*depth*dy);
H /= pow(D, 3.0f/2.0f);
// curvature dependent shift
OUT.color = depth + epsilon * H;
```

Listing 3.4. This pixel shader code performs one step in the iterative process of screen-space curvature flow filtering.

3.3.3 Foam and Layers

Up to now we have discussed the problem of how to create a surface for our water. What remains is to provide this surface with realistic shading and to add foam effects.

Figure 3.4. The three cases of foam formation that are handled by our rendering model: foam without water (left), foam on water (middle), and foam inside water (right).

Figure 3.5. The individual layers of our water model: back water layer (upper-left), foam layer with the two user-defined colors that define the look of the foam as inlay (upper-right), front water layer (lower-left), and reflections and specular highlights (lower-right).

We have investigated the different scenarios where foam occurs and have found three main cases for a single pixel: foam without water, foam in front with water behind, and foam inside water (see Figure 3.4). We disregard more complex scenarios, like multiple layers of foam, because in practice the visual difference compared with a single foam layer will be negligible. These cases can be cast into a three-layered model (see Figures 3.2 and 3.5).

3.3.4 Steps of the Algorithm

To put this model into practice, our algorithm separates water and foam particles and splats them into different buffers. The complete algorithm performs the following steps in each frame (see Figure 3.6):

- Update the physics simulation.

- Render the background scene into a depth and color buffer.

- Calculate foam depth by splatting foam particles into a depth buffer.

- Calculate the front water depth by splatting water particles that are in front of the foam.

- Calculate the filtered front water depth by applying adaptive curvature flow filtering.

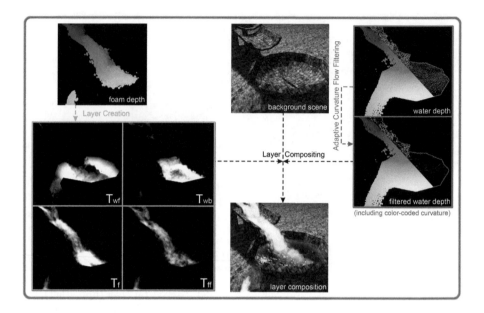

Figure 3.6. Overview of the buffers used in our method. T_{wf} denotes the thickness of the water in front of the foam, T_{wb} denotes the thickness of the water behind the foam, T_f denotes the foam thickness, and T_{ff} denotes the thickness of the front foam layer.

- Calculate the thickness of

  ∘ the foam T_f,

  ∘ the water in front of the foam T_{wf},

  ∘ the water behind the foam T_{wb},

  ∘ the front foam layer T_{ff}.

- Perform volumetric compositing

We use a sphere kernel for water particles and multiply the sphere kernel with a Perlin noise texture for foam particles to get more details. Smoothing is only applied to the front-most water layer, because the surface of water behind a layer of foam will be obfuscated anyway. The front foam layer thickness T_{ff} is an artificial construct that accumulates only foam particles within a user-defined distance behind the foam depth. We found this to create more interesting looking foam.

We have already discussed the basics behind each of the steps, except for the final one, volumetric compositing, that builds on top of all the other steps.

3.3.5 Volumetric Compositing

The difference between the usual compositing of layers and volumetric compositing is that we take the thickness of each layer into account to attenuate a viewing ray. Compositing along a viewing ray back to front, we have (see Figure 3.2):

$$
\begin{aligned}
C_{wb} &= \text{lerp}(c_{\text{fluid}}, C_{\text{background}}, e^{-T_{wb}}), \\
C_{\text{foam}} &= \text{lerp}(c_{fb}, \ c_{ff}, e^{-T_{ff}}), \\
C_f &= \text{lerp}(C_{\text{foam}}, C_{wb}, e^{-T_f}), \\
C_{wf} &= \text{lerp}(c_{\text{fluid}}, C_f, e^{-T_{wf}}),
\end{aligned}
$$

where c_{fluid} is the water color and c_{ff} and c_{fb} are two user-defined colors that are blended together to create more freedom in designing the look of the foam.

After attenuation, we calculate highlights at the front water surface, as well as reflection and refraction (including the Fresnel Term). Here, refraction considers the whole water (front and back water layer) as one volume, so $C_{\text{background}}$ is sampled from the scene background texture perturbed along the normal vector, scaled using $T_{wb} + T_{wf}$ [van der Laan et al. 09].

Figures 3.5 and 3.7 show the individual steps and colors used in the compositing, and Listing 3.5 shows the GLSL pixel shader.

Figure 3.7. User-defined colors (c_{fluid}, c_{ff}, c_{fb}), and resulting colors from the compositing steps ($C_{\text{background}}$, C_{wb}, C_{foam}, C_f, C_{wf}) (left) and final shading results (right).

3.4 Artist Control

We have introduced a number of user-controllable parameters into our algorithm to allow artists to produce a multiplicity of visual appearances (see Figure 3.1).

The visual appearance of water is controlled by the fluid/water color (c_{fluid}), which is combined during the composition depending on the different water thicknesses (t_{wb}, t_{wf}) and a user-defined falloff scale. Additionally, the specular color and specular shininess, as well as the Fresnel bias, scale, and power, which are

```
1  // surface properties (v = view vector, h = half angle vector)
2  float specular = pow(max(0.0, dot(normal, h)), fluidShininess);
3  // bias, scale, and power = user-defined parameters to tune
4  // the Fresnel Term
5  float fresnelTerm = bias + scale * pow(1.0 + dot(v, normal), power);
6  float3 c_reflect = texCUBE(cubeMap, mul((float3x3)invView,
7     reflect(-v, normal)));
8  ...
9  // attenuation factors (incl. user-defined falloff scales)
10 float att_wb = saturate(exp(-t_wb * falloffScale));
11 float att_foam = saturate(exp(-t_f * foamFalloffScale));
12 float att_ff = saturate(exp(-t_ff * foamScale));
13 float att_wf = saturate(exp(-t_wf * falloffScale));
14 // composition (frag = fragment position in screen space
15 float3 c_background = texRECT(scene, frag.xy+normal.xy*(t_wb+t_wf));
16 float3 c_wb = lerp(c_fluid, c_background, att_wb);
17 float3 c_foam = lerp(c_fb, c_ff, att_ff);
18 float3 c_f = lerp(c_foam, c_wb, att_foam);
19 float3 c_wf = lerp(c_fluid, c_f, att_wf);
20 // calculate factor to suppress specular highlights if
21 // foam is the frontmost visual element
22 float spw = saturate(1.0f - att_wf + att_foam) * (1.0f - att_wf);
23 // combine with fresnel and specular highlight
24 float3 surfaceColor = lerp(c_wf, c_reflect, min(fresnelTerm, spw))
25    + fluidSpecularColor * specular * spw;
```

Listing 3.5. Pixel shader for compositing along a viewing ray: lighting (lines 2–7), thickness dependent attenuation (lines 9–19), and final color (lines 20–25)

used to control the approximation of the Fresnel equations, are exposed to be used by artists. The approximation of the Fresnel equations is then used to combine the reflection and the thickness-dependent attenuation of our algorithm (see Listing 3.5).

The reflection itself can be influenced by an artist by modifying or replacing the cubic environment map (cubeMap) of the corresponding scene. Note that the cubic environment map has a large influence on the visual appearance of our algorithm because it is blended directly with the thickness-dependent attenuation and furthermore, it describes the static illumination of the scene.

The visual appearance of the foam is composed of a foam back color (c_{fb}) and a foam front color (c_{ff}), which are blended depending on the thickness of the front foam layer (t_{ff}) (see Figure 3.7) and a user-defined scale factor. Again, as for the water, a user-defined falloff scale is used to control the overall opacity of the foam. The final parameter that should be exposed to artists is the Weber number threshold. As mentioned earlier, this user-defined threshold controls how easily the simulated fluid forms foam.

3.5 Conclusion

We have presented a physically based water (fluid) and foam rendering algorithm that can handle arbitrary dynamic scenes where water is allowed to freely interact and flow everywhere, but which also allows artists to fine-tune the look of the result. This algorithm runs easily in real time (on average 16 ms rendering time) on modern hardware and integrates well with rendering engines (especially with deferred shading).

For more theoretical details and exhaustive benchmarks for the presented method, please refer to the paper [Bagar et al. 10] and the thesis [Bagar 10] on which this work is based.

Bibliography

[Bagar et al. 10] Florian Bagar, Daniel Scherzer, and Michael Wimmer. "A Layered Particle-Based Fluid Model for Real-Time Rendering of Water." *Computer Graphics Forum (Proceedings EGSR 2010)* 29:4 (2010), 1383–1389.

[Bagar 10] Florian Bagar. "A Layered Particle-Based Fluid Model for Real-Time Rendering of Water." Master's thesis (Diplomarbeit), Vienna University of Technology, Austria, 2010.

[Desbrun and Gascuel 96] Mathieu Desbrun and Marie-Paule Gascuel. "Smoothed Particles: A New Paradigm for Animating Highly Deformable Bodies." In *Proceedings of the Eurographics Workshop on Computer Animation and Simulation '96*, pp. 61–76. New York: Springer-Verlag New York, 1996. Available online (http://dl.acm.org/citation.cfm?id=274976.274981).

[Nvidia 11] Nvidia. "NVIDIA PhysX." http://developer.nvidia.com/physx, 2011.

[van der Laan et al. 09] Wladimir J. van der Laan, Simon Green, and Miguel Sainz. "Screen Space Fluid Rendering with Curvature Flow." In *I3D '09: Proceedings of the 2009 Symposium on Interactive 3D Graphics and Games*, pp. 91–98. New York: ACM Press, 2009.

4

II

CryENGINE 3: Three Years of Work in Review

Tiago Sousa, Nickolay Kasyan, and Nicolas Schulz

4.1 Introduction

For the game *Crysis 2*, the R&D team at Crytek created the acclaimed CryENGINE 3 (CE3) game engine. This latest engine iteration involved a large engineering team, took approximately three years to complete, and covered a number of technical areas including physics, AI, animation, graphics, and audio. For this chapter, we focus on a few key rendering topics.

Figure 4.1. A scene from *Crysis 2*.

We start with an introduction to the CE3 rendering pipeline and discuss the differences from previous iterations of the engine. We also cover individual topics, including gamma-correct HDR rendering, deferred lighting, shadows, batched HDR postprocessing for efficient multiplatform motion blur and bokeh DoF, stereo rendering, and advanced screen-space rendering methods. See Figure 4.1 for an example of a scene from *Crysis 2* rendered with CE3.

4.2 Going Multiplatform

In developing *Crysis 2* and CryENGINE 3, the team went out of its comfort zone. Virtually every team member had little or no prior console experience, most coming from a PC background.

Additionally, the design team decided early on to move away from Jungle-style environments, which Crytek has been so well known—for almost a decade—for creating. This time the challenge was to create a post-apocalyptic urban environment, an "Urban Jungle." This was a completely new experience for almost everyone on the team.

Our high-level goals were clear from the beginning: no lead platform, simultaneously shipping on all platforms (PS3, Xbox 360, and PC), and maximize quality on all platforms and all system specs, eliminating sloppy lower specs, as was common with *Crysis 1*. In *Crysis 1*, for example, we essentially disabled individual features for lower system specs, resulting in very poor quality results for the less capable systems. This time around, every single feature was re-engineered so that every platform configuration could support it to some degree.

Going multiplatform meant we had to pick our fights carefully and share as much base work as possible across platforms. This required us to generalize whenever feasible and to avoid custom techniques and optimizations for this or that platform—unless one proved to be a significant performance gain or visual improvement. Such an approach allowed us to minimize risks and time spent on quality assurance and debugging—though, of course, this was still a significant effort. This resulted in approximately three and a half years of learning and hard work for everyone at the company.

We essentially began the process by porting existing functionality across all platforms and checking that everything was in place and worked as expected. Very often we were shocked by how slowly certain processes were running. For example, we were surprised to find post processes taking up to 30 ms, particles taking up to 50 ms, and consoles running at 10 fps, with barely anything on the screen! (See Figure 4.2.)

After most of the key functionality was in place, we started a massive re-engineering and optimizing effort where our philosophy was in essence: "Every millisecond counts but so does visual quality."

Figure 4.2. Some of the very first CryENGINE 3 results on consoles PlayStation® 3 (left) and Xbox 360 (right). Notice the 10 fps on the PS3.

4.2.1 Multiplatform GPU High-Level Optimization Guidelines

Many lessons were learned during CryENGINE 3's development regarding GPU-side optimization. Even though these lessons are self-evident having gone through this process, they were not obvious just a couple of years ago. Here are some of the most important ones:

1. Generalize and always optimize for the worst case scenario.

    (a) Discover the biggest bottlenecks and address them by tackling the biggest time consumer. This means avoiding partial optimizations. An example from *Crysis 1* times: if the camera was static, then motion blur was disabled. If the camera was moving fast, then motion blur was enabled. This kind of bad optimization strategy resulted in big performance peaks and an inconsistent frame rate.

    (b) Once done, repeat *ad nauseam*!

2. Don't repeat work or do unnecessary work. For example:

    (a) Don't down-sample full-screen color targets or depth targets multiple times for different postprocessing functions.

    (b) Minimize the number of memory transfers, render target clears, and any redundant full-screen passes.

    (c) Such repeated or redundant work adds up very quickly. For example, a full-screen pass at 720 p costs ca. 0.25 ms on the Xbox 360 and ca. 0.4 ms on PS3. It is very easy to spend many milliseconds in a wasteful manner.

    (d) Batch as much as possible in a single pass.

3. Take advantage of interframe coherency. Amortize costs across frames:

   (a) This can provide a significant gain if done carefully, taking performance peaks and multi-GPU systems into account.

   (b) Distribute costs evenly. For example, if the HUD updates every nth frame, then every $n + 1$-th frame update some similar-costing render technique.

   (c) For screen-space ambient occlusion (SSAO) and the like, the cost can be distributed across frames.

4. In the end, the key words for most cases are: "share, share, share." Share as many computations and as much bandwidth as is reasonably possible in a single pass. We went through several steps, re-engineering several techniques so that certain dependencies would be eliminated and techniques could be batched.

4.2.2   Multiplatform Optimization: Best Practices

Streamline the optimization process; everyone in a company is responsible for performance and memory. Instead of programmers spending weeks or even months of work optimizing, sometimes it is much more efficient and productive for the art or design teams to spend a couple of hours optimizing the art resources to remove waste.

We achieved this kind of streamlining by helping each team keep within its budget by showing clearly where the cost of its work was located. We introduced a

Figure 4.3. Our GPU timers' view (left); lighting overdraw view (right).

few timers that showed where the GPU costs were located: e.g., shadows, lighting, post processes. We also employed other visualization tools such as lighting and scene overdraw visualization (see Figure 4.3).

Budgets are very important early on; they define clear limits for the project. It is important to ensure that the budgets are understood not only by programmers but also by art and design departments. Everyone must understand that budgets are guidelines that can be further adjusted, depending on a level's characteristics, since every level has its own requirements, for example an indoor or night level requires many light sources, while an outdoor daytime level requires mainly sunlight.

Another important step for us was to monitor performance regularly on all platforms, since on a very big team such as Crytek Frankfurt (300 colleagues), it is very easy for performance to run out of control. This meant that every week we made a couple of PIX/GPad captures at exact, repeatable locations as well as at any low-performance locations, and then we investigated the findings. By the end of the project this was done on almost a daily basis.

Last but not least, something new that we introduced at Crytek during *Crysis 2* production was visual regression tests. Whenever a programmer submitted code, an automated build/test was triggered that ran the new code changes at predefined camera locations. Performance was measured and a screenshot was captured. The results were uploaded to our automated test server and could be visualized through a user-friendly web interface. It was not fully automated; for example, no image comparison was done, but this simple measure allowed us to track visual or performance regressions much quicker. This is an area we will certainly continue to evolve for our next projects.

4.3 Physically Based Rendering

For CryENGINE 3 we wanted to take a step forward with more physically based rendering techniques, while still maintaining the minimal precomputation steps involved and also allowing for many dynamic light sources (a limitation of our previous engine).

We decided early on, that a certain degree of backward compatibility with our previous engine was required; hence, we opted for not moving to a fully deferred rendering engine, since current console hardware is still too limited for achieving the required material variety supported in CryENGINE. We used instead a variation of what is now commonly called deferred lighting, which was popularized by Naughty Dog's *Uncharted* series, allowing us to keep our material-variation flexibility, at the cost of an additional opaque rendering pass.

We use a minimal G-buffer setup, composed of depth/stencil (stencil used for tagging indoor areas), world-space best fit normals [Kaplanyan 10a], and material glossiness stored in the alpha channel. Additionally, we required an HDR

Target ID	R	G	B	A	Format (PC/Xbox 360/PS3)
DS	Depth + Stencil				D24S8
RT0	Normals + Glossiness				A8B8G8R8
RT0	Diffuse Accumulation				FP16, FP10, RGBK
RT1	Specular Accumulation				FP16, FP10, RGBK
RT0	Scene Target				FP16, FP10, RGBK

Table 4.1. G-buffer and render targets set up across different platforms (PC, Xbox 360, and PS3).

lighting buffer and an HDR scene target. Besides these, there are several other intermediate targets, used for many different purposes, including shadows, sprites, postprocessing, and other cases. This was one of the cases where generalization was not possible due to hardware limitations (see Table 4.1).

A typical frame starts with our G-buffer, rendering opaque geometry, then composing any alpha-blended layers on top of it (these can be decals, or deferred decals and terrain layers). Storing normals in world space helped minimize trouble with alpha blending since most of today's hardware still lacks programmable blending. This is still far from ideal since more complex normal encoding could help improve quality or storage costs but would not blend well on most hardware (see Figure 4.4).

Depth   Normals

Figure 4.4. G-buffer visualization.

G-buffer generation is followed by lighting-accumulation stages. At this point, ambient lighting, environment lighting probes, SSDO or SSAO, GI, real-time local reflections, and all light sources are applied (see Figure 4.5).

Shading is then done in forward passes. Lighting buffers are fetched and when required, albedo and specular maps are applied along with a per-material Fresnel term. Different shading models, (such as deferred skin shading, hair rendering with anisotropic highlights, cloth) may be used for each material.

Figure 4.5. Diffuse lighting accumulation (left) and specular lighting accumulation (right).

After the opaque shading passes, alpha-blended geometry is processed. This can be any alpha-blended pass, like glass, deferred fog passes, water surfaces, or particles. A frame ends by performing final tone mapping, postprocessed antialiasing, and a couple of game-dependent postprocessing steps such as the game 3D HUD or similar (see Figure 4.6).

Figure 4.6. Shading passes (linear space; left) and final tonemapped and postprocessed image (right).

4.3.1 The Importance of HDR

High dynamic range (HDR) [Reinhard et al. 10] is important for two main reasons: precision and range. HDR rendering allows for more accurate lighting ranges and minimizes banding and color clipping. The human eye cells are sensitive to a wide range of light wavelengths and our brain is trained from birth to recognize objects through color. Thus, humans are particularly sensitive to any kind of incorrectness in images, any kind of color clipping, improper range, or tone reproduction. The naïve observer may not know why an image doesn't look or feel

Figure 4.7. LDR (left; notice color clipping) and HDR (right; notice the much wider range tone reproduction).

real, but will be unconsciously aware of the many and common contributors for unnatural-looking images.

Such underrated features are the keys to opening the door to physically based rendering, and consequently into achieving more realistic images by more accurately simulating how the human eye or cameras behave. HDR imaging also allows for physically based postprocessing, including depth of field and motion blur, camera CMOS grain simulation, the common bloom, flares, streaks, and other effects (See Figure 4.7).

Additionally, one large benefit for a high dynamic range rendering pipeline is the improved art workflow, since the artists don't have to spend as much time working around the limitations of low dynamic range (for example, not being able to use dark textures or darker/denser fog, and certain decals). Of course, hardware limitations still apply, particularly on consoles where range and precision are still limited compared to PCs, so a bit of care and common sense should be exercised.

4.3.2 The Importance of Being Linear

It might surprise many to learn that the lighting and rendering in video games have been incorrectly implemented for a long time. In fact, entire art teams have been tweaking their materials and light setups incorrectly. Lighting correctly in linear space means that all rendering computations should happen in linear space: lighting in linear space, linear blending operations, and ensuring gamma correctness at the end of frame output.

Movie industry professionals have been aware that such mathematical correctness is also one of the main contributors to the realism of the final image. Larry

Figure 4.8. Incorrect linear rendering (left) and correct linear rendering (right).

Gritz (Pixar/Nvidia/Sony Pictures Imageworks) popularized this extremely important topic in video games [Gritz and d'Eon 08] (see Figure 4.8).

The main source of linear incorrectness is the input albedo and specular maps, which most DCC tools store in sRGB space due to precision benefits. Luckily this gamma curve is now supported natively by most hardware, with some differences across certain platforms. For instance, Xbox 360 has a custom piecewise linear (PWL) sRGB curve, hence additional care must be taken to ensure linear correctness across a regular sRGB curve to PWL [Vlachos 08]. This conversion could be done in shader code, instead of relying on hardware functionality, but due to the lack of programmable texture filtering, this would give nonlinear filtered results. Another multiplatform limitation is that DX9-level hardware and the PS3 do not support gamma-correct alpha blending so alpha blending targets must be stored in linear space for correct results.

Since we are rendering using HDR, we can store our render targets in linear space without worrying about the loss of precision. Thus, all we have to worry about is using sRGB texture reads and then all the resulting shading and blending are implicitly linearly correct.

After tone mapping, a final gamma 2.2 curve is applied in the tone-mapping shader. This helps eliminate any hardware differences across multiple platforms; all platforms perform the exact same math.

However, the Xbox 360 requires an additional final step, since it is performing a custom TV gamma for its final image output. This final step effectively undoes the implicit TV gamma. Ideally, this should be done in a tone-mapping shader,

```
float DegammaFuncTV( float f )
{
  return (f <= 0.0812f) ? f / 4.5f :
                          powf(( f+0.099f ) / 1.099f, 1.0f/0.45f);
}
```

Listing 4.1. Undoing TV gamma, according to XDK.

before any quantization happens, but for performance reasons we did it through the hardware gamma ramp functionality.

Our individual steps to modify the gamma ramp are convert to linear space (remove gamma 2.2), remove TV gamma, and reapply the gamma 2.2 curve (see Listing 4.1 and Figure 4.9).

Figure 4.9. Color output equalization on Xbox 360 (left) and PS3 (right).

4.3.3 Deferred Lighting

Our lighting accumulation passes are done into HDR render targets or encoded in RGBK (also popularized as RGBM) for PS3, due to that platform's poor floating-point render target performance. Lower precision formats are insufficient due to lack of range and precision and should be avoided, unless very restrictive conditions can be imposed on the art department (such as avoiding albedo/specular maps below certain luminance thresholds, for example).

Since we are using an encoded format on PS3, hardware blending cannot be used. Luckily, the PS3's GPU allows for a workaround. Blending can be performed in the pixel shader itself by sampling from the same render target into which you are rendering. This feature requires that a pixel be written only once on the same drawcall (no overdraw). Such functionality allows for a very handy form of programmable blending that most hardware (including DX11-level hardware) lacks.

Z-buffer depth caveats. Unlike previous engine iteration, we don't output linear depth into a separate render target. On consoles and on DX10.1/DX11-level hardware (and on certain DX9 hardware) we can access the depth buffer directly. This saves performance, but with a few caveats: first, the depth's hyperbolic distribution needs to be converted back to linear space before it is used in our shaders. Second, first-person objects, like first-person arms and weapons on CryENGINE (and typically every engine), have different depth ranges to avoid intersections with the world and have additional art control, like different FOV (see Listing 4.2).

```
ProjRatio.xy=float2(zfar/(zfar-znear),znear/(znear-zfar));
float GetLinearDepth(float fDevDepth)
{
  return  ProjRatio.y/(fDevDepth-ProjRatio.x);
}
```

Listing 4.2. Device depth to linear depth.

This was problematic particularly because deferred lighting did not work properly for first-person objects. In addition, this resulted in extreme shadowing artifacts. We tried multiple approaches, such as stencil masking or outputting a few depth layers, but ended up simply adjusting our depth reconstruction function to convert hardware depth to a linear depth, using a different depth scale for first-person objects (see Listing 4.3).

```
float GetLinearDepth(float fDevDepth)
{
    float bNearDepth = step(fDevDepth, g_PS_NearestScaled.z);
    float2 ProjRatio= lerp(g_PS_ProjRatio.xy,
                           g_PS_NearestScaled.xy, bNearDepth);
    float fLinearDepth = ProjRatio.y/(fDevDepth-ProjRatio.x);
    return fLinearDepth;
}
```

Listing 4.3. Final linear depth reconstruction.

Reconstructing world-space/screen-space position from depth. In order to reconstruct a world space or shadow space position from a depth sample, we linearly transform the screen-space VPos basis directly to the target homogeneous space. This approach is used for all our deferred techniques, such as lights, shadows, fog, and stereo. This is also the simplest way to render light volumes, since it is not possible to use perspective correct interpolators.

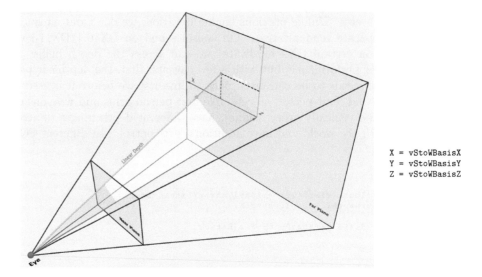

X = vStoWBasisX
Y = vStoWBasisY
Z = vStoWBasisZ

Figure 4.10. Position reconstruction visualization.

Geometric meaning of reconstruction. Essentially, position reconstruction from the depth buffer is achieved by rescaling the depth buffer's linear depth with the addition of three basis vectors. First vX and vY are scaled by screen coordinates (VPos) before addition. As the result of the addition of these three vectors, we have a view vector from the eye to the point on the far plane that corresponds to the specified X- and Y-screen coordinates. Simple scaling of this vector with the given linear depth from the depth buffer gives you the position in world space or in any homogenous space. This depends on the space in which the vX, vY, and vZ basis vectors are specified (see Figure 4.10 and Listing 4.4).

```
// projection ratio
float fProjectionRatio = fViewWidth/fViewHeight;
//all values are in camera space
float fFar = cam.GetFarPlane();
float fNear = cam.GetNearPlane();
float fWorldHeightDiv2 = fNear * cry_tanf(cam.GetFov()*0.5f);
float fWorldWidthDiv2 = fWorldHeightDiv2 * fProjectionRatio;
float k = fFar/fNear;
Vec3 vStereoShift = camMatrix.GetColumn0() * cam.GetAsymL();
// Apply matrix orientation
Vec3 vZ = (camMatrix.GetColumn1() * fNear + vStereoShift)* k;
// Size of vZ is the distance from camera pos to near plane
Vec3 vX = camMatrix.GetColumn0() * fWorldWidthDiv2 * k;
Vec3 vY = camMatrix.GetColumn2() * fWorldHeightDiv2 * k;
vZ = vZ - vX;
vX *= (2.0f/fViewWidth);
vZ = vZ + vY;
vY *= -(2.0f/fViewHeight);
```

```
// Transform basis to any local space (shadow space here)
vStoWBasisX = mShadowTexGen * Vec4 (vX, 0.0f);
vStoWBasisY = mShadowTexGen * Vec4 (vY, 0.0f);
vStoWBasisZ = mShadowTexGen * Vec4 (vZ, 0.0f);
vCamPos   = mShadowTexGen * Vec4 (cam.GetPosition(), 1.0f);

//Shader code:
float4 CalcHomogeneousPos(float SceneDepth, float2 WPos)
{
  float4 HPos = (vStoWBasisZ +
   (vStoWBasisX*VPos.x)+(vStoWBasisY*VPos.y) ) * fSceneDepth;
  HPos += vCamPos.xyzw;
  return HPos;
}
```

Listing 4.4. Computing the reconstruction basis.

Ambient passes. Lighting accumulation starts with hemisphere ambient-lighting passes. These can be the outdoor ambient light, which is rendered additively as a full-screen quad, or the indoor ambient light, which is rendered as stencil-tagged regions (which get set during the G-buffer passes), using an indoor volume bounding box. This functionality was helpful to designers, for setting up custom ambient lighting in an indoor area. Hemisphere lighting approximation is computed by warping the Z-component of the world-space normal and using this term to scale the ambient term, e.g., ambient * (N.z * 0.7 + 0.3) (see Figure 4.11).

Figure 4.11. Ambient passes: outdoor ambient lighting (left) and indoor ambient lighting (right). Notice the sharp transition between outdoor and indoor.

Environment lighting probes. Image-based lighting was one of the big novelties introduced in the latest version of our engine. It allows for more accurate diffuse and specular lighting, utilizing special light probe sampling locations that are carefully picked by the artists. At each sampling location an HDR cube map of the scene is captured. From this cube map we generate a low resolution (8×8) diffuse map and a specular cube map, encoded in RGBK. Such cube maps are preprocessed using the ATI CubemapGen tool [Sheuermann and Isidoro 05], which generates correct mip-map levels, taking into account cube map borders,

Figure 4.12. Environment lighting probes passes.

which avoids the noticeable seams that would otherwise result with a more naïve cube map generation.

These environment lighting probes are rendered as a light volume using linear blending and replacing existing ambient lighting. Because lighting artists can control the light multiplier, such lights can also act as "negative lights." G-buffer material glossiness is used for picking which mip level is sampled for the specular cube map to maintain consistency between image-based lighting and traditional specular lighting (see Figure 4.12).

Diffuse global illumination. Another novelty introduced for CryENGINE 3 is an approximation for real-time diffuse global illumination through light propagation volumes. This is an additive indirect ambient pass rendered into light buffers. We will not go into much detail on this feature since it has been covered in depth in previous publications [Kaplanyan 10b].

Contact shadows (SSDO). One of the greatest benefits of SSAO [Kajalin 09] is that it allows objects to appear more grounded by creating a slight drop shadow (sometimes called a "contact shadow") around them. However, since SSAO is meant to attenuate ambient light, it does not take into account any particular light direction. Screen-space directional occlusion (SSDO) [Grosch and Ritschel 10] improves upon this method by accumulating the lighting during the SSAO pass and discarding the light contribution if a given sample vector is occluded. This implicitly creates directional, colored shadows.

Sampling the lighting efficiently during the SSAO pass is not feasible for our deferred lighting pipeline, so we use a different more deferred approach that still gives us the directional and colored contact shadows for each light source. During the SSAO pass, in addition to the regular occlusion term, we also store the average unoccluded direction (usually known as a "bent normal"). The bent normal is just the normalized accumulation of all SSAO sample vectors weighted by each sample's occlusion amount. So if a sample is completely occluded, it does not contribute to the bent normal.

Figure 4.13. SSDO results. Notice the clear contact soft shadows (left). Bent normals target visualization (right).

During the lighting passes, the bent normal can be used to modulate the lighting intensity for each light source. We compute the directional lighting influence $N \cdot L$ as usual and then also compute $N' \cdot L$ using the bent normal (N'). The clamped difference of the two dot products is used to modulate the lighting intensity.

It is desirable that the SSAO shader use a large kernel radius so that the contact shadows are a reasonable size. Furthermore, it is essential that the SSAO implementation produces very clean results without any self-occlusion; otherwise lighting becomes incorrectly attenuated (see Figure 4.13).

Real-time local reflections (RLR). Accurate reflections are difficult to generate efficiently with rasterization-based rendering. The most common techniques for approximating reflections are to re-render the scene once for each planar reflection or create an environment map such as a cube map (which is only truly valid for computing reflections at a single position in space). Both of these techniques have in common that reflections are treated as a special case and will only work for a limited number of reflective objects.

For the *Crysis 2* DX11 upgrade we tried an old idea that we first considered at the beginning of the project: generating the reflections in screen space. The basic idea is simple. For each pixel on the screen, the reflection vector is computed using a per-pixel normal from the G-buffer. Then, in the pixel shader we ray march along the reflection vector to find out if and where the ray intersects the scene. Several samples are taken along the ray, and the z-coordinate of the ray is compared against the depth sampled from the depth buffer at the current step on the ray. If the difference is within a certain interval, we detect a hit and the computed world-space position is re-projected into the previous frame's back buffer to sample the reflection color.

The biggest benefit of this technique is that it can efficiently create accurate reflections on all kinds of visible geometry, even on complex curved surfaces.

Figure 4.14. RLR result. Notice reflections on most surfaces.

However, as the computation is performed in screen space, there are naturally a lot of limitations that need to be taken into account.

An inherent problem is that not all of the required information is available in screen space. The worst case occurs when the reflection vector points in exactly the opposite direction to the view vector. In this case, the back faces of the scene need to be reflected, and these are not visible from the camera's perspective. Instead of displaying an incorrect reflection color, we avoid this situation by smoothly fading out the reflections based on the dot product between the view and reflection vectors. A similar issue occurs when the reflected point is outside of the frame of the back buffer. To avoid hard popping when the perspective is changed, we smoothly fade out the reflections at the screen edges.

For ray marching, the number of samples makes a huge difference in the accuracy of the reflections, especially if a simple linear stepping scheme is used. In order to hide staircase artifacts, we apply some jittering to the length of the sampling steps. This also makes the reflections appear slightly glossy without requiring an additional blur step (see Figure 4.14).

Despite the numerous limitations, the technique can add a lot of visual quality if used carefully for nearby local reflections. It usually works fairly well on ground surfaces like a marble floor, where the reflection vector is pointing in the same direction as the view vector. Also, there are still several opportunities for future improvements. A more sophisticated ray-marching algorithm can be used to improve the reflection quality, and the glossiness of surfaces can be used to alter the sharpness of the reflections.

Light passes. We support point lights and projector light sources in CE3; the lighting model is limited to normalized Blinn-Phong lighting [Hoffman et al. 10].

Figure 4.15. Clip volume enabled (left) and disabled (right). Notice light leaking.

These lights are rendered as full screen quads with stencil volume prepasses if the viewer is inside the light source. Depending on the light's screen coverage, it might be converted into a convex light volume or simply a quad if the light is small enough, since using stencil volume prepasses can actually be slower in some cases. The light volumes are reconstructed in the vertex shader and the geometry used is a tessellated unit cube and frustum projection matrix depending on the light type.

We did several tests with different approaches such as interleaved light rendering or tiled rendering, but for our particular cases, such approaches did not pay off performance-wise and added additional complexity to further handling of lights and light leaking. Light leaking is particularly important, since we don't want a light source to bleed from a wall into an exterior area, but also it is not performance-friendly to have every light casting shadows. For such cases the lighting artists could specify a special clip box/volume shape to be attached to lights; such shapes are used for stencil culling (see Figure 4.15).

For performance reasons, the number of simultaneous shadow-casting lights was limited to four. On the Xbox 360 there was a constant cost penalty for each shadow map of about 0.5 ms due to EDRAM resolve/restore requirements, since all EDRAM regions were used during light accumulation stages. For high-end PCs, almost all lights cast shadows and there is no hard limit on the number of shadow casters, something that was impossible with our previous engine (where we limited the amount of shadow casters to 32).

Shadows. We have been using deferred shadows for the sun since CryENGINE 2 (back in the days of *Crysis 1*, we used just a shadow mask for the sun). Shadows for point lights and projectors are rendered directly into the light accumulation buffers. Shadows in our engine are shadow-map based, highly optimized, and fully dynamic. Point lights are supported by splitting them up into six projected light sources, which is both efficient and very simple to accomplish with our system (see Figure 4.16).

Figure 4.16. Visualizing the sun's shadow mask.

Cascaded shadow maps and point-light shadows. We switched to cascaded shadow maps during the development of *Crysis 1* since this solution better fit all our needs—our levels always consist of big environments with long view distances and everything cast shadows onto everything else. We tried to use different adaptive shadowing schemes that attempted to partially focus shadow maps on the specific areas that were visible to the camera, but this did not work well when the entire space around the camera both casts and receives shadows.

For local lights, a different approach must be used. We split omni-directional lights into six independent frustums. A shadow map for each projection was generated and its size was scaled independently of the other five projections and was based on its projected screen-space coverage. After scaling, a big texture atlas was used to pack all of the shadow maps for a given omni-light. This texture

Figure 4.17. Example scene with 10+ shadow-casting lights (left) and visualizing the shadow atlas (right).

atlas was allocated permanently, which helps avoid memory fragmentation (see Figure 4.17).

Cascade-splitting scheme. Our cascade frustum sizes are based on a logarithmic distribution and the orientation for each shadow frustum is fixed in world space (see Figure 4.18). Shadow frustums are adjusted also to cover camera view frustum conservatively.

More cascades allow better approximation of the logarithmical distribution and improve the density distribution of shadow map texels, thus improving shadow-acne problems for wide view ranges. Additionally, shadow space snapping helped us greatly reduce shadow flickering.

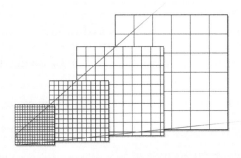

Figure 4.18. Visualizing the individual shadow cascades.

Deferred shadow passes. The shadow cascades are rendered in a deferred way, where potential shadow-receiving areas are selected by stenciling. Such a scheme

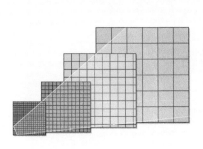

Figure 4.19. Visualizing the shadow cascade stenciling.

is better because the sophisticated splitting algorithm would make cascade selection in the shader too expensive. For the overlap regions of the cascade frustums, we always use the cascade with the highest shadow texels/world unit ratio. For optimizing the shadow-mask generation passes, stencil prepasses are used in order to avoid branching instructions in our shaders, which can be very expensive on consoles (see Figure 4.19).

Shadow cascade caching. For performance reasons, on consoles or on lower spec PCs, updates of shadow cascades are amortized over several frames. This allows us to have more cascades within the same performance restrictions, meaning better shadow-map density distribution. It works by updating more distant cascades less frequently. The most distant cascade uses VSM and is blended additively with the shadow mask. This allows us to have huge penumbras from huge distant objects.

Shadow acne. Shadow acne is typically caused by low shadow-map texel density and insufficient precision in shadow depth buffers (see Figure 4.20). We use different solutions for different cases to overcome issues due to low texel density during shadow-map rendering:

- *Sun shadows.* Render front faces only with slope-scaled depth bias.

- *Point light shadows.* Render back faces only (works better indoors).

- *Variance shadows for distant LODs.* Render both front and back faces to shadow maps due to very low shadow map texel density.

Additionally, a constant depth bias was used during deferred shadow passes to overcome precision problems.

Figure 4.20. Shadow acne example.

Figure 4.21. Particle casting transparent shadows.

Shadows and transparency. For transparent geometry, an additional forward rendering pass is performed for shadow-receiving geometry. For cascaded shadow maps, this means finding the affected geometry and figuring out which cascade frustums it uses. This is computed while processing shadow casters on the CPU. As it turns out, about 90% of the cases are affected by one cascade and the rest by two cascades.

For casting a transparent shadow, we generate a separate render target where we accumulate transparency alpha values (see Figure 4.21).

The steps for rendering translucency maps include:

1. Depth testing should be done using the regular opaque shadow map to avoid back projections.

2. Accumulate translucency alpha values. (Transparent objects can be sorted front to back to have proper accumulation of transparency alpha values.)

Finally the shadow depth map and the translucency alpha map are both used during a deferred shadow pass, computed as follows:

```
InShadow = max(translShadow, opaqueShadow).
```

4.3.4 Deferred Decals

Forward decals, especially projective forward decals, have quite a few drawbacks, which require additional memory (a big problem for consoles), mesh re-allocations (causing memory fragmentation), and CPU time for dynamic mesh creation. In

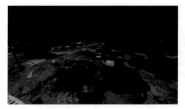

Figure 4.22. Deferred decals visualization. No decals (left), deferred decals layer (middle), and final composition (right).

addition, they are problematic with DX11 Tessellation + Displacement (intersections). Replacing the rendering of forward decals by deferred decals [Krassnigg 11] helped us to solve all these problems. Our deferred decals are rendered into a separate diffuse and normal buffer using a box volume shape. Such decals are applied to static geometry only, do not require any allocation for dynamic meshes, and reduce shader computation cost (see Figure 4.22).

All decals share the same shading and due to simplicity, they are very performance friendly, allowing designers to use a lot of them. They are shaded during forward shading passes by fetching the layer of accumulated deferred decals. Leaking through dynamic geometry and/or walls is the biggest problem with such an approach (see Figure 4.23). Besides only applying the approach to static geometry, we tried to further address this in several ways. For example, we used an adjustable decal volume and attenuation function based on a decal normal, and a world-space normal dot product.

Figure 4.23. Deferred decal leaking.

4.4 Forward Shading Passes

The biggest strength of deferred lighting (and weakness in performance terms), is that shading is done in an additional forward pass. This allows for a great deal of material variation and flexibility when compared to "vanilla" deferred rendering.

Lighting buffers are fetched as required (depending on material properties) albedo and specular maps are modulated as usual, and a per-material Fresnel term is applied (see Figure 4.24).

Figure 4.24. Shading composite overview.

To minimize the bandwidth impact due to so many full-screen targets being fetched, on the PS3, lighting buffers are stored in a 32-bit format using an RGBK encoding. On the Xbox 360, lighting buffers are resolved from A2B10G10R10F_EDRAM into A2B10G10R10 instead of A16B16G16R16F, since there is no corresponding FP10 texture format; this integer format is bitwise equivalent to FP10, and it is converted when sampled into a 7e3 floating-point format as proposed by Cook [Cook and Gould 08]. This allows us to minimize the resolve costs from 1.0 ms down to 0.5 ms and trade off bandwidth for ALU cost. Additionally, if a surface's material properties are mostly diffuse, then we only fetch from the diffuse lighting buffer to save on wasted bandwidth.

Deferred skin shading. The biggest strength of deferred lighting is material variation, and we tried to take advantage of it. One of our early ideas during development was to reuse all diffuse lighting accumulation for approximating subsurface scattering in UV, or even screen space. The idea was simply to project from screen space into UV space and to avoid redundant lighting computations, which are present in the vanilla approach [Borshukov and Lewis 03]. Although this worked, it still suffered from the limitations of the original algorithm: a need for a texture atlas into which all characters would be rendered, hence additional precious memory, additional geometry pass, unique UV texturing, and a constant

Figure 4.25. Deferred skin shading in action. (*Head model courtesy Infinite-Realities.*)

frame cost for each update. We were able to avoid UV space altogether by implementing our subsurface scattering approximation in screen space instead. This
worked around most limitations and does not require additional render target
memory, which was the biggest gain.

Screen-space subsurface scattering is implemented by performing a bilateral
blur, using a Poisson distribution for taps, during the geometry pass. The kernel
size is depth dependent. This might sound expensive, and it is, but because character faces and arms tend to be small on screen, it turns out that in practice, this
approach is quite affordable since the overall cost of the technique is proportional
to the number of screen pixels to which it is applied (see Figure 4.25).

Screen-Space self-shadowing. Self-shadowing still remains challenging for macro-
geometry details and particularly for character faces. However, self-shadowing
is an important visual hint and its significance should not be underestimated.
Many games achieve high-quality self-shadows for their characters by generating
a shadow depth map for each character—sometimes just for the closest few characters. This method works quite well but it requires additional memory for each
shadow map and a custom code path specialized for handling character shadows.

One idea we had during production, of which we were initially very skeptical,
was to approximate shadows in screen space for such cases. As it turned out,
this method works relatively well and has no additional memory requirements.
This approximation consists of ray marching through the depth buffer along the

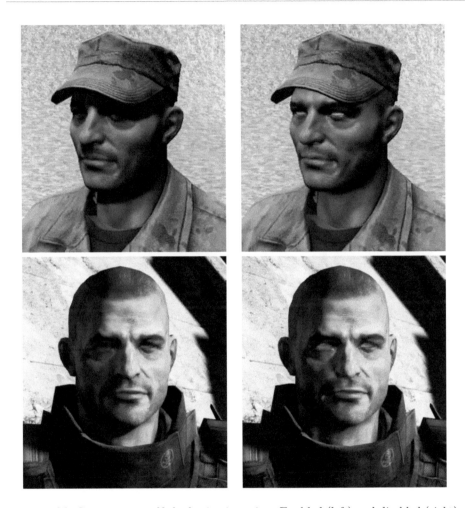

Figure 4.26. Screen-space self-shadowing in action. Enabled (left) and disabled (right).

screen-space light vector during the geometry pass. As in other screen-space techniques, the runtime cost of this approximation is proportional to its size on screen. Fortunately, for characters, only a small amount of screen space is required and this technique performs quite well. We ended up using screen-space self-shadowing for our character's skin, hair, and eye rendering (see Figure 4.26).

Soft alpha test. Efficient hair rendering is a big challenge, particularly on the current generation of console hardware. This challenge is made even more difficult when using deferred rendering techniques such as deferred fog and deferred shadows. Most games avoid using alpha blending for hair, either because it is too expensive or because it is incompatible with many deferred rendering techniques. Instead, most people chose to use alpha testing for hair. Unfortunately, alpha testing results in a cartoon-like look that spoils the realism of your characters.

One solution we came up with, again very early during the project, was inspired by existing image space motion-blur techniques. We attempted to smooth hair geometry along its per-pixel screen-space tangent vector. This is done during a separate geometry pass, which is still quite a bit cheaper than brute force alpha blending (which typically requires three passes for approximating back to front sorting). Once again, the cost of this screen-space technique is proportional to its size onscreen and for characters (who aren't extraordinarily hairy), this performs amazingly well (see Figure 4.27).

The exact same concept can be used for fur rendering but rather than smoothing along the tangent, for fur you should smooth along the screen-space surface normal.

Figure 4.27. Soft alpha test in action. Enabled (left) and disabled (right).

4.5   Batched HDR Postprocessing

The main goal for optimizing performance while postprocessing is to reduce, as much as possible, the amount of work that must be done and to share computations wherever possible.

Camera and object motion blur. One difference between our newest engine and the previous engine is that we rid ourselves of our old approach of using "a sphere around camera" to approximate camera motion blur. Our new approach computes camera motion blur in a single pass instead of several passes, which the old approach required.

For static geometry, reprojection is used since it is straightforward to compute how much a pixel has moved, compared to the previous frame. This is computed

Figure 4.28. Visualizing individual stages for motion blur and composition.

using a per-pixel depth value and the previous frame's view projection matrix to find the previous frame's pixel location and then using that to compute a delta (velocity) to the current frame's position. To handle dynamic geometry, like skinned characters, we have no choice but to output velocity to a render target.

The velocity values are used to do a directional blur. Performing such a directional blur at full resolution means at least 3 ms spent for blurring an LDR render target (this cost is even higher if blurring an HDR image), and not really much can be done to speed up the worst-case scenario.

Inspired by the *Killzone 2* approach [Valient 09], we ended up using a half-resolution buffer instead of a full-screen buffer. To save bandwidth, we store 2 RGBA/8 targets, one that uses RGBK encoded colors with the final blurred result and the other with the composition mask. On a PC, we fall back to straightforward 16-bit floating-point render targets with the mask in alpha.

Object velocity buffer dilation is done, in a similar way to what we did in *Crysis 1* [Sousa 08]. This avoids unpleasant sharp silhouettes by slightly dilating the values stored in the velocity buffer. One difference from our earlier approach is that we now do this on the fly, in the same pass in which we apply the motion blur, which proved to be good enough and allowed us to avoid additional passes and the associated resolves steps that would be necessary on the Xbox 360 (see Figure 4.28).

The directional blur is done in linear color space, using HDR values, before tone mapping, which is more physically accurate and allows for the propagation of bright streaks [Debevec and Malik 97]. For consoles, we limited our kernel to nine taps and clamped to a maximum range to avoid undersampling. For high-spec'd PCs, we allow up to 24 taps.

Bokeh DoF: just another kernel and weights. It turns out that DoF, or any blur, is just a special case of the previous directional blur. It is essentially just another

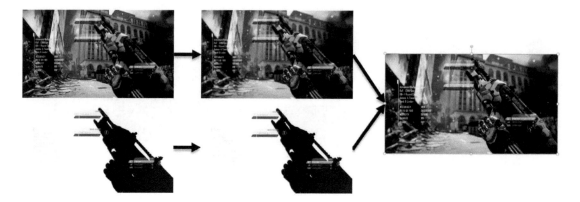

Figure 4.29. Visualizing individual stages for bokeh DoF and composition.

blur kernel with taps offsets in a disk-shaped pattern. The kernel size is scaled based on the circle of confusion (CoC) term—a term that is proportional to how "out of focus" a pixel is. In order to make this less expensive, we reuse the same nine taps (24 on PCs) mentioned above (see Figure 4.29).

Batching it all together. In the end, what we really want is to blur the image and to reuse all taps whenever possible in order to share as much work as possible. The kernel offsets are morphed based on the blur type: directional versus disk, masked blur, radial blur, distant DoF, and other cases.

The final composition is done in our tone-mapping pass. Note that this is not necessarily physically correct, since "final composite" should be done into an HDR target so that eye adaptation, bloom, and other stages are 100% correct. But we cheated to save performance at the cost of very minimal visual sacrifice. In the end, with one blur pass, we were able to achieve motion blur, depth of field, and many other blur-based effects for a constant frame cost of 1 ms on consoles.

Motion blur for ultra specs. For the DirectX 11 Ultra Upgrade, we added a very high-quality mode for certain effects. One of the effects that got a nice boost was motion blur (see Figure 4.30).

This mode is a single pass at full-screen resolution, using 12 taps (once again clamping the maximum range to limit undersampling). The alpha channel stores the objects' ID, and these are used to implement a directional blur masking scheme based on velocity and ID. For each tap we compute:

- If $||V|| >$ threshold then allow bleeding, else reject the tap.

- Early out if $||V|| <$ threshold.

Figure 4.30. Example of "ultra specs" motion blur (left); visualizing bleeding masking (center); and bleeding masking disabled (right).

Bokeh DoF for ultra specs. For the DirectX 11 Ultra Upgrade, we optimized the GPU-side so much that we had quite a bit of free performance to use (something in the order of 16 ms). One of the very high-quality modes with which we went a bit crazy was a technique commonly used in the movie industry to approximate high-quality DoF [Cyril, Sylvain, and Olivier 05]. Essentially, we render a quad/sprite per pixel in order to perform an arbitrarily sized masked blur (see Figure 4.31).

These quads are scaled by the circle-of-confusion factor using a geometry shader, and are additively accumulated into an intermediate render target. The quads can also feature a camera-aperture-shaped mask for different bokeh shapes (spherical, hexagonal, etc.). We employed dithering to minimize noticeable precision loss (see Figure 4.32).

Figure 4.31. DirectX 11 DoF with circular bokeh.

Figure 4.32. "Ultra Specs" DoF. Visualizing foreground and background layers.

There is no explicit depth masking, instead quads are sorted per background and foreground layers. Quad count is accumulated into a destination target alpha channel. During composite with the final scene, we normalize the accumulated color values by dividing by each pixel's alpha value. This technique provides a very high-quality, although physically incorrect, depth-of-field blur but it is also very expensive. The naïve implementation takes 100 ms for large defocus at 1080 p. Unfortunately, even high-end hardware is not currently fast enough to perform this technique at full-screen resolution.

Bokeh DoF for ultra specs: making it fast. In order to optimize our high-quality depth of field we first had to switch to performing it at quarter-resolution (half-width and half-height buffer). Additionally, quads were rejected using an inter-leaved pattern, which helped improve the fill-rate requirements of this technique. We also found that using "early out" conditions, both on the geometry shader and pixel shader side, and using a spherical aperture shape (which can be computed using ALU instructions in the shader instead of texture fetches) helped improve performance further. Although we did not do this, avoiding geometry shader usage could have helped performance as well, particularly on hardware that has weak geometry shader support.

After the front and back layers are generated, they are composited with the final scene as follows:

- Back layer is composited using full resolution CoC, computed based on full resolution depth target.

- Front layer is composited based on layer alpha, which works quite well, since the front layer should bleed into the background.

Merging quad-based bokeh DoF with motion blur. One idea that occurred to us late in the DX11 ultra upgrade project was to merge the DoF quad-based approach with motion blur in a single pass. This is achievable by simply extruding quad geometry and using geometry shader along the motion direction.

Figure 4.33. Screen space reprojection stereo in action (anaglyph output).

4.6   Stereoscopic 3D

With the recent success of 3D technology in the movie industry and a growing number of consumer devices that are capable of displaying 3D content, stereoscopic 3D is becoming increasingly important for video games. Although adding basic 3D support to an engine is straightforward in principle, in practice it can be challenging to get the performance right, and to ensure that the user can play the game comfortably over a longer period without eye strain (see Figure 4.33).

4.6.1   Generating the Stereo Image Pair

Stereo 3D (s3D) requires that the user be presented with two slightly different images, one for the left eye and one for the right eye. The standard way to generate this image pair is to render the scene two times from carefully shifted perspectives. While this approach is straightforward for a 3D engine and yields perfect results in terms of quality, it can be problematic for a graphics-heavy game that makes full use of the available hardware resources. If a game is GPU-bound, rendering the scene a second time will often mean that the frame rate will be cut in half—something that is usually unacceptable for a console title that must run at 30 fps. In order to overcome this performance issue, one must reduce the rendering resolution, the geometric detail, and the number of effects. Obviously, this can result in a very noticeable degradation of visual quality when entering 3D mode.

Reprojection. A completely different approach to achieving s3D is to generate the image pair from the existing nonstereo rendering data. When the depth for each pixel is available, it is possible to reproject each fragment into the space of the left and right eye cameras. Assuming that the scene was rendered from a regular "center" perspective, this is done by reconstructing the view space position for each pixel and applying the left and right camera view-projection matrices. The pixel is then plotted at the computed image-space location. Unfortunately, this point splatting approach requires data scattering, which is not efficient on current generation console GPUs. Furthermore, the generated images will contain holes at locations where no pixels were plotted. No information is available in the original image for these locations, so they need to be filled with some estimated color during a second pass.

Image displacement. As we required a fully gather-based approach that can be executed efficiently in a pixel shader, even on older console hardware, we ended up using a simple technique that can be considered a kind of image displacement. This technique is executed as a postprocessing step on the final back buffer, before the HUD is rendered.

We use two basic parameters for our s3D view setup: the maximum separation (MaxSeparation), which is the distance between the left and right eye cameras in normalized screen space; and the distance to the virtual screen plane, which we call zero parallax plane (ZPP). If the depth of a point is the same as the ZPP distance, it appears to be exactly on the screen, while a smaller or larger depth will make the point come out of or go into the screen.

The parallax is the distance on the ZPP between the positions of a point that was projected into the left and right views. Using Thales' theorem, the parallax is straightforward to compute (see Figure 4.34).

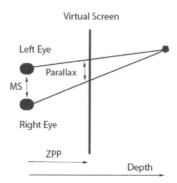

Figure 4.34. Parallax = MaxSeparation * (1 − ZPP / Depth).

The computed parallax is used as an offset to sample the back buffer. The parallax is added for the left eye and subtracted for the right eye. This creates two images that are displaced in a way that the brain expects; therefore, they will create the perception of 3D.

However, performing this displacement in image space reveals two basic problems: occlusion and disocclusion. Disocclusion occurs when a part of an object should be visible in the left or right eye view but is hidden in the original view. This issue is not handled explicitly or correctly with our solution. The center view is used for synthesizing the two images, so the error gets distributed for both eyes. Luckily, the brain seems to be quite forgiving of this kind of error if the stereo parameters are not too extreme.

The second issue, that of occlusion, can be more noticeable. It happens when a background object with a high parallax is occluded by a closer object with a lower parallax. In this case, the nearby object would be sampled by the background although the background should be sampled instead. Luckily this case is easy to detect by checking if the depth of the offset sample is closer. When this happens, the background can just be cloned. In our implementation, we simply search for a minimum depth in the MaxSeparation range and use that to compute the parallax. This works because a smaller depth results in a smaller offset for a positive parallax. A basic version of the s3D algorithm we use is shown in Listing 4.5.

```
const float samples[3] = { 0.5, 0.66, 1 };

float minDepthL = 1.0;
float minDepthR = 1.0;
float2 uv = 0;

for( int i = 0; i < 3; ++i )
{
    uv.x = samples[i] * MaxSeparation;
    minDepthL = min( minDepthL, GetDepth( baseUV + uv ) );
    minDepthR = min( minDepthR, GetDepth( baseUV - uv ) );
}

float parallaxL = MaxSeparation * (1 - ZPP / minDepthL );
float parallaxR = MaxSeparation * (1 - ZPP / minDepthR );

left  = tex2D( backBuf, baseUV + float2( parallaxL, 0 ) );
right = tex2D( backBuf, baseUV - float2( parallaxR, 0 ) );
```

Listing 4.5. Basic s3D algorithm.

Although the algorithm works surprisingly well for carefully chosen stereo parameters, there are some artifacts that are inevitable due to the nature of this screen-space approach. As the background is getting cloned in the case of occlusion, some halos can appear around objects. These can be fairly noticeable sometimes, but usually they do not disturb the perception of 3D. The screen edges need some special handling, as it is possible that the algorithm samples outside the image. This can easily be solved by cropping the image a bit at the sides. Finally, it needs to be noted that the technique does not work for transparent objects, as they usually do not write to the depth buffer. Transparent objects just get the depth of the background, which can look more or less wrong depending on the situation.

4.6.2 Viewing Comfort

Stereo 3D is essentially tricking the viewer's brain in order to produce the impression of depth. It is important that a few basic rules are not violated, otherwise the brain can get confused and the experience can result in uncomfortable side effects for the viewer.

For *Crysis 2* we decided that everything should have positive parallax and hence go into the screen, so that the screen is a window into the world. Not having any objects come out of the screen completely avoids window violations where an object with negative parallax would be cut by the screen borders, which would hurt the illusion. While negative parallax is considered as a "wow" effect in s3D movies, it can quickly fatigue the viewer as it requires strong refocusing and is hard to control in games.

One of the most important rules for keeping the s3D viewing comfortable is to avoid depth conflicts as much as possible. A depth conflict exists when the perceived stereo depth does not match the rendered depth. For example, if a crosshair is rendered on top of a wall, but the separation is higher than that of the wall, the brain will get confused by the wrong hints and can react with headaches and sickness after some time.

Avoiding depth conflicts. Giving a certain amount of depth to HUD elements and overlays can greatly improve the overall stereo experience. While static HUD elements can be placed carefully in s3D space to avoid intersections with the world, some more dynamic HUD elements may require additional effort. In *Crysis 2* the crosshair is located a few meters away from the weapon to look more convincing. However, when getting close to a wall, there will be an annoying depth conflict between the world and the crosshair. To avoid this, a ray-cast against the world is performed and in case of a hit, the crosshair is smoothly moved towards the viewer to avoid the intersection.

HUD elements usually get rendered after the scene without depth testing. Thus, there can be a depth conflict between the first-person weapon and the crosshair that is supposed to be in front of the gun. Although it is often just a few pixels that are conflicting, we wanted to get rid of that issue, as we found it to be disturbing enough while playing the game for a long time to warrant our attention. We ended up writing a mask for the weapon in the alpha channel of the left and right eye buffers during the stereo image generation. When drawing HUD elements located in the scene, a blend mode is used that fades out, and hence occludes pixels that are covered by the weapon mask.

In order to get enough depth for the scene, a reasonably high distance for the zero parallax plane must be chosen. This is problematic for a first-person shooter where the weapon is always very close and would come out of the screen. Not only does this look unnatural, it also makes the viewer exhausted as the eye needs to refocus a lot more. In order to avoid this, the weapon is pushed into the screen during the stereo image synthesis by offsetting and scaling the depth values.

Unfortunately, pushing the weapon artificially into the screen is a serious source of depth conflicts when getting close to objects. This is especially annoying in a shooter where the player can take cover. To avoid these depth conflicts, we try to find out when the player is close to some world geometry. The most accurate way to achieve this would be to analyze the depth buffer, however, for simplicity we just do a few ray casts. In case a potential depth conflict is detected, the ZPP distance is smoothly reduced based on the distance to the closest object. This reduces the overall depth of the scene without being very obvious to the player.

4.7 Conclusion

We have covered here only a very small part of the immense work that went into our latest engine during a period of almost three and a half years. We hope that this chapter has effectively conveyed the massive team effort that went into the creation of CryENGINE 3 and *Crysis 2*.

4.8 Acknowledgments

For their support and helpful feedback, we thank in particular Vaclav Kyba, Michael Kopietz, Carsten Wenzel, Vladimir Kajalin, Andrey Konich, Ivo Zoltan Frey, Marco Corbetta, Christopher Evans, Chris Auty, Magnus Larbrant, Pierre-Ives Donzallaz, and Christopher Oat.

Last but not least, we thank the entire Crytek Team.

Bibliography

[Borshukov and Lewis 03] George Borshukov and J. P. Lewis. "Realistic Human Face Rendering for 'The Matrix Reloaded'." In *ACM SIGGRAPH 2003 Sketches & Applications (SIGGRAPH '03)*, p. 1. New York: ACM, 2003.

[Cook and Gould 08] David Cook and Jason Gould,"Xbox Textures—Formats, Conversion, Fetching and Performance," Microsoft. Gamefest 2008. Available online (http://www.microsoft.com/download/en/details.aspx?displaylang=en&id=1166).

[Cyril, Sylvain, and Olivier 05] Pichard Cyril, Michelin Sylvain, and Tubach Olivier. "Photographic Depth of Field Blur Rendering." Available online (http://wscg.zcu.cz/wscg2005/Papers_2005/Short/H13-full.pdf). 2005.

[Debevec and Malik 97] Paul E. Debevec and Jitendra Malik. "Recovering High Dynamic Range Radiance Maps from Photographs." In *Proceedings of SIGGRAPH '97, Computer Graphics Proceedings, Annual Conference Series*, edited by Turner Whitted, pp. 369–378, Reading, MA: Addison Wesley, 1997.

[Gritz and d'Eon 08] Larry Gritz and Eugene d'Eon, "The Importance of Being Linear," In *GPU Gems 3*. Edited by Hubert Nguyen, pp. 529–542. Reading, MA: Addison Wesley, 2008.

[Grosch and Ritschel 10] Thorsten Grosch and Tobias Ritschel. "Screen-Space Directional Occlusion." *GPU Pro*. Edited by Wolfgang Engel, pp. 215–230. Natick, MA: A K Peters, 2010.

[Hoffman et al. 10] Natty Hoffman, Yoshiharu Gotanda, Ben Snow, and Adam Martinez. "Physically-Based Shading Models in Film and Game Production." SIGGRAPH course 2010.

[Kajalin 09] Vladimir Kajalin. "Screen-Space Ambient Occlusion." *ShaderX^7: Advanced Rendering Techniques*. Edited by Wolfgang Engel, pp. 412–424. Hingham, MA: Charles River Media, 2009.

[Kaplanyan 10a] Anton Kaplanyan. "CryENGINE 3: Reaching the Speed of Light." Crytek. Available online (http://www.crytek.com/cryengine/presentations/CryENGINE3-reaching-the-speed-of-light). 2010.

[Kaplanyan 10b] Anton Kaplanyan. "Real-time Diffuse Global Illumination in CryENGINE 3." Crytek. Available online (http://www.crytek.com/cryengine/presentations/real-time-diffuse-global-illumination-in-cryengine-3). 2010.

[Krassnigg 11] J. Krassnigg. "A Deferred Decal Rendering Technique." *Game Engine Gems 1*. Edited by Eric Lengyel, pp. 271–280. Sudbury, MA: Jones and Bartlett, 2011.

[Reinhard et al. 10] Erik Reinhard, Greg Ward, Sumanta Pattanaik, and Paul Debevec. *High Dynamic Range Imaging: Acquisition, Display, and Image-Based Lighting*. Second edition. San Francisco: Morgan Kaufmann, 2010.

[Sheuermann and Isidoro 05] Thorsten Scheuermann and John Isidoro. "Cubemap Filtering with CubeMapGen." AMD Developer Central. Available online (http://developer.amd.com/gpu_assets/GDC2005_CubeMapGen.pdf). 2005.

[Sousa 08] Tiago Sousa. "Crysis: Next Gen Effects." Crytek. Available online (http://crytek.com/cryengine/presentations/crysis-next-gen-effects). 2008.

[Tchou 07] Chris Tchou. "HDR The Bungie Way," Microsoft. Gamefest Unplugged (Europe) 2007. Available online (http://www.microsoft.com/download/en/details.aspx?displaylang=en&id=21523). 2007.

[Valient 09] Michal Valient. "Rendering Technology of Killzone 2." GDC 2009.

[Vlachos 08] Alex Vlachos, "Post Processing in The Orange Box," GDC 2008. Available online (http://www.valvesoftware.com/publications.html).

5

II

Inexpensive Antialiasing of Simple Objects

Mikkel Gjøl and Mark Gjøl

5.1 Introduction

In the age of mobile devices, every algorithm gets a second chance. This article explores a use of discontinuity edge overdraw [Sander et al. 01] for antialiasing simple objects on 3D-capable mobile devices. The essence of this technique is to render a "smooth" line on top of aliasing primitive edges in order to cover the aliasing edge.

The method is trivially useful for rendering objects whose outline is geometrically defined or easily derived. This applies to everything from GUI-elements to 2D objects positioned in 3D, or even simple 3D-objects—anything where the outline is defined by geometry. For textured 2D-elements, the usual way to deal with antialiasing is to use textures with a translucent edge, relying on texture-sampling to produce a smooth transition at the boundary. While this is a good solution, it requires careful construction of the mip-chain to avoid artifacts during scaling or when viewed at steep angles.

5.2 Antialiasing via Smoothed Lines

The founding observation of [Sander et al. 01] was that aliasing in 3D scenes appears mostly at geometric silhouette edges and crease edges, and so only pixels along these lines require antialiasing. As these boundaries can be described as lines, and since line smoothing is widely available in hardware, aliasing can be reduced by rendering smooth lines on top of the aliasing edges. The main contribution of [Sander et al. 01] was an algorithm to find the aliasing edges. For some applications, the potentially aliasing edges are trivially available, allowing us to use this method easily. It is worth noting that the resulting algorithm does not work for translucent objects, and does nothing to improve upon texture-aliasing,

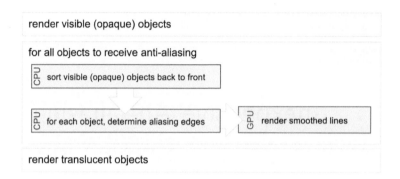

Figure 5.1. Basic rendering setup.

including aliasing when rendering 2D sprites. Hardware texture filtering mostly solves this issue however, and is available on the majority of modern mobile GPUs.

Applying the algorithm consists of just two steps (see Figure 5.1):

1. Determine the geometric edges that are causing aliasing.

2. Render aliasing edges as smooth lines.

In the general case it is not trivial to determine which edges cause aliasing, and we refer readers to the exhaustive discussion in [Sander et al. 01]. In summary, three sets of geometric edges should be considered for any visible object:

- silhouette edges,

- discontinuous edges, e.g., "hard" edges or texture seams,

- intersection-edges between geometric objects.

While discontinuous edges are typically static for a triangle mesh and can be precomputed, silhouette edges change with the viewer. Dealing with scenes constructed entirely of triangles, a geometric approach to finding silhouette edges is to locate all edges where one of the adjacent triangles faces towards the viewer and the other faces away. Computing exact intersections between geometric objects is computationally expensive, and a solution was not presented in [Sander et al. 01].

When rendering lines to cover the detected aliasing edges, "over" alpha-blending is applied (`src_alpha,one_minus_src_alpha`), and depth buffering is used to achieve correct occlusion. While the rendered lines are potentially subject to z-fighting, the fighting pixels have the same color as the object on which they are rendered. Since the main contribution of the smooth lines is outside the aliasing object, z-fighting causes minimal issues. Rendering multiple layers of alpha-blended pixels necessitates composition in a back-to-front manner. This is an issue only at the few pixels where the smooth lines overlap, making the errors caused by incorrect depth sorting mostly unnoticeable. Doing only an approximate per-object sort is sufficient for most purposes, and skipping sorting altogether could be considered.

Shading of the lines should be done identically to the aliasing edges, applying lighting and texturing as for the underlying object. The same vertex program and fragment program should similarly be applied during rendering of smoothed lines (see also Section 1.3.3). Since the aliasing edge is an edge in the rendered mesh, the original vertex data can be used for the smooth line. For ambiguous cases where multiple sets of vertex data are associated with an edge, one set must be selected. Again, we refer to [Sander et al. 01] for treatment of the general case, but in summary, blending between two versions of the edge data is needed in all but the trivial case in order to alleviate popping.

5.3 Rendering Lines

Lines and triangles are rasterized fundamentally differently: while triangles generate fragments where a fragment center is contained within the triangle, lines generate fragments where they pass through a "diamond" centered around the fragment center (see Figure 5.2). In the case of triangles, vertex values are linearly interpolated to the fragment center, while line-generated fragments always receive the value at the rasterized point projected onto the center of the line.

OpenGL|ES defines the coverage of a fragment to be the exact area of overlap between the fragment and the rectangle centered around the line. Rendered lines thus give perfect coverage values for the affected fragments, making them ideal for antialiasing purposes. It is worth noting that the specification does allow variations in the implementation, so the exact outcome may vary.

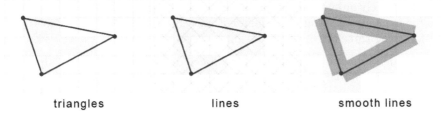

triangles   lines   smooth lines

Figure 5.2. Rasterization rules for various primitives.

5.3.1 OpenGL|ES 1.x

The OpenGL|ES 1.x specification includes the functionality of rendering smoothed points and lines, as also available in "regular" OpenGL (see Listing 5.1).

```
gl.glLineWidth(1.0f);
gl.glEnable(GL10.GL_LINE_SMOOTH);
gl.glBlendFunc(GL10.GL_SRC_ALPHA,GL10.GL_ONE_MINUS_SRC_ALPHA);
gl.glEnable(GL10.GL_BLEND);
```

Listing 5.1. Enabling line smoothing in OpenGL|ES 1.x

Implementations are not required to provide line widths beyond one pixel, however for this method wider lines are not required. While line smoothing is present on most phones exclusively supporting OpenGL|ES1.x, some phones supporting OpenGL|ES 1.x, as well as OpenGL|ES 2.x, did not provide line-smoothing functionality. The emulator for the iPhone provides smoothed lines, but alas the device itself does not [Flaherty 10].

5.3.2   OpenGL|ES 2.x

For OpenGL|ES 2.0, point- and line-smoothing were removed from the specification, and multisample-antialiasing (MSAA) was introduced, to allow for antialiasing of all primitives.[1] Not all OpenGL|ES2.x hardware supports MSAA, but where it is supported, it should be easily implemented and provides a very flexible solution.

Using multisampling does, however, significantly increase the number of processed fragments, while also increasing the memory used by depth and color buffers to store the multisampled buffers.[2] This overhead might not be acceptable for all applications, for reasons related to memory and performance, as well as to battery-life.

5.3.3   General Solution to Smoothed Line Rendering

Rather than rely on specific hardware capabilities, there are several methods available for manual rendering of antialiased lines [Bærentzen et al. 08, Texture 04]. The following three are of particular interest (see Figure 5.3):

1. Render an extra band of geometry along an edge, setting vertex alpha to 0 along the border.

2. Render with a masking alpha texture to smooth edges (optionally using a distance-field).

3. Analytically calculate the distance to a line segment in the pixel shader and use the mapped distance as an alpha-mask.

---

[1]MSAA is supported on the iPhone via the extension APPLE_framebuffer_multisample, while on Android EGL_SAMPLE_BUFFERS is passed to eglChooseConfig to determine the number of samples.

[2]Note that on some architectures, there is no memory overhead [IMG 11].

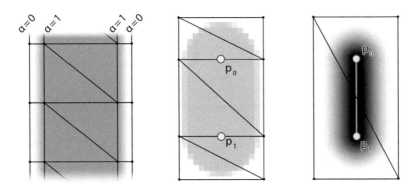

Figure 5.3. Vertex-alpha (left), texture-alpha (middle), and analytical distance (right).

For rendering lines with a width of only a few pixels like the ones sought here, rendering an extra strip of translucent vertices is impractical as it generates numerous small, thin triangles. First, it is not guaranteed that any fragment centers are contained within the triangles, requiring wide falloffs to guarantee smoothness. Second, because hardware often shades pixels in quads of 2×2 pixels, processing may be wasted on nonvisible fragments. Additionally, the method does not deal correctly with endpoints. At best, adding an end segment would produce bi-linearly interpolated areas, causing unsightly artifacts.

Using a simple alpha texture as a mask relies on the texture filtering and pre-filtered mip-maps to produce a smooth result. Using a texture easily allows us to specify a custom falloff for the line, allowing increased control over the smoothness. As the texture can be very small, e.g., a grayscale 32×32 pixels, memory is not a concern. In order to produce properly filtered lines at all scales, it is important to provide a mip-map for the texture. Applying the alpha texture can be done using either shaders or register combiners—having the final texture combiner replace the alpha for the masked texture alpha.

The third option for analytically calculating the distance provides the most accurate result, but can only be easily implemented using shaders. While the per-fragment distance calculations require more ALU instructions than using a texture lookup, it is still a viable option, as only a few fragments are touched using this shader. If the base shader is bandwidth bound, it may even be the preferred option. A hybrid of the second and third methods is possible, sampling a distance texture and mapping it to an alpha value, potentially providing yet more control over the falloff.

It is worth noting the importance of generating lines with a constant screen-space antialiasing footprint. Also, the rendered lines should have valid depths to be useful for depth culling. The following options are available for producing the needed geometry:

1. Project all points to screen space, extrude line geometry, and project back to world space.

2. Directly render collapsed triangles in world space, and do the expansion after projection within the vertex-shader.

3. For hardware with geometry-shaders, render line segments and expand vertices in the geometry shader.

Depending on hardware and the specific case, any of these methods could be preferable. The second method requires access to shaders, and results in only a small memory overhead to store vertex IDs. Geometry shaders, while not currently available on mobile hardware, would provide the most flexible solution, requiring very few changes compared to ordinary line rendering. In order to maintain backwards compatibility, we opted for generating all line geometry directly in world space, on the CPU. The downside to this is the overhead of creating new positions and texture coordinates whenever the view changes.

The method for generating line geometry is fairly straight forward, but is provided here for completeness (see Figure 5.4):

For each aliasing line segment $\{p_0, p_1\}$

1. Project $\{p_0, p_1\}$ to the near plane $\{p_0^{np}, p_1^{np}\}$.

2. Expand $\{p_0, p_1\}$ to eight vertices v_{n0-n7} forming lines on the near plane.

3. Generate plane P from the three points p_0, p_1, and $p_0 + \vec{v} \times (p_0 - p_1)$, where $\vec{v}$ is the view vector in world coordinates.

4. Project v_{n0-n7} on to P, thus obtaining world-space vertices.

Recalling that triangle rasterization only affects fragments whose center lies within the triangle, it is necessary to render lines wider than the targeted width, in order to affect the same fragments touched by smooth line rendering. The minimum line width required to affect the same fragments as a 1-pixel antialiased

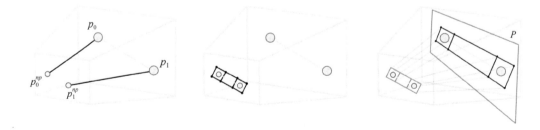

Figure 5.4. Generating world-space line geometry in three stages.

line depends on angle and offset. To cover the worst case, a width of $2\sqrt{2} = 2.8$ pixels can be used. If desired, a bias towards a smoother result can be introduced by artificially increasing the width of the lines.

During rendering, we want the alpha mask texture interpolation to happen in screen space. In other words, we want to do screen-space linear interpolation of the texture coordinates. OpenGL|ES does not currently support `noperspective` interpolation, but the same result is achievable using shaders, by negating the perspective transform as follows, see [Bærentzen et al. 08]: in the vertex shader, multiply the `texcoords` with the w-component of the clip space vertex position— then in the fragment shader, multiply the interpolated texture coordinates by the interpolated $1/w$.

Recalling that the lines should be rendered with the same lighting and textures as the object itself, it is generally sufficient to bind an extra vertex stream supplying the texture coordinates for the masking texture. If using shaders, specific variants of the vertex and fragment programs should be created that apply the extra alpha mask.

5.4 Discussion

Manual rendering of smooth lines was implemented in the Android application *Floating Image*. The application renders simple photos in a gallery-type manner. All potentially aliasing edges are static, and thus this application lends itself well to this particular method of antialiasing. It is a very simple application, and several other methods of antialiasing could also have been used—the simplest

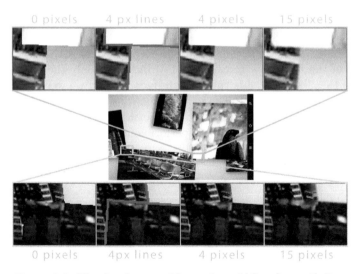

Figure 5.5. Floating image with varying widths of smooth lines.

	9 photos(no AA)	9 photos+AA (36 lines)	AA Cost
HTC Magic (320x480)	56Hz	22Hz	27.59ms
Nexus One (480x800)	52Hz	49Hz	1.17ms
Samsung Galaxy S (480x800)	56Hz	56Hz	"0ms"
	27 photos (no AA)	27 photos+AA (108 lines)	AA Cost
HTC Magic (480x320)	25Hz	9Hz	71ms
Nexus One (480x800)	34Hz	32Hz	1.8ms
Samsung Galaxy S (480x800)	56Hz	56Hz	"0ms"

Table 5.1. Performance timings on various Android devices. MSAA was not supported on these devices for comparison.

being to introduce a band of one translucent pixel around the edge of every mip-level in the photo texture. While occlusions could, and normally should, be handled using the depth buffer, *Floating Image* does manual compositing via the painter's algorithm for device-compatibility reasons, rendering all objects back-to-front.

The implementation uses an alpha texture to render smooth lines, and slightly biases towards blurriness by using a texture with a large falloff and oversized lines. Figure 5.5 shows the result achieved, along with a much over-blurred version. It is worth noting that the method always slightly expands the silhouette of objects: whereas a lot of FSAA techniques blend with a background pixel of a color assumed identical to one of the pixel neighbors, discontinuity edge overdraw always adds occluding pixels on top.

Due to the choice between generating lines directly in world space and rendering via a texture alpha mask, vertex-buffer data needs to be regenerated per frame. Opting for performance over compatibility, vertex-shader expansion of the lines could be used for line expansion, similar to what is often done for billboards.

We have tested the implementation on several devices with varying capabilities. None of the devices were capable of MSAA, and only the Nexus One supported GL_LINE_SMOOTH. Using the smooth lines method we were able to achieve antialiasing on all the devices. The performance has only been tested naïvely, by varying the number of photos displayed and noting the framerate (see Table 5.1). Adding smooth edges hardly impacts performance of the Nexus One, while the HTC is likely CPU-bound due to the line-expansion. The fastest of the devices remains capped at refresh-rate.

5.5   Conclusion

The main drawback of the algorithm is that it depends on the geometric complexity of the rendered scene. Traversing all geometry very quickly becomes impractical, thus limiting use of the method to reasonably simple setups. Furthermore, the need to track aliasing lines per frame makes it necessary to keep all geometry accessible to the CPU. Even though many modern mobile GPUs use a shared memory architecture, the APIs make it difficult to get around duplicating data.

While the algorithm is not complicated to set up, and is arguably trivial if line smoothing is available in hardware, it is challenging to make it scale with increasing geometric complexity. Any object where outlines are trivially found, or as in our example, are entirely static, is an obvious candidate. In general, 2D elements lend themselves well to the technique, whether in screen space or positioned in a 3D scene. For complex 3D scenes, other solutions will likely yield better results.

5.6 Acknowledgments

We would like to thank José Esteve, Romain Toutain, and Andreas Bærentzen for their feedback on this chapter.

Floating Image is available on the Android Market at https://market.android.com/details?id=dk.nindroid.rss and source code is available under GPL at http://code.google.com/p/floatingimage/.

Bibliography

[Bærentzen et al. 08] Jakob Andreas Bærentzen, Steen Munk-Lund, Mikkel Gjøl, and Bent Dalgaard Larsen. "Two Methods for Antialiased Wireframe Drawing with Hidden Line Removal." *Proceedings of the Spring Conference in Computer Graphics*, edited by Karol Myszkowski, pp. 171–177. Bratislava, Slovakia: Comenius University, 2008.

[Flaherty 10] Adam Flaherty. "How to Render Anti-Aliased Lines with Textures in iOS 4." O'Reilly Answers. June 24, 2010. Available at http://answers.oreilly.com/topic/1669-how-to-render-anti-aliased-lines-with-textures-in-ios-4/.

[IMG 11] "POWERVR Series5 Graphics: SGX Architecture Guide for Developers." Imagination Technologies. July 5, 2011. Available at http://www.imgtec.com/powervr/insider.

[OpenGL 08] "OpenGL ES Common/Common-Lite Profile Specification: Version 1.1.12." Edited by David Blythe, Aaftab Munshi, and Jon Leech. The Khronos Group and Silicon Graphics. April 24, 2008. Available at http://www.khronos.org/registry/gles/specs/1.1/es_full_spec_1.1.12.pdf.

[OpenGL 10] "OpenGL ES Common Profile Specification: Version 2.0.25." Edited by Aaftab Munshi and Jon Leech. The Khronos Group. November 2, 2010. Available at http://www.khronos.org/registry/gles/specs/2.0/es_full_spec_2.0.25.pdf.

[Rasterization 11] "Rasterization Rules (Direct3D 10)." *msdn*. Microsoft. 2011. Available at http://msdn.microsoft.com/en-us/library/cc627092(v=vs.85).aspx.

[Sander et al. 01] P. Sander, H. Hoppe, J. Snyder, and S. Gortler. "Discontinuity Edge Overdraw." In *I3D '01 Proceedings of the 2001 Symposium on Interactive 3D Graphics*, pp. 167–174. New York: ACM Press, 2001.

[Texture 04] "Texture AntiAliasing." Apple. 2004. Available at http://homepage.mac.com/arekkusu/bugs/invariance/TexAA.html.

Global Illumination Effects

The global illumination section is a permanent part of this series of books, underlining the importance of realistic shading techniques and, more specifically, global illumination effects in real-time applications. The section contains three articles addressing very different phenomena, each using dedicated data structures and algorithms in order to achieve the desired performance. The techniques range from screen-space approximations to using splat-based representations and spatial index structures.

The first chapter in this section is "Ray-Traced Approximate Reflections Using a Grid of Oriented Splats," by Holger Gruen. In this chapter, Gruen exploits the features of DX11-class hardware to render approximate ray-traced reflections in dynamic scene elements. His method creates a 3D grid containing a surface splat representation on-the-fly and then ray marches the grid to render reflections in real time. Gruen also outlines further improvements, for example, using hierarchical grids, for future hardware.

Our next chapter is "Screen-Space Bent Cones: A Practical Approach," by Oliver Klehm, Tobias Ritschel, Elmar Eisemann, and Hans-Peter Seidel. Ambient occlusion computed in screen space is a widely used approach to add realism to real-time rendered scenes at constant and low cost. Oliver Klehm and his coauthors describe a simple solution to computing bent normals as a byproduct of screen-space ambient occlusion. This recovers some directional information of the otherwise fully decoupled occlusion and lighting computation. The authors further extend bent normals to bent cones, which not only store the average direction of incident light, but also the opening angle. When preconvolving distant lighting, this results in physically more plausible lighting at the speed and simplicity of ambient occlusion.

The last chapter in this section is "Real-Time Near-Field Global Illumination Based on a Voxel Model," by Sinje Thiedemann, Niklas Henrich, Thorsten Grosch, and Stefan Müller. Thiedemann and her colleagues describe a method for computing one-bounce (near-field) indirect illumination with occlusion in dynamic scenes. It is based on a fast texture atlas-based generation of scene voxelizations for visibility, and reflective shadow maps (RSM) to sample directly lit surfaces. The indirect illumination is computed using Monte-Carlo integration using the voxel representation to find the closest intersection for a secondary ray within a user-defined search radius (the near-field). The indirect light is then obtained from projecting the intersection into the RSM.

—Carsten Dachsbacher

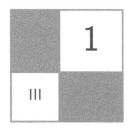

Ray-Traced Approximate Reflections Using a Grid of Oriented Splats

Holger Gruen

1.1 Overview

This chapter introduces a method to generate approximate ray-traced reflections of dynamic scene elements. It uses a dynamic 3D grid containing lists of oriented surface splats to generate these reflections on DX11-class GPUs. It is shown how a straightforward implementation of this technique allows for real-time frame rates for low to moderate grid sizes. The resulting reflections are plausible for rough reflectors. The chapter further describes a future implementation that utilizes a flat hierarchical grid to improve the quality of the reflections while keeping the memory requirements for the 3D grid at an acceptable level.

1.2 Introduction

Real-time reflections in dynamic scenes are still one of the most desired features for real-time 3D applications like computer games, and they pose a really challenging problem in the general case. Recent advances in programmable hardware allow real-time rendering into data structures that capture properties of dynamic scene elements (see e.g., [Yang et al. 10]). This chapter makes use of these capabilities to construct a data structure that allows for computing approximate reflections of dynamic scene elements.

Until now, real-time reflections have been realized by one or a combination of the following techniques:

1. *Flat Reflectors*. Mirror the camera to render a reflection texture.

2. *Reflections through a set of environment maps.* An approximation of the real reflections seen at a specific surface point in the scene is generated. Usually environment maps are used to realize reflections of distant objects.

3. *Screen space reflections.* An approximation is generated that ignores reflections from objects that are not visible onscreen.

4. *Image-based reflections.* Examples are the billboard reflections in the last Unreal Engine 3 demo presented at GDC 2011.

The DX11 rasterizer is used to generate a splat-based intermediate representation of the dynamic objects' surfaces in a scene. In the context of this chapter, the minimum set of attributes stored for each splat are the 3D position of the center of the splat, a surface normal, and some other surface properties used for lighting. This approach shares some of the benefits of image-based rendering, as there is no longer a need to access the full scene geometry. The rasterizer also eliminates some of the geometric complexity of the scene, as small triangles that do not straddle the center of a pixel will not generate any splats.

The use of the rasterizer makes it possible to render exactly the same geometry that is used by other rendering passes of the 3D application. As a result, no memory for an additional scene representation is needed.

GPU-based ray tracing of the full-scene geometry can also be used to generate high-quality reflections. However, ray tracing of fully dynamic scenes is not yet fast enough for a real-time solution. Also, ray-tracing algorithms can become memory limited if they need to parse the full geometric complexity of the scene. This can be especially bad for nonplanar reflectors, as reflected rays in general do not show good coherence.

1.3   The Basic Algorithm

The basic algorithm for generating approximate splat-based reflections works in three phases. These will be now described in detail. Please note that all phases must be carried out per frame for all dynamic scene elements.

1.3.1   Phase 1: Generating a Grid of Splats

In order to generate a good set of point splats, one renders a set of orthogonal views of the geometry in question. Typically three views, for example, a top view, a front view, and a side view are used. To render these views efficiently, we use hardware instancing to replicate the geometry for each of the views . The DX11 system value `SV_InstanceID` is used inside the vertex shader to select what view matrix and what orthogonal projection matrix are to be used.

DX11-class graphics hardware allows for scattering pixel shaders. In other words, a pixel shader can write data to an arbitrary location inside a buffer.

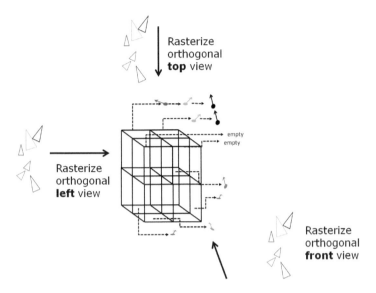

Figure 1.1. Rasterizing oriented splats for a set of orthogonal views into a 3D grid of single linked lists.

When rendering the splats, one needs to disable depth tests and backface culling, and one doesn't actually bind any valid render target but only two output buffers for scattering writes. These output buffers are used to represent a 3D grid with a list of splats in each grid cell (see [Yang et al. 10]). We typically use a $64 \times 64 \times 64$ grid around the dynamic scene elements to capture splats.

We set up a viewport that is big enough to generate a reasonable number of splats along each view direction, and then the scattering pixel shader is used to insert a splat entry for each pixel into the 3D grid. Please consult Figure 1.1 for a high-level abstraction of this process.

In fact, we construct a small bounding box around each pixel in the pixel shader and add the oriented splat to all grid cells that are touched by the bounding box. This avoids popping artifacts for dynamic objects. The size of the bounding box is typically chosen to be around 25% of the world-space size of a grid cell for our demo implementation.

The splat entry for each pixel can contain every piece of information that may be needed by later rendering operations. The minimum set of attributes is:

1. the 3D position of the splat,

2. the surface normal of the splat,

3. surface properties used for lighting the splat.

Listing 1.1 shows an implementation of the scattering pixel shader mentioned above. Please note that the shader uses a shadow map to apply a shadow term to the coloring of the splats.

```
#define CELLS_XYZ 64

struct LINKEDSPLAT
{
  float3 pos;
  float3 n;
  float3 col;
  uint   prev;
};

struct PS_RenderSceneInput
{
  float4 f4Position            : SV_POSITION;
  float4 f4Diffuse             : COLOR0;
  float2 f2TexCoord            : TEXTURE0;
  float3 f3WorldSpacePos       : TEXTURE1;
  float3 f3WorldSpaceNormal    : TEXTURE2;
};

RWStructuredBuffer<LINKEDSPLAT> LinkedSplatsBuffer;
RWByteAddressBuffer             StartOffsetBuffer;

uint offset( uint3 pos )
{
    return ( pos.x + pos.y * CELLS_XYZ +
             pos.z * CELLS_XYZ * CELLS_XYZ );
}

void PS_RenderSplats( PS_RenderSceneInput I )
{
  // compute initial splat color
  float4 f4Col = I.f4Diffuse* g_txCurrentObject.Sample(
                     g_SampleLinearWrap, I.f2TexCoord );

  // compute shadow term
  float4 f4SMC = mul(float4(I.f3WorldSpacePos.xyz, 1.0f ),
                          g_f4x4WorldViewProjLight );
  float2 rtc   = float2( 0.0f, 1.0f ) +  float2( 0.5f, -0.5f ) *
                   ( (1.0f).xx + ( f4SMC.xy / f4SMC.w ) );
  float  fShadow = filter_shadow(float3(rtc, f4SMC.z/f4SMC.w) );

  LINKEDSPLAT ls;

  ls.pos = I.f3WorldSpacePos.xyz;
  ls.n   = normalize( I.f3WorldSpaceNormal.xyz );
  ls.col = 1.3f * saturate( fShadow + 0.3f ) * f4Col.xyz;

  // compute position normalized to grid coord system
  // g_LBFbox holds left, bottom, front corner of box of grid
  float3 f3GridP = max( I.f3WorldSpacePos - g_LBFbox.xyz,
                     (0.0f).xxx );

  // set up small bounding box around splat (EPS = small number)
  float3 f3TLBF = max( f3GridP - EPS * g_GridCellSize.xyz,
                     (0.0f).xxx );
  float3 f3TRTB = max( f3GridP + EPS * g_GridCellSize.xyz,
                     (0.0f).xxx );
```

```
// figure out the range of cells touching the bb
float3 f3Start = min( (float(CELLS_XYZ-1)).xxx,
                 max( f3TLBF * g_InvGridCellSize.xyz,
                 (0.0f).xxx ) );
float3 f3Stop  = min( (float(CELLS_XYZ-1)).xxx,
                 max( f3TRTB * g_InvGridCellSize.xyz,
                 (0.0f).xxx ) );

// compute integer range of grid cells to iterate over
uint3  start = uint3( f3Start );
uint3  stop  = uint3( f3Stop );

// iterate over cells
for( uint zi = start.z; zi <= stop.z; ++zi )
{
  for( uint yi = start.y; yi <= stop.y; ++yi )
  {
    for( uint xi = start.x; xi <= stop.x; ++xi )
    {
      uint oldOffset;

      // alloc new offset
      uint newOffset = LinkedSplatsBuffer.IncrementCounter();

      // update grid offset buffer
      StartOffsetBuffer.
      InterlockedExchange( 4 * offset(uint3(xi,yi,zi) ),
                           newOffset, oldOffset );

      ls.prev = oldOffset;

      // add splat to the grid cell
      LinkedSplatsBuffer[ newOffset ] = ls;
    }
  }
}
```

Listing 1.1. Scattering pixel shader that adds splat information to all grid cells touching a small box around the splat.

1.3.2   Phase 2: Lighting of the Splats

Depending on the lighting requirements of the application, it may be necessary to perform deferred lighting operations on the splats stored in the grid. All deferred light sources and shadow operations must be carried out on the splats to compute the final lit color of each splat.

If the lighting model is simple, then one can carry out these steps in Phase 1 as set forth in Listing 1.1. The simple proof-of-concept implementation that accompanies this article also does carries out a diffuse lighting operation and a shadow map lookup in Phase 1 to immediately arrive at a lit and shadowed color for each splat.

1.3.3 Phase 3: Ray Tracing the Grid of Splats

Now we use the grid of splats for speeding up ray casting to compute where reflected rays hit dynamic scene geometry.

It is of course possible to trace a ray along the reflected view direction even for forward rendering applications. Nevertheless it is more efficient to run this operation on a full-screen g-buffer that has been generated while rendering the main scene.

Using the camera position, the surface normal, and the position at each g-buffer-pixel, the direction to trace along for finding reflections is computed. The pixel shader then traces a ray through the grid starting at the surface position stored in the g-buffer.

For each grid cell entered by the ray, a weight is assigned to each splat in the cell. The lit color of each splat is multiplied by the weight and the weighted colors and weights of all splats are accumulated.

The weights chosen will be zero for splats that point away from the current g-buffer pixel and also take the distance of the center of the splat from the traced ray into account. As a consequence, splats that are too far away will receive a zero weight as well.

If the resulting sum of weights is above zero, the shader assumes that the ray has hit a surface splat and it returns the ratio of the accumulated weighted color and the accumulated weight as the color for the reflection.

Listing 1.2 shows the implementation of the weighting function used in the demo for this chapter. Please note that in order to make efficient use of ALU resources, four splats are handled simultaneously by this shader function.

```
float4
intersect_splats( float3 orig, float3 dir,
                  LINKEDSPLAT s0,
                  LINKEDSPLAT s1,
                  LINKEDSPLAT s2,
                  LINKEDSPLAT s3,
                  float4 f4Mask )
{
    float4 w, denom, k, dw;

    // compute initial weights
    w.x = saturate( dot( normalize( orig - s0.pos ), s0.n ) );
    w.y = saturate( dot( normalize( orig - s1.pos ), s1.n ) );
    w.z = saturate( dot( normalize( orig - s2.pos ), s2.n ) );
    w.w = saturate( dot( normalize( orig - s3.pos ), s3.n ) );

    // compute closest distance to splat
    // ( ( orig + k * dir ) - s.pos ) * s.n = 0
    // s.n * orig + k * dir * s.n  - s.pos * s.n = 0
    // k = ( s.pos * s.n - orig * s.n ) / ( dir * s.n )
    denom.x = dot( dir, s0.n );
    denom.y = dot( dir, s1.n );
    denom.z = dot( dir, s2.n );
    denom.w = dot( dir, s3.n );
```

```
k.x = dot( ( s0.pos - orig ), s0.n );
k.y = dot( ( s1.pos - orig ), s1.n );
k.z = dot( ( s2.pos - orig ), s2.n );
k.w = dot( ( s3.pos - orig ), s3.n );

k /= denom;

k *= ( denom != (0.0f).xxxx ? (1.0f).xxxx : (0.0f).xxxx );

w *= ( k > ( 0.0f ).xxxx ) ? ( 1.0f ).xxxx : ( 0.0f ).xxxx;

// change w to reflect distance from splat center
float3 temp0 = orig + k.x * dir - s0.pos;
dw.x = 0.001f + dot( temp0, temp0 );
float3 temp1 = orig + k.y * dir - s1.pos;
dw.y = 0.001f + dot( temp1, temp1 );
float3 temp2 = orig + k.z * dir - s2.pos;
dw.z = 0.001f + dot( temp2, temp2 );
float3 temp3 = orig + k.w * dir - s3.pos;
dw.w = 0.001f + dot( temp3, temp3 );

// combine weights
w *= ( dw < (0.08f).xxxx ? 1.0f : 0.0f ) * f4Mask;

// compute result
return float4( w.x * s0.col + w.y * s1.col +
               w.z * s2.col + w.w * s3.col,
               dot( w, (1.0f).xxxx ) );
}
```

Listing 1.2. Computing a weighted combined color for four splats.

1.4 Results

The proof-of-concept implementation for this technique renders splats to a low-resolution grid of $64 \times 64 \times 64$ cells. In order to generate a good frame rate ($>$ 60 fps), we have chosen to generate reflections for only one out of four pixels of the scene image. Intermediate values are generated using bilateral upsampling [Tomasi and Manduchi 98].

The way the weights are chosen for each splat leads to the perception that the grid contains a sphere-based scene representation. In order to hide this fact—in the end an artifact that comes from the use of a low-resolution grid—we use a bilateral blurring operation to blur the reflections. The resulting blurry reflections look plausible if one assumes rough reflectors.

Figures 1.2–1.4 show screenshots from our demo—all are taken on an AMD HD6870 GPU at frame rates above 60 Hz.

Figure 1.2. Screenshot 1 using a $64 \times 64 \times 64$ grid of splats.

Figure 1.3. Screenshot 2 using a $64 \times 64 \times 64$ grid of splats.

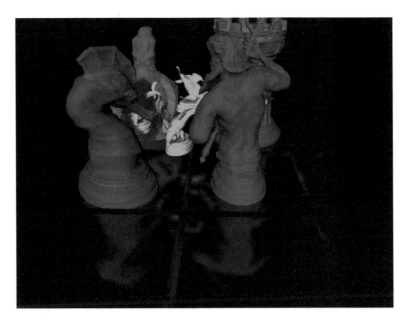

Figure 1.4. Screenshot 3 using a $64 \times 64 \times 64$ grid of splats without ground textures.

1.5 Future Work

We hope that in the future, we will overcome the quality limitations that stem from the use of a fairly low-resolution grid. To do so, we must meet two requirements:

1. Increase the resolution of the grid without making its memory footprint prohibitively high.

2. Keep the ray-traversal performance at a level similar to the one in the low-resolution grid.

The most obvious idea is to make use of a hierarchical grid that only uses memory to store a subgrid for nonempty cells of the coarser grid cells. The following steps describe details of how to implement such an approach:

1. When rendering the splats, one just adds them to an append buffer A. At the same time, the scattering pixel shader doing the append marks the grid cells of a coarse level-0 low-resolution grid as occupied. Also, one needs to allocate a buffer B that is big enough to hold an offset for each cell of the level-0 low-resolution grid.

2. Next, run a compute shader pass to store a valid offset to a subgrid (e.g., 32×32) into the cells of offset buffer B for all nonempty grid cells of the level-0 grid.

   Each cell of the subgrid initially contains an empty list of splats.

3. Another compute shader pass runs over the splats in the buffer (from Step 1) and inserts them into the nonempty subgrids accessible via B.

4. When casting rays, we traverse the coarse grid and only descend into subgrids if the coarse grid cell is nonempty.

Implementing all these steps will result in heavily reduced memory requirements and should enable a jump in image quality. Also, the two-level hierarchical grid should keep ray-traversal speed close to speeds achieved by the demo using just a grid. DX11-class hardware already allows for implementing this approach. The most optimal implementation is still a topic of active research, which will be presented in a later publication. At this point in time it is easy to realize the expected memory savings, yet it is hard to reach the performance of the simple nonhierarchical prototype.

Bibliography

[Tomasi and Manduchi 98] C. Tomasi and R. Manduchi. "Bilateral Filtering for Gray and Color Images." In *Proceedings of the Sixth International Conference on Computer Vision (ICCV '98)*. pp. 839–846. Washington, DC: IEEE Computer Society, 1998.

[Yang et al. 10] J. Yang, J. Hensley, H. Gruen, and N. Thibieroz. "Dynamic Construction of Concurrent Linked-Lists for Real-Time Rendering." Presented at *Eurographics Symposium on Rendering*, 2010.

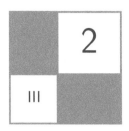

Screen-Space Bent Cones: A Practical Approach

Oliver Klehm, Tobias Ritschel,
Elmar Eisemann, and Hans-Peter Seidel

2.1 Overview

Ambient occlusion (AO) is a popular technique for visually improving both real-time as well as offline rendering. It decouples occlusion and shading, providing a gain in efficiency. This results in an average occlusion that modulates the surface shading. However, this also reduces realism due to the lack of directional information. Bent normals were proposed as an amelioration that addresses this issue for offline rendering. Here, we describe how to compute bent normals as a cheap byproduct of screen-space ambient occlusion (SSAO). Bent cones extend bent normals to further improve realism. These extensions combine the speed and simplicity of AO with physically more plausible lighting.

2.2 Introduction

AO is a physically incorrect but perceptually plausible approximation of environmental lighting and global illumination (GI). It has been used in many games, in particular when implemented in screen space. AO achieves high performance by averaging occlusion that modulates the surface shading instead of respecting the directionality of the lighting. However, the lack of directionality can be visually unpleasant and leaves room for improvement.

   To this end, Landis [Landis 02] introduced so-called bent normals. While AO stores the average occlusion, bent normals are modified normals bent according to an estimate of the direction that is most disoccluded, in other words, the average unblocked direction. Using these bent normals in shading—for example, with preconvolved environment maps—leads to improved lighting. Usually, bent

Figure 2.1. Lighting computed using bent cones: 2048×1024 pixels, $60.0\,\text{fps}$, including direct light and DOF on an Nvidia GF 560Ti.

normals can be easily integrated in rendering engines; the only required change is to apply a bending of the normal. Adjusting the length of the bent normal by multiplying it with the corresponding AO value leads to automatically integrating AO in the shading evaluation.

Computing AO in screen space (SSAO) is one popular implementation of the approach [Mittring 07, Shanmugam and Arikan 07, Bavoil et al. 08, Ritschel et al. 09, Loos and Sloan 10]. In this chapter, we will describe a technique to extend SSAO. Our idea is to keep the simplicity of SSAO by relying on a screen-space solution, but to add the advantages of bent normals. Additionally, a new extension to further improve accuracy is introduced: bent cones. Bent cones capture the distribution of unoccluded directions by storing its directional average and variance.

2.3   Ambient Occlusion

Ambient occlusion [Zhukov et al. 98] decouples shading and visibility by moving visibility outside of the integral of the rendering equation [Kajiya 86]:

$$L_{o}(\mathbf{x}, \omega_{o}) \approx AO(\mathbf{x}) \int_{\Omega^{+}} f_{r}(\mathbf{x}, \omega \to \omega_{o})\, L_{i}(\mathbf{x}, \omega)\, (\mathbf{n} \cdot \omega)\, d\omega,$$

$$AO(\mathbf{x}) := \frac{1}{2\pi} \int_{\Omega^{+}} V(\mathbf{x}, \omega)\, d\omega,$$

where $L_o(\omega_o)$ is the outgoing radiance in direction ω_o, Ω^+ is the upper hemisphere, f_r is the bidirectional reflectance distribution function (BRDF), $\mathbf{n}$ is the surface normal, L_i is the incoming light, and V is the visibility function that is zero when a ray is blocked and one otherwise. We assume that the diffuse surfaces f_r are constant and then ω_o can be dropped. Applying AO, light from all directions is equally attenuated by the average blocking over all directions.

Landis [Landis 02] used Monte-Carlo integration based on ray tracing to compute the hemispherical integral of AO. The idea of *bent normals* also dates back to the work of Landis, where it was proposed as a generalization of AO. Bent normals are the mean free direction scaled by the mean occlusion and are used for shading instead of the normals. Different from AO, their definition includes the direction ω inside the integral:

$$N(\mathbf{x}) := \frac{1}{\pi} \int_{\Omega^+} V(\mathbf{x}, \omega)\, \omega \, d\omega.$$

For lighting computations, bent normals simply replace the surface normal and the visibility term:

$$L_o(\mathbf{x}) \approx \frac{1}{\pi} \int_{\Omega^+} L_i(\mathbf{x}, \omega)\, (N(\mathbf{x}) \cdot \omega) \, d\omega.$$

In the case of bent normals, the visibility has to be multiplied with the direction using Monte-Carlo computation of bent normals $N(\mathbf{x})$, which is computationally simple and efficient compared to AO alone.

AO—in particular in screen space—has become a key ingredient in the shading found in a range of contemporary games [Mittring 07, Shanmugam and Arikan 07,

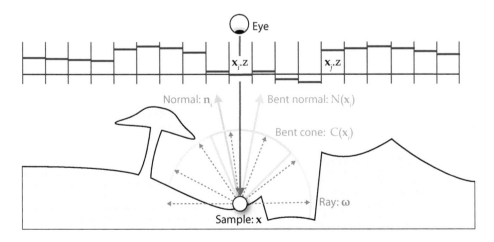

Figure 2.2. Overview: AO, bent normals, and bent cones in flatland.

Bavoil et al. 08, Ritschel et al. 09, Loos and Sloan 10]. SSAO is based on deferred shading [Mittring 09]. We propose to use bent cones, which are easy to integrate and program, and result in smooth illumination at high speed.

Usually, SSAO (Figure 2.2) is computed for a pixel i by counting occlusion of random point samples S. We ignore the 2D structure of the image for a moment, and enumerate all pixels using a 1D index i. The samples are chosen within a sphere, respectively, hemisphere (if the normal at i is known) centered at the point in world space that corresponds to pixel i (its back projection). The sphere corresponds to a pixel neighborhood, which can either be of constant size in screen space or be scaled according to the distance to the camera, thereby having constant world-space radius. Each sample is tested against the depth buffer to check for an occlusion by objects that are closer to the camera. If the samples S are distributed in the upper hemisphere, each sample S_i itself is tested for occlusion. Whereas, if the samples S are directly chosen in a pixel neighborhood of i, it is checked to see if the back-projected point of S_i occludes the back-projected point of i. For now, we stick to the latter.

For a pixel i, we compare its camera space location $\mathbf{x}_i$ with other pixels' camera space position $\mathbf{x}_j$ in a pixel neighborhood $P_i \subset \mathbb{N}$:

$$AO_{\mathrm{ss}}(i) := \frac{1}{|P_i|} \sum_{j \in P_i} d(\Delta_{ij}), \qquad (2.1)$$

where $\Delta_{ij} := \mathbf{x}_j - \mathbf{x}_i$. Intuitively, this function is 0 for blocking pixels, and 1 otherwise, depending on their relative position, most particularly, their relative depth. One possible implementation of $d(\Delta)$ is $d_{\mathrm{x}}(\Delta)$, defined as

$$d_{\mathrm{x}}(\Delta) := \begin{cases} 0 & \text{if } \Delta.z > 0, \\ 1 & \text{otherwise.} \end{cases}$$

Improvements are possible by accounting for outliers that should not cast shadows [Shanmugam and Arikan 07, Ritschel et al. 09, Loos and Sloan 10] if $\Delta.z$ is greater than z_{max}, and by including the normal at the ith pixel [Ritschel et al. 09]:

$$d_{\mathrm{xn}}(\Delta, \mathbf{n}) := \begin{cases} 0 & \text{if } z_{\mathrm{max}} > \Delta.z > 0 \text{ and } (\Delta \cdot \mathbf{n}) > 0, \\ 1 & \text{otherwise.} \end{cases}$$

It is further possible to replace the binary function d by some falloff function [Filion and McNaughton 08] depending on the distance and angle of the occluder, which results in smoother AO.

The underlying assumption of SSAO is that summing occlusion of "nearby" occluders approximates true visibility. However, visibility is a nonlinear effect: two occluders behind each other in one direction do not cast a shadow twice. Hence, other approaches find the correct occlusion for a set of directions in screen space via ray marching in the depth buffer. Alternatively, one can also compute a horizon angle [Bavoil et al. 08]. As an in-between solution, others [Szirmay-Kalos et al. 10, Loos and Sloan 10] considered the free volume over a height field of depth values inside a sphere around a pixel as a better approximation.

2.4 Our Technique

In this section, we will describe our approach for interactive AO and GI based on screen-space bent normals. We will first introduce their computation (Section 2.4.1), and then generalize them to bent cones (Section 2.4.2).

2.4.1 Bent Normals

Our technique is mostly orthogonal to the used type of SSAO. We will describe here the basic implementation along the lines of the original Crytek SSAO [Mittring 07]. Instead of just computing AO at the ith pixel (Equation (2.1)), we additionally compute a new normal N_{ss}. The basic principle behind our approach is that when computing AO in screen space, the direction Δ_{ij} is known and can be used to accumulate an unblocked direction that defines the bent normal. Thus, we simply sum up the normalized unoccluded directions defined by our samples, and divide the resulting vector by the number of nonblocked directions:

$$N_{\text{ss}}(i) := \Big(\sum_{j \in P_i} d(\Delta_{ij}) \Big)^{-1} \sum_{j \in P_i} \frac{\Delta_{ij}}{|\Delta_{ij}|} \, d(\Delta_{ij}) \approx N(\mathbf{x}_i). \qquad (2.2)$$

The resulting bent normal is the mean of the unoccluded directions at $\mathbf{x}_i$.

2.4.2 Bent Cones

Bent cones are bent normals augmented by an angle (Figure 2.2). As the mean of the unoccluded directions gives the bent normal, the variance defines the angle. However, directions require the use of directional statistics instead of linear statistics in Euclidean spaces. To this end, we use an approach similar to the computation of variance in von Mises-Fisher (vMF) distributions. There, variance is approximated from the length of the non-normalized bent normal as computed in Equation (2.2). While vMF distributions are defined for spheres, we estimate a distribution on a hemisphere. This leads to a simple estimation of angle, corresponding to the variance of the unoccluded directions as

$$C(i) := (1 - \max(0, 2\,|N_{\text{ss}}(i)| - 1))\,\frac{\pi}{2}.$$

Bent normal and bent cone define a certain spherical cap of visibility. Figure 2.3 shows possible unblocked directions and the resulting bent normal and cone. We use this cap in combination with shading methods that compute the incoming

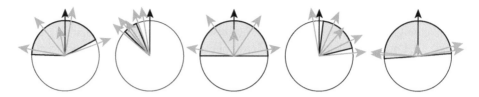

Figure 2.3. Resulting bent normal and cone of different visibility configurations. Blue arrows show unblocked directions within the hemisphere centered around the normal (black). Bent normals form the average direction (orange). The length of the bent normal describes the variance of the unblocked directions and is used to calculate the angle of the bent cone with the bent normal as center (darkened sector of circle).

light inside a spherical cap, such as preconvolved environment maps [Heidrich and Seidel 99] or irradiance volumes [Greger et al. 98]. Note that the clamping ensures that the length of the bent normal of an unoccluded point is mapped to a cone that covers the entire hemisphere.

We only use the bent cone to limit the directions from which we gather light. The cone does not describe a concrete visibility approximation. We still use AO to estimate the overall visibility. One can think of the cone as describing the illumination color whereas the AO controls brightness. This also allows that a cone does not need to match the actual visibility configuration very accurately. Using a cone with an angle of 90 degrees means a fallback to illumination with bent normals only. In Section 2.4.3, we describe how to use the cones to evaluate the incoming illumination.

2.4.3   Shading

For shading using bent cones, preconvolved environment maps are used [Heidrich and Seidel 99], which are indexed using bent cones. The same concept applies to irradiance volumes [Greger et al. 98]. Such precomputations are done at application start-up or once per frame, and avoid needing to do computations when shading each pixel. The convolutions involved are known to give very smooth results without noticeable noise, which fit well with the perceptual requirements of games.

Preconvolution of environmental illumination computes a directional function $L_p(\mathbf{n})$. For every possible normal $\mathbf{n}$, it convolves the BRDF (a constant for the diffuse surfaces we consider, therefore there is no dependence on ω_o), the geometric term, and the environmental illumination $L_i'(\omega)$:

$$L_p(\mathbf{n}) := \frac{1}{\pi} \int_{\Omega^+} L_i'(\omega') \, (\omega' \cdot \mathbf{n}) \, d\omega'.$$

To query this convolved environment map, the bent normal is used in place of $\mathbf{n}$: the computation reduces to a lookup in the preconvolved environment map and

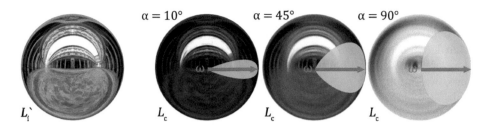

Figure 2.4. Preconvolution of environmental lighting (left) into a series of triple products of light, BRDF, and visibility of cones with varying angle α (left to right, 10, 45, and 90 degrees).

a multiplication with SSAO, which accounts for visibility:

$$L_o(\mathbf{x}) = AO(\mathbf{x})\, L_p(N(\mathbf{x})).$$

However, the preconvolution has to assume that no shadows occur as the point $\mathbf{x}$ and its visibility configuration are not known at preconvolution time. With bent cones, we propose to include a proxy visibility inside the preconvolution leading to a trivariate function

$$L_c(\mathbf{n}, \alpha) := \frac{1}{\pi} \int_{\Omega^+} L_i'(\omega')\, \bar{V}(\omega', \mathbf{n}, \alpha)\, (\omega' \cdot \mathbf{n})\, \mathrm{d}\omega'$$

that stores the outgoing radiance for a bent cone in direction $\mathbf{n}$ with angle α (Figure 2.4). The function $\bar{V}$ returns one if ω' and $\mathbf{n}$ form an angle smaller than α and zero otherwise. Note that by doing so, with increasing α the preconvolved values get larger. To include bent cones, we look up the appropriate convolved environment map. The term becomes

$$L_o(\mathbf{x}) = AO(\mathbf{x})\, L_c(N(\mathbf{x}), C(\mathbf{x}))\, (1 - \cos(C(\mathbf{x})))^{-1}.$$

The last part of the equation is a "normalization" of the preconvolved incoming light. The reason for this is that we do not use the cone as the actual visibility approximation of the visibility configuration at $\mathbf{x}$, which is usually much more complicated than a simple cone. Instead, we use it as a proxy to select directions from which we gather light. AO is then used to account for the average visibility. By doing so, we shift the lighting to the correct result compared to a convolution over the entire hemisphere. Only if AO and the cone angle match ($AO(\mathbf{x}) = 1 - \cos(C(\mathbf{x}))$), we get the same result as using the cone as visibility approximation. Due to the decoupling, bent cones are even able to handle visibility configurations, which cannot be well represented with a cone. Note that by our definition of the cone angle, the spherical cap is usually larger than or of equal size as AO ($AO(\mathbf{x}) \leq 1 - \cos(C(\mathbf{x}))$).

In practice, we move the normalization term to the preconvolution step to account for a given angle α. We thereby limit the sampling to the cone, such that $\bar{V}(\omega', \mathbf{n}, \alpha)$ returns one, and the normalization is included implicitly. Therefore, we can skip the normalization $((1 - \cos(C(\mathbf{x})))^{-1})$ during lighting. During preconvolution, one can do the sampling exactly by looping over all pixels, resulting in a complexity of $O(n^2)$, where n is the number of pixels. For every output pixel, a loop computes a cone-weighted sum of all other pixels. Samples are ignored if $\bar{V}(\omega', \mathbf{n}, \alpha)$ returns zero. Alternatively, one can use a Monte-Carlo approach with a fixed set of samples, which turns complexity into $O(nm)$, where m is the number of Monte-Carlo samples and $m \ll n$. This can help to reduce precomputation time, especially for high-resolution environment maps. Further, it is very easy to distribute the Monte-Carlo samples in a way that $\bar{V}(\omega', \mathbf{n}, \alpha)$ returns one and no samples need to be ignored. However, m has to be chosen carefully, depending on the frequency of the environment map and its resolution.

2.4.4   Geometric Term

We use a heuristic to combine the geometric term (cosine of incoming light and normal) with our bent cones. The geometric term must be a part of the preconvolution because the incoming light per direction is only known at this moment.

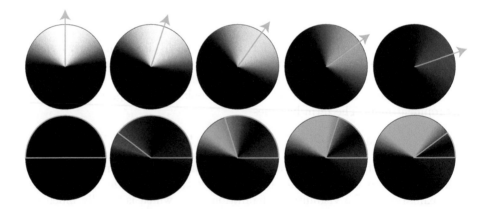

Figure 2.5. A 2D showcase of the effect of the approximation of the geometric term. The heuristic is shown in the top row, error is shown in the bottom row (compared to a normal with direction upward (left)). Red color encodes overestimation and green encodes underestimation compared to the correct geometric term. The bent normal is increasingly rotated in the images to the right. If normal and bent normal point to the same direction, the heuristic weights all directions correctly (left). The more normal and bent normal diverge (images to the right), the greater the error becomes. However, at the same time, the angle of the bent cone becomes smaller and so the error within the cone remains low. Note that the bent cone can have a different size than shown.

Correctly integrating the geometric term would be five dimensional: 2D for the mean direction (bent normal), 1D for the cone angle, and 2D for the surface normal. However, we can approximate the correct geometric term by

$$(\omega \cdot \mathbf{n}) \approx (\omega \cdot N(\mathbf{x}))\,(N(\mathbf{x}) \cdot \mathbf{n}).$$

Figure 2.5 illustrates the heuristic for different angles between $\mathbf{n}$ and $N(\mathbf{x})$. If $(N(\mathbf{x}) \cdot \mathbf{n}) \approx 1$, we can use the cosine between bent normal and incoming light and, thus, our heuristic approximates the geometric term very well. In the other case, if $(N(\mathbf{x}) \cdot \mathbf{n}) < 1$, using the bent normal only would result in visible arti-facts. Fortunately, if normal and bent normal diverge, we have a concentration of the incoming light and also the angle of the bent cone is small, thus, $(\omega \cdot \mathbf{n}) \approx (N(\mathbf{x}) \cdot \mathbf{n})$. We also tried to interpolate between both versions $((\omega \cdot N(\mathbf{x}))$ and $(N(\mathbf{x}) \cdot \mathbf{n}))$ depending on $(N(\mathbf{x}) \cdot \mathbf{n})$, which is known at runtime, but this underes-timates the geometric term and causes artifacts. Instead, the multiplication uses the original normal and should be preferred to only using $(\omega \cdot N(\mathbf{x}))$. The heuris-tic avoids a 5D preconvolution and gives correct results for unoccluded points (where $\mathbf{n} = N(\mathbf{x})$).

2.5 Implementation

Variants. Our approach can be used in conjunction with different SSAO tech-niques. Differences remain small, mostly depending on the sampling radius (Figure 2.6).

Crytek2D SSAO [Mittring 07] uses a 2D sampling pattern to distribute sam-ples in screen space. For higher quality, we perform jittering and reject samples outside the unit disc.

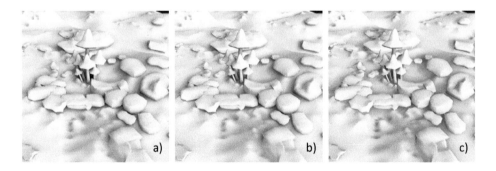

Figure 2.6. Our approach is largely orthogonal to the particular SSAO implementation used. Bent normals implemented with: (a) fixed screen-space radius (Crytek2D), (b) fixed world-space radius (Crytek3D), (c) horizon-based ray marching (HBAO). Note, that the results are very similar.

`Crytek3D` [Mittring 09] uses a 3D sampling pattern to distribute samples in space that are projected to screen space. We generate samples in a hemisphere, which is then transformed using an orthonormal basis according to **n**. Optionally, we add ray marching (multiple AND-combined samples per random 3D direction), which drastically improves AO and bent normal quality, even for a low number of marching steps (two to three) and a reduced number of ray directions. Here, the samples are distributed on the unit hemisphere to get random directions, and randomized starting points per direction turn aliasing into more eye-pleasing noise.

`HBAO` [Bavoil et al. 08] uses random 3D directions that are marched to find the highest intersection. We generate samples on the unit disc, apply randomized offsets, and then transform them according to **n**.

We rely on OpenGL 3 and store all sample patterns in uniform variables. If a large pattern or many samples are required, we store the data in a texture. Listing 2.1 gives pseudocode showing how AO and bent normals are computed in a pixel / fragment shader.

Filtering. Interleaved sampling [Keller and Heidrich 01] in combination with filtering of illumination guided by positions and normals [Laine et al. 07] is used to compute AO and bent normals using only a small number of samples per pixel. At a resolution of 2048×1024, downsampled 2×2 for antialiasing, three to six samples are enough for AO when applying an 8×8 joint-bilateral filtering. However, bent cones usually require at least six samples to avoid visible artifacts. Obviously, the quality of the filtering depends on the coherence of the neighboring pixels.

Instead of interpolating the bent normal directly, we compute the difference between normal and bent normal and filter this difference. The change is then added back to the original high-frequency normals per-pixel. Thus, the details in the normal field itself are preserved as shown in Figure 2.7 and the bent information is propagated.

Figure 2.7. Fine geometric details, for example, those due to bump maps, are lost when directly filtering bent normals (left). When filtering the change-of-normals instead, details are preserved (right).

```
void main() {
  // get point properties at pixel i
  vec3 positionX = backproject(depthTexture(pixelCoordinateI),
                               inverseViewProjectionMatrix );
  vec3 normalX = normalTexture(pixelCoordinateI);
  // get ONB to transform samples
  mat3 orthoNormalBasis = computeONB(normalX);
  // select samples for pixel out of pattern
  int patternOffset = getPatternOffset(pixelCoordinateI);

  float ao = 0.0;
  int validAODirectionCount = 0;
  vec3 bentNormal = vec3(0.0);
  float unoccludedDirections = 0.0;

  for(int index=0; index<sampleCount; ++index) {
    vec3 sampleDirection = orthoNormalBasis *
                   getSampleDirection(index, patternOffset);
    bool isOutlier = false;
    // use float instead of bool and
    // apply a fall-off function to get smooth AO
    float visibility = 1.0;
    // this function tests for occlusion in SS
    // depending on the actual technique
    // and sample distribution,
    // the implementation of this function varies
    checkSSVisibilityWithRayMarchingSmooth(
      sampleDirection, maxOccluderDistance,
      depthTexture, inverseViewProjectionMatrix ,
      positionX, normalX,
      rayMarchingSteps, rayMarchingStartOffset ,
      visibility, isOutlier);

    // we have insufficient information in SS
    // here, we simply ignore samples,
    // which cannot be handled properly
    if(!isOutlier) {
      validAODirectionCount ++;
      ao += visibility;
    }

    // for bent normals, we assume,
    // that outlier occluders are NOT real occluders!
    // sum up unoccluded directions
    // direction may be partially visible
    // => only counts accordingly
    bentNormal += normalize(sampleDirection) * visibility;
    unoccludedDirections += visibility;
  }

  ao /= float(validAODirectionCount );
  bentNormal /= unoccludedDirections;
}
```

Listing 2.1. Fragment shader pseudo-code for screen-space bent cones.

Preconvolved lighting. For preconvolved environment maps, we store L_p as a floating-point cube texture. Preconvolution including visibility L_c is trivariate and can be stored most efficiently using the recent cube map array extension of OpenGL [Bolz et al. 09]. This extensions stores an array of cube maps, which can be accessed with a direction and an index. We discretize α to eight levels and apply linear filtering between the levels. The preconvolved environment maps require a high dynamic range, which is why we chose to use RGB 16 bit floating-point textures. Due to the convolution, low resolution cube maps provide sufficient quality, resulting in $\sim$7 MB of storage for a typical 64 $\times$ 64 cube-map array with eight layers. More efficiently, in the context of glossy reflections Kautz and McCool [Kautz and McCool 00] propose to store the third dimension in cube-map MIP levels. This could even allow for a fully dynamic convolution of the environment map at reduced quality, but also reduced storage costs.

Practical considerations. Bent normal and cones integrate very well in an existing deferred shading rendering pipeline. The bent normal easily replaces the normal without requiring special handling. Further, the bent normal can be scaled with AO. Using the scaled bent normal for shading, AO is included automatically, also avoiding further storage requirements. For bent cones, no extra storage is required in addition to that for the bent normal and AO. A special preconvolution step is required for a number of possible cone angles.

2.6   Results

In this section, we present our results that increase accuracy while adding only a small performance penalty when compared to previous SSAO techniques.

A typical performance breakdown at resolution 2048 $\times$ 1024 of Figure 2.1 on an Nvidia Geforce 560Ti is as follows: 6.0 ms for AO and bent normals (16 $\times$ 16 pattern, four samples per pixel, two ray-marching steps per sample), 5.2 ms for geometry-aware blurring, 1.0 ms for the cone computation and environment map lookup, 1.5 ms for the deferred shading buffer, and 1.6 ms for direct light with 2 $\times$ 2-sample PCF shadows (shadow map resolution 4096 $\times$ 4096). The overhead for bent cones compared to only AO with the same number of samples is 6 % for the computation and 25 % for the blur, in total less than 9 %. We still see some room for engineering improvements, depending on the actual quality and performance constraints in real applications. For example, using data packing and 8 bits for bent normals may especially improve the blur speed.

Lighting using our bent normals is closer to a reference solution than AO alone (see Figure 2.8 (a)–(c)). It can be seen how AO decouples lighting and visibility, which leads to gray shadows that are perceived as a change of reflectance, rather than an effect of lighting. The reference solutions were created using path-tracing using several hundred samples. Our screen-space bent normals are similar to real bent normals (see Figure 2.8 (d)–(f)), which leads to only a small difference

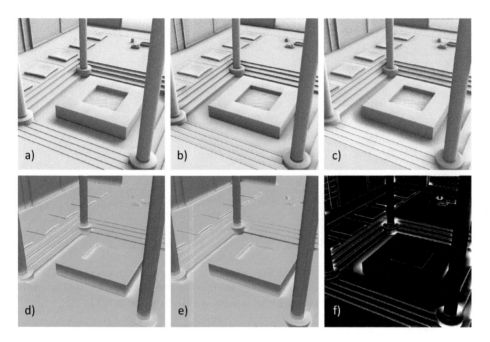

Figure 2.8. Top row: (a) Comparison between lighting using ray tracing, (b) SSAO, and (c) SS bent normals. Bottom row: (d) ray-traced bent normals, (e) SS bent normals, and (f) the 8 × angle difference. Note that SS bent normals is similar to ray tracing in quality, while performance is similar to SSAO. Further, the shadow's shapes are more similar to the reference.

when comparing lighting using accurate bent normals and our bent normals. Additionally, it shows that testing visibility in screen space is sufficient in most cases.

Bent cones further improve the directionality of lighting, which is limited with bent normals as their input remains the incoming light from all directions of a hemisphere (see Figure 2.9). Ritschel et al. [Ritschel et al. 09] apply a brute-force sampling for unblocked directions, which is inefficient in two ways. First, the additional texture lookup in the SSAO shader causes an overhead of about 10% in our tests. Second, more samples are required per pixel to avoid noise. Even with a randomization pattern and a postprocessing blur, at least 16 to 24 samples are required to avoid block noise in the final image. For high-resolution and high-frequency illumination this number is much higher. In contrast, bent cones return smooth results with a very small number of per-pixel samples (see Figure 2.10). In our experiments we were able to use eight samples at a minimum with similar minor artifacts. The cone does not need to be very accurate and AO is smooth anyway, which is why the sample count can be low. We also compared

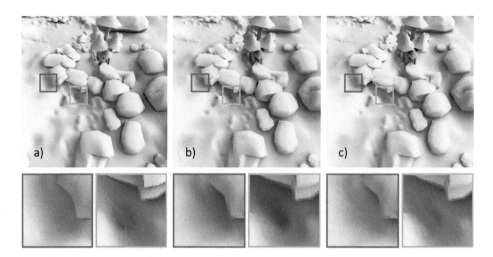

Figure 2.9. Left to right: (a) Lighting using ray tracing, (b) SS bent normals, and (c) SS bent cones. Applying cones, shadows are more colored and appear similar to the Monte-Carlo reference, because only visible light is gathered (see insets).

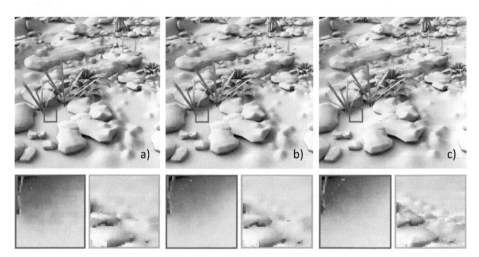

Figure 2.10. Left to right: (a) Environment map importance sampling, (b) SSDO [Ritschel et al. 09], and (c) SS bent cones. Importance sampling required 32 samples per pixel (18.8 ms), SSDO 16 samples (14.1 ms), and bent cones only eight samples (6.0 ms for bent normal, 0.7 ms for single bent cone environment map sample) to achieve the results. We set the sample count such that all techniques produce similar results with acceptable minor noise (red inset). For all techniques, we applied an 8×8 randomization pattern and a geometry-aware blur. Bent cones allow for blurring the change, which preserves normal details (green inset). In all cases, we used three ray-marching steps per sample for the SS visibility tests and computed lighting at a resolution of 1024×1024 to create the images.

bent cones to importance sampling, which in our tests required at least 24 to 32 samples for an equal quality. However, in contrast to sampling-based techniques, bent cones are not able to handle high-frequency illumination.

We removed high-frequency illumination changes in our test cases to allow for a fair comparison. Since bent cones simply blur the high frequencies, the brute-force sampling technique [Ritschel et al. 09] requires many more samples (up to hundreds), and the importance sampling requires at least 64 samples.

2.7 Discussion and Conclusion

Screen-space bent normals improve accuracy of shading without imposing much additional computation cost. The bent cones further improve on the directionality of lighting. Bent cones can limit the spherical cap depending on the variance of the unoccluded directions. The success clearly depends on whether the actual visibility configuration fits a cone. The cone is chosen such that it mostly includes unblocked directions, possibly overestimating the overall visibility. The overestimation is not a problem as we still rely on AO to account for the actual overall visibility. As a worst case, bent cones compare to lighting with bent normals. While screen-space directional occlusion [Ritschel et al. 09] achieves similar results, it requires the evaluation of shading for every sample. This is closer to screen-space Monte-Carlo rendering involving many samples, but does not agree with the original goal of AO to decouple shading and visibility as much as possible. In contrast, our approach keeps shading and visibility separated, leading to a significant speedup.

Bent normals and cones are most suitable for lighting techniques that compute lighting within a spherical cap, such as environmental lighting with light coming from many directions. They are less useful for direct illumination of very directed light such as from the common directional, spot, or point-light sources. Consequently, bent normals and cones are not able to handle high-frequency illumination changes.

We showed that our extension is mostly orthogonal to the particular SSAO implementation used [Mittring 07, Bavoil et al. 08], and thus can be easily integrated in existing implementations. It is intended to be used as part of a deferred shading pipeline, most interestingly for real-time applications. By performing the visibility test in screen space, only an incomplete scene representation is available, sharing the screen-space limitations with previous SSAO techniques. However, the screen-space visibility test could be replaced with a more accurate test, such as testing against a voxel representation of the scene.

In future work, we plan to investigate dynamic convolution of cube maps, other representations of the occlusion function, new interpolation methods, and a combination with irradiance volumes [Greger et al. 98] for local prefiltered directional occlusion.

2.8   Acknowledgments

This work was partly funded by the Intel Visual Computing Institute at Saarland University and the ANR iSpace & Time of the French government.

Bibliography

[Bavoil et al. 08] Louis Bavoil, Miguel Sainz, and Rouslan Dimitrov. "Image-Space Horizon-Based Ambient Occlusion." In *ACM SIGGRAPH 2008 Talks.* New York: ACM, 2008.

[Bolz et al. 09] Jeff Bolz, Yunjun Zhang, Bill Licea-Kane, Graham Sellers, Daniel Koch, and Mark Young. "ARB_texture_cube_map_array." OpenGL Extension, Available at http://www.opengl.org/registry/specs/ARB/texture_cube_map_array.txt, 2009.

[Filion and McNaughton 08] Dominic Filion and Rob McNaughton. "Starcraft: Effects & Techniques." In *Advances in Real-Time Rendering in 3D Graphics and Games Course*, edited by Natalya Tatarchuk, Chapter 5, pp. 133–164. ACM, 2008.

[Greger et al. 98] G. Greger, P. Shirley, P. M. Hubbard, and D. P. Greenberg. "The Irradiance Volume." *IEEE Computer Graphics and Applications* 18:2 (1998), 32–43.

[Heidrich and Seidel 99] Wolfgang Heidrich and Hans-Peter Seidel. "Realistic, Hardware-Accelerated Shading and Lighting." In *Proceedings of SIGGRAPH '99, Computer Graphics Proceedings, Annual Conference Series*, edited by Alyn Rockwood, pp. 171–178. Reading, MA, 1999.

[Kajiya 86] J. T. Kajiya. "The Rendering Equation." *Proc. SIGGRAPH '86, Computer Graphics* 20:4 (1986), 143–150.

[Kautz and McCool 00] Jan Kautz and Michael D. McCool. "Approximation of Glossy Reflection with Prefiltered Environment Maps." In *Graphics Interface*, pp. 119–126. Toronto, Canada: Canadian Human-Computer Communications Society, 2000.

[Keller and Heidrich 01] Alexander Keller and Wolfgang Heidrich. "Interleaved Sampling." In *Proceedings of the 12th Eurographics Workshop on Rendering Techniques*, pp. 269–276. London: Springer-Verlag, 2001.

[Laine et al. 07] Samuli Laine, Hannu Saransaari, Janne Kontkanen, Jaakko Lehtinen, and Timo Aila. "Incremental Instant Radiosity for Real-Time Indirect Illumination." In *Proceedings of Eurographics Symposium on Rendering 2007*, pp. 277–286. Aire-la-Ville, Switzerland: Eurographics Association, 2007.

[Landis 02] Hayden Landis. "Production-Ready Global Illumination." In *RenderMan in Production, SIGGRAPH Course*, pp. 87–102. New York: ACM, 2002.

[Loos and Sloan 10] Bradford James Loos and Peter-Pike Sloan. "Volumetric Obscurance." In *Proceedings of the 2010 ACM SIGGRAPH Symposium on Interactive 3D Graphics and Games, I3D '10*, pp. 151–156. New York: ACM, 2010.

[Mittring 07] Martin Mittring. "Finding next gen: CryEngine 2." In *Advanced Real-Time Rendering in 3D Graphics and Games, SIGGRAPH Course*, edited by Natalya Tatarchuk, pp. 97–121. NY: ACM, 2007.

[Mittring 09] Martin Mittring. "A Bit More Deferred – CryEngine 3." In *Triangle Game Conference*, 2009.

[Ritschel et al. 09] Tobias Ritschel, Thorsten Grosch, and Hans-Peter Seidel. "Approximating Dynamic Global Illumination in Image Space." In *Proceedings of the 2009 Symposium on Interactive 3D Graphics and Games, I3D '09*, pp. 75–82. New York: ACM, 2009.

[Shanmugam and Arikan 07] Perumaal Shanmugam and Okan Arikan. "Hardware Accelerated Ambient Occlusion Techniques on GPUs." In *Proceedings of the 2007 Symposium on Interactive 3D Graphics and Games, I3D '07*, pp. 73–80. New York: ACM, 2007.

[Szirmay-Kalos et al. 10] L. Szirmay-Kalos, T. Umenhoffer, B. Tóth, L. Szécsi, and M. Sbert. "Volumetric Ambient Occlusion for Real-Time Rendering and Games." *IEEE Computer Graphics and Applications* 30 (2010), 70–79.

[Zhukov et al. 98] S. Zhukov, A. Iones, G. Kronin, and G. Studio. "An Ambient Light Illumination Model." In *Rendering Techniques '98, Proceedings of the Eurographics Workshop in Vienna, Austria, June 29–July 1, 1998*, pp. 45–56. New York: Springer, 1998.

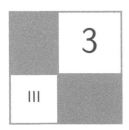

3

III

Real-Time Near-Field Global Illumination Based on a Voxel Model

Sinje Thiedemann, Niklas Henrich,
Thorsten Grosch, and Stefan Müller

3.1 Introduction

In real-time applications, displaying full global illumination is still an open problem for large and dynamic scenes. A recent trend is to restrict the incoming light to the *near-field* around the receiver point, which allows approximate one-bounce indirect illumination at real-time frame rates. Although plausible results can be achieved, several problems appear since the recent methods work in *image-space*: only occluders and senders of indirect light visible in the current image contribute to the final illumination. This results in shadows and indirect light that appears and disappears, depending on camera and object movement. On the other hand, several real-time *voxelization* methods were developed recently that enable the generation of a coarse scene description within milliseconds. At first glance, the voxel model seems to be a solution for the visibility problems, but in fact the voxel model is view-dependent as well: since the voxelization methods are based on rendering, gaps appear in the voxel model for polygons that are viewed from a grazing angle by the voxelization camera. To solve both problems, we introduce *voxel-based global illumination* (VGI) [Thiedemann et al. 11]. The basic idea is to generate a dynamic, view-independent voxel model from a *texture atlas* that provides visibility information (see Figure 3.1). In combination with reflective shadow maps (RSM), one-bounce indirect light can then be displayed with correct occlusion inside the near-field at real-time frame rates. We first describe our new voxelization method and a ray-intersection test with the voxel model. We then explain the one-bounce global illumination with voxel-based visibility, and evaluate our method with several test scenes.

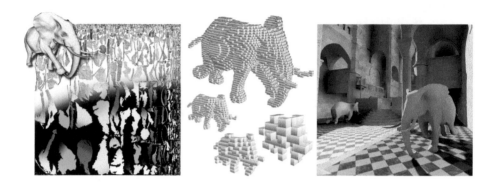

Figure 3.1. Voxel-based global illumination starts by generating an atlas of the dynamic scene that contains the 3D positions as texel colors (left). By rendering a point for each atlas texel, we obtain a hierarchical voxel model (center), which serves as visibility information in a real-time global illumination simulation (right). The indirect light is exaggerated in this example.

3.2   Binary Boundary Voxelization

In this section, we present our new boundary voxelization method, which turns a scene representation consisting of discrete geometric entities (e.g., triangles) into a three-dimensional regular-spaced grid. There are several approaches to creating the voxel grid. Methods based on slicing intersect all triangles of the scene with each plane of the three-dimensional voxel grid to successively fill each layer [Crane et al. 07, Fang and Chen 00]. Alternative methods use depth-peeling [Li et al. 05, Passalis et al. 07] for this process. The method presented by Eisemann and Décoret [Eisemann and Décoret 06] utilizes the depth of a rasterized fragment to set the appropriate cell in the voxel grid. The grid itself is represented by a 2D texture, where the bits of the RGBA channels encode the presence of the voxelized geometry. A similar approach presented by Dong et al. [Dong et al. 04] better handles geometry that lies parallel to the viewing direction.

The key idea of our approach is that a texture atlas discretizes the surface of an object. This discretization is used to create the voxel grid. The algorithm consists of two main steps (see Figure 3.2). In a first step, all objects are rendered to one or several atlas-texture images. In the second step, one vertex is generated for each valid atlas texel and inserted into a voxel grid. In this way, a voxelization of deforming objects is possible. Our method can create a *binary* voxelization, where the bits of the RGBA channels of a two-dimensional texture are used to encode the voxels, as done by [Eisemann and Décoret 06]. It can also create a *multivalued* voxel grid, where the information is stored in a three-dimensional texture (one texel per voxel). With the help of a multivalued voxelization, any

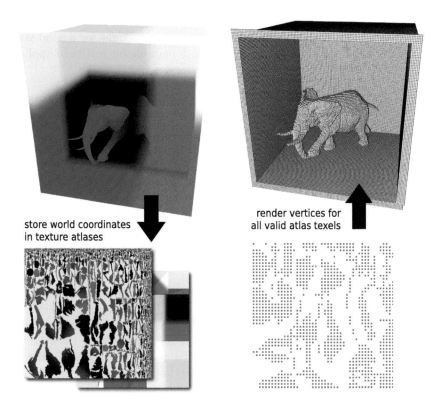

store world coordinates
in texture atlases

render vertices for
all valid atlas texels

Figure 3.2. Atlas-based voxelization. The scene is rendered to texture atlases capturing the three-dimensional world positions. All valid atlas texels correspond to full voxels that are inserted into the grid by point rendering.

type of data (e.g., radiance for diffuse objects, normals, or BRDF) can be stored in a voxel grid. As the following description will focus on the binary voxelization approach, please see [Thiedemann et al. 11] for further details on the multivalued voxelization.

In contrast to voxelization approaches based on depth peeling, the presented algorithm is independent of the depth complexity of the scene. Compared to the boundary voxelization method presented by Eisemann and Décoret [Eisemann and Décoret 06], our method does not exhibit problems with polygons parallel to the voxelization direction and creates a voxel-model that tightly fits the bounding volume of the scene. Our algorithm requires that each object to be voxelized is already mapped to a texture atlas. It is applicable for dynamic rigid bodies as well as moderately deforming models because these just need one atlas mapping.

Furthermore, as it only creates a boundary voxelization, it imposes no further restrictions on the objects (e.g., objects must be watertight for a solid voxelization). Due to its performance the algorithm is suitable for real-time applications in dynamic scenes.

3.2.1 Algorithm

The voxelization starts by rendering the scene into one or multiple texture atlases. If every object has its own atlas the scene composition is more flexible because objects can be added or removed without having to recompute the whole atlas. Having the texture atlas of the object currently to be voxelized bound as a render target, the object is rendered, passing its texture-atlas coordinates by glTexCoord2f to the shader built-in variable gl_MultiTexCoord0. The vertex shader (see Listing 3.1) transforms the coordinate into normalized device coordinates and outputs the object's vertex at this position. It passes the world-space position to the fragment shader, which then simply writes this value to the texture atlas.

Afterwards, all valid entries in the texture atlas are inserted into the grid storing the voxel data by point rendering. For this purpose, one vertex has to be generated for each valid texel of the atlas texture. As most mappings from objects to a texture atlas leave unused space in the atlas texture, the atlas texture contains several invalid texels that have to be omitted. To identify the invalid texels, the texture atlas is cleared with a value that lies outside of the range of the values that are going to be captured. This value can then be used as a threshold to select the valid texels.

The selection process is done as a preprocess on the CPU. After an initial atlas rendering, the content of the texture atlas is read back and a display list containing only the vertices for the valid texels of the texture atlas is created. The

```
varying vec3 P;

void main()
{
  // Transform atlas texture coordinate into NDC
  gl_Position = vec4(gl_MultiTexCoord0.xy * 2.0 - vec2(1.0),
                     0.0, 1.0);

  // Pass world-space position to fragment shader
  P = (gl_ModelViewMatrix * gl_Vertex).xyz;
}
```

Listing 3.1. Render to texture atlas (vertex shader).

display list can then be invoked at any time to insert the vertices into the voxel grid. This selection process can also be done on the fly on the GPU. Vertices are generated for all atlas texels. Either the geometry shader emits only valid vertices, or the vertex shader assigns a position that gets clipped in the rendering pipeline to all invalid vertices.

As a binary voxelization approach is employed, the bits of the RGBA channels of a two-dimensional texture are used to encode the voxels as done by Eisemann and Décoret [Eisemann and Décoret 06]. Before inserting the vertices into the grid, the graphics pipeline has to be prepared for this task. First, the texture storing the voxel grid has to be bound as a render target. Second, a logical OR operation has to be defined for the framebuffer:

```
glLogicOp(GL_OR);
glEnable(GL_COLOR_LOGIC_OP);
```

Third, a camera whose frustum defines the coordinate system of the voxel grid has to be set up. Please note that the position and orientation of this voxelization camera are completely arbitrary.

After the rendering pipeline is prepared, each vertex is rendered. The vertex shader performs a vertex texture fetch (see Listing 3.2) reading the world-space position from the texture atlas. This value is used to transform the vertex into the coordinate system of the voxel grid according to the voxelization camera. A linear depth value is computed and passed on to the fragment shader. The task of the fragment shader (see Listing 3.3) is to determine the position of the

```
uniform sampler2D textureAtlas;
uniform mat4 viewProjMatrixVoxelCam;

varying float mappedZ;

void main ()
{
  // Incoming vertices have positions in the range
  // of [0..atlasWidth-1]x[0,atlasHeight-1].
  // Fetch world space position from atlas
  vec3 pos3D = texelFetch2D(textureAtlas,
                            ivec2(gl_Vertex.xy),0).rgb;

  // Transform into voxel grid coordinates
  gl_Position = viewProjMatrixVoxelCam * vec4(pos3D, 1.0);

  // map z-coordinate to [0,1]
  mappedZ = gl_Position.z * 0.5 + 0.5;
}
```

Listing 3.2. Fill voxel grid (vertex shader).

```
uniform usampler1D bitmask;
varying float mappedZ;

varying out uvec4 result;

void main()
{
  // Set bit in voxel grid
  result = texture1D(bitmask, mappedZ);
}
```

Listing 3.3. Fill voxel grid (fragment shader).

bit that represents the voxel in the voxel grid. This is done with the help of a one-dimensional texture, created on the CPU beforehand (please see the source code or [Eisemann and Décoret 06] for full details). The lookup texture maps a depth value to a bitmask representing a full voxel at that certain depth interval. The fragment shader writes this bitmask to the render target and thus sets the corresponding bit in the voxel grid. To avoid texture fetches, a bit-shift operation can also be used to create the bitmask from the depth value, but we did not observe any timing differences because the texture cache works well in this case.

Figure 3.3. Atlas-based voxelization of the elephant model (84 K triangles) with two different atlas resolutions. The resolution of the voxel grid is 128^3. The image on the left shows the voxel grid generated from an atlas of too low resolution: 112^2 (6K points, 0.18 ms for atlas rendering and voxelization). On the right, a sufficient atlas resolution of 368^2 (65K points, 0.27 ms) was used. Nevertheless, the voxel surface is not perfect. As you can see on the right, a few voxels might be missing.

Voxel-grid resolution	Time (ms)	Vertices	Atlas resolution
$64^2 \times 128$	0.21	24k	224×224
$128^2 \times 128$	0.27	65k	368×368
$256^2 \times 128$	0.60	285k	768×768
$512^2 \times 128$	1.22	790k	1280×1280

Table 3.1. Timings for a binary voxelization of the elephant model shown in Figure 3.3. We use a single 2D texture encoding the voxels as bits in the RGBA-channels, so the depth resolution is fixed to 128. Columns from left to right: voxel grid resolution, time in ms to create the voxel grid (including atlas rendering), number of vertices that were needed to insert the valid texels of the atlas into the grid and the resolution of the texture atlas. For all resolutions, creating the custom mip-maps took less than 0.1 ms.

3.2.2 Performance

The performance of the algorithm largely depends on the number of voxels that must be drawn. This number in turn depends on the resolution of the texture atlas. An ideal atlas resolution is reached if one atlas texel covers roughly the same surface area in world space as does one voxel of the voxel grid. If a lower resolution is used, holes can appear in the voxel grid. If the resolution is too high, several vertices are drawn that cover the same voxel. This overdraw fills some voxels more than once and can therefore lead to a decline in performance. See Figure 3.3 for a visual comparison of different atlas resolutions and the resulting voxel grid. In Table 3.1 some example timings for different atlas and voxel resolutions are shown. Our test system is an Nvidia GTX 570 (1280 MB RAM), Intel Core2Duo CPU (2 × 2,16 GHz), 3 GB RAM, Windows XP 32 bit. In some cases it might be best to manually try to find a sufficient atlas resolution that gives the best trade-off between quality and rendering time.

To speed up the voxelization process in dynamic scenes, a prevoxelization can be used. At start-up, the static parts of the scene are voxelized and stored in a voxel grid. At runtime, only the dynamic objects have to be voxelized in each frame. The voxel grid storing the dynamic parts can then be joined with a copy of the static voxel grid. Depending on the ratio of dynamic vs. static parts of the scene, this approach can lead to a significant speedup.

3.3 Hierarchical Ray/Voxel Intersection Test

The basic idea of the intersection algorithm is to use a hierarchical representation of a binary voxelized scene to quickly compute the intersection of a ray with the voxel grid. Using the hierarchical representation allows us to decide on a coarse level if an intersection is to be expected in a region of the voxel grid or if the region can be skipped entirely.

The developed algorithm borrows ideas from [Forest et al. 09] but was given some improvements to increase its performance and functionality. For example, a different traversal method is used that does not need the additional overhead of an octree. Furthermore, the presented method is not only able to determine the visibility between two points in space, but can also determine the first intersection point along a ray.

3.3.1   Data Structure

The method is based on a binary voxelization, stored in a 2D texture. Each bit of a texel encodes the presence of geometry at a certain depth along the voxelization direction (negative z-axis of the voxelization camera). Therefore, a texel represents a "stack" of voxels along the negative z-axis. The texture is used to build a hierarchical structure, which is essentially a mip-map hierarchy where the texels along the x- and y-axis are joined. The depth resolution along the z-axis is kept at each mip-map level (see Figure 3.4). The high depth resolution at each level of the structure allows us to decide more precisely if the traversal of the hierarchy can be stopped early. The hierarchy itself is stored in the different mip-map levels of a 2D texture. The mip-map levels are generated manually. For this task, four adjacent texels of one mip-map level are joined with a logical OR operation, representing a texel at the next mip-map level.

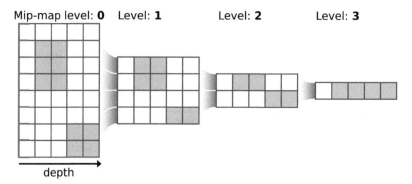

Figure 3.4. Construction of the mip-map hierarchy in two dimensions (1D voxel texture of width 8 with a depth resolution of 5). The depth resolution is identical for all mip-map levels. Each new texel is created with a logical OR-operation of two texels of the previous level.

3.3.2   Overview

The traversal starts at the texel of the hierarchy that covers the area of the scene in which the starting point of the ray lies. To determine this texel, the starting point of the ray is projected along the inverse voxelization direction onto the 2D texture. If the texel is found, it has to be tested if the ray hits any voxels inside the region of the voxel grid represented by this texel. As the bitmask stored at each texel represents a *stack* of voxels along the direction of depth, a bounding box covering this volume can be computed. The size of the corresponding bounding box depends on the current mip-map level. For example, at the maximum mip-map level, the hierarchy consists of only one texel, covering the whole scene. After the bounding box corresponding to the current texel of the hierarchy is computed, the ray is intersected with it. The intersection results in two depth

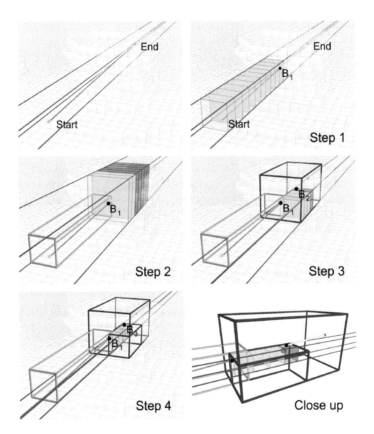

Figure 3.5. Hierarchy traversal for a simple case. In this example, the intersection test starts at mip-map level one. The blue lines visualize the bounding box of the voxels stored at the active texel. The bitmask of the active texel is represented by green (empty) and red (nonempty) voxels. The green and red cuboids show the history of the traversal (green = no hit, red = possible hit) for the given texel.

values: one value where the ray enters the bounding box and another depth value where it leaves it. With the help of these two values, a so called *ray bitmask* can be generated, representing the voxels the ray intersects within the bounding box. This ray bitmask and the bitmask stored in the texel of the mip-map hierarchy are used to determine if an intersection occurs. If no intersection occurs, the starting point of the ray is advanced to the last intersection point with the bounding box and the mip-map level is increased. If an intersection occurs, the mip-map level has to be decreased to check whether the intersection still occurs on a finer resolution of the voxelization until the finest resolution of the hierarchy (mip-map level 0) is reached. The algorithm stops if a hit is detected or the length of the remaining ray segment becomes zero.

An example of a simple case is given in Figure 3.5. In the first step, the intersection (B_1) of the ray with the bounding box of the active texel is computed. The bitmask for this segment of the ray (orange) is created and compared to the bitmask stored at the texel. As this yields no hit, the starting point of the ray is advanced to B_1 and now only the remaining segment (yellow) of the ray has to be checked. The mip-map level is increased (second step) and a bitmask for the yellow segment is created and checked for a possible intersection. As this results in a possible hit, a finer resolution of the mip-map is chosen. The entry and exit point $(B_1$ and $B_2)$ at the finer resolution are computed and the bitmask for this ray segment is retrieved. The bitmask test also results in a possible intersection so the mip-map level is decreased again (third step). In the fourth step, the finest mip-map level is reached. The intersection of the ray segment with the bounding box leads to the box intersection point B_3. As the bitmask for the ray segment up to B_3 compared with the bitmask stored at this texel results in an intersection, the algorithm terminates.

3.3.3   Algorithm

The algorithm starts by fetching the world-space position of the current fragment from the g-buffer. This is going to be the starting point of the ray (*origin*). The direction of the ray is generated by sampling the hemisphere above the starting point with a cosine-weighted distribution. To avoid self-intersections, the starting point of the ray is advanced by an offset along the ray direction and the normal (please refer to the code for more details). The extent of the ray direction (`dir`) is limited to a user-defined radius (see Section 3.4 for more details). Afterwards, the ray is transformed into the unit cube $[0\ldots1]^3$ and the ray traversal starts.

Before the algorithm enters the main loop (see Listing 3.4), the exit point of the ray with the bounding box of the scene is computed (this limits the ray extent). For practical reasons, the hierarchy traversal itself will not start at the coarsest mip-map level; instead it starts at a finer resolution (e.g., mip-map level 3 for a 128^3 volume), which turned out to be faster. The hierarchy is traversed as long as no hitpoint is found and the ray parameter `tNear` is smaller than `tFar`.

```
float tNear = 0.0;
float tFar = 1.0;

// Compute the exit position of the ray with the scene's BB
if(!IntersectBox(vec3(0.0), vec3(1.0), tFar))
  // IntersectBox modifies tFar, so set a proper value
  tFar = 1.0; // test whole ray

// Set current position along the ray to the ray's origin
vec3 posTNear = origin;

bool intersectionFound = false;
uvec4 intersectionBitmask = uvec4(0);

// It's faster to not start at the coarsest level
int level = 3;

for(int i = 0; (i < MAXSTEPS) && (tNear < tFar)
                          && (!intersectionFound); i++)
{
  float newTFar = 1.0;

  if(IntersectHierarchy(level, posTNear, newTFar,
                        intersectionBitmask))
  {
    // If we are at mipmap level 0 and an intersection occurred,
    // we have found an intersection of the ray with the volume
    intersectionFound = (level == 0);

    // Otherwise we have to move down one level and
    // start testing from there
    level --;
  }
  else {
    // If no intersection occurs, we have to advance the
    // position along the ray. Furthermore, add a small offset
    // computed beforehand (see the code for more details)
    tNear = newTFar + offset;
    posTNear = origin + tNear * dir;

    // Move one level up
    level ++;
  }
}
```

Listing 3.4. Main loop of the hierarchy traversal.

Furthermore, we have included a user-defined variable called MAXSTEPS. With the help of this variable the user can limit the total number of iterations (and therefore the computation time) the algorithm is allowed to search for a hitpoint. Please note that if this value is set too low, a hitpoint might be missed.

During each iteration, the hierarchy is tested for an intersection at the current mip-map level. The function IntersectHierarchy, described later on, determines if an intersection of the ray at the current level of the hierarchy is present. It further computes a new value for newTFar, which stores the exit point of the ray with the bounding box of the current texel of the hierarchy at the given level. If the method found an intersection and the finest mip-map level is reached, the algorithm can stop. Otherwise, if a possible intersection at a coarser level is found, the next finer mip-map level is tested. If no intersection occurs, the inspected part of the hierarchy can be skipped by advancing the starting point of the ray to the exit position stored in `newTFar`. A small offset is added to avoid precision problems. The search for a hitpoint along the remaining ray segment then continues on a coarser mip-map level.

The main part of the algorithm consists of the method `IntersectHierarchy`, shown in Listing 3.5. The first step is to determine the active texel of the hierarchy. This is done by projecting the current position on the ray, stored in `posTNear`, to the image plane. As the ray was transformed to the unit cube beforehand and the scene was voxelized along the negative z-direction, the projection is achieved by multiplying the x- and y-position of the ray with the current resolution of the hierarchy. Afterwards, the axis-aligned bounding box (AABB), belonging to the active texel, is constructed and its intersection with the ray is computed. As the current position `posTNear` on the ray is always at `tNear`, we

```
bool IntersectHierarchy(in int level, in vec3 posTNear,
  inout float tFar, out uvec4 intersectionBitmask)
{
  // Calculate pixel coordinates ([0,width]x[0,height])
  // of the current position along the ray
  float res = float(1 << (maxMipMapLevel - level));
  ivec2 pixelCoord = ivec2(posTNear.xy * res);

  // Voxel width and height in the unit cube
  vec2 voxelWH = vec2(1.0) / res;

  // Compute voxel stack (AABB) in the unit cube
  // belonging to this pixel position
  vec2 box_min = pixelCoord * voxelWH; // (left, bottom)

  // Compute intersection with the bounding box
  // It is always assumed that an intersection occurs and
  // that the position of posTNear remains the same
  tFar = IntersectBoxOnlyTFar(vec3(box_min, 0.0),
      vec3(box_min + voxelWH, 1.0));

  // Now test if some of the bits intersect
  float zFar = tFar*dir.z + origin.z ;

  // Fetch bitmask for ray and intersect with current pixel
  return intersectBits(
      texture2D(bitmaskRays, //stores all possible bitmasks
      vec2(min(posTNear.z, zFar), max(posTNear.z, zFar))),
      pixelCoord, level, intersectionBitmask);
}
```

Listing 3.5. Ray/hierarchy intersection test.

only have to compute a value for `tFar`. With the help of `tFar`, the depth values for the ray segment intersecting the AABB are computed. These depth values are used to construct a bitmask with bits set to one that represent the voxels covered by the ray segment. For this task, a 2D texture (`bitmaskRays`) is created at start-up which stores all the possible ray bitmasks for any given combination of depth values. The bitmask is read from this texture and passed to the method `intersectBits` as well as the coordinates of the active texel and the current mip-map level.

The method `intersectBits` simply uses these values to retrieve the voxel bitmask belonging to the active texel from the 2D texture storing the hierarchy and uses a logical AND operation to test for an intersection (see Listing 3.6). The result of this operation is stored in `intersectionBitmask`, which will be used later on to identify the exact position of the hitpoint. The result of the method `IntersectHierarchy` is used in the main loop to determine if the algorithm has found an intersection or if it has to continue its search.

```
bool intersectBits(in uvec4 bitRay, in ivec2 texel,
                   in int level, out uvec4 intersectionBitmask)
{
    // Fetch bitmask form hierarchy and compute intersection
    intersectionBitmask = (bitRay &
                          texelFetch2D(voxelTex, texel, level));

    return (intersectionBitmask != uvec4(0));
}
```

Listing 3.6. Bitmask intersection test.

3.3.4   First Intersection Point along a Ray

The described intersection test can only tell if there is an occluder anywhere in space along the ray. We extend the algorithm to determine the position of the first intersection along the ray as well. This can be done by finding the first bit that is set in the bitmask `intersectionBitmask` returned by the method `IntersectHierarchy` (see Listing 3.5). Please note that "first bit" denotes the most significant bit, "last bit" the least significant bit. The position of the bit inside the mask is used to determine its depth in the unit cube. The depth can then be used to calculate the position of the intersection along the ray in world coordinates. To find the foremost bit, a logarithm to the base 2 can be used. If the ray direction is opposite to the direction of the voxelization, the position of the last bit has to be found. As this case is more involved, we will describe it in more detail.

```
// get the position of the lowest bit
for(int  v = 3;  x == 0 && v >= 0;  v--) { // a b g r
  x = int(intersectionBitmask[v]);
  if(x != 0) {
    int pos32 = int(log2(float(x & ~(x-1)))+0.5);
    bitPosition = (3-v)*32 + pos32;
  }
}
```

Listing 3.7. Determining the hit position.

The algorithm (see Listing 3.7) iterates over each color channel of the bitmask in reverse order. If a channel with a nonzero bitmask is found, the last bit has to be isolated. This can be achieved with the operation x AND NOT(x-1). Afterwards, the position of the bit is computed with a logarithm to the base 2. To deal with floating-point rounding issues, a value of 0.5 is added prior to this operation. As this yields the position of the bit in the respective color channel only, the position of the bit in the whole bitmask composed of all four color channels is computed in the last step. The determined position can then be used to compute the world-space position of the hitpoint (please see the source code for full details).

3.4 Near-Field Indirect Illumination

For a fast near-field illumination, we generate a reflective shadow map (RSM) [Dachsbacher and Stamminger 05] that contains direct light, position, and normal for each pixel, viewed from the light position. We render one shadow map for a spotlight and a cube map for a point light. To obtain the indirect light for a pixel in the camera image, we use a gathering approach to compute one-bounce near-field illumination. Therefore, we compute N rays starting from the receiver position $\mathbf{x}$ with a maximum distance r, as shown in Figure 3.6. We noticed that splitting up the computation into multiple passes with one pass per ray increases rendering speed. For each ray, we use our proposed intersection test to determine the first intersection point. If we hit a voxel along the ray we need to determine the direct radiance $\tilde{L}_i$ at this point. This can be implemented by a back-projection of the hitpoint into the RSM, which allows us to read the direct radiance stored in the RSM pixel. This direct radiance is valid if the distance between the 3D position of the hitpoint and the position stored in the RSM pixel is smaller than a threshold ϵ. Otherwise, the direct radiance is set to zero because the hitpoint is in the shadow of the light source. The threshold ϵ has to be adjusted to the voxelization discretization v, the RSM pixel size s, the

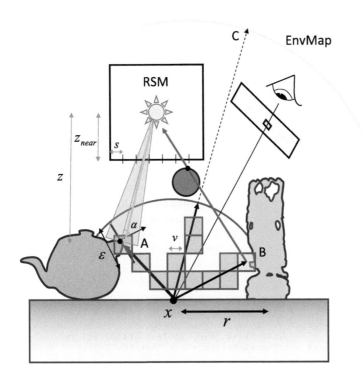

Figure 3.6. Near-field indirect light. To compute the indirect light at a point $\mathbf{x}$, several rays are shot into the upper hemisphere. The voxels along each ray are traversed until a hitpoint is found. The hitpoint is then back-projected into the RSM to obtain the direct radiance at this point. Indirect light is gathered from hitpoint A, because it is visible from the light source. The distance from hitpoint A to the RSM pixel position is smaller than the threshold ϵ. Hitpoint B is in the shadow of the direct light, because its position is different from the position stored in the RSM pixel. If no intersection point is found within the search radius r, the radiance can optionally be read from an environment map, to simulate directional occlusion (point C).

perspective projection, and the normal orientation α. As shown in Figure 3.6, this leads to $\epsilon = \max(v, \frac{s}{\cos\alpha} \cdot \frac{z}{z_{\text{near}}})$. Using Monte-Carlo integration, the radiance L_o at the receiver point $\mathbf{x}$ can then be computed as

$$L_o(\mathbf{x}) \approx \frac{\rho(\mathbf{x})/\pi}{N} \sum_{i=1}^{N} \frac{\tilde{L}_i(\mathbf{x}, \omega_i)\cos\theta}{p(\omega_i)}, \tag{3.1}$$

where $\rho(\mathbf{x})/\pi$ is the diffuse BRDF at the receiver point and ω_i are N sample directions. The value $\tilde{L}_i(\mathbf{x}, \omega_i)$ is the radiance that is visible at the hitpoint in sample direction ω_i. The sample directions are generated from a cosine density function $p(\omega_i) = \cos\theta/\pi$, where θ is the angle between ω_i and the surface normal. For this density, the term $\cos\theta/\pi$ cancels out and only $\frac{\rho(\mathbf{x})}{N}\sum_{i=1}^{N}\tilde{L}_i(\mathbf{x}, \omega_i)$ needs to be computed.

Listing 3.8 shows the fragment shader that computes a single radiance value $\tilde{L}_i(\mathbf{x}, \omega_i)$ for the near-field illumination. First, we get the 3D position from the buffer storing the intersection points of the shot rays with the voxel structure and transform it into light space using a transform matrix (`mapLookupMatrix`). Since we use a spotlight in this example, the back-projection can be implemented using a `texture2DProj` command. When reading the reflective shadow map, we extract the position (`position`), direct light (`color`), and normal (`normal`) at the reprojected texture coordinate `projCoord`. The `normalCondition` uses a dot

```
void main()
{
    // initialize resulting radiance with black
    result = vec3(0);

    // get intersection point with voxel scene
    // and transform it into spot light space
    vec3 hitPos = texture2D(hitBuffer, gl_TexCoord[0].st).xyz;
    vec4 projCoord = mapLookupMatrix * vec4(hitPos, 1.0);

    // fetch RSM values
    vec4 position = texture2DProj(positionSpotMap, projCoord);
    vec4 color = texture2DProj(colorSpotMap, projCoord);
    vec3 normal = texture2DProj(normalSpotMap, projCoord).rgb;

    // compute ray from hit position to g-buffer position
    vec3 ray = normalize(texture2D(positionBuffer,
                         gl_TexCoord[0].st).xyz - hitPos);
    float lightZ = position.w;
    float pixelSide = pixelSide_zNear * lightZ;

    // only front faces are lit and senders of indirect light
    bool normalCondition = dot(normal, ray) >= 0.0;
    float cosAlpha = max(0.001, dot(normal, spotDirection));

    // check if the hitpoint is valid
    if((hitPos.z < 100.0) && (projCoord.w > 0.0) &&
       distance(hitPos, position.xyz) < min(10.0*voxelDiagonal,
       max(voxelDiagonal, pixelSide/cosAlpha*distanceEpsScale))
       && normalCondition)
    {
        // output radiance
        // sampleContrib = (user-def. contrast / numberOfSamples)
        result = color.rgb * sampleContrib;
    }
}
```

Listing 3.8. Near-field illumination (fragment shader).

product to check if we found a front-facing sender of indirect light. To check whether a reprojected sample contains a valid source of indirect light, several tests are performed. Projection behind the spotlight is handled by checking the homogenous coordinate of the projected coordinate. If a valid intersection point has been found, `hitPos.z` is inside a maximum range (set to 100 in this example). Next, the distance between the hit position `hitPos` and the reprojected position `position.xyz` must be within a tolerance region. Due to the perspective projection of the spotlight, this tolerance region grows with distance and slope. The minimum tolerance we have to allow is the diagonal size of a voxel. To avoid light bleeding, we introduce a maximum distance, which is set to ten voxel diagonals in this example. Additionally, the normal condition is included. If all these tests succeed, we return the sender radiance (`color`), otherwise the sender radiance is set to zero. This shader is called for each sample direction to compute Equation (3.1).

3.5 Results

Voxel-based global illumination enables one-bounce global illumination in dynamic scenes. Keeping the search radius r for intersections small leads to real-time frame rates. All our example images were created using an Nvidia GTX 570 (1280 MB RAM). Figure 3.7 shows VGI and the voxel model. Similar to many other real-time methods, indirect light has to be computed on a lower resolution. We use standard techniques like *interleaved sampling* and a *geometry-aware blur* filter to compute indirect light only on a subset of all pixels. Figure 3.8 shows the "raw" image data and the image after applying the filter. To obtain the final image, we multiply with the reflectance value of the texture and add the direct light.

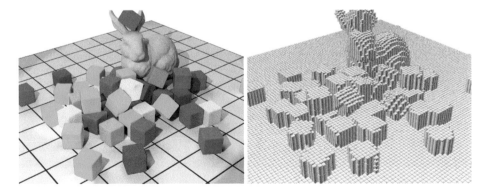

Figure 3.7. Voxel-based global illumination and the underlying voxel model.

Figure 3.8. Unfiltered image, 48 fps (left). The filtered image and the final image, including textures and direct light, 36 fps (right).

Figure 3.9. Changing the voxel resolution. $32^2 \times 128$ (47 fps) (left), $64^2 \times 128$ (36 fps) (center), $128^2 \times 128$ (28 fps)(right). Image resolution is 1024×768, with eight rays per pixel.

Figure 3.10. Changing the radius from $r=1.5$ (37 fps)(left) to $r=4.0$ (27 fps)(center) to the whole scene (21 fps)(right)

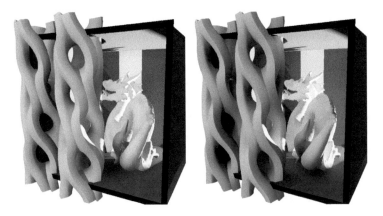

Figure 3.11. Using a screen-space method (SSDO), the color bleeding arising from the wall behind the columns disappears (left). VGI correctly displays such effects (right).

Changing the voxel resolution affects both the quality and the rendering speed. As shown in Figure 3.9, small details in the shadow disappear and the shadow appears too dark if a coarse voxel model is used. Since the image-space blur removes some of the small details, these parameters have to be adjusted manually.

Figure 3.10 shows images with a varying radius r. The frame rate drops for a large radius, but the color bleeding can be displayed over large regions in the scene. In contrast to image-space approaches, the voxel-space method does not depend on the camera position. Senders and blockers that are invisible in the camera image are always detected, as can be seen in Figure 3.11.

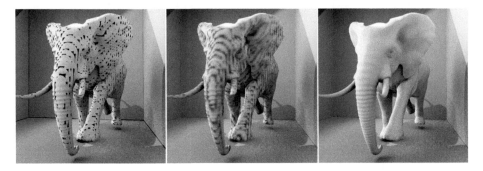

Figure 3.12. No ray offset is used, resulting in the dark artifacts (left). An offset along the ray direction is used but no offset along the normal (center). An offset is used both along the ray and normal direction, removing the self-occlusions (right).

Due to the spatial discretization introduced by the voxel model, an offset must be used for the ray-intersection test. Otherwise, wrong self-occlusions appear. Figure 3.12 shows renderings with and without an offset.

We found that the voxel discretization and also the image-space blur prevent the use of glossy materials: inside the reflective material, the voxel structure becomes visible and the filter changes the shininess. So we only use diffuse BRDFs and generate the rays from a cosine density function. Although the accuracy of the reprojection decreases in distant regions of the light source (due to the perspective projection of the RSM), we found the resulting error acceptable because of the quadratic falloff of the light source.

As future work, we would like to improve the temporal coherence and extend our method to larger scenes. One possibility would be a hierarchical voxel model that adapts to the viewpoint as well as to important regions in the scene. This would also improve the appearance of glossy materials. A recent publication by Crassin et al. [Crassin et al. 11] using Giga Voxels shows promising results in this direction.

Bibliography

[Crane et al. 07] Keenan Crane, Ignacio Llamas, and Sarah Tariq. "Real-Time Simulation and Rendering of 3D Fluids." In *GPU Gems 3*, edited by Hubert Nguyen, pp. 633–675. Reading, MA: Addison-Wesley Professional, 2007. Available online (http://developer.download.nvidia.com/books/gpu_gems_3/samples/gems3_ch30.pdf).

[Crassin et al. 11] Cyril Crassin, Fabrice Neyret, Miguel Sainz, Simon Green, and Elmar Eisemann. "Interactive Indirect Illumination Using Voxel Cone Tracing: A Preview." Poster ACM SIGGRAPH Symposium on Interactive 3D Graphics and Games (I3D), 2011. Available online (http://artis.imag.fr/Publications/2011/CNSGE11).

[Dachsbacher and Stamminger 05] Carsten Dachsbacher and Marc Stamminger. "Reflective Shadow Maps." In *I3D '05: Proceedings of the 2005 Symposium on Interactive 3D Graphics and Games*. New York: ACM, 2005. Available online (http://www.vis.uni-stuttgart.de/~dachsbcn/download/rsm.pdf).

[Dong et al. 04] Zhao Dong, Wei Chen, Hujun Bao, Hongxin Zhang, and Qunsheng Peng. "Real-time Voxelization for Complex Polygonal Models." In *Pacific Conference on Computer Graphics and Applications*, pp. 43–50. Washington, DC: IEEE Computer Society, 2004. Available online (http://www.mpi-inf.mpg.de/~dong/download/PG04.pdf).

[Eisemann and Décoret 06] Elmar Eisemann and Xavier Décoret. "Fast Scene Voxelization and Applications." In *ACM SIGGRAPH Symposium on Interactive 3D Graphics and Games*, pp. 71–78. New York: ACM, 2006. Available online (http://artis.imag.fr/Publications/2006/ED06).

[Fang and Chen 00] Shiaofen Fang and Hongsheng Chen. "Hardware Accelerated Vox-elization." *Computers and Graphics* 24:3 (2000), 433–442. Available online (http://www.cs.iupui.edu/~sfang/vg99.pdf).

[Forest et al. 09] Vincent Forest, Loic Barthe, and Mathias Paulin. "Real-Time Hierar-chical Binary-Scene Voxelization." *Journal of Graphics, GPU, & Game Tools* 14:3 (2009), 21–34.

[Li et al. 05] Wei Li, Zhe Fan, Xiaoming Wei, and Arie Kaufman. "Flow Simula-tion with Complex Boundaries." In *GPU Gems 2: Programming Techniques for High-Performance Graphics and General-Purpose Computation*, edited by Matt Pharr and Randima Fernando, pp. 747–764. Reading, MA: Addison-Wesley, 2005. Available online (http://http.developer.nvidia.com/GPUGems2/gpugems2_chapter47.html).

[Passalis et al. 07] Georgios Passalis, Theoharis Theoharis, George Toderici, and Ioan-nis A. Kakadiaris. "General Voxelization Algorithm with Scalable GPU Implemen-tation." *Journal of Graphics, GPU, & Game Tools* 12 (2007), 61–71.

[Thiedemann et al. 11] Sinje Thiedemann, Niklas Henrich, Thorsten Grosch, and Ste-fan Müller. "Voxel-based Global Illumination." In *Proceedings of I3D '11 Symposium on Interactive 3D Graphics and Games*, pp. 103–110. New York: ACM, 2011. Available online (http://www.rendering.ovgu.de/rendering_media/downloads/publications/VoxelGI.pdf).

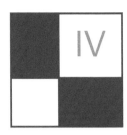

IV
Shadows

In this section, we explore algorithms for generating shadow data. Shadows are the dark companions of lights and although they can each exist on their own, in games they should always be together. Achieving good visual results in rendering shadows is considered a particularly difficult task for graphics programmers.

The first chapter in this section is "Efficient Online Visibility for Shadow Maps" by Oliver Mattausch, Jiri Bittner, Ari Silvennoinen, Daniel Scherzer, and Michael Wimmer. The authors introduce an algorithm that makes shadow-map rendering efficient, and that is particularly useful for shadow mapping in large-scale outdoor scenes. This algorithm quickly detects and culls the geometry that does not contribute to shadows in final images. The solution presented by Mattausch and his coauthors uses camera-view visibility information to create a mask of potential shadow receivers in the light view, which restricts the area in which shadow casters have to be rendered. There are four main steps in the algorithm: determine the shadow receivers, create a mask of shadow receivers, render shadow casters using the mask for culling, and compute shading. The authors note that their basic principle is easy to integrate into existing game engines.

The second chapter in this section is "Depth Rejected Gobo Shadows" by John White. In this chapter, White describes a technique to provide soft shadows using a simple texture sample. This approach extends the basic projected gobo texture concept by removing the incorrect projections on objects closer to the light source.

—Wolfgang Engel

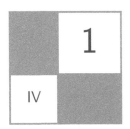

1

IV

Efficient Online Visibility for Shadow Maps

Oliver Mattausch, Jiri Bittner, Ari Silvennoinen, Daniel Scherzer, and Michael Wimmer

1.1 Introduction

Standard online occlusion culling is able to vastly improve the rasterization performance of walkthrough applications by identifying large parts of the scene as invisible from the camera and rendering only the visible geometry. However, it is of little use for the acceleration of shadow-map generation (i.e., rasterizing the scene from the light view [Williams 78]), so that typically a high percentage of the geometry will be visible when rendering shadow maps. For example, in outdoor scenes typical viewpoints are near the ground and therefore have significant occlusion, while light viewpoints are higher up and see most of the geometry.

Our algorithm remedies this situation by quickly detecting and culling the geometry that does not contribute to the shadow in the final image. Note that from the geometry visible from the light, only a small fraction will remain (for

 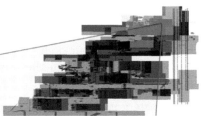

Figure 1.1. The shadow-map geometry rendered for a particular *Left 4 Dead* view (left) and the corresponding light-view visualization (right), where the rendered shadow casters are shown in red.

example, the red parts in Figure 1.1). The main idea is to use camera-view visibility information to create a mask of potential shadow receivers in the light view, which restricts the areas where shadow casters have to be rendered. This algorithm makes shadow-map rendering efficient by providing the important property of *output sensitivity* (i.e., the complexity depends only on what is visible from the camera and not the size of the scene).

The method is easy to integrate into an existing rendering engine that already performs occlusion culling for rasterization. It is orthogonal to the particular occlusion-culling algorithm being used. We used the CHC++ algorithm [Mattausch et al. 08] in our implementation, but in principle any state-of-the-art occlusion-culling algorithm can benefit from our method. Likewise, our method does not pose any restriction on the shadow-mapping algorithm being used. It was tested successfully with different algorithms like uniform shadows, LiSPSM, or cascaded shadow maps.

Our method is particularly useful for shadow mapping in large-scale outdoor scenes. In terms of overall render time (i.e., the whole pipeline until the final shaded image is rendered), the algorithm achieves a speedup of up to ten in real-world city scenes compared to the naïve use of occlusion culling. It also brings a significant speedup of up to two in real game scenes (e.g., a *Left 4 Dead* level as shown in Figure 1.1).

1.2   Algorithm Overview

The algorithm consists of the following four main steps, as also shown in Figure 1.2. Steps 1 and 4 constitute the standard approach for deferred shading (including shadow mapping); the main contributions of our algorithm are Steps 2 and 3.

Step 1: Determine shadow receivers. First we use occlusion culling to render the scene from the camera. This gives us the visible geometry, which corresponds to the potential shadow receiver geometry. Such an initial depth pass is a common practice in rendering engines. Our implementation uses a deferred shading approach, where other attributes like the geometry normals are stored in separate render targets for subsequent shading together with the depth buffer. We use a bounding volume hierarchy over the geometry as input to our occlusion-culling algorithm, and the potential shadow receivers correspond to the leaves of this hierarchy. Note that this step provides a conservative estimate of the visible geometry.

Step 2: Create a mask of shadow receivers. Next we render the potential receivers from the light view to generate a so-called receiver mask. During shadow-map rendering, shadow map updates are restricted to this mask. We can further tighten the receiver mask and restrict shadow-map rendering to only those shadow map texels that correspond to visible receiver

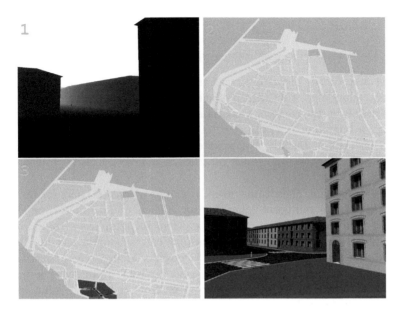

Figure 1.2. Steps of our algorithm. (1) Determine the potential shadow receivers and compute the depth buffer. (2) In light view, create a mask from the potential receivers containing only those fragments that contribute to a pixel in camera view (shown in green). (3) Determine visible subset of shadow casters using occlusion queries against the mask, and rasterize them into a shadow map. (4) Shade image using the depth buffer and the shadow map.

pixels. For this purpose, we make an additional lookup into the camera depth buffer when rendering into the shadow map (this step can be seen as a *reverse shadow test*).

Step 3: Render shadow casters using the mask for culling. After using the potential receivers for mask creation, we rasterize the rest of the scene geometry in order to complete the shadow map, i.e., the *potential shadow casters*. Our receiver mask allows us to quickly reject geometry that does not contribute to the final image, and significantly reduces the number of rendered shadow casters. This is done using hierarchical occlusion culling from the light view, issuing fast hardware occlusion queries to test if a node affects any masked pixels. Note that the speedup of our method is achieved in this step.

Step 4: Compute shading. Finally, we use the shadow map generated in the previous step to perform shadow mapping to find those pixels that are visible from the light source, and shade them accordingly. Note that this step is not altered by our approach.

1.3 Detailed Description

1.3.1 Determine Shadow Receivers

The first step of our algorithm consists of rendering the scene using an online occlusion-culling algorithm, which efficiently detects and culls the geometry that is not visible from the camera. Occlusion queries are issued on cheap proxy geometry (e.g., a bounding box) in order to determine the visibility of the contained complex geometry. Luckily a hardware implementation of occlusion queries is available [Cunniff et al. 07], which returns the number of visible fragments after a small latency.

Occlusion-culling algorithms usually employ front-to-back rendering, and make heavy use of temporal coherence for efficiency and minimizing the query overhead. Culling becomes particularly efficient if it employs a spatial hierarchy to quickly cull large groups of shadow casters, e.g., a bounding volume hierarchy in the case of the CHC++ algorithm. Occlusion culling is less effective for extreme bird's eye views, as much of the scene is visible from such views. Hence, for a typical light view (consider shadows cast from the sun) it is not feasible to use naïve occlusion culling.

Besides determining the depth buffer, such an occlusion pass also gives a good estimate of the geometry visible in the current frame and hence the potential shadow receiver geometry (as of course we are only interested in shadowing the visible geometry). We will use both depth buffer and visible geometry as input to our receiver-masking algorithm.

1.3.2 Create a Mask of Shadow Receivers

The general idea of our method is to create a mask of visible shadow receivers, i.e., those objects determined as visible in the first camera-rendering pass (Step 1). In order to create the mask, we rasterize the actual geometry of the visible shadow receivers into a render target. The creation of the mask happens in a separate pass before rendering the shadow map, but already generates parts of the shadow map itself as well, simplifying the subsequent shadow-map rendering pass. Note that this method alone would already create a valid receiver mask (shown in Figure 1.3 (left)).

However, we can do even better and create a tighter mask by considering the fact that not all of the potential receiver fragments are visible from the camera view. This is because visibility in the camera view is only determined on a per-object basis, while for some objects, only a few pixels are actually visible. The invisible pixels can be detected and discarded using a *reverse shadow test* (see Listing 1.1[1]), leaving only the fragments actually visible in the camera view (depicted in orange in Figure 1.3 (left)). The shader tests whether the current

---

[1]Note that all code segments are given in the Cg shading language.

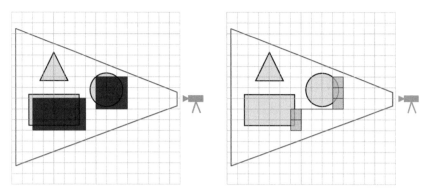

Figure 1.3. The mask is created by rasterizing the potential receiver geometry from the light view (dark-blue fragments, left). With an additional depth buffer lookup, we can discard all potential receiver fragments which are not visible from the camera (leaving only the orange fragments in the mask, right).

fragment lies within the screen-space boundaries and passes the depth test with respect to the camera view. It outputs the test result to a color channel.

```
Fragment ReverseShadowTest(fragin IN,
                           uniform sampler2D depthBuffer)
{
  Fragment OUT;
  // post-projection screen-space position of current fragment
  float4 screenSpacePos = IN.screenSpacePos;
  screenSpacePos /= screenSpacePos.w;

  // the depth of this fragment from the camera
  float fragmentDepth = screenSpacePos.z;
  // the depth of the current pixel from the camera
  float4 depth = tex2D(depthBuffer, screenSpacePos.xy).x;

  // depth comparison: is current fragment visible?
  bool visible = fragmentDepth <= depth + 1e-4f;
  // is fragment inside screen boundaries?
  bool inside = all(saturate(screenSpacePos) == screenSpacePos);

  // if fragment contributes to shading, add to mask
  OUT.color.x = (visible && inside) ? 1.0f : .0f
  return OUT;
}
```

Listing 1.1. The depth buffer of the camera is used to test the visibility of shadow-map fragments. This can be seen as a reverse shadow test that reverses the role of camera and light view.

```
Fragment OcclusionQuery(fragin IN, uniform sampler2D fragMask)
{
  Fragment OUT;
  // post-projection position in receiver mask
  float2 texCoord = IN.maskPos.xy / maskPos.w;
  // lookup corresponding fragment mask value
  float maskVal = tex2D(fragMask, texCoord).x;

  // discard if current fragment not masked
  if (maskVal < .5f) discard;
  return OUT;
}
```

Listing 1.2. Fragment shader for the receiver-mask lookup of an occlusion query.

1.3.3 Render Shadow Casters Using the Mask for Culling

In the shadow-map rendering pass, we rasterize the rest of the geometry as potential shadow casters. The mask is used in this pass to cull those potential shadow casters that do not contribute to the visible shadows. When issuing a hardware occlusion query, we use the fragment mask as a lookup texture and discard all fragments lying outside the mask (as shown in Listing 1.2).

Note that the lookup into the mask creates a minor overhead as compared to a standard occlusion query, which could be avoided if it were possible to directly write to the stencil buffer within the fragment shader in order to create a stencil mask. However, a suitable OpenGL extension (GL_ARB_shader_stencil_export) is already available and hopefully this feature will be better supported in the future.

1.4 Optimization: Shadow-Map Focusing

For very large scenes, the shadow-map resolution can become critical for maintaining a reasonable shadow quality. Shadow-map warping algorithms like LiSPSM [Wimmer et al. 04] and shadow-map partitioning algorithms like cascaded shadow maps [Engel 06, Zhang et al. 06] provide a better distribution of shadow map texels between near and far geometry, and in addition focus the shadow map in order not to waste shadow-map space on geometry not within the view frustum. However, if the distance to the far plane is very large compared to the near plane, the shadow quality can still become unacceptable due to lack of resolution. While cascaded shadow maps improve shadow quality significantly by slicing the view frustum and computing a shadow map for each slice individually, the problem still remains that a lot of shadow resolution can be wasted for areas that cannot be seen from the camera [Lauritzen et al. 11].

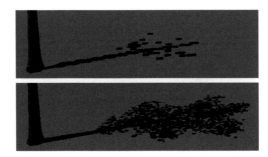

Figure 1.4. The shadow quality of an unfocused shadow map (top) can be greatly improved by focusing the shadow map on the visible geometry (bottom).

Since we collect the geometry visible from the camera in the first step of our algorithm anyway, we get all the information necessary for effectively focusing the shadow map for free. In particular, instead of the usual approach of intersecting the view frustum with the scene boundaries and focusing the shadow map on the resulting polytope, we intersect the view frustum with the union of the bounding boxes of all visible objects.

This algorithm can significantly improve the shadow quality in cases where there is sufficient occlusion (Figure 1.4). Focusing can also improve shadow-map rendering times due to more accurate shadow-frustum culling. However, the increase in the effective shadow-map resolution and the more accurate shadow-frustum culling gained from focusing are both temporally unstable. This temporal instability is potentially manifested by flickering shadow artifacts due to varying shadow-map resolution and incoherent shadow-map rendering times. The former is hard to control, although one could use temporal coherence and careful level design to mitigate the effect. The latter is an example of a non–output-sensitive process and at worst, a single visibility event can make the focused culling dependent on the whole scene. In contrast to simple shadow-frustum culling, our receiver-masking technique is output sensitive and hence the shadow-map rendering times are always predictable. Focusing as a stand-alone algorithm is not a reliable acceleration technique and should always be used in combination with receiver-masking.

1.5 Results

We implemented the presented algorithm in OpenGL and C++ and evaluated it using a GeForce 480 GTX GPU and a single Intel Core i7 CPU 920 with 2.67 GHz. For the camera-view render pass, we used an 800×600 32-bit RGBA render target (to store color and depth) and a 16-bit RGB render target (to store the normals). For the light-view render pass, we used a 32-bit depth texture.

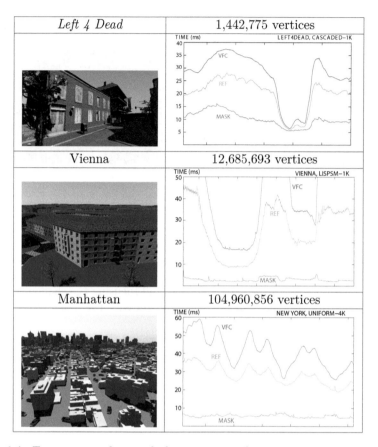

Table 1.1. Test scenes and example frame times with varying shadow parameters.

We compared the proposed receiver-mask algorithm (MASK) to view frustum culling (VFC) and a reference method (REF), which uses our unmodified occlusion culling algorithm for both light and camera views, and we plotted the total frame-rendering times for different test scenes in Table 1.1.

As can be observed from the timings, our algorithm works particularly well in the two city environments: a model of Manhattan and the town of Vienna, which were populated with various scene objects. This is because they are large, containing open scenes with a high cost for shadow mapping. We get a lower speedup of 1.4–2 in the *Left 4 Dead* game scene (rendered at 720p resolution and using four cascaded shadow maps with 1 K resolution each), partially explained by the overall lower geometric complexity. However, keep in mind that a two times speedup in a scene otherwise highly optimized for fast rendering is very worthwhile. The dependence of the algorithm performance on the shadow-map

SM type	LISPSM			UNIFORM		
Shadow size	1K	2K	4K	1K	2K	4K
Scene	Vienna					
Reference	21.6	22.3	22.4	28.7	28.7	29.2
Our method	2.9	3.5	6.1	2.9	3.4	5.9
Scene	Manhattan					
Reference	36.6	35.9	35.1	44.2	43.9	41.8
Our method	4.5	5.4	9.0	4.5	5.3	8.6

Table 1.2. Average frame times for two of the tested scenes (in ms).

resolution (1 K–4 K) and the used shadow-mapping algorithm (LiSPSM [Wimmer et al. 04] and uniform shadow maps) can be seen in Table 1.2.

1.6 Conclusion

We presented an algorithm for fast, output-sensitive shadow mapping in complex scenes. The proposed method generalizes trivially over a wide class of occlusion-culling algorithms as long as they are compatible with receiver masking, a property that holds for all rasterization-based algorithms. The basic principle is easy to integrate into existing game engines, especially if the engine is already using occlusion culling for the main view. We demonstrated the benefits of the algorithm using a reference implementation in the context of large directional light sources and note that the small overhead of generating the receiver mask is easily compensated by the performance gains during shadow-map generation.

1.7 Acknowledgments

We would like to thank Jiri Dusek for an early implementation of shadow map culling ideas; Jason Mitchell for the *Left 4 Dead 2* model; Stephen Hill and Petri Häkkinen for feedback. This work has been supported by the Austrian Science Fund (FWF) contract no. P21130-N13; the Ministry of Education, Youth, and Sports of the Czech Republic under research program LC-06008 (Center for Computer Graphics); and the Grant Agency of the Czech Republic under research program P202/11/1883.

Bibliography

[Cunniff et al. 07] Ross Cunniff, Matt Craighead, Daniel Ginsburg, Kevin Lefebvre, Bill Licea-Kane, and Nick Triantos. "ARB_occlusion_query." *OpenGL Registry*. Available online (http://www.opengl.org/registry/specs/ARB/occlusion_query.txt).

[Engel 06] Wolfgang Engel. "Cascaded Shadow Maps." In *ShaderX⁵: Advanced Rendering Techniques*, edited by Wolfgang Engel, pp. 197–206. Hingham, MA: Charles River Media, 2006.

[Lauritzen et al. 11] Andrew Lauritzen, Marco Salvi, and Aaron Lefohn. "Sample Distribution Shadow Maps." In *Symposium on Interactive 3D Graphics and Games, I3D '11*, pp. 97–102. New York: ACM Press, 2011.

[Mattausch et al. 08] Oliver Mattausch, Jiří Bittner, and Michael Wimmer. "CHC++: Coherent Hierarchical Culling Revisited." *Computer Graphics Forum (Proceedings of Eurographics 2008)* 27:2 (2008), 221–230.

[Williams 78] Lance Williams. "Casting Curved Shadows on Curved Surfaces." *Computer Graphics (SIGGRAPH '78 Proceedings)* 12:3 (1978), 270–274.

[Wimmer et al. 04] Michael Wimmer, Daniel Scherzer, and Werner Purgathofer. "Light Space Perspective Shadow Maps." In *Rendering Techniques 2004 (Proceedings Eurographics Symposium on Rendering)*, pp. 143–151. Aire-la-Ville, Switzerland: Eurographics Association, 2004.

[Zhang et al. 06] Fan Zhang, Hanqiu Sun, Leilei Xu, and Lee Kit Lun. "Parallel-Split Shadow Maps for Large-Scale Virtual Environments." In *Proceedings of the 2006 ACM International Conference on Virtual Reality Continuum and its Applications*, pp. 311–318. New York: ACM Press, 2006.

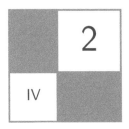

2
IV

Depth Rejected Gobo Shadows

John White

2.1 Introduction

This chapter describes a technique to provide soft shadows using a single texture sample in environments where the objects casting shadows and the objects receiving shadows are disjoint. This is common in games where the lighting on the static environment is prebaked into lightmaps and dynamic objects are later combined into the world.

Note that the soft shadows using this technique will only be cast onto prelit environment surfaces and not on themselves (i.e., self shadowing) or from one dynamic object to another. In these cases you need to use standard soft-shadowing techniques such as percentage closest filtering (PCF), variance [Donnelly and Lauritzen 06] or exponential shadows maps [Salvi 08]; otherwise the object will receive nonfiltered blocky shadows.

2.2 Basic Gobo Shadows

Before we discuss the technique, it is worthwhile to take a step backwards and describe a very simple technique for soft shadows using gobo projected textures.

A gobo is a theatrical term that refers to a cutout shape that can be placed in front of a spotlight light bulb. When the spotlight is turned on, the gobo cutout will partially block some light and the resultant shape will be projected onto the scene.

In games we can apply the same trick by applying a similar black or white texture to a projected light. The result is a soft image that casts onto the world. This texture can therefore be used to fake a shadow from an object. A common example of this in games is to have the light source in a wired cage; the gobo is then used to fake the shadow from the cage onto the world. As in the theater, the trick relies on the fact that any moving objects cannot move in between the light source and the world object from which the gobo is used to fake shadows (see Figure 2.1).

Figure 2.1. A gobo texture and its projection.

In games, this gobo can be generated upfront and loaded in and used statically. It can also be generated per frame by rendering the objects using a black shader onto a white surface, and then applying a blur filter afterwards to smooth the edges to fake the penumbra from the area light source.

Figure 2.2. A correct and an incorrect projection.

The main problem with basic gobo shadowing, especially for infinitely far directional shadowing such as from the sun, is that it is often impossible to guarantee that there is no surface between the light source and the gobo-casting object. This will lead to the gobo incorrectly projecting onto closer objects that should be fully in light. Figure 2.2 shows a wall closer to the light source with an incorrect gobo projection on it.

2.3 Depth Rejected Gobo Shadows

We can now extend the basic projected gobo technique to remove these incorrect projections on objects closer to the light source. We will do this by using standard shadow mapping to store depth values so that we can detect these incorrect back projections.

The basic algorithm in a nutshell is as follows:

1. Render a shadow map as usual but ensure that written pixels are tagged in the stencil buffer or in the second channel of a two-channel texture.

2. Apply a separable blur to the shadow maps to blur the stencil buffer and dilate out the depth values. The output is a two-channel depth + gobo texture.

3. Apply the blurred shadow map to the environment during a forward render pass. Use the depth component as the typical binary depth test with the blurred stencil component as the softness (i.e., penumbra) of the shadow. This shadow map can and should be sampled using a bilinear filter and not a point/nearest filter.

2.3.1 Stage 1: Shadow-Map Rendering

Shadow map rendering is performed as in typical games except that when we clear the depth stencil buffer to `ZFar` we also clear the stencil to zero. On hardware where we cannot read back the depth buffer afterwards, we can render the shadow map into a two-channel 16-bit texture, such as G16R16. The accompanying demo renders into a texture of this form.

We then render all objects into the shadow map with the computed depth stored in the R channel and we set the green to 1. In the case of rendering to a depth stencil texture, simply set the stencil states to always set the 8-bit stencil value to 255. This allows for the double speed Z only rendering on the consoles. It is possible to perform standard shadow mapping without the need for a separate channel, but by doing so it allows for a simple blurring stage afterwards.

A difference from common shadowing is that the Z-Buffer runs in reverse; 0.0f is as at the far plane and 1.0 is at the near plane with the depth test changed to a GREATER mode. This is used to allow for some optimizations when later blurring the shadow map in the next stage.

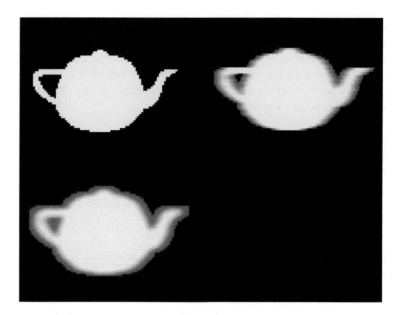

Figure 2.3. Gobo shadow map (top left), after horizontal blur (top right), and after vertical blur (bottom left).

2.3.2 Stage 2: Shadow-Map Blurring

In the next stage, the shadow map is blurred using a modified separable Gaussian blur.

This pass will do a standard Gaussian blur on the gobo component and will perform a weighted average of the depth values for any pixels that are equal to ZFar. That is, the blur will dilate out depth values into the initially empty unwritten space. Any pixels that already have a nonzero depth value written out during Stage 1 will not be affected. In the example, I use a G16R16 texture to store this information. You could also use two separate textures to store the depth and gobo components with different bit depths if the hardware allows for such rendering using MRTs.

Figure 2.3 shows the process of blurring the shadow map. Note that the red channel is the depth and these values are dilated out without blurring. The green channel is subject to a Gaussian blur.

2.3.3 Stage 3: Applying Shadows

In the forward render shader, the shadow map is tapped using a bilinear filtered texture sampler. The gobo component is made up of the shadow softness amount and the depth as a binary test to see if we need to use the softness at all, i.e.,

whether to set the gobo component to zero because the pixel is known to be fully
in light. The basic code is given in Listing 2.1.

```
float2 depthGobo = tex2D(shadowSampler, LightSpaceUV)

if(depthGobo.x < lightspaceZ) // Reject gobo if too close
    depthGobo.y = 0.0;

float keylightVisibility = 1.0 Ũ depthGobo.y;
```

Listing 2.1. Applying the gobo shadows.

The value stored in `keylightVisibility` can be used to modulate the key-
light $N \cdot L$ result. It is possible to remove the conditional using the code given
in Listing 2.2.

```
// Tune the 100 to sharpen the fadeout
depthGobo.y *=  saturate((depthGobo.x - lightspaceZ) * 100;
```

Listing 2.2. Removing the conditional.

The best way to think about this new shadowing is that rather than use depth
values in the shadow map to identify pixels that are in shadow, the depth is used
to indicate which pixels are *not* in shadow.

2.4 Extensions

2.4.1 Variable Penumbra

Instead of doing a binary comparison to see if pixels are in shadow or not, and
using the blurriness channel as is for the penumbra amount, the difference between
the stored Z value in the shadow map and the Z value from the surface in shadow
can be used to adjust the contrast on the softness value. So as the comparison gets
smaller, the contrast value increases to sharpen the shadow value. In extreme
cases, this can lead to very sharp shadows like shadow volumes. To allow the
penumbra to increase further, the prefiltered shadow maps can be mip-mapped.
If the distance to the receiver value is over a certain threshold, then an extra tap
is read from the mip-chain and this softness value can be used instead. However,
in these cases the blurriness value has to be conservatively blurred inwards to
avoid hitting failure cases where shadow casters start to overlap more in light
space (see Figure 2.4).

Figure 2.4. Variable penumbra by applying contrast based on the distance from receiver to caster.

2.5   Failure Case

The algorithm works best in large, relatively flat worlds. This is because the technique relies on the premise that shadow-casters are usually disjoint (i.e., not connected) when viewed in light space. There are cases where casters will overlap in shadow-map space with a receiver in-between. In these cases, the receiving surface will receive a blocky shadow from the caster that is overlapping with a more distant caster in light space. Generally these cases are very rare and hence these issues were ignored in games that shipped with this technique. In the demo there is an area where objects are rendered that exhibit this problem. A potential solution to this artifact is to render the world into the shadow map but with the stencil-write off. This will stop the more-distant shadow caster from being written into the shadow map with stencil-writes on.

Bibliography

[Donnelly and Lauritzen 06] William Donnelly and Andrew Lauritzen. "Variance Shadow Maps." Available at http://www.punkuser.net/vsm, 2006.

[Salvi 08] Marco Salvi. Exponential Shadow Maps, GDC 2008.

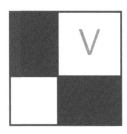

3D Engine Design

Welcome to the 3D Engine Design section of this edition of *GPU Pro*. The chapters you will find here cover various aspects of engine design, such as quality and optimization, in addition to high-level architecture.

First, Pascal Gautron, Jean-Eudes Marvie, and Gaël Sourimant present us with the article, "Z^3 Culling," in which the authors suggest a novel method to optimize depth testing over the Z-buffer algorithm. The new technique adds two "depth buffers" to keep the early-Z culling optimization even on objects drawn with states that prevent early-Z culling (such as alpha testing).

Next, Dzmitry Malyshau brings his experience of designing a quaternion-based 3D engine in his chapter, "Quaternion-Based Rendering Pipeline." Malyshau shows the benefits of using quaternions in place of transformation matrices in various steps of the rendering pipeline based on his experience of a real-world 3D-engine implementation.

In the article, "Implementing a Directionally Adaptive Edge AA Filter using DirectX 11," Matthew Johnson improves upon the box antialiasing filter using a postprocessing technique that calculates a best fit gradient line along the direction of candidate primitive edges to construct a filter that gives a better representation of edge information in the scene, and thus higher quality antialiased edges.

Finally, Donal Revie describes the high-level architecture of a 3D engine in the article "Designing a Data-Driven Renderer." The design aims to bridge the gap between the logical simulation at the core of most game engines and the strictly ordered stream of commands required to render a frame through a graphics API. The solution focuses on providing a flexible data-driven foundation on which to build a rendering pipeline, making minimal assumptions about the exact rendering style used.

I would like to thank the authors who contributed to this section for their great work. I would also like to thank my wife Suzan and my brother Homam for their wonderful support. I hope you find these articles inspiring and enlightening as you undertake your rendering and engine development work.

—Wessam Bahnassi

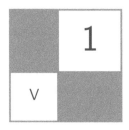

Z³ Culling

Pascal Gautron, Jean-Eudes Marvie, and Gaël Sourimant

1.1 Introduction

Virtual worlds feature increasing geometric and shading complexities, resulting in a constant need for effective solutions to avoid rendering objects invisible for the viewer. This observation is particularly true in the context of real-time rendering of highly occluded environments such as urban areas, landscapes, or indoor scenes.

Figure 1.1. In highly occluded scenes many fragments potentially cover a single pixel of the final image. Each of those fragments being shaded before getting eventually discarded by depth testing, this overlap results in a waste of computational power.

In those cases, even though many elements of the scene are occluded, the visibility tests are performed on the output of the shading stage. Complex shading is then evaluated for fragments that are eventually discarded by the depth tests (Figure 1.1).

This problem has been intensively researched in the past decades, resulting in numerous optimizations building upon the well-known Z-buffer technique. Among them, extensions of graphics hardware such as early-Z culling [Morein 00] efficiently avoid shading most of the invisible fragments. The only drawback of this technique is its reduced applicability range: early-Z culling is disabled if the fragment shader discards fragments or modifies their depth values, or if alpha testing is enabled [Nvidia 08]. While easily usable with simple shaders, more complex and costly shading techniques such as relief mapping [Policarpo and Oliveira 06] cannot benefit from such optimization. The principle of the programmable culling unit [Hasselgren and Akenine-Möller 07] solves this problem by introducing a specific programmable culling stage in the graphics pipeline. However, this stage is not yet embedded within current graphics hardware.

We introduce Z^3 culling for fast and programmable per-pixel visibility at the fragment-shading stage using alternate render buffers containing color and depth information. This method effectively avoids shading hidden fragments in a single pass, hence reducing the overall rendering costs while not introducing limitations

Figure 1.2. The overlapped fragments (shown in red) can be efficiently detected and discarded before shading, using Z^3 culling for increased performance. Unlike the early-Z culling approach, Z^3 culling is independent from shading operations, typically supporting programmable fragment discard and alteration of fragment depth, as well as alpha testing in this example.

on shader operations (Figure 1.2). Z^3 culling is also complementary with the existing culling stages of graphics hardware and could be easily integrated as an additional stage of the graphics pipeline.

1.2   Principle

Z^3 culling is a simple method for early detection of occluded fragments within the fragment shader. A first issue is the access to the occluder geometry: such detection requires the fragment shader to determine its own visibility compared to the rest of the scene. While the visibility is usually solved using the Z-buffer algorithm, most graphics APIs forbid binding the current depth buffer as a texture for use in the fragment shader.

We solve this problem using alternate render buffers: when rendering into a given buffer, depth information regarding previously rendered fragments is available in another buffer. The visibility of the fragments can then be evaluated efficiently using simple, cache-friendly texture fetches. We amortize the cost of swapping the render buffers by rendering object batches whose size can be adapted by real-time performance analysis.

Another key for the efficiency of the algorithm is the availability of relevant depth information: a reliable visibility information for a given fragment can be obtained only if all the potentially occluding geometry had been previously rendered. Based on this observation the object batches are ordered to optimize the occlusion detection.

1.3   Algorithm

The overall principle of Z^3 culling is illustrated in Figure 1.3. After allocating two RGBA buffers B_1 and B_2, B_2 is chosen as the current render target and B_1 is the source for existing color and depth. As shown in Algorithm 1.1, a batch of objects is rendered into B_2. For each fragment, the algorithm fetches the existing depth value stored in B_1 corresponding to the current location of the fragment. As B_1 is empty for this first batch, each fragment of the batch gets shaded: the resulting color and depth are stored into one RGBA value, in which the alpha channel encodes the depth of the fragment.

Then, B_1 becomes the current render target while B_2 holds the existing depth information. During the rendering of a second batch, the depths of the fragments are tested against the values stored in B_2: if the existing depth is smaller than the depth of the current fragment the fragment is not shaded, hence reducing the rendering time. The buffers are then swapped again for each object batch.

As buffers B_1 and B_2 only contain parts of the final image, the buffers are merged by selecting the pixels with the lowest depth value. Section 1.4 contains technical details for the implementation of Z^3 culling.

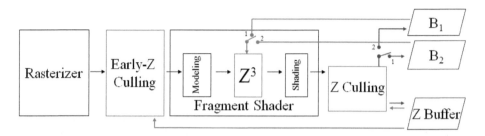

Figure 1.3. Z^3 culling is an additional, programmable depth-culling step at the fragment-shader stage. While rendering into B_2, the culling is performed using the partial depth information available in B_1 (Step 1). The buffers B_1 and B_2 are then swapped, hence maintaining information in both buffers (Step 2).

1.4   Implementation

Based on the high-level description of Z^3 culling presented in Algorithm 1.1, this section provides technical insights regarding buffer allocation and binding, splitting of the scene into batches, programmable culling, and buffer merging.

1.4.1   Framebuffer Setup and Binding

As current graphics APIs do not generally allow using the same memory area for both reading and writing, Z^3 culling considers two render buffers: a "read" buffer B_1 containing the closest previously rendered fragments, and a "write" buffer B_2 receiving the currently rendered fragments. Each of those buffers contain color information as well as depth values for each pixel: the combined color and depth information can be stored within a single floating-point RGBA buffer, where the alpha channel encodes the depth of the closest fragment.

Compared to a classical frame-buffer setup, this technique only introduces two additional render buffers, while keeping the classical color and Z-buffer untouched. Once the buffers are created, the read/write alternation can be performed by rendering the potentially visible objects as a set of batches: we first bind B_1 as the current render target and render a first object batch. Then, B_2 is bound as the render target while B_1 gets bound as a texture to serve as the source for previous fragment information. The second batch is then rendered, and the process is repeated for every batch of potentially visible objects.

At the end of the rendering of a frame, each render buffer contains a subset of the pixels of the final image. Each pixel contains both color and depth information. The final image is then obtained by combining B_1 and B_2, keeping only the closest pixels. To this end a screen-covering quad is rendered into the framebuffer, and a fragment shader outputs the pixels corresponding to the low-

---

Algorithm 1.1. (Z^3 culling.)

Initialization:
Create render buffers $B1$ and $B2$

Main loop:
for each frame **do**
   readBuffer $= B1$
   writeBuffer $= B2$
   for all object batch b **do**
      Bind writeBuffer as the render target and readBuffer as a texture[1]
      for all object o $\in$ b **do**
         for all fragment covered by o **do**
            // Compute fragment depth
            $d_{cur} = $ fragmentDepth(...)
            // Fetch the depth of the closest existing fragment
            $d_{ref} = $ readBuffer[fragmentCoord].a)
            // Compare current and reference depths
            if $d_{cur} < d_{ref}$ **then**
               // Shade current fragment and output its depth
               writeBuffer[fragmentCoord].rgb $= $ shade(...)
               writeBuffer[fragmentCoord].a $= d_{cur}$
            else
               // Abort fragment shading
            end if
         end for
      end for
      swap(writeBuffer, readBuffer)
     end for
     finalImage $= $ combine(writeBuffer, readBuffer)
   end for

---

est depth values (Listing 1.1[2]). Note that the fragment shader not only outputs the color of the pixels, but also their depth. This enforces the consistency of the depth buffer, hence allowing Z^3 culling to be used in conjunction with other rendering strategies. For example, opaque objects can be rendered using Z^3 culling, and transparent objects may be rendered with the classical back-to-front sorting, using the same depth buffer for visibility determination.

While the goal of the algorithm is the avoidance of overlapping fragments, objects within a given batch may overlap. In this case all the fragments of the

---

[1]The binding is typically performed using **glFramebufferTexture2D** and **glBindTexture** calls in OpenGL.
[2]The shader pseudocode follows the GLSL syntax.

```
uniform sampler2D B1, B2;

void main()
{
    // Fetch the color and depth information in each buffer
    vec4 colDepth1 = texture2D(colorDepth1, fragmentCoord);
    vec4 colDepth2 = texture2D(colorDepth2, fragmentCoord);

    // Compare the depths of each pixel of B1 and B2
    // and output depth and color of the closest pixel
    if ( colDepth1.a <= colDepth2.a)
    {
        gl_FragColor = vec4(colDepth1.rgb, 1.0);
        gl_FragDepth = colDepth1.a;
    }
    else
    {
        gl_FragColor = vec4(colDepth2.rgb, 1.0);
        gl_FragDepth = colDepth2.a;
    }
}
```

Listing 1.1. Combination of both render buffers to obtain the final image.

batch are rendered, relying on the classical depth test to determine the closest fragment after shading. The conservativeness of Z^3 culling is then ensured at the cost of some unnecessary computations for intra-batch visibility.

1.4.2   Depth Batching

As for early-Z culling, the basis of Z^3 culling is the knowledge of the depth of previously rendered fragments. Therefore, object ordering is as important as for early-Z culling. In a worst case scenario, the objects are rendered from back to front: in this case the current fragment is always closer to the viewpoint than the previously rendered fragments, hence preventing early culling.

In the spirit of early-Z culling, the object batches are roughly sorted from front to back to avoid this scenario. This is typically achieved by fast sorting of the bounding boxes of the objects. Besides the gain of culling efficiency, in many scenes objects with similar depths tend to be spread over image space (Figure 1.4). This observation subtends another performance increase: the more pixels are covered by a batch, the more information is available for culling the fragments of further batches.

Once the set of potentially visible objects has been divided into depth-sorted batches, the batches can be efficiently rendered into alternate render buffers using Z^3-enabled fragment shaders (see Figure 1.5).

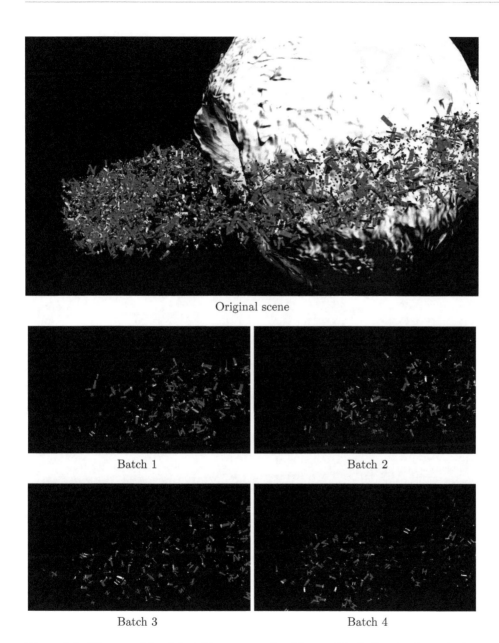

Original scene

Batch 1

Batch 2

Batch 3

Batch 4

Figure 1.4. The use of depth batching groups the objects with similar depths, reducing the overall amount of overlaps while spreading the rendered objects over large parts of the image space.

Figure 1.5. Once the object batches have been rendered using buffer alternation, approximately half of the rendered pixels is contained in each buffer, while the Z-buffer contains the depth information for the entire scene (top). The final image is obtained by compositing B_1 and B_2, keeping only the closest pixels (bottom).

1.4.3   Programmable Culling

Culling information is obtained using a simple texture fetch within the source for previous fragment information. Listing 1.2 provides a trivial implementation of the classical early-Z culling using Z^3 culling.

```
uniform sampler2D readBuffer;

void main()
{
    // Fetch previous depth information
    float refDepth = texture2D(readBuffer, fragmentCoord).a;
    float fragDepth = gl_FragCoord.z;

    // Compare current and previous depths
    if (fragDepth > refDepth )
    {
        // If occluded, discard the fragment
        discard;
    }
    else
    {
        // Otherwise perform shading
        gl_FragColor.rgb = shade(...);
        // and output the fragment depth in the alpha channel
        gl_FragColor.a = fragDepth;
    }
}
```

Listing 1.2. Naïve implementation of early-Z using Z^3 culling.

This example raises an important observation: a fragment determined as occluded is discarded, thus not generating any data in the framebuffer. However, the main principle of Z^3 culling is to populate both render buffers to allow for efficient visibility culling. A discard operation thus corresponds to a missed opportunity to add relevant information into the current render buffer. More precisely, let us consider the example depicted in Figure 1.6: An object O_1 is rendered into B_1, and an object O_2 is rendered into B_2. A fragment of O_2 occluded by O_1 is then discarded, leaving the corresponding location in B_2 empty. Then,

```
// Compare current and previous depths
if (fragDepth > refDepth )
{
    // If occluded, replicate the reference
    gl_FragColor = refFragment;
    gl_FragDepth = refDepth;
}
else
{
    // Otherwise perform shading
    gl_FragColor.rgb = shade(...);
    // and output the fragment depth in the alpha channel
    gl_FragColor.a = fragDepth;
}
```

Listing 1.3. Optimized early-Z using Z^3 culling with fragment replication.

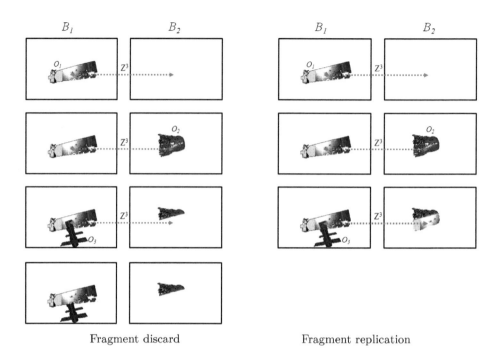

Fragment discard   Fragment replication

Figure 1.6. The information generated by rendering an object O_1 into a buffer B_1 (left, top row) is used to discard fragments of O_2 subsequently rendered into B_2 (left, second row, in red). When rendering O_3 into B_1, no information is available in B_2. The fragments of O_3 are then rendered (left, third row) and discarded after shading using the Z-buffer (left, bottom row). Replacing the fragments of the occludee O_2 by the fragments of the occluder O_1 propagates depth information across render buffers and avoids unnecessary shading of O_3 (right).

a fragment of an object O_3 rendered into B_1 is occluded by O_1. Due to the lack of information in B_2, Z^3 culling cannot detect the occlusion. The visibility test is then performed after shading using the classical Z-buffer.

To overcome this problem the discard operation can be advantageously replaced by a simple copy of the reference color and depth information. Relevant visibility is then propagated across buffers at virtually no cost, increasing the overall performance of the algorithm. In addition, the discard operation tends to introduce non-negligible costs into fragment shading, even on recent graphics hardware. Avoiding this call further reduces the execution time of the shader. Listing 1.3 provides the comparison and shading part of the implementation of early-Z culling.

Note that the culling and fragment replication can be performed at any stage of the shader to allow for fine performance tuning. For example, a shader con-

```
// Compare current and previous depths
if (fragDepth > refDepth )
{
    // If occluded, replicate the reference
    gl_FragColor = refFragment;
    gl_FragDepth = refDepth;
}
else
{
    // Otherwise compute alpha value
    float alpha = evalAlpha();
    // and perform Z3-friendly alpha test
    if (alpha < alphaThreshold)
    {
        gl_FragColor = refFragment;
        gl_FragDepth = refDepth;
    }
    else
    {
      // Evaluate costly shading if needed
        gl_FragColor.rgb = shade(...);
      // and output the fragment depth in the alpha channel
        gl_FragColor.a = fragDepth;
    }
}
```

Listing 1.4. Z³ culling with optimized alpha test.

taining complex alpha evaluation for alpha testing as well as complex shading may contain several exit paths (Listing 1.4).

Note that in this case the built-in alpha test is disabled to take full advantage of Z³ culling within the fragment shader: if the fragment does not pass the test, the shader propagates the fragment information from the reference buffer. In this regard Z³ culling takes particular advantage of situations where early-Z culling cannot be applied, making those approaches complementary.

More complex shaders can make further use of this technique. For example, a shape-altering algorithm such as relief mapping can perform culling at several stages to avoid unnecessary computations.

1.5 Performance Analysis

Z³ culling has been implemented within fragment shaders using an Nvidia GeForce GTX480. The presented scenes contains 15 K and 70 K objects featuring complex, early-Z unfriendly fragment shaders. The images are rendered into floating-point render buffers with a resolution of 1280×720. Compared to classical Z-buffering, Z³ culling provides performance increases of 8 to 50% using batches of 50 objects (Table 1.1), while remaining applicable in any context.

Scene	# triangles	# objects	Z	Early-Z	Z^3
Forest	70M	50K	90 ms	N/A ms	44.5 ms
Asteroids	35M	15K	215 ms	N/A ms	198 ms

Table 1.1. Render time comparisons between regular post-shading depth test and Z^3 culling (50 objects per batch). Due to the complexity of the shaders, early-Z culling is not applicable in this case.

The Z^3 culling technique provides significant speedups by introducing an alternation of render buffers as well as an early detection of occlusions within the fragment shader. In the remainder of this section, we analyze the costs of those operations and compare our technique with the built-in early-Z culling.

The alternation of render buffers described in our technique may generate pipeline stalls: rendering a batch into a buffer requires finishing all the previous operations on the reference buffer. In our test scenes the average cost of buffer swapping is around 25 μs per swap, typically representing an overhead of 5 ms (2.5%) per frame in the Asteroids scene with batches of 50 objects. We amortize the cost by adjusting the size of the object batches. This size can be adjusted either manually or automatically using a simple convergence based on the render time of the last frame. While the overhead does not completely vanish, the savings due to Z^3 culling remain significant, especially in scenes containing many objects. However, note that on certain platforms the use of a render target as a texture requires a "resolve" operation copying the contents of the render target into the texture. The cost of this operation must be taken into consideration while implementing our technique on such platforms.

Another overhead is the additional branching within the fragment shader: as shown in the above listings, the behavior of any shader using Z^3 culling depends on a depth test. This branching does introduce a cost, however this cost must be compared to the complexity of the shaders. In particular, Z^3 culling performs better on scenes containing very complex shaders, which typically also involve branching. This makes our approach complementary with early-Z culling: simple, nonbranching shaders without alpha testing or depth modification take full benefit of the built-in culling technique. Conversely, the rendering of objects featuring more complex shaders can be drastically optimized by Z^3 culling. In this regard, outputting the depth of the selected fragments at the end of rendering (Listing 1.1) proves particularly useful: simply-shaded objects can be rendered using classical techniques and combined with more complex shaders whose visibility is evaluated using Z^3 culling.

The analysis of the performance of Z^3 culling also requires a comparison with early-Z culling. However, as mentioned above, the test scenes shown in this chapter feature shaders containing instructions not compliant with early-Z culling.

Scene	# triangles	# objects	Z	Early-Z	Z^3
Forest	70M	50K	88 ms	18 ms	42 ms
Asteroids	35M	15K	214 ms	135 ms	195 ms

Table 1.2. Degrading the shaders by removing the instructions incompatible with early-Z culling makes the final image unusable, as this process alters the appearance of the objects. However, this table provides a comparison of the rendering times for classical depth testing, early-Z culling, and Z^3 culling. The values confirm the high efficiency of the hard-wired early-Z culling for simple shaders. Both culling methods are then complementary depending on the type of shaders used in the scene.

To provide a fair comparison we degraded the shaders to avoid such instructions. While the final image gets altered and non-usable, Table 1.2 provides an informative analysis of the performance of early-Z culling and Z^3 culling. As expected the built-in early-Z culling outperforms Z^3 culling when the shading remains simple, making those approaches complementary: simply-shaded objects can be rendered using early-Z culling, while more complex shaders can leverage Z^3 culling for higher efficiency.

Another aspect of this technique is the potential false negatives in the occlusion detection: for a given fragment, the expensive shading step is carried out only if the fragment is determined as visible. However, the available visibility information is inherently approximate as each of the additional buffers holds only a part of the rendered fragments. Consequently, some fragments may be erroneously considered as visible. As for the intra-batch occlusion, this results in some unnecessary computations but ensures the conservativeness of our visibility algorithm. Note that this solution does not introduce artifacts, as the occluded fragments eventually get discarded after shading by classical depth testing.

1.6 Conclusion

This chapter introduced Z^3 culling for simple and programmable elimination of occluded fragments before shading. Based on an alternation of render buffers, this technique provides significant performance increases especially in highly occluded scenes containing numerous objects with complex shading. We believe further performance could be achieved by implementing Z^3 culling in an additional stage in future graphics hardware for programmable fragment elimination, potentially taking advantage of the hierarchical representation of depth buffers.

Bibliography

[Hasselgren and Akenine-Möller 07] Jon Hasselgren and Tomas Akenine-Möller. "PCU: The Programmable Culling Unit." *SIGGRAPH '07, Transactions on Graphics* 26:3 (2007), 92.

[Morein 00] S. Morein. "ATI Radeon Hyper-Z Technology." Hot3D Proceedings (talk), ACM SIGGRAPH/Eurographics Workshop on Graphics Hardware, 2000.

[Nvidia 08] Nvidia. "GPU Programming Guide Version for GeForce 8 and Later GPUs." http://developer.download.nvidia.com/GPU_Programming_Guide/GPU_Programming_Guide_G80.pdf, 2008.

[Policarpo and Oliveira 06] Fabio Policarpo and Manuel M. Oliveira. "Relief Mapping of Non-Height-Field Surface Details." In *ACM SIGGRAPH Symposium on Interactive 3D Graphics and Games*, pp. 55–62. New York: ACM Press, 2006.

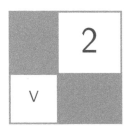

2

A Quaternion-Based Rendering Pipeline

Dzmitry Malyshau

2.1 Introduction

A matrix is the first thing every graphics developer faces when building an engine. It is a standard data object for representing 3D affine and projection transformations—covering most of the game developer's needs. Matrix operations have even been implemented in hardware used by a 3D graphics API like OpenGL. However, this is not the only way to represent transformations.

Quaternions were introduced by Sir William Rowan Hamilton in the middle of the nineteenth century, at a time when vector analysis did not exist. A quaternion is a hypercomplex 4D number of the form: $w + xi + yj + zk$. There are rules for quaternion multiplication, inversion, and normalization. Quaternions can effectively represent spatial rotations, by applying them to 3D vectors or when converted into 3×3 rotation matrices.

This chapter aims to explain pitfalls and advantages of the quaternion approach for graphics pipelines. There are many articles describing quaternion mathematics, such as [Void 03] and [Gruber 00], which we will not cover here, assuming that the reader is familiar with the basics. We will describe the KRI Engine (see [Malyshau 10a]) as a sample implementation of a complete quaternion-based rendering pipeline.

2.2 Spatial Data

Spatial transformation data combine *rotation*, *position*, and *scale*. Let's compare the most popular representation (i.e., a homogeneous matrix) with a new representation based on a quaternion (see Table 2.1).

We can conclude that quaternion representation is much more complex with regard to transformations in shaders, the manual perspective transform, and other

Type	Matrix	Quaternion (fixed handedness)
struct Spatial (*1)	mat3 rotation_scale; vec3 position;	quaternion rotation; vec3 position; float scale;
vectors to store (four-component)	three	two
understanding difficulty	easy	medium
interpolation flexibility (*2)	low	high
combining transforms cost	high	medium
applying transforms cost	low	medium
hardware support (*3)	high	medium
non-uniform scale support	yes	no
perspective transform	can be added easily, resulting in mat4	manual only

*1. Hereafter we use GLSL types (vec3,vec4,mat3,mat4,etc.).

*2. For the quaternion approach, you can use spherical linear interpolation (SLERP) or use dual-quaternion representation with little to no difficulty.

*3. Currently, there is no shading language with direct support of quaternions operations. The only exception is the normalization operator, which uses a fast built-in function for vec4. However, other operations are easily written via traditional built-in cross and dot vector products (see quat_v.glsl).

Table 2.1. Comparison of homogeneous matrix versus quaternion transformation.

issues, but that it provides definite benefits like interpolation flexibility and more efficient storage, which are critical for dynamic graphics scenes.

2.3   Handedness Bit

One of the major differences between rotation matrices and quaternions is the handedness property. Matrices operate freely between right-handed and left-handed coordinate systems. Quaternions do not have this property (always preserving the given handedness upon transformation), so we need to define the corresponding matrix handedness globally and store the actual value together with the quaternion itself. For an orthonormal matrix M, handedness is equal to the determinant and computed as follows:

$$H = \text{Handedness}(M) = \det(M) = ((\text{Row}(0, M) \times \text{Row}(1, M)) \cdot \text{Row}(2, M)).$$

$$(2.1)$$

The handedness of an orthonormal matrix can be either $+1$, in which case it is right-handed, or -1, in which case it is left-handed. Assuming we defined quaternions to correspond to right-handed matrices with regard to the vector rotation, we can implement the matrix conversion routines as well as the direct point transformation by a quaternion. Rotation matrix handedness is usually fixed in 3D editors (this applies to Blender and 3DsMax), so our initial assumption is not an issue. However, when a matrix is constructed from arbitrary basis vectors (e.g., tangent space), its handedness can also be arbitrary—and that is a problem.

The issue can be resolved by adding a bit of information to the quaternion: the handedness bit. The algorithm for the matrix processing in the quaternion approach is given in Algorithm 2.1.

Algorithm 2.1. (Calculating and applying the handedness bit.)

---

1. Given basis vectors, construct matrix M

2. Calculate handedness H, using Equation (2.1)

3. We have to make sure that M is right-handed before converting it to a quaternion. In order to achieve this we are going to multiply the first row of the matrix by the scalar H: Row(0,M) = Row(0,M) * H. This would not change the right-handed matrix (H == 1), but it would flip the handedness of a left-handed one (H == −1)

4. Transform to quaternion, Q = Quaternion(M)

5. Store (Q,H), instead of a matrix M

6. V'T(V) = Rotate(Q,V) * (H,1,1), negating x-coordinate of the transformation vertex V'

We give here some example Blender API Python code that converts a tangent space into the quaternion:

```
bitangent = normal.cross(tangent.normalized())       # derive the bitangent from the mean
                                                     # tangent and a normal
bitangent *= vertex.face.handedness                  # compensate for the opposite handedness
tangent = bitangent.cross(normal)                    # orthogonalize the tangent, defer
                                                     # handedness multiplication to the
                                                     # shader
tbn = mathutils.Matrix((tangent,bitangent,normal))   # composing ortho-normal right-handed
                                                     # tangent space matrix
vertex.quaternion = tbn.to_quaternion().normalized() # obtain the quaternion representing
                                                     # the vertex tangent space
```

2.4 Facts about Quaternions

Here we address some facts and myths about quaternions in an attempt to correct the common misunderstandings of their pros and cons and to provide needed information for using quaternions.

2.4.1 Gimbal Lock

According to Wikipedia, gimbal lock is the loss of one degree of freedom in a three-dimensional space that occurs when the axes of two of the three gimbals are driven into a parallel configuration, "locking" the system into rotation in a degenerate two-dimensional space. Gimbal lock is an attribute of the Euler angle representation of the rotation. Contrary to what some people believe, gimbal lock has nothing to do with either matrices or quaternions.

2.4.2 Unique State

There are always two quaternions (−Q, component-wise negative) that produce exactly the same rotation, thus representing the same state.

2.4.3   No Slerp in Hardware

Graphics hardware can linearly interpolate values passed from the vertex geometry into the fragment shader. One may conclude that quaternions should not be
interpolated this way, because spherical linear interpolation is the only correct
way to do that.

In fact, after normalizing the interpolated quaternion in the fragment shader
we get normalized Lerp (or Nlerp), which is very close to Slerp. According to
[Blow 04] it follows the same minimal curve; it just does not keep the constant
velocity. So for 3D meshes, it is perfectly fine to use hardware for interpolation
of quaternions.

It's important to note that Nlerp produces a larger error, the larger the angle
is between quaternions as four-component vectors. While this may seem to be a
problem, in fact the error is just four degrees for a 90-degree angle, according to
calculations by [Kavan et. al 06]. In practice, we need this HW interpolation for
vertex data, and your rendered mesh is not going to look smooth anyway if its
normals differ by more than 90 degrees on a single face.

2.4.4   Hypercomplex Four-Dimensional Number

You don't need to know the complete mathematical background of quaternions in
order to use them. Knowledge of the following operations is sufficient for graphics
developers: inversion, multiplication, interpolation, and applying rotation to a
vector.

The GLSL code for a sample rotation application is given below:

```
vec3 qrot(vec4 q, vec3 v)   {
    return v + 2.0*cross(q.xyz, cross(q.xyz,v) + q.w*v);
}
```

2.5   Tangent Space

Tangent space is an orthonormal coordinate system of a surface point, constructed
from the tangent, bi-tangent, and normal. It is used for normal mapping as the
basis for normals stored in the texture. Object-space normal maps suffer from
reduced reusability across different meshes (and mesh parts—for texture tiling)
in comparison to tangent-space normal maps. The latter also support skinning
and morphing of the object that is normal-mapped; the only requirement is not to
miss the tangent space while processing the vertex position. Quaternions are very
effective for representing the tangent space. We will show this by comparing the
traditional pipeline (via a tangent-space matrix, also known as TBN—an acronym
for tangent, bi-tangent, normal) with a new pipeline based on quaternions.

2.5.1   TBN Pipeline

A 3D modeling program may provide both normal and tangent vectors, or just
a normal vector for exporting. In the latter case, your engine has to generate
tangents based on UV coordinates (exactly those used for normal mapping): in
this case, the tangent is calculated as a surface parametrization following the
orientation of the U-axis of the UV. Each vertex stores both normal and tangent
resulting in two vectors or six floats.

In the case of direct Phong lighting calculations, we just need to transform
a few vectors into the tangent space (namely the light vector and the view/half
vector). Then, the GPU pipeline interpolates them between vertices. We evaluate
the lighting using these two vectors and a surface normal fetched from a map.
The tangent space matrix is constructed by simply crossing the normal with the
tangent (their length and orthogonality can be ensured by the engine):

```
mat3 tbn = mat3(Tangent, cross(Normal,Tangent) ,Normal);
```

But there are scenarios where you need to interpolate the basis itself, for
example to store it in textures for particles or hair to be generated from it afterwards. First, if you need to store the basis, it will occupy two textures, seriously
affecting the storage requirements. Second, interpolated basis vectors are neither
orthogonal (in general) nor do they have unit lengths. The construction of the
TBN matrix is more costly in this case:

```
in vec3 Normal,Tangent;
vec3 n = normalize(Normal);
vec3 t = normalize(Tangent);
vec3 b = cross(n, t);
t = cross(b,n); //enforce orthogonality
mat3 tbn = mat3(t,b,n);
```

2.5.2   Quaternion Pipeline

The TBN matrix can be replaced by the pair: (quaternion, handedness). Each
vertex stores a single quaternion and a handedness bit: This requires 1+ vectors
or four floats and one bit. For example, the KRI engine stores handedness in the
Position.w component, supplying an additional quaternion as **vec4** for TBN.

Note that the normal is no longer needed—only the quaternion is provided by
the exporter and expected to be present for the renderer. This change introduces
a difficulty for the handling of objects with no UV coordinates, because we can't
compute either tangents or quaternions for them. Hence, it will be impossible to
compute even regular Phong lighting in contrast with the traditional approach
where the normal vector is always available. This limitation can be alleviated
by making all objects UV-mapped before exporting. Another solution is to have
a hybrid pipeline that switches between quaternion-rich and normal-only inputs,
but the implementation of such a dual pipeline is complex.

For direct Phong lighting calculations, we rotate vectors by our quaternion and apply the handedness bit as described in Algorithm 2.1. Computation-wise, it is not much more costly than the matrix pipeline, especially taking into account the general low cost of vertex shader computations (assuming that the number of fragments processed is significantly greater than the number of vertices, which should be the case for a properly designed engine).

In a more complex scenario, as in deferred lighting calculation, or baking the world-space surface basis into UV textures, the quaternion approach shows its full power. Storing the surface orientation requires only one texture (if you supply handedness in the position). Interpolation of the quaternion requires a special one-time condition to be met (an algorithm to accomplish this is presented below). At runtime an interpolated quaternion requires just a single normalization call:

```
in vec4 Orientation;
vec4 quat = normalize(Orientation);
```

Note that it is possible to not keep handedness as a vertex attribute (and pass it as a uniform instead) if one decides to split the mesh into two, each part containing all faces of the same handedness. In this case we would need to draw two meshes instead of one for each mesh consisting of faces with different handedness. This would save us a single floating-point operation in vertex attributes, but it would almost double the number of draw calls in a scene.

We can therefore conclude that quaternions require special handling: additional common routines in shaders, an additional preparation stage in the exporter (see Algorithm 2.2), and correct handedness application. But if they are handled properly, quaternions significantly reduce the bandwidth utilization and storage requirements. In advanced scenarios, they are extremely cheap computation-wise, compared to matrices.

2.6   Interpolation Problem with Quaternions

The interpolation problem originates from the fact that Q and $-Q$ represent exactly the same orientation (Q is any quaternion). Hence, by interpolating between the same orientation represented with different signs, we produce a range of quaternions covering the hypersphere instead of just a constant value. In practice, this means that in a fragment shader the quaternion interpolated between vertex orientations will, in general, be incorrect.

The solution for this problem is a special preprocessing technique on the mesh, performed during the export stage. The technique ensures that $dot(Q1,Q2)>=0$ for each two orientations of vertices in the triangle, forcing all vertices of the triangle to be in the same four-dimensional hemisphere. The algorithm for processing each triangle is given in (Algorithm 2.2).

Algorithm 2.2. (Triangle preprocessing that guarantees correct quaternion interpolation.)

---

let Negative pair = a vertex pair, whose quaternions produce a negative dot product.
let N = number of negative pairs in the current triangle.
to Negate quaternion = multiply all its components by −1.
if N==0: OK, exit
if N==2: clone the common vertex (between two given negative pairs), negate the cloned
quaternion; go to N==0 case
if N==3: clone any vertex, negating the quaternion; go to N==1 case
if N==1: divide the edge between a negative pair by inserting a vertex in the middle
with attributes averaged from the pair (including quaternion); go to N==0 case.

As you can see, this procedure duplicates some vertices and even creates some faces. This doesn't look good at first, because we don't want to complicate meshes for drawing. However, the actual number of vertices added is quite small. For example, the test 10 K vertex mesh gains only 7.5% additional vertices and 0.14% additional faces.

While interpolation with quaternions is a complicated process, a solution is available preprocessing the data as described in Algorithm 2.2. Additionally, you may not need to interpolate the TBN of the vertices at all. For Phong lighting, for example, you can interpolate the light and camera vectors in tangent space. Interpolation of TBN quaternions (aside from being handy) is needed when lighting and normal extraction are separated (as for deferred techniques). When using this algorithm, the handedness becomes a property of a face as well as a property of a vertex, because each face now links vertices of the same handedness.

2.7 KRI Engine: An Example Application

The KRI engine's rendering pipeline works in the OpenGL 3 core context and does not contain matrices, but instead uses quaternions for both spatial transformations and tangent spaces.

2.7.1 Export

The exporter from Blender is written in Python. It computes a (normal, tangent) pair for each vertex, producing a (quaternion, handedness) pair. A special stage (Algorithm 2.2) duplicates a small number of vertices and faces in order to ensure the correct quaternion interpolation for the rendering. Transformation matrices for each spatial node are also converted into (quaternion, position, scale) form, ensuring uniform scale and uniform handedness across the scene.

2.7.2   Storage

Tangent space for vertices (as a quaternion) is stored as a `float vec4` attribute, and the handedness occupies the `Position.W` component. Spatial data uses the (quaternion, position, scale) form and is passed to the GL context as two vectors.

2.7.3   Skinning

Vertex data is skinned in a separate stage using transform feedback. Bone transformations are interpolated (on the CPU) and weighted (on the GPU) using a dual-quaternion representation (this is optional). Smaller spatial structure size allows the passing of 50% more bones in the shader uniform storage.

2.7.4   Render

A special GLSL object file (`quat_v.glsl`) is attached to each program before linking. It contains useful quaternion transformation functions that are missing from the GLSL specification. There are render components that use forward and deferred Phong lighting, as well as surface baking into UV textures (e.g., emitting particles/hair from the mesh surface, as used in [Malyshau 10b]).

An example of typical vertex transformation GLSL code (excluding projection) is given here:

```
uniform struct Spatial  {
    vec4 pos, rot;         // camera->world and model->world transforms
}s_cam, s_model;
// vertex attributes of position and quaternion
in vec4 at_vertex, at_quat;
// forward transform of a vertex (from quat_v.glsl)
vec3 trans_for(vec3,Spatial);
// inverse transform of a vertex (from quat_v.glsl)
vec3 trans_inv(vec3,Spatial);
. . .
vec3 v_world = trans_for(at_vertex.xyz, s_model); // world-space position
vec3 v_cam = trans_inv(v_world, s_cam);     // camera-space position
```

2.8   Conclusion

The OpenGL 3 core / ES 2.0 pipeline no longer pushes the programmer to use matrices. In this article, we showed some advantages of using quaternions and pointed out the complexities associated with them. We also used the KRI engine as a proof-of-concept for the idea of using quaternions as a full-scale matrix replacement in a real-world game engine scenario. We believe that quaternions will have a future much brighter than their past.

Bibliography

[Banks 94] Dadid C. Banks. "Illumination in Diverse Codimensions." In *Proceedings of SIGGRAPH '94, Computer Graphics Proceedings*. Annual Conference Series, edited by Andrew Glassner, pp. 327–334, New York: ACM Press, 1994.

[Blow 04] Jonathan Blow. "Understanding Slerp, Then Not Using It." *The Inner Product*. Available at http://number-none.com/product, Apr 2004.

[Gruber 00] Diana Gruber. "Do We Really Need Quaternions?" Game Dev.net. Available at http://www.gamedev.net/page/resources/_/do-we-really-need-quaternions-r1199, Sept 2000.

[Hast 05] Anders Hast. "Shading by Quaternion Interpolation." In WSCG (Short Papers), 53–56, 2005. Available at http://wscg.zcu.cz/wscg2005/Papers_2005/Short/B61-full.pdf.

[Kavan et. al 06] Ladislav Kavan, Steven Collins, Carol O'Sullivan, and Jiri Zara. "Dual Quaternions for Rigid Transformation Blending." Technical report TCD-CS-2006-46, Trinity College, Dublin, 2006.

[Malyshau 10a] Dzmitry Malyshau. "Quaternions." *KRI Engine*. Available at http://code.google.com/p/kri/wiki/Quaternions, 2010.

[Malyshau 10b] Dzmitry Malyshau. "Real-Time Dynamic Fur on the GPU." GameDev.net. Available at http://www.gamedev.net/page/resources/_//feature/fprogramming/real-time-dynamic-fur-on-the-gpu-r2774, Oct 2010.

[McMahon 03] Joe McMahon. "A (Mostly) Linear Algebraic Introduction to Quaternions." Program in Applied Mathematics, University of Arizona, Fall 2003.

[Svarovsky 00] J. Svarovsky. "Quaternions for Game Programming." In *Game Programming Gems*, edited by Mark DeLoura, pp. 195–299. Hingham, MA: Charles River Media, 2000.

[Void 03] Sobeit Void. "Quaternion Powers." GameDev.net. Available at http://www.gamedev.net/page/resources/_/reference/programming/math-and-physics/quaternions/quaternion-powers-r1095, Feb 2003.

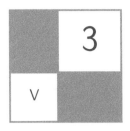

Implementing a
Directionally Adaptive Edge
AA Filter Using DirectX 11
Matthew Johnson

3.1 Introduction

With the advent of DirectX 10 and beyond, more and more features are being offloaded from fixed-function hardware to programmable shaders. Until recently, the lack of flexible access to the sample information in antialiased (AA) buffers required developers to rely on fixed-function hardware filtering to convert these buffers to single-sample representations. Now, with access to sample information, developers seek even higher quality results with the same memory footprint. This allows the creation of new techniques to balance the performance and quality of the rendered images being generated.

This chapter describes a postprocessing AA technique, directionally adaptive edge antialiasing, based on the paper by [Iourcha et al. 09]. In this technique, the sample information is used to calculate a best-fit gradient line along the direction of candidate primitive edges to construct a filter that gives a better representation of edge information in the scene.

3.1.1 Standard Multisampling

Unlike supersampling, multisampling occurs at pixel (not sample) frequency for color samples, using the coverage information at discrete sample points to resolve[1] to a single sample texture. In the center of a triangle where the scan converter is rendering an interior pixel, there is no image quality advantage with multisampling aside from the texture filtering/interpolation. At primitive edges,

---

[1]The process of taking a buffer with multiple samples per pixel and generating a buffer with a single sample per pixel is defined as *resolving* the buffer.

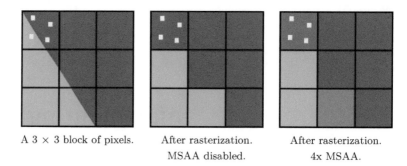

A 3 × 3 block of pixels.   After rasterization.   After rasterization.
                           MSAA disabled.   4x MSAA.

Figure 3.1. A 3 × 3 region of pixels.

however, the hardware has access to the neighboring samples as well as coverage information. The standard resolve operation will blend the color value of every sample in a pixel using a simple box filter.

The performance win in multisampling is not necessarily in memory (a multisampled surface at 4x MSAA can be four times the size), but in performance. Ideally (unlike supersampling), there is no need to execute the pixel shader more than once per pixel.

When multisampling is disabled, any pixel center inside a triangle is drawn. This is shown in Figure 3.1. When multisampling is enabled, if one or more samples are covered by the triangle, then the pixel shader is executed once and the resultant color is replicated for all covered pixels. In Direct3D 10.1 and above, a pixel shader can also run at sample rate; however, this feature is orthogonal to adaptive edge AA.

As shown in Figure 3.1, the 4x MSAA sample pattern in the upper left pixel shows three out of four samples that are covered (e.g., an edge pixel). A simple box filter resolve will calculate the final pixel color as

$$\frac{3 \times \text{red} + 1 \times \text{blue}}{4}. \tag{3.1}$$

Although the box filter is sufficient in many cases, it is not a panacea: the box filter resolve utilizes no information about neighboring samples to determine an even closer estimate of the actual slope of the primitive edge being rendered. With additional information, an even better antialiasing filter can be constructed.

3.1.2   Directionally Adaptive Edge Multisampling

As demonstrated in Equation (3.1), a simple box filter only averages the samples available to it in each individual pixel. This limitation is especially noticeable at steep edges or low-frequency data, in which the gradual changes in gradient between adjacent pixels can be lost. In the example of one red and one blue tri-

Red	Blue
0%	100%
25%	75%
50%	50%
75%	25%
100%	0%

Table 3.1. Color permutations in Figure 3.1 (4x MSAA).

angle being rendered, Table 3.1 shows that the number of unique color gradations along the edge is limited by the total sample count.

An alternative AA filter is called *directionally adaptive edge antialiasing*. The key difference is that instead of evaluating a simple box filter, it evaluates an edge filter by finding a best-fit "gradient" vector perpendicular to the triangle edge.

Figure 3.2 visualizes a close-up of a triangle edge rasterized with no AA, with 4x MSAA, and with adaptive edge AA. The quality improvement with directionally adaptive AA is more pronounced on longer, straighter edges. Along the triangle edge, the color value is the average of red and blue. Perpendicular to the edge, the color value varies smoothly between solid red and solid blue.

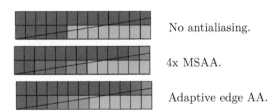

No antialiasing.

4x MSAA.

Adaptive edge AA.

Figure 3.2. Close-up of triangle edge rasterization.

3.1.3 Adaptive Edge Equation

Iourcha, Yang, and Pomianowski constructed an approximation equation for the estimated color value $f(v)$ of any sample position by taking into account the slope of the triangle edge and a "gradient" perpendicular to the triangle edge [Iourcha et al. 09]:

$$f(v) \approx \tilde{f}(\vec{g} \cdot v) = C_1(\vec{g} \cdot v) + C_0, \qquad (3.2)$$

where $v, \vec{g} = [x, y] \in \mathbb{R}_2$, constants $C_0, C_1 = [\text{red}, \text{green}, \text{blue}] \in \mathbb{R}_3$, and $\tilde{f}$ is an approximation function that inputs a scalar and returns a color. The gradient $\vec{g}$ is a 2D vector and is perpendicular to the rasterized triangle edge. Although not a true gradient, this vector points in the direction of the color gradation. Position v is any arbitrary 2D pixel or sample coordinate on the Cartesian grid.

This approximation equation allows us to estimate the color of any sample position in a given pixel, instead of the set of sample colors bounded by the MSAA sample count.

To solve for $\tilde{f}$ in this equation, it is necessary to find the gradient vector. For easier calculation, Equation (3.2) is centered by substituting $v_i = v_i - \bar{v}$ and $f(v_i) = f(v_i) - \overline{f(v)}$ such that

$$\sum_{i=0}^{n} v_i = 0 \quad \text{and} \quad \sum_{i=0}^{n} f(v_i) = 0,$$

where n is the number of color samples, v_i is the raster sample position (x, y), $\bar{v}$ is the mean of all sample positions, and $\overline{f(v)}$ is the mean of all color samples. Then $C_0 = 0$ and C_1 is a constant relative to the original C_0. Because the gradient is a vector and vectors are directionally invariant to translation, this is a valid substitution. Now, Equation (3.2) can be solved by finding the least squares fit,

$$F = \sum_{i=0}^{n} ||C_1(\vec{g} \cdot v_i) - f(v_i)||^2. \tag{3.3}$$

To solve this least squares fit, treat it like a vector minimization problem in calculus by solving for the derivative of F and setting each component equal to 0. Because this is a vector-valued function, that gives us $[\text{red}, \text{green}, \text{blue}]^{\text{T}}$ color values, the partial derivative of each color component is set to 0. Because $f(v_i)$ and v_i are centered, $C_0 = 0$ and Equation (3.2) becomes

$$f(v) \approx \tilde{f}(\vec{g} \cdot v) = C_1(\vec{g} \cdot v).$$

Let F be the sum of the least square difference between color value $f(v_i)$ and $f(\vec{g} \cdot v)$:

$$F = \sum_{i=0}^{n} ||\tilde{f}(\vec{g} \cdot v_i) - f(v_i)||^2. \tag{3.4}$$

The easiest way to evaluate this equation is to examine each component separately. Focus on the red component (subscript r):

$$f(v)_{\text{r}} \approx \tilde{f}(\vec{g} \cdot v)_{\text{r}} = \text{red}(\vec{g} \cdot v),$$

because the red component of C_1 is scalar r. Equation (3.4) becomes

$$F(r) = \sum_{i=0}^{n} (\tilde{f}(\vec{g} \cdot v_i)_{\text{r}} - f(v_i)_{\text{r}})^2$$

$$= \sum_{i=o}^{n} (r(\vec{g} \cdot v_i) - f(v_i)_{\text{r}})^2,$$

and

$$\frac{dF(r)}{dr} = \sum_{i=0}^{n} 2(\text{red}(\vec{g} \cdot v_i) - f(v_i)_{\text{r}})(\vec{g} \cdot v_i)$$

$$= 2\,\text{red}\sum_{i=0}^{n}(\vec{g} \cdot v_i)^2 - 2\sum_{i=0}^{n} f(v_i)_{\text{r}}(\vec{g} \cdot v_i).$$

Solving for the minimum by setting $dF(r)/dr = 0$ and then solving for the red component gives

$$\text{red} = \frac{\sum\limits_{i=0}^{n} f(v_i)_{\text{r}}(\vec{g} \cdot v_i)}{\sum\limits_{i=0}^{n}(\vec{g} \cdot v_i)^2}.$$

This is also done for the other two color components. Solving for C_1 yields

$$C_1 = \begin{bmatrix} \text{red} \\ \text{green} \\ \text{blue} \end{bmatrix} = \frac{1}{\sum\limits_{i=0}^{n}(\vec{g} \cdot v_i)^2} \begin{bmatrix} \sum\limits_{i=0}^{n} f(v_i)_{\text{r}}(\vec{g} \cdot v_i) \\ \sum\limits_{i=0}^{n} f(v_i)_{\text{g}}(\vec{g} \cdot v_i) \\ \sum\limits_{i=0}^{n} f(v_i)_{\text{b}}(\vec{g} \cdot v_i) \end{bmatrix}$$

$$= \frac{\sum\limits_{i=0}^{n} f(v_i)(\vec{g} \cdot v_i)}{\sum\limits_{i=0}^{n}(\vec{g} \cdot v_i)^2}. \tag{3.5}$$

Substituting Equation (3.5) into Equation (3.3) gives us the function to minimize. Expanding Equation (3.3) by using the vector form of the law of cosines and simplifying gives[2]

$$\sum_{i=0}^{n} ||f(v_i)||^2 = \frac{\left\|\sum\limits_{i=0}^{n} f(v_i)(\vec{g} \cdot v_i)\right\|^2}{\sum\limits_{i=0}^{n}(\vec{g} \cdot v_i)^2}. \tag{3.6}$$

Because the first sum is constant, only the second term should be maximized (giving us the minimum value because this term is negative):

$$\frac{\sum\limits_{i=0}^{n} ||f(v_i)||^2(\vec{g} \cdot v_i)^2}{\sum\limits_{i=0}^{n}(\vec{g} \cdot v_i)^2}. \tag{3.7}$$

---

[2]The derivation for this substitution is given in the appendix (Section 3.4).

The expression in Equation (3.7) is the ratio of two positive quadratic forms of $\vec{g}$,

$$\frac{\mathbf{A}\vec{g}\cdot\vec{g}}{\mathbf{B}\vec{g}\cdot\vec{g}},$$

where

$$\mathbf{A} = \mathbf{C}^{\mathrm{T}}\mathbf{C},$$

$$\mathbf{C} = \sum_{i=0}^{n} f(v_i)v_i{}^{\mathrm{T}} = \sum_{i=0}^{n} \begin{bmatrix} R_i \\ G_i \\ B_i \end{bmatrix} \begin{bmatrix} x_i & y_i \end{bmatrix},$$

$$\mathbf{B} = \sum_{i=0}^{n} v_i v_i{}^{\mathrm{T}} = \sum_{i=0}^{n} \begin{bmatrix} x_i \\ y_i \end{bmatrix} \begin{bmatrix} x_i & y_i \end{bmatrix}. \tag{3.8}$$

The vectors are column vectors.

Because each sample position in the set is centered, matrix $\mathbf{B}$ is a 2×2 matrix with a similar construct as a covariance matrix. If the sample positions in the sample pattern are constant relative to every pixel, it can be precalculated. If they are taken at integer pixel locations only, e.g.,

$$\begin{bmatrix} 0 \\ 0 \end{bmatrix}, \begin{bmatrix} \pm 1 \\ 0 \end{bmatrix}, \begin{bmatrix} 0 \\ \pm 1 \end{bmatrix}, \begin{bmatrix} \pm 1 \\ \pm 1 \end{bmatrix},$$

then $\mathbf{B}$ is $s\mathbf{I}$, where s is the distance in pixels from the center pixel. In the case of a 3×3 block of pixels, $s = 14$; hence,

$$\mathbf{B} = \mathbf{I} = \begin{bmatrix} 1 & 0 \\ 0 & 1 \end{bmatrix}.$$

Using a 3×3 pixel region is sufficient to calculate the gradient with reasonable speed and accuracy. Thus, it is only necessary to solve for $\mathbf{A}$. Because each sample position and color value is centered, matrix $\mathbf{A}$ is a 2×2 matrix with a similar construct as a covariance matrix. The value $\mathbf{A}\vec{g} \cdot \vec{g}$ is maximized when the resultant vector is parallel to $\vec{g}$. This occurs when $\mathbf{A}\vec{g} = \lambda\vec{g}$, where λ is an arbitrary scalar factor, turning it into an eigenproblem.

Let

$$\mathbf{A} = \begin{bmatrix} a & b \\ c & d \end{bmatrix};$$

then, solving for the characteristic equation, we have

$$\det \begin{bmatrix} a - \lambda & b \\ c & d - \lambda \end{bmatrix} = (a - \lambda)(d - \lambda) - bc$$

$$= \lambda^2 - (a + d)\lambda + (ad + bc). \tag{3.9}$$

Thus there are two solutions for the eigenvalues:

$$\lambda = \frac{a+d}{2} \pm \frac{\sqrt{4bc + (a-d)^2}}{2}.$$

With this matrix, we are interested only in the largest eigenvalue (the positive term), because its corresponding eigenvector is in the direction of the gradient. Solve for the eigenvector:

$$(\mathbf{A} - \lambda\mathbf{I})\vec{g} = 0, \quad \vec{g} \neq [0, 0, 0]^{\mathrm{T}}.$$

So $(\mathbf{A} - \lambda\mathbf{I})$ is singular. Within some application-defined epsilon, if $c \neq 0$, then

$$\vec{g} = \begin{bmatrix} \lambda - d \\ c \end{bmatrix};$$

else if $b \neq 0$, then

$$\vec{g} = \begin{bmatrix} b \\ \lambda - a \end{bmatrix}.$$

If both $b = c = 0$, the matrix is already diagonalized and $\vec{g}$ is any arbitrary 2D vector and should therefore be masked out. This occurs when the discriminate in Equation (3.9) is close to or equals 0.

3.1.4 Edge Pixels

Identifying edge pixels using an MSAA buffer is relatively simple. In DirectX 10 and beyond, you can iterate through all the samples and see if any of the sample color values differ; if they do, it is an edge pixel. This works pretty well, but because of texture coordinate extrapolation or precision issues the rasterizer may calculate a slightly different sample color on the same pixel for each triangle rendered that shares the same primitive edge. One way to filter out these small differences is to use an epsilon as shown in Listing 3.1.

```
bool compareSample(float3 c0, float3 c1)
{
    static const float eps = 0.001f;

    float3 d = abs(c0 - c1);

    return (d.r > eps) || (d.g > eps) || (d.b > eps);
}

float4 PS_EDGE_DETECT(VS_OUTPUT In) : SV_Target
{
    float width;
    float height;
    float sampleCount;
```

```
        tMs.GetDimensions(width, height, sampleCount);

        uint2 e;
        e.x = In.TexCoord.x * width;
        e.y = In.TexCoord.y * height;

        bool edgePixel = false;

        float3 c[4];
        c[0] = tMs.Load(e, 0);
        c[1] = tMs.Load(e, 1);
        c[2] = tMs.Load(e, 2);
        c[3] = tMs.Load(e, 3);

        if (compareSample(c[0], c[1]) ||
            compareSample(c[1], c[2]) ||
            compareSample(c[2], c[3]))
        {
            edgePixel = true;
        }

        if (edgePixel == false)
        {
            discard;
        }

        return float4(1.0f, 1.0f, 1.0f, 1.0f);
}
```

Listing 3.1. Detecting edge pixels with 4x MSAA.

Another way to check is to use centroid sampling and check SV_Position in the pixel shader (which is in screen space). If the position has shifted from the center, it is an edge pixel. In DirectX 11 you can also check SV_Coverage as input to the PS and verify that the mask is unequal to (1 << sampleCount) - 1. In the case of 4x MSAA, a pixel is an edge pixel if the coverage is not equal to 0xF. Unfortunately, while both of these techniques are valid, they will also pick up interior triangle edges as well (though the threshold pass may be able to filter these out).

3.1.5   Masking

Knowing the edge pixels from the previous pass, further pixels can be eliminated from processing by comparing every pixel in the scene by a set of masking patterns.

As shown in Figure 3.3, every center pixel can be validated against a set of 3×3 sample pattern masks to ensure that the pixel lies across a flat or diagonal edge that can be processed by this filter. If it does not match any of these patterns, then filtering is skipped and a standard resolve is used instead; for example, if the center pixel is the only edge pixel, the algorithm skips this pixel because it does not belong to a "dominate" edge [Iourcha et al. 09]. With DirectCompute,

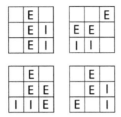

Figure 3.3. Sample masking patterns: E = edge pixel, I = interior pixel.

many of these passes can be combined. This will be discussed in the DirectX 11 implementation in Section 3.2.

3.1.6 Thresholding

Isolines are paths on a graph along which a particular value is constant. In this paper, the term is overloaded to include paths along edges of the image identified by the edge detect pass. Because this is a linear approximation filter, the best results are obtained when the isoline is flat and not curved.

To detect this scenario and eliminate further pixels, it is necessary to implement thresholding. The benefits of thresholding include that it

- speeds up postprocessing by focusing only on edges that will see quality improvements using the adaptive edge filter,

- avoids excessive blurring of corner features in the image,

- tweaks the amount that can be tweaked on a per-app basis.

For thresholding, we need to exclude pixels in which the curvature is too high. For the target pixel grids that benefit from this filter, simply use the standard MSAA resolve. Assuming v_i and $f(v_i)$ are centered, the difference between the actual color value and the estimated color value at a sample position (relative to our edge equation) is

$$\delta(v_i) = f(v_i) - C_1(\vec{g} \cdot v_i).$$

Because $\delta(v_i)$ is a vector, we want to calculate the total threshold as a magnitude of all these differences:

$$\sum_{i=0}^{n} ||\delta(v_i)|| = \sum_{i=0}^{n} ||f(v_i) - C_1(\vec{g} \cdot v_i)||. \tag{3.10}$$

Equation (3.10) can be solved by a simpler approximation. For example, it is easier to experimentally derive a threshold value across all pixels that look good for a particular application [Iourcha et al. 09]:

$$\frac{\sum\limits_{i=0}^{n} ||\delta(v_i)||^2}{\sum\limits_{i=0}^{n} ||f(v_i)||^2} \leq \text{threshold}^2, \tag{3.11}$$

where a pixel is rejected if Equation (3.11) is greater than the squared threshold.

3.1.7   Final Pixel Color

When you are calculating the final color, it is not necessary to actually solve for C_0 or C_1. Instead, for every pixel color, several samples are weighted among a 3×3 pixel grid, as shown in Figure 3.4.

To find this weight value for every sample position v_i, the procedure in Figure 3.4 constructs a line along the orthogonal of the gradient (the isoline) that intersects each sample position in the dashed rectangle in Figure 3.4. This rectangle is inscribed in the pixel region, aligns with the slope of the line, and bounds a set of sample positions that we are interested in weighting. Note that along this line, the color value does not change (because $(\vec{g} \cdot v_i) = 0$ and only C_0 remains), so the sample weight is influenced only by the slope of the line, not the distance between the sample position and the center pixel.

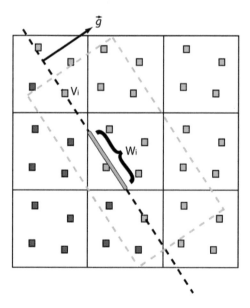

Figure 3.4. Sample weights along each isoline.

Finally, clip this line along the pixel boundaries. The length of this clipped line is the weight value. For every sample i, the weight is calculated as

$$w_i = ||(v_i + t_i \vec{g}_\perp||,$$

where n is the total number of color samples used for the approximation, v_i is the sample position in the inscribed rectangle, and $t_i = [t_{min}, t_{max}]$ are the floating-point minimum and maximum intersection values after the isoline is clipped to the center pixel boundary. These weight values are not normalized and may be greater than 1, so it is necessary to normalize the final color by the sum of all the weights:

$$color = \frac{\sum_{i=0}^{n} w_i f(v_i)}{\sum_{i=0}^{n} w_i}.$$

Every color sample k yields a unique clipped isoline, so t_{min} and t_{max} vary per sample. Weighting each color sample by the length of each clipped isoline acts as an integration model to yield the final pixel color [Iourcha et al. 09].

3.2 Implementation

3.2.1 DirectX 10 Implementation

The original paper by Iourcha, Yang, and Pomianowski describes a multipass approach that is useful for a DirectX 10 implementation [Iourcha et al. 09]. The following full-scene passes are described:

1. Identify edge pixels using MSAA buffer. Seed framebuffer by performing standard resolve.

2. Mask out candidate pixels using edge patterns.

3. Compute edge gradients for all masked pixels. Perform thresholding to further eliminate pixels.

4. Calculate the final framebuffer color as described in Section 3.1.7. Reading from the original MSAA surface, weight every sample color value in a 3×3 pixel grid for each candidate pixel.

3.2.2 DirectX 11 Implementation

According to [Thibieroz and Cebenoyan 10], compute shaders should target pixel shaders with a heavy texture or ALU bottlenecks. Because this algorithm is heavy on both, this is a potential candidate for compute shader optimizations.

As always, experimentation is needed to determine which path has the highest performance depending on the target platform. Dividing the full screen into 8×8 pixel blocks allows for the execution of 64 threads in parallel; this is the maximum number of threads per wavefront on current ATI hardware:

```
pDevice11->Dispatch(backBufferWidth/8, backBufferHeight/8, 1);
```

The following Compute Shader 5.0 pass is proposed:

1. Ensure the swap chain was created with DXGI_USAGE_UNORDERED_ACCESS bind flags. Seed by performing a standard resolve.

2. In the compute shader, create group shared memory to cache an 8×8 block of pixels, including room for border pixels outside the immediate block as shown in Listing 3.2.

```
struct Pixel
{
    float3 color[MsaaCount];
    bool   isEdgePixel;
};

groupshared Pixel pixelBlock[8+w][8+h];

[numthreads(8, 8, 1)]

void CSMain(uint2 blockIndex : SV_GroupThreadID,
            uint2 pixelIndex : SV_DispatchThreadId)
{

...

}
```

Listing 3.2. Shared memory for caching pixel blocks.

3. For a 3×3 pixel block, we only need a border of one pixel on each boundary side, so $w = h = 2$. To reduce thread-group shared memory (TGSM) in Shader Model 5.0, you can also pack colors in uint instead of float4 and pack edge pixel bitmasks (1 bit per pixel) in uint instead of bool, at the expense of more ALU operations. For example, you would need to use InterlockedAnd to clear the correct bitmask and InterlockedOr to set only the packed part; however, this could cause contention if multiple threads are operating atomically on the same shared memory location.

4. For each compute thread,

    (a) populate the color array with all the colors from the MSAA texture color,

    (b) compute whether the pixel is an edge pixel and store it in isEdgePixel.

5. Issue a GroupMemoryBarrierWithGroupSync to ensure all prior thread work has completed.

6. Mask out the candidate pixel using edge patterns, and continue if it passes the test. Masking is achieved by looking at the isEdgePixel of each pixel in the 3 ×3 neighborhood of the candidate pixel and comparing it to the edge mask pattern.

7. Compute the edge gradient for each pixel.

    (a) As an optimization, the number of samples n in Equation (3.8) can be reduced to nine: one pixel in each 3×3 pixel grid. Edge pixels that have different sample colors can be averaged out. In practice, this does not affect the accuracy of the calculated gradient [Iourcha et al. 09].

    (b) Perform thresholding to see if the pixel should be eliminated.

8. If the target pixel is not eliminated, calculate the final framebuffer color as described in Section 3.1.7.

    (a) Weight every sample color value in a 3×3 pixel grid for each candidate pixel.

    (b) Output the color to the framebuffer (bound as a UAV).

There are a few advantages to using a compute shader. Texture fetches are reduced because compute shader fetches are cached and stored in TGSM for a 10×10 pixel block $(8 + w, 8 + h)$. For every compute thread (each pixel), the 3×3 neighborhood of pixels can be cached in temporary registers to avoid fetching from TGSM more than once. This could reduce fetch overhead because the edge detect, edge gradient, and final color calculations require access to the same 3×3 neighborhood of color samples. On some architectures, flow control can save time by early exit of a complete 8×8 thread block. If an 8×8 thread block does not have any candidate pixels after thresholding, the final pass (Step 8) is skipped. Finally, API and driver overhead are eliminated by collapsing all passes into a single compute shader postprocess pass.

3.2.3 DirectX 11 Implementation on Downlevel Hardware

On some 10.x hardware platforms (such as the ATI Radeon 48xx series), a restricted form of Compute Shader is supported. Compute Shader 4.0 and 4.1 have the following restrictions:

- Only a single raw or structured UAV may be bound.

- Group shared memory is limited to 16 Kb.

- Group shared memory can be written only to an area indexed by SV_Group-Index.

- Only one group-shared variable may be declared.

- No access to atomic instructions, append/consume, double-precision, etc.

The difference between Compute Shader 4.0 and 4.1 is that the latter has access to Vertex Shader 4.1 model instructions.

The algorithm for downlevel hardware works similarly to the Compute Shader 5.0 model; however, there is no way to output to a Texture2D directly from a UAV. To work around this limitation, output to a buffer resource and then render a full-screen pass using a pixel shader to read from the buffer resource.

Another restriction (as already mentioned) is that group shared memory needs to be indexed by SV_GroupID when writing to it. Sixty-four compute threads are not enough to cover the whole 8×8 block with border pixels (in the case of a 3×3 region, this is a 10×10 pixel block). Therefore the numthreads will need to be increased (in the 10×10 case, 100 threads per thread group). Only compute threads that are in the 8×8 pixel block and that will write to the structured resource (e.g., the border pixel threads are only used to populate group shared memory). This restriction might necessitate adjusting the block size to have better performance for the target hardware; for example, one could divide the scene into 6×6 blocks, leaving 8×8 pixel blocks including the border pixels. To check support for Compute Shader 4.0, call CheckFeatureSupport with D3D10_X hardware options. If ComputeShaders_Plus_RawAndStructuredBuffers_Via_Shader_4_x is true, then downlevel computing is supported.

3.3   Conclusion

This paper describes a directionally adaptive edge antialiasing reference implementation for improving image quality with the same memory footprint of multisampling. It offers a clear and thorough mathematical derivation to fully explain the approach, so that any necessary adaptations can be made for quality or performance trade-offs. This work also gives an overview of DirectX 10 and DirectX 11 paths. AA research is a constantly moving field; newer and newer techniques are being developed continuously that have various performance and quality trade-offs. Understanding of different approaches paves the way for developing an algorithm that is the best fit for your game or application. Consult the bibliography and appendix for additional implementation or theoretical details.

3.4   Appendix

Substituting Equation (3.5) into Equation (3.3) gives us the function to minimize:

$$||A - B||^2 = ||A||^2 - 2A \cdot B + ||B||^2,$$

where

$$||A||^2 = ||C_1||^2 \sum_{i=0}^{n} (\vec{g} \cdot v_i)^2,$$

$$-2A \cdot B = -2C_1 \cdot \sum_{i=0}^{n} f(v_i)(\vec{g} \cdot v_i),$$

$$||B||^2 = \sum_{i=0}^{n} ||f(v_i)||^2.$$

The expression $2A \cdot B$ is simplified by moving the C_1-term outside the summation because

$$(s \cdot \vec{a}_0) + (s \cdot \vec{a}_1) + \ldots + (s \cdot \vec{a}_n) = s \cdot (\vec{a_0} + \vec{a}_1 + \ldots + \vec{a}_n)$$

and $(\vec{a}s \cdot \vec{b}) = (\vec{a} \cdot s\vec{b})$. Next, substitute the value of C_1 from Equation (3.5) and simplify:

$$||A||^2 = \left|\left|\frac{\sum_{i=0}^{n} f(v_i)(\vec{g} \cdot v_i)}{\sum_{i=0}^{n}(\vec{g} \cdot v_i)^2}\right|\right|^2 \sum_{j=0}^{n}(g \cdot v_j)^2,$$

$$-2A \cdot B = -2\left(\frac{\sum_{i=0}^{n} f(v_i)(\vec{g} \cdot v_i)}{\sum_{i=0}^{n}(\vec{g} \cdot v_i)^2}\right) \cdot \sum_{j=0}^{n} f(v_j)(\vec{g} \cdot v_j),$$

$$||B||^2 = \sum_{j=0}^{n} ||f(v_j)||^2.$$

To simplify the $||A||^2$ term, in general,

$$\frac{\sum_{j=0}^{n} a_j^2}{\left|\left|\sum_{i=0}^{n} a_i^2\right|\right|^2} = \frac{1}{\sum_{i=0}^{n} a_i^2},$$

because $i = j$ and n is the same. To simplify the $2A \cdot B$ term, note that

$$\sum_{i=0}^{n} \vec{a}_i \cdot \sum_{j=0}^{n} \vec{a}_j = \sum_{i=0}^{n} \vec{a}_i^2$$

because $i = j$, n is the same, and $(\vec{a} \cdot \vec{a}) = ||\vec{a}||^2$.

Moving $||B||$ to the left, simplifying, and combining like terms, we get Equation (3.6).

Bibliography

[Iourcha et al. 09] Konstantine Iourcha, Jason C. Yang, and Andrew Pomianowski. "A Directionally Adaptive Edge Anti-Aliasing Filter." In *Proceedings of the Conference on High Performance Graphics*, pp. 127–133. Edited by Stephen N. Spencer, David McAllister, Matt Pharr, and Ingo Wald. New York: ACM, 2009.

[Larson et al. 98] Ron Larson, Robert P. Hostetler, and Bruce H. Edwards. *Calculus with Analytic Geometry*, Sixth Edition. Boston: Houghton Mifflin, 1998.

[Lengyel 03] Eric Lengyel. *Mathematics for 3D Game Programming & Computer Graphics*, Second edition. Hingham, MA: Charles River Media, 2003.

[Thibieroz 09] Nicolas Thibieroz. "Shader Model 5.0 and Compute Shader." Game Developers Conference 2009. Available online (http://developer.amd.com/documentation/presentations/Pages/default.aspx).

[Thibieroz and Cebenoyan 10] Nicolas Thibieroz and Cem Cebenoyan. "DirectCompute Performance on DX11 Hardware." Game Developers Conference 2010. Available online (http://developer.amd.com/documentation/presentations/Pages/default.aspx).

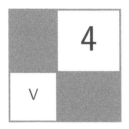

Designing a Data-Driven Renderer

Donald Revie

4.1 Introduction

Since the advent of hardware acceleration, rendering 3D graphics has been almost entirely achieved through the use of a handful of APIs. It is thus accepted that almost all engines that feature real-time 3D visuals will make use of one or more of these. In fact, as computing complexity and power increase, it becomes inconceivable that a single development studio could create proprietary code to access the abilities of hardware or implement all the newest techniques in fields such as physics and AI. Thus, engine development focuses more and more on integrating functionality exposed by APIs, be that hardware, OS features, or middleware solutions [Bell 10].

Each API is built using its own model and paradigms best suited to a specific problem domain, expressing in higher-level terms the structures and concepts of that domain. Graphics APIs are no different in this respect, typically exposing the hardware as a virtual device that must send relatively large amounts of information to the hardware when rendering each frame.

The engine itself can also be thought of as an interface, exposing a superset of the functionality found in all its components in a consistent manner. This interface forms the environment within which the core logic of the game or simulation is implemented. Thus, the engine must adapt the concepts and functionality of its constituent APIs to its own internal model, making them available to the game logic.

This chapter explores designing a renderer to bridge the gap between the logical simulation at the core of most game engines and the strictly ordered stream of commands required to render a frame through a graphics API. While this is a problem solved by any program used to visualize a simulated scene, the solution presented here focuses on providing a flexible data-driven foundation on which to build a rendering pipeline, making minimal assumptions about the exact rendering style used.

The aim is to provide a solution that will decouple the design of the renderer from the engine architecture. Such a solution will allow the rendering technology on individual projects to evolve over their lifetime and make it possible to evaluate or develop new techniques with minimal impact on the code base or asset pipeline.

4.2   Problem Analysis

So far we have defined our goal as exposing the functionality of a graphics API in a way consistent with our engine, placing emphasis on flexibility of rendering style. As a top-level objective this is sufficient but provides very little information from which to derive a solution. As already stated, every API is designed to its own model requiring its own patterns of use coinciding to a greater or lesser extent with that of the engine. To determine this extent and thus the task of any renderer module, both the API and the intended engine interface must be explored in detail. Discussion of these matters will be kept at a design or conceptual level, focusing on the broader patterns being observed rather than on the specifics of implementation in code. In this way the problem domain can be described in a concise manner and the solution can be applicable to the widest possible range of graphics API and engine, regardless of language or other implementation details.

4.2.1   Graphics API Model

Most graphics APIs belong to one of two groups, those based on the OpenGL standards [Shreiner et al. 06] and those belonging to Microsoft's Direct3D family of libraries [Microsoft 09]. At an implementation level, these two groups are structured very differently: OpenGL is built on the procedural model informed by its roots in the C language, and Direct3D has an object-oriented structure using the COM (Component Object Model) programming model. Despite this, the underlying structure and patterns of use are common to both groups [Sterna 10] (and most likely all other APIs as well). Above this implementation level we can work with the structures and patterns common to all graphics APIs and define a single model applicable to all.

No doubt many of these concepts will be very familiar to most graphics programmers, however in programming how a thing is thought about is often more important than what that thing is. Therefore, this section is intended to achieve a consensus of view that will form the foundation for the rest of the chapter. For instance, this section is not concerned with what the graphics API does, only the patterns of interaction between it and the application.

Graphics device. The graphics API is designed to wrap the functionality of hardware that is distant from the main system architecture, be it an expansion card with self-contained processor and memory or a completely separate computer accessed via a network connection; communication between the main system and the graphics hardware has historically been a bottleneck. This distance is addressed by the concept of a virtual device; the exact term varies between APIs. Differing hardware devices, and even software in some cases, are exposed as a uniform set of functionality that can be roughly divided into three groups:

1. *Resource management.* This controls the allocation and deallocation of device-owned memory, typically memory local to the hardware device, and controls direct access to this memory from the main system to avoid doing so concurrently from both the main system and the graphics hardware.

2. *State management.* Operation of the graphics hardware is too complicated to pass all pertinent information as parameters to the draw function. Instead, execution of the draw command is separated from the configuration of the device. Calling such functions does not modify the device resources in any way and their effects can be completely reversed.

3. *Execution.* This executes a draw or other command (such as clearing a framebuffer) on the current device configuration. The results may permanently modify resources owned by the device.

Graphics pipeline. The main function of the graphics device is to execute draw commands, thus much of the device is dedicated to this task. The core of the device is structured as a series of stream processing units (Figure 4.1), each with

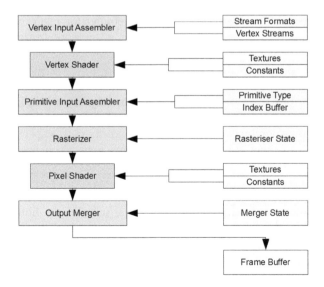

Figure 4.1. Pipeline (DX9).

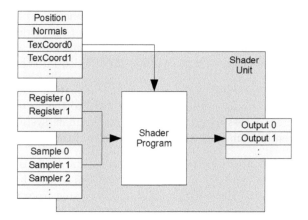

Figure 4.2. Shader unit.

its own specific function in transforming streams of vertex information into pixels
in the framebuffer. For the purposes of this chapter two distinct types of unit
comprise the stages of the pipeline.

Fixed function units such as the raster, merge, and triangle assembler stages
are characterized by having a set of specific state values used to configure operations during that stage of the pipeline. For instance, the raster stage supports
various culling conditions that may determine the face winding during rasterization or may mask off a subsection of the framebuffer for rendering. The various
different states and their descriptions fall outside the scope of this chapter—it is
enough to simply define them as a group of hard-coded device states.

In contrast, the programmable shader units (Figure 4.2) have various generic
resources associated with them. The nature of each unit remains fixed by its place
in the pipeline, but the exact function is defined by the shader program loaded
into the unit at the time a draw call is made. To accommodate this flexibility,
the resources associated with shader units are not fixed to a specific meaning like
the state values of other stages; instead, they are general-purpose resources that
are made visible to both the shader program and application. These resources
include the following:

- *Input streams.* Multiple streams of equal length may be attached to the
  shader, and the program is executed once for each element. These are the
  only values that can change across all iterations of the shader in a single
  draw call.

- *Output streams.* Each execution of the shader program will output a value
  into one or more output streams.

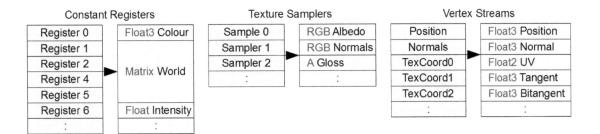

Figure 4.3. Parameter naming.

- *Constant registers.* Each shader unit has a number of constant registers that may be set before a draw call is made; the values stored will remain constant for all iterations of the shader.

- *Texture samplers.* Textures allow the shader access to multidimensional arrays of data. This data can be randomly indexed into, using various filtering options.

While increasing flexibility, these generic resources pose a problem. Without imposing a standardized mapping of resources between the shader and the engine, there is little indication telling the engine which values to associate with a given register, sampler, or stream index. Enforcing such a standard would conflict with the stated goal of maximizing flexibility and thus is not acceptable.

Fortunately high-level shading languages such as HLSL, Cg, and GLSL provide a simple and elegant solution (Figure 4.3). They expose these resources as named parameters that can be defined within the shader program, either on a global scope or as arguments. Each parameter must be identified with a type and name and, in some cases, can be given an optional semantic, too. This information is also exposed to the engine, providing the same amount of detail as the fixed function state with the flexibility of being defined in data (shader code). Thus, emphasis moves from interfacing with a finite set of standardized state values to an unlimited set of values defined by a combination of type and name and/or semantic, creating a very different challenge for engine design.

It should also be noted that the structure of the pipeline is not fixed across all APIs. With each generation of hardware, new features are exposed, extending and altering the layout of the pipeline (Figure 4.4). Over the last four generations of the Direct3D API, there has been a substantial movement from fixed function to programmable stages. It can be assumed that this trend will continue in the future, and any solution should acknowledge this.

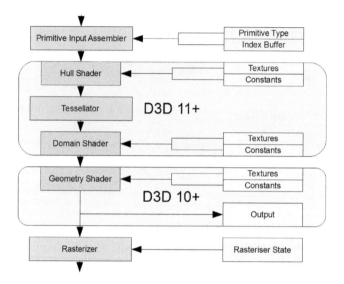

Figure 4.4. Pipeline expansions.

Command buffer. As the device is merely sending commands to the graphics hardware, these are not carried out immediately but are instead queued in a command
buffer to be sent to the graphics hardware for execution. By examining the command buffer, we can clearly discern a pattern of use across the whole frame (Figure 4.5). Several state-setting commands are followed by the execution of a draw
(or clear) command. Each recurrence of this pattern involves the configuration
of the pipeline for a single draw call followed by its execution.

For the purposes of this chapter, this recurring pattern is defined as a *batch*.
A batch describes a single unit of execution on the device, that contains all the
state setting commands required to configure the pipeline and the draw command
itself. Therefore, the rendering of a frame can be described as a series of batches
being executed in order (Figure 4.6).

Summary. In summary, it can be said that the modern graphics API does not
recognize higher-level concepts that might be associated with rendering such as

Figure 4.5. Command buffer.

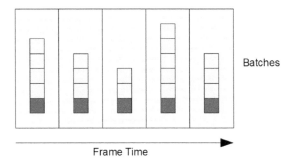

Figure 4.6. Batches.

lights, characters, sprites, or postprocesses. Instead, it focusses on providing a homogenizing interface exposing a uniform set of features on a range of hardware. A typical pattern of use involves

- over the course of a session, managing resources in device memory to ensure they are available during rendering;

- over the course of a frame, constructing batches by assigning appropriate shaders to the programmable units and then gathering both fixed function state information and shader parameters from the application. These batches must then be executed in the correct order to generate a command buffer for the frame.

4.2.2 Engine Model: Intended Pattern of Use

Every engine follows a design model dictated by the personal requirements and tastes of its authors; thus, in contrast to the graphics API, it is very difficult to define a general model that will fit all engines. It is, however, possible to select common examples of rendering during a typical game or simulation and from these derive patterns that could be expected to exist in most engines. By combining and refining these patterns, a general model for all rendering can be derived. These examples of rendering may often be considered the domain of separate modules within the engine, each using a model of rendering that best suits that domain. They may even be the responsibility of different authors, each with their own style of system design. By providing a single interface for rendering at a level above that of the API, it is much simpler to create rendering effects that cross the boundaries between these systems or to build new systems entirely.

3D scene rendering. Rendering 2D images of increasingly complex 3D scenes has been the driving force behind graphics development for many years now. Graphics

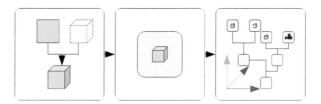

Figure 4.7. 3D scene creation.

APIs like OpenGL and Direct3D were originally designed with 3D rendering in mind. The older versions of the pipeline were entirely fixed function, consisting of stages like the *transformation* and *lighting* of vertices, focusing on processing 3D geometric data. This rigidity has been largely superseded by the flexibility of the programmable pipeline, but the focus on processing 3D geometry is still prevalent. Typically in real-time 3D applications, a complete visual representation of the scene never actually exists. Instead, the simulation at the core of the engine approximates the scene as a collection of objects with a visual representation being composited only upon rendering.

The visual representations of objects within the scene are usually constructed in isolation as part of the asset-creation process and imported into the simulation as data (Figure 4.7). Many simulated objects—entities—of a single type may reference the same visual representation but apply their own individual attributes, such as position and orientation, when rendering. The visual scene itself is constructed around the concept of nested local spaces defined relative to one another. Meshes are described as vertex positions relative to the local space of the whole mesh, visible entities are described as a group of meshes relative to the entity's local origin, and that entity may be described relative to a containing space, all such spaces ultimately being relative to a single root origin. This system has the great advantage of allowing many entities to share the same mesh resources at different locations within the scene. By collapsing the intervening spaces, the vertex positions can then be brought into the correct world-space positions.

Rendering involves the further step of bringing these world-space vertices into the 2D image space of the framebuffer (Figure 4.8). To do this we need to define

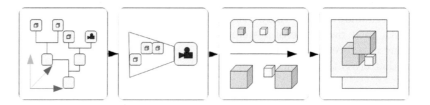

Figure 4.8. 3D scene rendering.

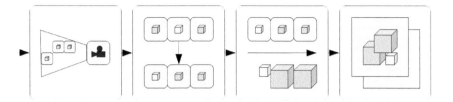

Figure 4.9. Order-dependent rendering.

a point of view within the scene and a space representing the visible volume of the scene to be projected. These additional transforms are encapsulated within the camera or view frustum entity. Similarly, output information needs to be specified regarding to which framebuffer and, if necessary, to which subsection of that framebuffer the scene is to be rendered. This information could be added to the camera object or embodied in further objects. Most importantly, it illustrates a key disjoint between the representational information stored within or referenced by the individual entities and the output information responsible for compositing the scene as an image.

In some cases, such as the rendering of transparent geometry within the scene, there are further constraints placed on the order in which entities may be rendered (Figure 4.9). This is due to the use of linear interpolation when compositing such entities into the existing scene. To achieve correct composition of the final image, two additional criteria must be met. Transparent entities must be rendered after all opaque parts of the scene, and they must be ordered such that the transparent entities furthest from the camera render first and those closest render last.

There are occasions, such as rendering real-time reflections, where rendering the scene from the main viewpoint will be reliant on output from a previous rendering of the scene, typically from another viewpoint. This creates a scenario where the entire pipeline for rendering is instantiated multiple times in a chain. This could even occur dynamically based on the contents of the scene itself, with later instances of the pipeline being dependent on the results of those prior (Figure 4.10).

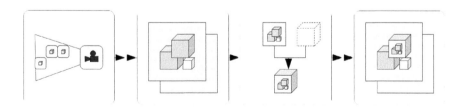

Figure 4.10. Result-dependent rendering.

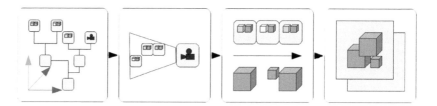

Figure 4.11. Differing representations.

In some cases it is possible that the required output will not be identical to that of the main viewpoint. For instance, rendering a shadow map from the perspective of a light should result in only depth information. To use the same resources, such as shaders and textures, needed to produce a fully colored and lit image would be highly inefficient. Therefore, multiple potential representations need to be referenced by any given entity and selected between based on the required output (Figure 4.11).

Postprocessing. The previous section focused on projecting geometric shapes from 3D space into a 2D framebuffer. The postprocessing stage is instead mostly concerned with operations in image space. Modifying the contents of previous render targets, postprocessing systems often reference the high-level concept of image filtering [Shodhan and Willmott 10].

However, the graphics hardware is unable to both read from and write to a single framebuffer, with the exception of specific blending operations. This necessitates a pattern of use whereby the postprocessing system accesses the results of previous framebuffers as textures and writes the modified information into a new framebuffer (Figure 4.12). Each stage within postprocessing typically requires rendering as little as a single batch to the framebuffer. This batch will likely not represent an object within the simulation; it will merely consist of a screen-aligned quad that will ensure that every pixel of the source image is processed and output to the framebuffer. More complex postprocesses may require a number of stages to create the desired effect. This will result in a chain of dependent batches each using the output of one or more previous framebuffers. Upon examination it can

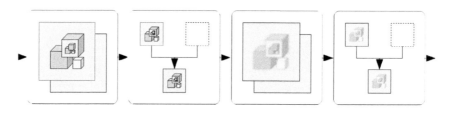

Figure 4.12. Postprocessing.

then be said that the required functionality for postprocessing is not dissimilar to that required for reflection or shadow map creation as described in the 3D scene rendering section. In fact, with regard to effects such as heat haze, there is some overlap between the two areas of rendering.

GUI rendering. In contrast to 3D scene rendering, the GUI system typically is not interested in projecting 3D entities but operates in a much more confined volume of space encapsulating the screen. This space is populated with various objects each of which might represent a single element of the interface. There may be a wide range of elements, from active elements such as text or status bars to interactive elements such as buttons, all of which represent elements of the logical if not physical simulation, or static decorative elements.

While these elements and the space within which they exist are often assumed to be inherently 2D in nature, in composing a working interface it is often necessary to layer multiple elements one atop the other in a single area of the screen. For instance, a text element may appear in front of a decorative sprite, thus adding a strict order of rendering that must be observed. This ordering can be represented by adding depth to the space and the position of elements (Figure 4.13). In practice it might be more effective to construct the GUI as any other 3D scene containing transparencies, treating GUI elements as normal entities, thus making effective use of the structures already implemented for such scenes. This approach has the added benefit of addressing the difficulties of constructing interfaces that work well when rendering in stereographic 3D.

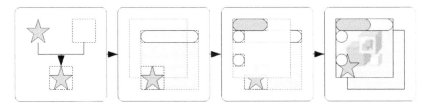

Figure 4.13. GUI rendering.

Summary. In summary, it can be said that by broadening the definitions of entity, scene, space, and camera, the same structures required for rendering 3D scenes can be extended for use in postprocessing and GUI rendering. Any object that needs to be rendered should be defined as an entity within a scene regardless of whether it is a character, terrain section, postprocessing stage, or GUI element. Similarly, all scenes must be rendered through the use of a pipeline of objects that provide

- contextual information for shaders (such as view and projection matrices),

- culling information about the volume being rendered,

- a correct rendering order of entities,

- output information on the render area and framebuffer to be used.

This investigation of potential rendering patterns is by no means exhaustive. It is therefore important that any solution be extensible in nature, allowing for additional patterns to be readily integrated.

4.2.3 Renderer Model

The graphics API and a potential engine-level interface for rendering have been examined, and simplified models have been constructed to describe typical patterns of activity in both. By combining the two models it is possible to accurately describe the desired behavior of the renderer. At various points in the execution of the application, the renderer will be required to perform certain functions.

Session. All visible elements of the game should be represented by entities that provide a single interface for rendering regardless of whether they are 3D, 2D, or a postprocessing stage. Each visible entity will need to reference resources in the form of shaders, meshes, textures, and any other information that describe its visual representation in terms of batch state (Figure 4.14).

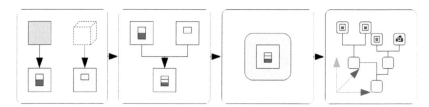

Figure 4.14. Session setup.

Frame. Over the course of each frame, various targets must be rendered to in a specific order creating multiple stages of rendering. Each stage requires rendering for the previous stage to be complete, perhaps to allow for a change to a new framebuffer or viewport or for constrictions on the composition of the current one such as transitioning from opaque to transparent entities.

Stage. Each stage forms a pipeline consisting initially of a camera object that filters entities from the scene it is observing, culling based on its own criteria. The resulting group of entities can then be sorted using the operation specified in this particular stage. Once correctly ordered, the entities are queried for any representative data relevant to this stage (Figure 4.15).

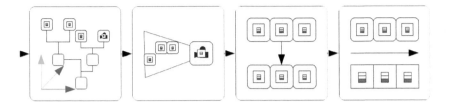

Figure 4.15. Stage rendering.

Batch. Representative data from an entity is used to form the basis for a single batch. The other elements of the rendering stage then provide the remainder of the batch's state, such as the correct viewport dimensions and framebuffer. This batch can now be executed before moving onto the next (Figure 4.16).

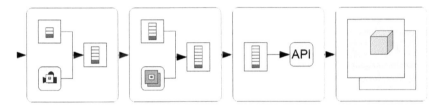

Figure 4.16. Batch rendering.

4.2.4   Further Considerations

Having defined the basic operations of the renderer, there are a number of additional requirements to consider during its development.

Exposing diverse API features. Though APIs employ the same general model, some useful features will be unique to certain APIs and new features will become available as hardware advances. It is important to allow the renderer to be quickly extended to expose these.

Supporting multiple rendering techniques. An entity with specific visual properties may exist in multiple projects with different rendering styles (e.g., forward/deferred shading) or in the same project across multiple platforms with differing hardware features. It is important to be able to choose between different implementations of a single visual effect, preferably from a single data set.

Extensible architecture. New graphics techniques are constantly being developed, and it is important that any new patterns of rendering be easily integrated into the renderer with minimal impact to code or data formats.

Resource management. Device resources are finite and any solution should attempt to minimize duplication of resources wherever possible. A comprehensive resource management scheme, however, is beyond the scope of this chapter.

4.3   Solution Development

Before outlining an exact design for the renderer, it is a good idea to determine a general approach to the implementation, which can further inform decisions.

4.3.1   Object-Based Pipeline

The design of the renderer and additional constraints lend themselves well to a highly modular implementation. By examining the model derived in Section 4.2.3, we can see a pattern emerging where the functions of the renderer are independent operations performed in series to construct a single batch. This design pattern is often defined as a *pipeline* or *pipes and filters* pattern [Buschmann et al. 96]. Rather than encapsulating functionality in a monolithic object or function, a system is constructed as a series of autonomous components sharing a single interface where the output of one object becomes the input for the next. The same pattern can also be observed in many asset pipelines used by developers to process assets before loading them into an engine and in the graphics pipeline described in the API section. In some ways the renderer pipeline can be thought of as a continuation of these two pipelines, bridging the gap between the assets and the device state. Such fine-grained modularity allows for the decoupling of the composition of the pipeline as data and the function of its components as code with numerous benefits.

Accessibility. With a little explanation, artists and other asset creators should be able to understand and modify the data set used to configure the renderer without programmer intervention. This process can be further improved by providing tools that will allow users to author a renderer configuration via a visual interface.

Flexibility. It should be possible to change the structure of the renderer quickly by modifying the data set from which it is created, even while the engine is running. This allows for quick testing of various configurations without affecting the project's work flow and also for opportunities to optimize rendering as requirements may vary over a session.

Extensibility. Objects allow the architecture to be extended by adding new object types that match the same interface but bring new behaviors, thus providing a degree of future proofing with regards to new rendering patterns or to exposing new API features.

4.3.2   Device Object

It has already been posited that all graphics APIs have a central device object, whether explicitly, as in the case of the Direct3D libraries, or implicitly. To improve the portability of the renderer code, it makes sense to write its components to use a single interface regardless of the underlying API. Equally, it makes sense for this interface to formalize the concept of the device object, even if such a concept already exists in the API.

To properly abstract all possible APIs, the device object must expose a superset of all the functionality provided. If a feature is not supported on a given API, then it would need to be emulated or, because the renderer is configured through data, it could warn that the current data set is not fully supported. As new features become available, the device interface would need to be extended before additional renderer components could be written to expose them.

4.3.3   Deriving State from Objects

As described previously, when rendering each batch, the renderer will iterate over the list of objects forming the entity and the pipeline, deriving from each a portion of the state required to render that batch. It is important to differentiate between the various types of states found in the graphics pipeline (Section 4.2.1) and also between the objects representing entities within the simulation and those representing the pipeline (Section 4.2.3). Iteration will ensure that objects get access to the device for state setting.

Fixed function state. Objects that contain fixed function state are simple to manage. When iteration reaches such a node in the pipeline or entity, the node will be able to access the device and make the correct calls.

Shader parameters. Correctly setting the values of shader parameters is a considerably more difficult challenge. Each parameter is identified by a type and a name and an optional semantic (where semantics are supported by the shading language); there is a certain amount of redundancy between the name and semantic values. While the semantic quite literally represents the meaning of the parameter, a good name should be equally expressive; in practice, the name is quite often a shorthand version of the semantic (for instance, a world-view matrix might have the semantic WORLDVIEW but have the abbreviated name WVm).

It is usually enough to match either the name or semantic rather than both; each has its own benefits and drawbacks. Names are a requirement of any parameter and thus are guaranteed to be available in all shader code; however, naming conventions cannot be guaranteed and would have to be enforced across a whole project. There exists a Standard Annotations and Semantics (SAS) initiative that looks to solve this problem by standardizing the use of semantics between applications.

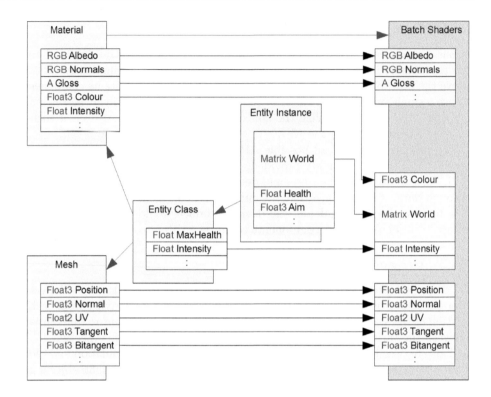

Figure 4.17. Parameter setting.

To correctly set the parameter, an equivalent variable must be found within the logic of the program. Unfortunately, compilation usually strips the context from variables, preventing us from simply performing a search of each object's member variables by type and name (Figure 4.17). Two possible solutions might be considered:

- Build a search function into any object that provides such variables; it will return a pointer to the member variable that best matches the parameter (or a NULL pointer if none can be found) [Cafrelli 01]. This approach may be best suited to existing engines that use an inheritance hierarchy of entity types. It has the drawback of enforcing a fixed naming or semantic vocabulary in code.

- Define entity types using data aggregation instead of classes; each object can store its variables as a structure of nodes that can actually be searched based on type and name or semantic. This may not be realistic in many engine architectures, but it has the added benefit of flexibility, allowing new data to be inserted into an entity and to be automatically picked up by the assigned shaders.

Due to the cost of searching for data, these links between shader parameters and variables should be formed once per session when initializing the entity and its shaders rather than per frame. These links can be divided into two groups, those involving data that represent the entity and those involving the current context or configuration of the pipeline at the time of rendering.

Representational objects. Every visible object is represented by a single unique entity within the scene; however, that entity can reference resource objects that may be shared by any number of other entities. Collectively, these objects provide information required to represent the entity as one or more batches under various different conditions. This information is limited to values that remain static across the period of a frame (such as the entities' absolute positions in the world space). It is taken in isolation and further information is required to dictate how the entity will appear at the exact moment of rendering (such as the position of the particular camera in use). For each of its potential batches, the entity stores links between all the shader parameters and variables used to set them. Where the relevant data is available within the entity or one of its referenced resources, this is used.

Contextual/pipeline objects. Where data is not available directly to the entity, it can be referenced from a global context entity. This entity is unique and contains all the variables needed to describe the current state of the pipeline from within a shader. As the pipeline changes over the course of a frame, its components modify the variables stored in the context entity, thus ensuring any batches rendered will gain the correct inputs.

4.4 Representational Objects

As stated, the visual representation of a single entity is built up from multiple objects. Each object references a more general resource and adds an extra layer of specificity, progressing from generic shared resources to a unique instance of an entity. In effect, this creates a hierarchy with resources becoming more specific as they near the root (Figure 4.18).

The exact nature of these resources is somewhat arbitrary, and the structures used could easily vary between engines. The criteria for their selection is to group states roughly by the frequency with which they change between batches; a shader might be used multiple times with different parameters, thus it will change with a lower frequency. As the specificity of an object increases so does the frequency with which it will change.

As each successive layer of the hierarchy is more specific, any values provided by it will take precedence over those from more general resources.

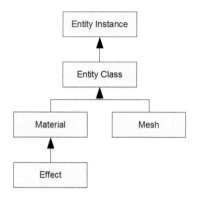

Figure 4.18. Hierarchy of resources.

4.4.1   Effect

The concept of the effect makes aspects of the programmable graphics pipeline accessible in a way that does not require deep knowledge of graphics or API programming. It does this by encapsulating these elements in a structure based not on their purpose within the pipeline but on the end result, a unique visual quality (Figure 4.19).

While the structure of the effect is fairly well standardized, interpretation of the components involved is quite open. In this chapter, the interpretation is informed by the meaning of component names, documentation provided by APIs in which effects are a feature, and existing sources on the subject [St-Laurent 05].

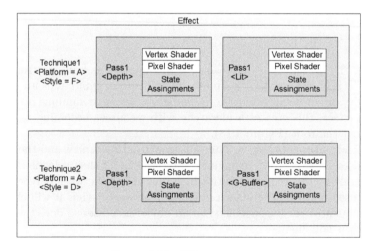

Figure 4.19. Effect structure.

Techniques. The visual quality embodied by any particular effect can often be achieved in a number of ways, each with various trade-offs and requirements. Each technique within the effect is a different method for achieving comparable results. By applying annotations to the individual techniques, it is possible to group them by various criteria, such as features required or relative cost, allowing the renderer to algorithmically select the appropriate technique depending on the circumstances.

Passes. It may not always be possible to achieve an effect with a single batch, instead requiring multiple successive batches that may render at various points throughout the frame. Each technique is constructed from one or more passes; these passes can be annotated to direct the renderer to execute them at the correct point within the frame.

Passes contain states with a similar frequency of change, such as shaders or state assignments, which are rarely useful taken individually due to their interdependence on one another to create an overall pipeline configuration. Therefore, each pass within the technique combines shaders and state assignments but omits many of the shader parameter values, effectively creating an interface to the graphics pipeline allowing the effect as a whole to be parameterized.

Default values. Having the effect provide default values for all its parameters reduces the time required to implement new techniques. It minimizes the number of values that need to be overridden by more specific resources to just those that are strictly necessary, many of which may be automatically provided.

4.4.2 Assets

Assets further specialize a particular effect by providing inputs to some of the parameters. They are typically authored, at least in part, using tools external to the engine. The end result is a visual representation of an object in isolation.

Although the terms *material* and *mesh* are typically used in 3D asset creation, these are equally applicable to GUI or postprocess rendering.

Material. Typically, the material consists of constant and texture information that specializes the effect to emulate the qualities of a certain substance. More generally, to extend the concept to postprocessing, it can be considered an authored configuration or tuning of the effect with static values.

Mesh. A mesh is the set of all vertex data streams and indexes and thus encapsulates all the varying input for an effect. There are many cases in which this information is not used directly as provided by asset creation tools. Instead, systems within the engine will generate or modify vertex streams before transferring them to the graphics device—this could include animation of meshes, particle effects, or generating meshes for GUI text.

A more complete resource management system would likely support instancing of these resources to improve efficiency. However, such details are beyond the scope of this chapter.

4.4.3 Simulation

Where resources in the assets section were largely concerned with the visual attributes of batches, this section is concerned with objects representing the logical attributes.

Entity class. As part of the game design process, archetypal entities will be described in terms of visual and logical attributes shared by many individual entities. These attributes do not vary between individual entities and do not vary over the course of a game session, so they can be safely shared.

Entity instance. Individual entities are instances of a specific class; they represent the actual simulated object. As such they contain all the values that make each instance unique, those which will vary over the course of a game session and between individual instances.

4.5 Pipeline Objects

The pipeline is made up of a series of interchangeable objects, each of which observes the same interface. This pipeline controls the rendering of a group of entities during one stage of the frame (Figure 4.20).

4.5.1 Contextual Objects

Contextual objects provide values to the effect in a similar way to representative ones. However, there is a level of indirection involved; the effect parameters are linked to values defined within a global context object, and these values are manipulated over the course of the frame to reflect the current context in which batches are being rendered.

The values are specific to each object only; they cannot provide concatenations of these with any belonging to the entity currently being rendered, although this functionality could be added as an additional stage in rendering.

Camera. The camera object will also likely be an entity within the scene, though perhaps not a visible one. It is responsible for the transforms used to project entities from their current space into that of the framebuffer. The camera may also provide other information for use in effects, such as its position within world space. The exact details are at the discretion of those implementing the system.

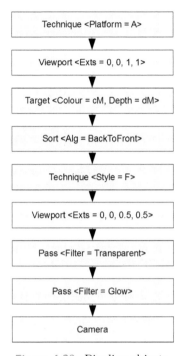

Figure 4.20. Pipeline objects.

Viewport. The viewport defines a rectangular area of the framebuffer in which to render, the output image being scaled rather than cropped to fit. The viewport could be extended to work using relative values as well as absolute ones, decoupling the need to know the resolution of any particular target when authoring the pipeline. This could be further extended to permit nesting of viewports, with each child deriving its dimensions relative to those of its immediate parent.

Target. The render target defines the contents of the framebuffer to be used, referencing either a client area provided by the platform or textures that may be used in further stages of rendering.

4.5.2 Control Objects

In contrast, control objects do not set the states of effect parameters. Instead, they control the order and selection of the batches being rendered.

Camera. In addition to providing contextual data during rendering, the camera object may also perform culling of entities before they are queried for representational data.

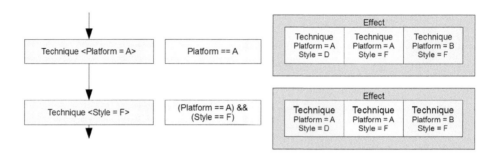

Figure 4.21. Technique filters.

Layer. Layers can be used for course-grained control of rendering across a single render target. This forces one set of batches to be rendered only after the previous set has completed. As the name suggests, they are analogous with layers in art packages like Photoshop or GIMP.

Sorting algorithm. Defining a sorting algorithm for the pipeline will force entities to be sorted by arbitrary criteria before any rendering is performed. This is a requirement for compositing semitransparent batches onto a single layer of rendering, but it can also be used to gain additional performance by sorting batches based on material or approximate screen coverage.

Technique filter. Technique filters can be applied to provide additional information for choosing the correct technique from an effect. Each filter can provide values in one or more domains, such as platform, required features, or rendering style. Each domain can only have a single value at any point in the frame, and these are matched to the domain values specified by the effect techniques available to select the best suited (Figure 4.21).

The domains and values are not defined anywhere in the code and only appear in the pipeline configuration and effect files, allowing each project to define their selection. Technique filters are largely optional, being most useful for larger projects and those using extensive effect libraries.

Pass filter. Pass filters are a requirement for the pipeline to operate correctly. These work differently from the technique filters in that each filter just has an identifying value and any number of pass filters can be active at a single point in the frame. When rendering an entity, all passes within the current technique that match an active filter will be rendered. The order in which they are presented in the technique will be observed regardless of any sorting algorithm in use (Figure 4.22). If no passes match the active filters, then nothing will be rendered.

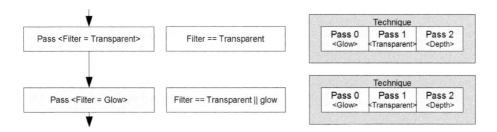

Figure 4.22. Pass filters.

4.6   Frame Graph

The configuration of the pipeline varies from stage to stage over the course of each frame. As with the representative resources, the components of the pipeline vary with different frequencies. It is therefore possible to describe the pipeline over the course of a whole frame as a graph of the various components (Figure 4.23).

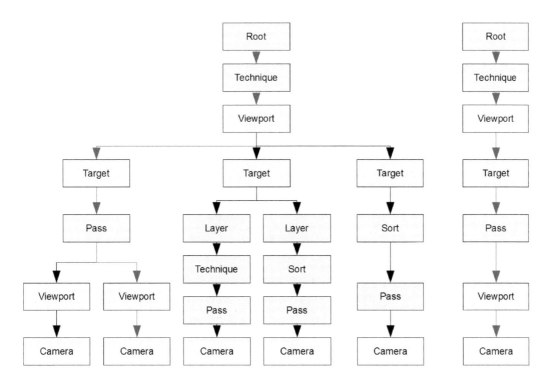

Figure 4.23. Frame graph iteration and derived pipeline.

This graph effectively partitions the frame based on the current stage of rendering, with the nodes being active pipeline components. The components touched by iterating through the graph from root to leaf form the pipeline at that stage of the frame. Each leaf node represents a complete pipeline configuration for which rendering must occur. By traversing the graph depth first, it is possible to iterate through each of the pipeline configurations in sequence, thus rendering the entire frame.

As each node in the graph is iterated over, it is activated and modifies the context object or the control state of the pipeline. Once the leaf node is reached, the camera object begins the rendering of that stage, iterating over the scene graph and processing the visible entities based on the pipeline state. Upon completion of the stage, iteration returns back through the graph undoing the changes made by the various nodes in the graph.

While the concept of the pipeline remains valid, this behavior of modifying global states makes the implementation of the system more akin to a stack. Changes are pushed onto the stack as each node is visited and then popped from the stack upon returning. This reduces the frequency of certain state changes immensely, making it considerably more efficient than having each batch iterate along the full pipeline as it is being rendered.

4.7   Case Study: Praetorian Tech

Praetorian is Cohort Studio's proprietary engine technology. It was developed to provide the studio with a solid platform on which to build full titles and prototypes across multiple platforms (Figure 4.24).

Figure 4.24. Prototypes developed by Cohort Studios: *Wildlife* (left) and *Pioneer* (right).

Figure 4.25. Various rendering styles tested on the *Me Monstar* motion prototype: custom toon shading defined by Andreas Firnigl (left), soft ambient lighting (center), and deferred shaded fur (right).

4.7.1 Motivation

Praetorian was developed with the intention of maximizing code reuse across multiple simultaneous projects. With this in mind, it made sense to define those features unique to each project through data and scripts instead of engine code, allowing artists, designers, and gameplay programmers to control the look and feel of their project in great detail (Figure 4.25). As described earlier, effect files were a natural solution to exposing programmable graphics via data. Being compatible with a large range of art packages meant that many artists were already familiar with their use and in some cases with authoring them. However, it was soon discovered that more advanced visual effects required multiple passes throughout the course of a frame, something which effect files alone could not define. A data structure was needed that could map out the frame so as to give points of reference and control over the order of rendering at various levels of granularity.

4.7.2 Implementation Details

Praetorian's design was based on the concepts described in the introduction to this chapter. At its core lies a highly flexible architecture that split the functionality of objects, as provided by the engine's subsystems, from the raw data stored in the central scene graph. As such all entities within the scene were represented in code by a single class that stored a list of data objects, with distinctions. An entity containing references to a mesh and material could be drawn; one with a physics object would be updated by the physics simulation; and so on. Thus, a single conceptual entity such as a character or light could be represented as a single entity in the scene or by a subgraph of entities grouped under a single root node. Such details were largely informed by the assets produced by artists and designers rather than led by code.

This approach made it simple to add subgraphs to the scene that could embody many of the renderer concepts discussed in this chapter. The design described throughout this chapter is a refinement of the resulting architecture.

4.7.3 Analysis

The purpose of the renderer design was to separate graphics development from that of the engine, exposing through data the functionality of the graphics API beyond that already provided by effect files. In this it proved highly successful, initially in moving from forward to deferred shading on our main project and then in experimenting with a number of styles and variations including deferred and inferred lighting, various forms of cell shading, and other nonphotorealistic rendering methods. All this could occur in parallel to the main development of the projects with the roll-out of new styles being performed gradually to ensure that builds were unharmed by the introduction of potential bugs.

Another area where the design proved successful was in the definition of postprocessing techniques; these benefited from the same development environment as other effects but also from being fully configurable across multiple levels within the same project.

As with any design decisions, there were trade-offs made when developing the renderer, some of which have been addressed to various degrees in the revised design. To a certain extent, the data-driven nature of the renderer became a limitation in its initial and continuing development. In the case of some simple tasks, it took considerably longer to design and implement an elegant way to expose functionality through data than it would to do so through code. Once such structures are in place, however, the savings in time can quickly make up for the initial investment. Praetorian's initial structure was significantly more rigid than that described in this chapter—this made adding special-case behaviors, such as shadow frustum calculations or stereographic cameras, more difficult to implement.

As the renderer configurations became more complex so too did the XML files used to describe them. This had the undesired effect of reducing the system's accessibility and increasing the likelihood of errors occurring. One solution would have been to create a visual editor to interpret the files, something that is highly recommended to anyone implementing a similar renderer design.

The generalized nature of the architecture also had the effect of making optimization more difficult. By making minimal assumptions about the batches being rendered, it can be difficult to maximize efficiency. The greatest gains were made in performing as much processing as possible during loading or as part of the asset pipeline, moving the workload away from the time of rendering. This had an impact on the runtime flexibility of the system, forcing entities to be reinitialized if data was added or removed, but overall it was necessary to maintain realistic frame rates.

4.8   Further Work and Considerations

4.8.1   Optimization: Multithreaded Rendering Using Thread-Local Devices

Some APIs support the creation of multiple command buffers on separate threads. Where this is available, it would be possible to have multiple threads process the frame graph simultaneously. Each thread would iterate until it reached a leaf node. It would then lock the node before processing the resultant pipeline as normal. Should a thread reach an already locked node, it would simply skip that node and continue iteration until it discovered an unlocked leaf node or the end of the frame graph.

To make this approach safe from concurrency errors, each thread would have a local device with a subset of the functionality of the main device. This would also require thread-local context entities to store the state of the current pipeline; as no other objects are modified during rendering, the scene and pipeline objects can be accessed concurrently.

4.8.2   Extension: Complex Contextual Data

Some shaders will require data that does not exist within a single entity, such as a concatenated world-view-projection matrix. This data can be created in the shader from its constituent parts but at a considerably higher performance cost than generating it once per batch. Thus, a system could be added to perform operations on values in the context entity and the entity being rendered to combine them prior to rendering. In its most advanced state, this could take the form of executable scripts embedded in an extended effect file, a kind of *batch shader*.

4.8.3   Debugging: Real-Time Toggling of Elements in Pipeline

Shaders for displaying debug information can be added to entities by inserting additional techniques into their effects. These techniques can then be activated by adding the correct filters to the frame graph, and these sections can then be toggled to render various entities under different conditions, showing information such as normals, overdraw, or lighting. As the renderer automatically binds shader parameters to entity data it is possible to visualize a wide range of information by modifying only the shader code. This debugging information is strictly controlled by data, and as such it is simple to introduce and remove, allowing individual developers to tailor the output to their specific needs and then remove all references before shipping.

4.9   Conclusion

The renderer described in this chapter successfully decouples the details of graphics rendering from engine architecture. In doing so it tries to provide an interface that better fits the needs of graphics programmers and asset creators than those currently available—one that takes its lead from the incredibly useful effect structure, attempting to expand the same data-driven approach to the entire rendering pipeline.

The principles discussed have been used in several commercial game titles and various prototypes, being instrumental in the rapid exploration of various graphical styles and techniques that could be freely shared across projects. In the future it might even be possible to expand on these concepts to create a truly standardized notation for describing graphics techniques in their entirety, regardless of the application used to display them.

4.10   Acknowledgments

Thanks to everyone who worked at Cohort Studios over the years for making my first real job such a great experience. I learned a lot in that time. All the best wherever the future finds you. Special thanks go to Andrew Collinson who also worked on Prætorian from the very beginning, to Bruce McNeish for showing a lot of faith in letting two graduate programmers design and build the beginnings of an engine, and to Alex Perkins for demanding that artists should be able to define render targets without programmer assistance, even if they never did.

Bibliography

[Bell 10]   G. Bell. "How to Build Your Own Engine and Why You Should." *Develop* 107 (July 2010), 54–55.

[Buschmann et al. 96]   F. Buschmann, R. Meunier, H. Rohnert, P. Sommerland, and M. Stal. *Pattern-Oriented Software Architecture*. Chichester, West Sussex, UK: John Wiley & Sons, 1996.

[Cafrelli 01]   C. Cafrelli. "A Property Class for Generic C++ Member Access." In *Game Programming Gems 2*, edited by Mark DeLoura, pp. 46–50. Hingham, MA: Charles River Media, 2001.

[Microsoft 09]   Microsoft Corporation. "DirectX SDK." Available at http://msdn.microsoft.com/en-us/directx/default.aspx, 2009.

[Shodhan and Willmott 10]   S. Shodhan and A. Willmott. "Stylized Rendering in Spore." In *GPU Pro*, edited by Wolfgang Engel, pp. 549–560. Natick, MA: A K Peters, 2010.

[Shreiner et al. 06]   D. Shreiner, M. Woo, J. Neider, and T. Davis. *OpenGL Programming Guide*, Fifth edition. Upper Saddle River, NJ: Addison Wesley, 2006.

[St-Laurent 05] S. St-Laurent. *The COMPLETE Effect and HLSL Guide.* Redmond, WA: Paradoxal Press, 2005.

[Sterna 10] W. Sterna. "Porting Code between Direct3D9 and OpenGL 2.0." In *GPU Pro*, edited by Wolfgang Engel, pp. 529–540. Natick, MA: A K Peters, 2010.

VI

GPGPU

With the latest advances in computer graphics, the use of general compute APIs such as CUDA, OpenCL, and DirectX 11 compute shaders has now become mainstream. By allowing modern GPUs to go far beyond the standard processing of triangles and pixels, the power of the graphics processor is now open to domains reaching far beyond those of visualization or video games. The latest advances in GPU technologies now allow the implementation of various parallel algorithms such as AI or physics. With the parallel nature of the GPU, such algorithms can generally run order of magnitudes faster than their CPU counterparts. This section covers chapters that present techniques that go beyond the normal pixel and triangle scope of GPUs and take advantage of the parallelism of modern graphics processors to accomplish such tasks.

The first chapter, "Volumetric Transparency with Per-Pixel Fragment Lists" by László Szécsi, Pál Barta, and Balázs Kovács, presents an efficient approach to rendering multiple layers of translucency by harnessing the power of compute shaders. By implementing a simple ray-tracing approach in a computational shader, they can determine the appropriate color intensity for simple particles. The approach can then be taken further and extended to even account for visual effects such as refraction and volumetric shadows.

In the second chapter, "Practical Binary Surface and Solid Voxelization with Direct3D 11" by Michael Schwarz, a new real-time voxelization technique is presented. This technique is efficient and tackles some of the problems, such as voxel holes, that occur in rasterization-based voxelization algorithms. The resulting voxels can then be used in the application of a variety of techniques such as collision detection, ambient occlusion, and even real-time global illumination.

And finally, in "Interactive Ray Tracing Using the Compute Shader in DirectX 11" by Arturo García, Francisco Ávila, Sergio Murguía, and Leo Reyes, a novel technique is presented to allow for real-time interactive ray tracing using a combination of the GPU and CPU processing power. This implementation properly handles glossy reflections as global illumination. An efficient bounding volume hierarchy is also offered to accelerate the discovery of ray intersections.

—Sebastien St-Laurent

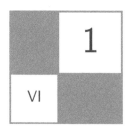

Volumetric Transparency with Per-Pixel Fragment Lists

László Szécsi, Pál Barta, and Balázs Kovács

In this chapter we describe the *volumetric transparency* method for rendering transparent objects that departs from classic alpha blending. Instead, it builds per-pixel lists of surface fragments and evaluates illumination analytically between neighboring pairs. This new approach allows object transparency and color to depend on material thickness, and transparent objects are allowed to intersect. Thus, the method is geared at the most prevalent application of transparency: particle system rendering, where it avoids all popping and clipping artifacts characteristic of alpha-blended billboard clouds. We also show how texturing, shadows, or light shafts can be added.

1.1 Introduction

In transparent objects and media, light interactions do not happen only on object surfaces but also within its volume. Accurate computation of these, under general conditions, requires costly *ray-marching* [Bunyk et al. 97, Szirmay-Kalos et al. 11] or *slicing* [Ikits et al. 04] algorithms. These use, directly or indirectly, a large number of point samples to find the color of each pixel. Thus, they can be implemented most straightforwardly for voxel grid data; other representations are usually converted to this.

A much more lightweight technique, *alpha blending* allows us to add transparency to regular surface rasterization. However, it requires surface elements to be rendered in a back-to-front order, does not instantly allow for transparency to depend on object thickness, and works poorly with Z-testing. In the case of particle systems rendered with transparent particle billboards, the most distressing problems are addressed by *spherical billboards* [Umenhoffer et al. 06], also called *soft particles*. This method uses pixel shaders to actually compute visible thickness, clipped by opaque surfaces, and to adjust transparency and color accordingly. However, ordering of billboards is still required, and when the order of the billboards changes between two animation frames, visible popping still occurs. This is less pronounced if there are more particles, or if they appear similar. However, in certain circumstances—for example, in fire-and-smoke scenarios, or when shadows are cast onto the medium—particle colors and saturations may be varied, and popping becomes more visible.

The *megaparticles* technique [Bahnassi and Bahnassi 06] eliminates billboard artifacts, rendering actual spheres instead of billboards. This allows particles to be shaded and depth-tested the same way as solid geometry. Their volumetric nature is lost, but the effect can be reintroduced in an image-space distortion and blurring pass. The technique can render stunningly shaded dense smoke, and, with some sorting required, even solid objects are allowed to intersect. However, mixing of low-opacity particles and proper depth-dependent transparency are not addressed. Megaparticles and our volumetric transparency method share the concept of using a few complex volumetric particles rather than thousands of billboards.

The method of this chapter can be grasped both as a special case of ray casting and a generalized case of alpha blending. From the ray-casting point of view, what we do is assume a piecewise homogeneous medium and thus replace costly point sampling with the evaluation of an analytic formula. Compared to spherical billboards, our volumetric transparency method does not only clip the volume thickness against opaque objects, but also accurately handles intersection between particles. Mixing the two media together, it completely eliminates the possibility of popping artifacts.

1.2 Light Transport Model

In rendering algorithms, we need to find *radiance* incoming at the eye along rays through every pixel. Transparent objects and participating media exhibit volumetric lighting effects (see Figure 1.1): they let through some of the background

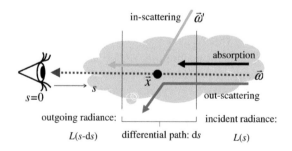

Figure 1.1. Volumetric lighting effects in participating media.

light toward the eye, *absorb* or *scatter out* another part, and *scatter in* light from light sources toward the eye. Emissive media also *emit* light. The chance that a photon gets absorbed or scattered while traveling a small distance ds is $\tau \cdot ds$, where τ is called the *extinction coefficient* or *optical density*. If the incoming radiance is L, then $\tau L \cdot ds$ is the amount lost over distance ds.

How much light is emitted or scattered toward the eye depends on the medium emissivity, on the lighting conditions, and on the scattering properties of the medium. We are going to assume that this contribution is constant over every object volume. For this to be true, lighting must be uniform and the medium must be homogeneous. These, and more, are also assumed in classic alpha-blended transparency. In practice, this means that we use ambient or unattenuated directional lighting, discarding multiple scattering and volumetric self-shadowing effects.

The contribution of the medium to eye-directional radiance over a small distance ds is $g \cdot ds$, where g is called the *source term*. This contribution includes emission and in-scattering due to ambient or directional lighting, and it is influenced by lighting parameters. If value g is given for the RGB wavelengths, it can be intuitively interpreted as the color of the medium.

Thus, the absorption and out-scattering terms are characterized by extinction coefficient τ and the emission and in-scattering are covered by source term g. We will call these two together the *optical parameters* of the medium. With these, the change of radiance dL over distance ds can be written as

$$dL = g \cdot ds - \tau L \cdot ds,$$

yielding the differential equation

$$\frac{dL}{ds} = g - \tau L, \tag{1.1}$$

for which the particular solution with $L(0) = L_{\text{background}}$ is

$$L(s) = \frac{g \cdot (1 - e^{-s\tau})}{\tau} + L_{\text{background}} \cdot e^{-s\tau}. \tag{1.2}$$

This formula gives us the radiance contribution of a homogenous medium segment of thickness s and the attenuation factor for the background radiance. Note that the analytic solution of the differential equation is possible because we assume that the medium is homogeneous. With linear or quadratic functions for $\tau(s)$ and $g(s)$, we would get integral formulas, the evaluation of which would no longer appear beneficial, having ray marching as an alternative.

1.3 Ray Decomposition

In order to find the color of a pixel, we need to evaluate the radiance along the ray shot from the eye through the pixel. The scene objects are either opaque or

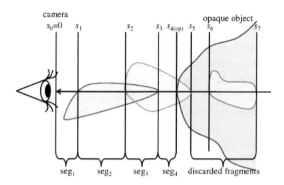

Figure 1.2. Ray decomposition into homogenous segments.

homogenously transparent solids. Let us consider the ray interval between the
eye and the first intersected opaque surface. As depicted in Figure 1.2, this interval is divided into homogenous segments by the points where the ray intersects
surfaces of transparent objects. Such a segment may be empty, contain medium
from one object, or have multiple objects overlapping. Our goal is to identify
all these segments, compute the optical properties for them, and evaluate their
contributions to the observed radiance.

Where two objects overlap, the optical parameters of the mixed medium must
be found. If the chance that a photon travels the distance ds without collision is
$1 - \tau_A \cdot ds$ in one medium and $1 - \tau_B \cdot ds$ in the other, the probability of no collision
in either is the product $(1 - \tau_A \cdot ds)(1 - \tau_B \cdot ds)$, meaning collision probability $\tau \cdot ds$
for the combined medium is $\tau_A \cdot ds + \tau_B \cdot ds - \tau_A \tau_B \cdot (ds)^2$. Dividing by ds gives
us the extinction coefficient we must use in the differential equation, but there,
as the remaining ds term approaches zero, this simply becomes $\tau = \tau_A + \tau_B$. It
can be said that the chance that a photon would collide with both media must
not be considered over an infinitesimal distance. Following the same reasoning,
the source terms g_A and g_B can also simply be added to get the mixed medium
source term g.

Let us denote the distances where the ray intersects the surfaces of transparent
objects in increasing order by s_i, with $i = 1 \ldots n$, where n is the number of
intersections, and prepend $s_0 = 0$ to this ordered list. The intersections divide
the ray into homogenous segments. Let τ_i and g_i be the extinction coefficient and
source term of the combined medium in segment $[s_i, s_{i+1})$. As explained above,
these are simply the sums of the medium parameters of the objects overlapping in
the segment. Along the ray, $\tau(s)$ and $g(s)$ increase at every *entry point*, at which
the ray enters an object, and decrease at every *exit point*, at which it leaves one.
The change is equal to the optical parameters of the entered or exited object.
Let us denote the changes at s_i with $\Delta \tau_i$ and Δg_i, respectively. The values are

positive for entry points and negative for exit points. The optical parameters at the eye can be found as the negated sum of all changes, as all objects are finite and both parameters are zero at infinity:

$$\tau_0 = -\sum_{i=1}^{n}\Delta\tau_i, \quad g_0 = -\sum_{i=1}^{n}\Delta g_i.$$

Consequent segment parameters can simply be found by applying the changes due to entered or exited objects:

$$\tau_i = \tau_{i-1} + \Delta\tau_i, \quad g_i = g_{i-1} + \Delta g_i. \tag{1.3}$$

If $L(s_n)$ is the background radiance that enters at the end of the last segment, and $L(s_i)$ is the radiance that leaves segment $[s_i, s_{i+1})$ toward the eye, then using Equation (1.2) we can write for $i < n$ that

$$L(s_i) = \frac{g_i \cdot \left(1 - e^{(s_{i+1}-s_i)\tau_i}\right)}{\tau_i} + L(s_{i+1})e^{(s_{i+1}-s_i)\tau_i},$$

which yields a recursive formula for $L(s_0)$, the incoming radiance at the eye. We can evaluate this formula in an iterative manner, by accumulating the contribution of segments into variable L while maintaining the total transparency of all processed segments in variable T. We start with $L = 0$ and $T = 1$, and for every segment, in order, we perform

$$L \leftarrow L + T \cdot \frac{g_i \cdot \left(1 - e^{(s_{i+1}-s_i)\tau_i}\right)}{\tau_i},$$

$$T \leftarrow T \cdot e^{(s_{i+1}-s_i)\tau_i}.$$

After the last segment has been processed, L will contain the radiance at the eye. Note that the process can be terminated early when T becomes negligibly small, meaning that the processed segments completely occlude any features further away.

1.4 Finding Intersections with Ray Casting

In order to render an image like the one in Figure 1.3, the radiance has to be evaluated as described above, for every pixel. Thus, for every pixel, we need to assemble an ordered list of all intersections with transparent object surfaces, storing intersection distances s_i. Optical parameter changes $\Delta\tau_i$ and Δg_i can either be stored directly in the list records or just be referenced by the object ID and an enter/exit flag. If the objects are such that ray–object intersection is easy to compute, building this ordered list can be done in a pixel shader when rendering a full-viewport quad.

Figure 1.3. Transparent spheres in the *Crytek Sponza* scene [Dabrovic and Meinl 02].

In this section, we discuss an algorithm for the case when the transparent objects are spheres. This is an important special case, because sets of spheres can be used to render particle systems. Although overlapping is allowed, presorting the spheres can help minimize local shader memory usage and sorting overhead, because it allows us to process partial intersection lists. The algorithm renders a frame as follows:

1. We render opaque scene color and depth into a texture. This texture is accessible for later shaders.

2. Spheres are sorted according to their distance from the camera, in ascending order. Note that this is not the distance to the sphere center, but the distance to the sphere, which is one radius less. The sorted array is uploaded to the GPU.

3. A full-viewport quad is rendered. For every pixel, the shader does the following:

   (a) Running variables extinction coefficient τ, source term g, and radiance contribution L are initialized to zero. Aggregate transparency T is initialized to one.

(b) For every sphere in the array, the following is true:

    i. The sphere is intersected with the ray through the pixel. Intersected intervals are clipped to between zero and the opaque depth. Intersection records (s_i, sphere ID, and an enter/exit flag) are inserted into a list ordered by depth. This list is short and it is stored in a fixed-sized local-memory array.

    ii. *Safe* intersection records are those intersections in the list that are within the eye-to-sphere distance of the next, yet unprocessed, sphere (in the *safe zone*). As spheres are ordered, intersections with further spheres cannot precede the safe ones. For these safe intersections, the radiance contribution L and the transparency T are accumulated. The extinction coefficient and source term are maintained in the running variables, adding the $\Delta\tau_i$ and Δg_i terms as the intersection points are processed. The processed intersections are discarded from the ordered list. If no spheres are left, we can evaluate all remaining intersections.

(c) We return L as the pixel color, adding T times the opaque surface color.

We store the elements of the ordered list in the local-memory array in reverse order. Elements are removed simply by decreasing the element count. For every intersected sphere we need to insert two records in known order, meaning records of a lesser distance have to be moved only once.

The fixed-size local memory array may be insufficient to hold intersections from too many overlapping spheres, forcing us to discard some intersections or, preferably, process nonfinal ones. This creates a trade-off between performance and the amount of overlapping we can handle robustly. However, as intersection records can be kept small, typical particle system scenarios can be handled easily.

The above brute force algorithm can be accelerated dramatically, if we render a set of smaller quadrilateral tiles that cover the viewport instead of a single viewport-sized quad. For every such tile, we can find in advance those spheres that intersect the frustum defined by the tile and the eye position. Only these spheres have to be considered for intersection in the shader. This allows the method to scale to higher particle counts and smaller particle diameters.

Other tweaks are also possible. Note that the shader now implicitly computes the optical properties at the eye in every pixel. These could be precomputed, but then we should handle intersections behind the eye as a special case, producing a more complex shader and more divergent execution. Likewise, intersections with spheres that happen completely in the safe zone could be processed immediately, skipping the list. This could save us a few operations, but at the cost of introducing new conditionals.

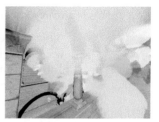

Figure 1.4. Particle system rendered with plain spheres (left), with impostors (center), and with colorful particles (right).

1.5 Application for Particle System Rendering

Using the above ray-casting algorithm, we are able to render perfect, intersecting, transparent spheres without billboard artifacts. We no longer require a large number of billboards to approximate a continuous effect. However, constant-density spheres have sharp apparent boundaries, and we cannot hope to compete with the detail of billboard rendering without texturing.

We can get rid of sharp sphere contours by artificially attenuating particle density near the edges. A sophisticated way of adding detail through textures is to use a *distance impostor* cube map [Szirmay-Kalos et al. 05], which can define the geometry of particles. Intersection with the sphere is then replaced by intersection with the distance impostor. Particle data sent to the shader can be augmented with a particle orientation quaternion, used to rotate the impostor providing proper 3D behavior. (See Figure 1.4 for results.) We found that executing a single iteration step of the intersection algorithm is sufficient to provide the required detail. In our implementation, we query the distance map with the intersection point on the sphere, and re-execute ray–sphere intersection with the obtained radius, as depicted in Figure 1.5. The sphere center is de-

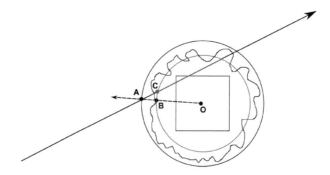

Figure 1.5. Using a distance impostor to add detail to particles.

noted by O, the original intersection point is A, the cube map texture is queried to return the distance OB, and the actual intersection point is approximated as C.

1.6   Finding Intersections with Rasterization

The ray-casting approach is only feasible if the transparent objects can be defined by few primitives, and even then an acceleration structure—like the tile decomposition described above—is necessary. For arbitrary-shaped objects, defined by manifold triangle meshes, we need to exploit the power of hardware rasterization. Gathering a list of fragments for image pixels is possible with Shader Model 5 hardware, as it has been demonstrated in the Order-Independent Transparency (OIT) method [Everitt 01]. In the OIT method the fragments are gathered so that they can be sorted by depth to evaluate alpha-blending-like transparency. We are going to use similar fragment lists to evaluate volumetric transparency, realizing that the front-face fragments correspond to entry points while back-face fragments are exit points.

The algorithm consists of three passes. First, we render the opaque scene into a render target texture, also storing surface distance from the eye. Second, we render transparent objects, collecting fragments into linked lists. Then, in the final pass, the lists are sorted and evaluated using the volumetric transparency method to get the pixel colors.

1.6.1   Data Structures

We store the fragment records in a *read/write structured buffer* called the *fragment&link buffer*. This contains linked list elements complete with an index referencing the buffer element that is the next in the linked list. This index is set to -1 in the final element of a list. The locations of the head elements of linked lists for specific pixels are given by *byte address buffers* called *start offset buffers*. The start offset buffer must have as many elements as there are pixels in the framebuffer.

When rasterizing the transparent objects, we need to be able to insert elements into these linked lists. This means adding new elements to the fragment&link buffer, which is possible using the built-in, synchronized-increment counter for structured buffers (consult the Direct3D documentation for details), in which we will maintain the element count. The buffer has to be large enough to accommodate all fragments. The required size can be estimated as the number of pixels multiplied by the average depth complexity.

Every fragment record in the fragment&link buffer stores the s_i distance, a front/back facing flag, and an index of the rendered object, allowing access to optical properties stored in a constant buffer.

1.6.2 Shader Passes

The first shader pass is called the *deferring* pass, as it is similar to the first pass of *deferred shading* [Policarpo and Fonseca 05]. It simply renders opaque scene elements with regular shaders into a render target texture and stores the eye-to-surface distance in the alpha channel. Regular Z-buffering is used, producing scene depth in the depth buffer.

The second pass (called the *storing* pass, as it stores the fragments into linked lists) renders transparent objects. There is no render target set; the frag-ment&link buffer is accessible as an initially empty, zero-element-count, unordered-access resource. Culling is disabled to get back-facing fragments. Depth writes are disabled, and depth tests might be enabled to discard frag-ments behind opaque objects. In the pixel shader, a new record is allocated in the fragment&link buffer by incrementing the buffer counter. The eye-to-surface distance, the facing flag, and the object ID are combined into this new fragment record, which is inserted as the new head element into the linked list of the pixel. For this, the index of the former head record in the start address buffer must be exchanged with the address of the new record. As multiple fragments for the same pixel might be processed at the same time, we need to use an *inter-locked exchange* operation, which is also a feature of Shader Model 5 structured buffers.

The third, *sorting and rendering* pass renders a full-viewport quad onto the framebuffer. The pixel shader traces linked lists reading fragments into a local array and sorts them according to their distance. Finally, it evaluates volumetric transparency for the segments between the fragments just like in the ray-casting case.

The sorting algorithm needs to work well with relatively few—surely less than 100—fragments. Thus, computational complexity is trumped by less storage and administration overhead, making insertion sort the optimal choice [Estivill-Castro and Wood 92].

If the camera is allowed within transparent objects, the optical properties at the eye—or rather, in this case, at the near clipping plane—are required. Find-ing them in the shader is possible if all fragments between the near clipping plane and infinity have been rendered into the linked lists: changes at the in-tersections have to be summed and negated. This requires that depth testing is disabled in the storing pass (meaning longer linked lists to store and sort) and that transparent objects do not extend over the far clipping plane. If we do not want to make these concessions, we need an extra pass that renders transpar-ent geometry, blend-adding optical properties into a texture and yielding near-plane optical properties for every pixel. The storing pass can also be modified to produce this texture if the depth test is performed in the shader, filtering hidden fragments from the linked list but letting them through to the render target.

Figure 1.6. Transparent objects with added surface reflection.

1.7 Adding Surface Reflection

Surfaces of transparent objects may also reflect light, just like opaque ones. To handle this, the surface reflection must be evaluated in the storing phase, and fragment records must store the additional radiance reflected toward the eye from the intersection point. When processing the intersections in the sorting and rendering pass, these also have to be added to the total radiance, weighted by the accumulated transparency. Figure 1.6 shows some examples.

1.8 Shadow Volumes

We assumed the source term to be constant in objects, meaning that lighting is uniform everywhere. However, we can maintain the concept of a piecewise-constant source term if the lighting is not uniform but piecewise constant itself. This is the case for directional or distant unattenuated point-like light sources. To augment the original algorithm, we need to factorize the source term to a product of the medium *albedo* α and the lighting irradiance I. Both of these can simply be added where multiple objects or lighted volumes overlap. Thus, optical properties τ, α, and I are handled just like τ and g were before. Naturally, a transparent object contributes nothing to lighting, making ΔI_i at intersections zero.

For a light source, the volume that it illuminates is given by its shadow volume [Yen Kwoon 02]. Shadow volumes can be rendered in the storing pass just like regular transparent objects. They contribute nothing to the extinction coefficient or the albedo, thus $\Delta\tau_i$ and $\Delta\alpha_i$ are zero. However, entering a shadow volume decreases irradiance by the value associated with the light source, and exiting increases it by the same. Irradiance at the eye is the sum of the changes along a ray added to the total irradiance due to all light sources.

Figure 1.7.   Volumetric shadows on transparent objects.

Note that the shadow volumes can be rendered by sending mesh-adjacency-enabled shadow caster geometry to the GPU and extruding silhouette edges in the geometry shader (see Figure 1.7 for screenshots).

1.9   Conclusion

Rendering complex transparent objects in real time became possible with Shader Model 5 and order-independent transparency. In this chapter, we have shown how the approach can be extended to volumetric transparency, and even intersecting objects. The algorithm can also be used—even with ray casting instead of linked-list rasterization—to render particles systems, thus eliminating all intersection and popping artifacts and reducing the required particle count to represent continuous volumetric phenomena. Thus, volumetric transparency can be seen both as a relatively low-cost improvement to order-independent transparency and as a sophisticated approach to replace billboards in particle rendering. Figure 1.8 shows a complex scene where the method performs in real time.

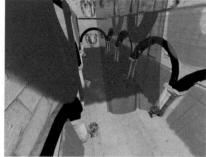

Figure 1.8.   A complex scene with transparent objects.

Bibliography

[Bahnassi and Bahnassi 06] H. Bahnassi and W. Bahnassi. *ShaderX⁵: Advanced Rendering Techniques*, Chapter Volumetric Clouds and Mega-Particles, pp. 295–302. Hingham, MA: Charles River Media, 2006.

[Bunyk et al. 97] P. Bunyk, A. Kaufman, and C. T. Silva. "Simple, Fast, and Robust Ray Casting of Irregular Grids." In *Scientific Visualization Conference*, pp. 30–30. Los Alamitos, CA: IEEE, 1997.

[Dabrovic and Meinl 02] M. Dabrovic and F. Meinl. "Crytek Sponza Model." http://www.crytek.com/cryengine/cryengine3/downloads, 2002.

[Estivill-Castro and Wood 92] V. Estivill-Castro and D. Wood. "A Survey of Adaptive Sorting Algorithms." *ACM Computing Surveys (CSUR)* 24:4 (1992), 441–476.

[Everitt 01] C. Everitt. "Interactive Order-Independent Transparency." *Nvidia* 2:6 (2001), 7. White paper.

[Ikits et al. 04] M. Ikits, J. Kniss, A. Lefohn, and C. Hansen. *Volume Rendering Techniques*, pp. 667–692. Reading, MA: Addison Wesley, 2004.

[Policarpo and Fonseca 05] F. Policarpo and F. Fonseca. "Deferred shading tutorial." Technical report, 2005.

[Szirmay-Kalos et al. 05] L. Szirmay-Kalos, B. Aszódi, I. Lazányi, and M. Premecz. "Approximate Ray-Tracing on the GPU with Distance Impostors." *Computer Graphics Forum (Eurographics '05)* 24:3 (2005), 695–704.

[Szirmay-Kalos et al. 11] L. Szirmay-Kalos, B. Tóth, and M. Magdics. "Free Path Sampling in High Resolution Inhomogeneous Participating Media." In *Computer Graphics Forum*. Wiley Online Library, 2011. Available online (onlibrary.wiley.com).

[Umenhoffer et al. 06] T. Umenhoffer, L. Szirmay-Kalos, and G. Szijártó. "Spherical Billboards and their Application to Rendering Explosions." In *Graphics Interface*, pp. 57–64. Toronto: Canadian Information Processing Society, 2006.

[Yen Kwoon 02] Hun Yen Kwoon. "The Theory of Stencil Shadow Volumes." http://www.gamedev.net/reference/articles/article1873.asp, 2002.

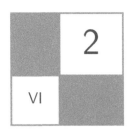

2

VI

Practical Binary Surface and Solid Voxelization with Direct3D 11

Michael Schwarz

2.1 Introduction

Regular, discrete representations of potentially complex signals are routinely used in many fields. They provide a comfortable domain in which to work, often facilitate processing, and are largely independent from the represented signal's complexity. In computer graphics, we encounter such representations mainly in the form of two-dimensional images, like the final rendering result or a shadow map. Their three-dimensional analog, and the focus of this chapter, is *voxelizations* stored in voxel grids. They offer a volumetric representation of a scene, where each grid cell, referred to as a *voxel*, encodes that part of the scene that is located within the cell. In case of a *binary voxelization*, this encoding is particularly simple: merely two states are distinguished, where a set voxel indicates the presence of some, and an unset voxel the absence of any, scene object.

Largely orthogonal to this encoding, two main flavors of voxelizations can be distinguished (see Figure 2.1). In a *surface voxelization* (also called boundary voxelization), the scene is interpreted as consisting solely of surfaces, that is, all closed objects are assumed hollow. Therefore, only voxels overlapped by a surface (like a scene triangle) will be nonempty. By contrast, a *solid voxelization* treats all objects as solids, and hence, any voxel interior to an object will be set. Note that this basically requires the objects to be closed.

Binary voxelizations are useful for many applications, ranging from collision detection [Zhang et al. 07, Eisemann and Décoret 08] to ambient occlusion [Reinbothe et al. 09], soft shadows [Forest et al. 10], area light visibility [Nichols et al. 10], and volumetric shadows [Wyman 11]. Unless confined to static settings, they all mandate that the voxelization be created on the fly at real-time speed. This chapter describes how this goal can be achieved using Direct3D 11, covering the process of turning an input scene, given as a collection

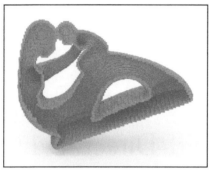 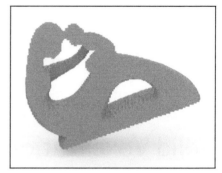

(a) Surface voxelization.   (b) Solid voxelization.

Figure 2.1. In a surface voxelization (a), the voxels overlapping the scene's surfaces are set, whereas in a solid voxelization (b), the voxels that are inside a scene object are set. (For illustration purposes, the fronts of the voxelizations have been cut away, revealing the interiors.)

of triangles, into a binary surface or solid voxelization. We first discuss implementations that build on the standard graphics pipeline and its rasterization stage; these are rather simple and easy to implement but also suffer from several shortcomings. Addressing some of them, we subsequently investigate alternative realizations that employ DirectCompute.

2.2 Rasterization-Based Surface Voxelization

With surface voxelization basically being a three-dimensional extension of rasterization, it is natural to try to pose this process in terms of rasterization and harness the according existing hardware units. Assuming a target voxel grid of size $w \times h \times d$, a simple approach is to render the scene into a deep framebuffer of resolution $w \times h$ with (at least) d bits per pixel (see Figure 2.2). Hence, for each triangle, all pixels covered are determined, and a fragment is generated for each of them. In the invoked pixel shader, those voxels within the voxel column represented by the according deep pixel are identified that are actually covered by the triangle. The resulting voxel-column pixel value is then output by the shader and incorporated into the existing framebuffer.

2.2.1 Challenges

Unfortunately, this appealing approach faces several problems in practice. A major issue is that in ordinary rasterization, a pixel is only considered to be covered by a triangle if the triangle overlaps the pixel's center. This implies that no fragments are generated for all those pixels that a triangle partially overlaps without simultaneously overlapping their centers. Consequently, no voxels are

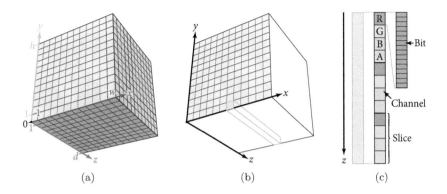

Figure 2.2. (a) We assume a voxel grid of size $w \times h \times d$ and define the *voxel space* such that each voxel has a footprint of size 1^3 and the grid covers the range $[0, w] \times [0, h] \times [0, d]$. (b) The grid can be thought of as a 2D image with deep pixels (each representing a voxel column). (c) These deep pixels may be encoded in multiple multichannel texture slices.

set in these cases, making resulting voxelizations routinely suffer from gaps and miss thin structures (see Figure 2.3). The situation can be somewhat alleviated by rendering the scene not just from one side of the grid (xy) but from three orthogonal sides (xy, xz, and yz) [Forest et al. 10]. This necessitates additional temporary buffers and a merging step, though, and still easily misses many voxels. The only real solution is to always generate a fragment if any part of a pixel's area is overlapped by a triangle. Current hardware, however, does not provide for this so-called *conservative rasterization*. While it can be emulated in software by enlarging each triangle appropriately [Hasselgren et al. 05] (e.g., in the geometry shader), this obviously incurs a significant overhead. Therefore, it is not surprising that an according voxelization algorithm [Zhang et al. 07] turns out to often be rather slow (and it also suffers from some robustness issues). For now, we will simply ignore this problem, but we will tackle it later in Section 2.4 when adopting a compute-based approach.

Another issue arises from updating the voxel grid to incorporate the voxel column output for a fragment. For correct results, obviously a bitwise OR operation is needed. One solution is to realize the deep framebuffer by multiple multichannel render targets, using the single bits of all the channels for encoding the voxel states (see Figure 2.2(c)), and to perform bitwise-OR blending. This was first demonstrated by Dong et al. [Dong et al. 04] (using additive blending, though); the specific framebuffer encoding is sometimes referred to as *slicemap* [Eisemann and Décoret 06]. While this approach works well when using OpenGL, it is not possible with Direct3D, as recent versions no longer expose the hardware's still-existing bitwise blending functionality (also known as logical pixel operations), which once was used for color-index rendering.

(a) Rasterized (1 dir).   (b) Rasterized (3 dirs).   (c) Conservative.

Figure 2.3. (a) If surface voxelization is performed with ordinary rasterization, voxels are frequently missed, leading to perforated surfaces and unconnected voxel clouds. (b) Executing this process from three orthogonal directions and combining the results helps in the case of closed surfaces (like the torus knot), but generally still fails badly if thin structures are involved (like in the leaf-deprived Italian maple). (c) By contrast, conservative voxelization yields correct results.

2.2.2 Approach

Fortunately, Direct3D 11 introduces the ability to write to arbitrary positions of a resource from within the pixel shader and further supports atomic updates to this end. These new features finally allow for pursuing a rasterization-based surface voxelization approach with Direct3D. The basic idea is to replace the bitwise blending of the pixel shader output into the deep framebuffer by performing atomic bitwise update operations on the voxel grid within the pixel shader.

This leads to the following overall approach: First, a resource for storing the voxel grid of size $w \times h \times d$, along with an according unordered access view (UAV), needs to be created. This can be a texture (array) or a buffer, with the latter

```
RWBuffer<uint> g_rwbufVoxels;

struct PSInput_Voxelize {
  float4 pos     : SV_Position;
  float4 gridPos : POSITION_GRID;
};

PSInput_Voxelize VS_Voxelize(VSInput_Model input) {
  PSInput_Voxelize output;
  output.pos = mul(g_matModelToClip, input.pos);
  output.gridPos = mul(g_matModelToVoxel, input.pos);
  return output;
}

float4 PS_VoxelizeSurface(PSInput_Voxelize input) : SV_Target {
  int3 p = int3(input.gridPos.xyz / input.gridPos.w);
  InterlockedOr(g_rwbufVoxels[p.x * g_stride.x + p.y * g_stride.y +
                              (p.z >> 5)], 1 << (p.z & 31));

  discard;
  return 0.0;
}
```

Listing 2.1. Vertex and pixel shaders for rasterization-based surface voxelization.

being the best choice for most applications. As for data format, a 32-bit integer type has to be chosen to allow for atomic updates. Furthermore, either a render target or a depth/stencil target of minimum size $w \times h$ needs to be available.

For creating the voxelization, this target is bound as the only output-merger-stage target, and a viewport of size $w \times h$ is set. Moreover, the voxel grid is reset by clearing its UAV with zeroes, and this UAV is bound. We then render the scene, using the vertex and pixel shaders from Listing 2.1, which adopt the buffer layout shown in Figure 2.4 as a concrete example. The vertex shader transforms

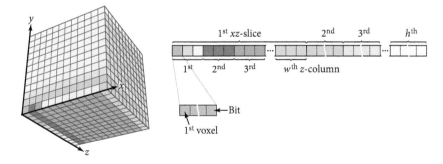

Figure 2.4. To store the voxel grid in a buffer, we linearize it first along the z-direction, packing 32 consecutive voxels into the bits of a 32-bit (unsigned) integer buffer value, then along the x-direction, and finally along the y-direction.

the vertex position into clip space, mapping the grid's xyz-extent to the clip volume (i.e., to $[-1, 1]^2 \times [0, 1]$), and into voxel space, mapping the grid's xyz-extent to $[0, w] \times [0, h] \times [0, d]$. Based on the clip-space coordinates, each triangle is rasterized, and a fragment is generated for each pixel (voxel column) whose center is overlapped. In the pixel shader, the voxel-space coordinate is used to directly set the according voxel in the voxel grid with an atomic OR operation. Subsequently, the fragment is discarded. Note that even though the render or depth/stencil target is thus never updated, it is still required, as otherwise no fragments would be generated.

2.2.3 Discussion

Compared to approaches using bitwise blending, confining them to OpenGL, the presented technique is similarly easy to implement and has both advantages and disadvantages. On the downside, it is often somewhat slower, especially in case of larger voxel grids. This is because random atomic updates to the voxelization are less optimized and efficient than blending executed by the graphics hardware's dedicated raster operation (ROP) units.

A big advantage of the described approach, however, is that the data organization is significantly nicer. Using a buffer resource and storing the voxel grid as a linearized 3D array, each voxel can be easily accessed via simple indexing into this buffer. In particular, this makes working with the generated voxelization rather straightforward. Moreover, it decouples the voxel grid from the side of the grid from which the scene is rendered. Consequently, if the scene is rendered from all three axis directions in order to reduce the artifacts resulting from non-conservative rasterization, a single voxelization buffer can be shared, both saving space and avoiding a final merging step.

By contrast, a deep framebuffer consisting of multiple multichannel render targets, typically stored in a texture array, makes addressing cumbersome because within a render target (texture slice) individual channels cannot be accessed via indexing; instead, conditional expressions are required. Furthermore, as the concrete number of render targets and channels depends on d, supporting variable grid depths d necessitates multiple pixel shaders—one for each render target count. Finally, for large values of d, the needed number of render targets can exceed the maximum number supported by the hardware, requiring multiple passes to fill the voxel grid.

2.3 Rasterization-Based Solid Voxelization

In solid voxelization, we seek to determine all voxels that are interior to some object. Typically, a voxel is considered interior if its center is interior, and we adopt this criterion, too. This leaves us with the task of computing, for each voxel center, whether or not it is located inside some scene object. Assuming that the

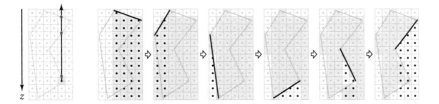

Figure 2.5. A voxel is inside an object if a ray shot upward from its center intersects the scene an odd number of times (far left). These intersection parities can be determined by rendering all triangles, each time flipping all voxels whose centers are below the respective triangle.

scene consists solely of closed, watertight objects and that no object is contained in another one, a point can be classified accordingly by shooting a ray from this point in an arbitrary direction and counting the number of intersections with the scene. If this number is even, the ray entered as many objects as it exited, and hence, the point must be outside. Conversely, an odd count indicates that the point is interior.

Instead of shooting a ray from each voxel center, the parity of the intersection count can be determined equally well using the following approach [Fang and Chen 00, Eisemann and Décoret 08]: First, all voxels are initialized to unset. Subsequently, we loop over all triangles. For each, the state of all voxels whose center is "below" this triangle is flipped. This accounts for the fact that if a ray would be shot from such a center "upward," it would intersect the triangle, increasing the intersection count and hence flipping its parity. Consequently, the final voxel state correctly reflects the parity of the total intersection count and thus the voxel's inside/outside classification (see Figure 2.5).

Using ordinary rasterization from the voxel grid's xy-side, identifying the voxels "below" a triangle is straightforward: for each fragment, corresponding to a whole voxel column, we merely have to select all voxels in this column whose z-index is larger than the fragment's voxel-space z-coordinate minus 0.5.[1]

Consequently, for a practical implementation, the same code as for the surface voxelization can be used. The only modification required affects the pixel shader: instead of setting the voxel corresponding to the fragment's voxel-space coordinates via a bitwise OR, we now have to flip the state of all voxels whose center is below the fragment via atomic XOR operations. Moreover, depth clipping should be turned off (or the clip-space z-coordinate set to a constant $\tilde{z} \in [0, 1]$ in the vertex shader); otherwise, some intersections may be missed if part of the scene is in front of the grid, potentially leading to wrong results.

Note that because a voxel's state is determined solely by the inside/outside classification of its center, accurate results are obtained with ordinary rasteri-

---

[1]This half-voxel adjustment is because we consider the voxel's center.

zation. This is unlike the situation with surface voxelization, where, instead, conservative rasterization is generally required for correctness.

2.4   Conservative Surface Voxelization with DirectCompute

Having seen that using the existing rasterization hardware for voxelization is rather simple, we now turn to an alternative approach based on DirectCompute.[2] It basically boils down to writing our own 3D software rasterizer, which is directly executed on the GPU. This allows us to adapt the rasterizer to the specific problem of voxelization and to exploit arising optimization potential. Being no longer bound to the design decisions and behavior of the graphics hardware's rasterizer, we are, in particular, free to adopt any criterion we want to determine whether a triangle covers a pixel or voxel. Consequently, the fundamental problem of surface voxelization encountered in Section 2.2 can be addressed, namely that the hardware rasterizer does not generate fragments for pixels that are partially covered without their respective centers being covered. Recall that this causes many voxels to incorrectly not be set, severely restricting the usefulness of according techniques.

2.4.1   Approach

Our software surface voxelizer processes all scene triangles in parallel, spending one thread per triangle. In the executed compute shader, at first, the triangle's vertices are fetched and transformed into voxel space. The bounding box of the transformed triangle is then determined and subsequently clipped against the voxel grid. In the case that the clipped bounding box is empty, the triangle is entirely outside the voxel grid, and we are done. Otherwise, the shader loops over all voxels within the bounding box that are potentially overlapped by the triangle. For each of these candidate voxels, an overlap test is performed, and, if the test passes, the voxel is set with an atomic OR operation.

To facilitate a practical implementation of this basic approach, some details should be pointed out. Firstly, the input scene geometry may be made available to the voxelizer in various forms. This could be a list of transformed vertex triplets, each representing a triangle, possibly collected in a stream-output buffer after vertex processing with an ordinary vertex shader. Another possibility is to provide a vertex buffer and an index buffer, and to perform any vertex processing in the compute shader together with the transformation into voxel space.

The chosen set of potentially overlapped voxels may basically be any superset of the actually overlapped voxels. Thus, a simple, conservative approach is just to consider all voxels that are (partially) within the triangle's bounding box. As

---

[2]This approach heavily builds on our previous CUDA-based work [Schwarz and Seidel 10].

each candidate voxel needs to be further investigated, subjecting it to an overlap test, and this test is far from free, performance benefits from better strategies that reduce the number of tested voxels that fail the test and that, hence, would ideally not have been considered in the first place. We will come back to this in Section 2.4.2.

Concerning the overlap test, we are fairly free to choose any criterion we like to define when an overlap occurs. For instance, by testing whether the triangle overlaps the voxel's 3D extent at least partially, a *conservative surface voxelization* is obtained. An according fast triangle/voxel overlap test is detailed in Section 2.4.2.

Finally, when looping over multiple voxels that are represented by different bits of the same 32-bit buffer value, it is advantageous to not immediately update the voxelization buffer for each set voxel among them. Instead, these updates should be buffered in a local 32-bit register and, once the last voxel has been processed, collectively written to the voxelization buffer with a single atomic OR operation.

2.4.2 Triangle/Voxel Overlap Testing

For conservative surface voxelization, we need to determine which voxels are at least partially overlapped by a certain triangle. To this end, we adopt a triangle/box overlap test [Schwarz and Seidel 10] that lends itself to a GPU implementation. It comprises several simpler tests that all have to succeed for an overlap to occur; if any of them fails, the voxel is not covered by the triangle.

Bounding box overlap. Given a triangle T and a voxel V, it is first checked whether the bounding box of T and V overlap. Since, by construction, we only test voxels that are (at least partially) within T's bounding box, this check is redundant and can be omitted.

Plane overlap. Subsequently, we have to test whether the plane of T overlaps V. Suppose that T has the three vertices $\mathbf{v}_0$, $\mathbf{v}_1$, and $\mathbf{v}_2$, all specified in voxel-space coordinates, and that V is located at index (x, y, z) within the voxel grid, thus corresponding to the box defined by the two voxel-space corners $\mathbf{x} = [x, y, z]$ and $\mathbf{x}' = [x+1, y+1, z+1]$. We then compute the normal $\mathbf{n}$ of T and determine that pair of opposing voxel corners $(\mathbf{c}_1, \mathbf{c}_2)$ that best aligns with $\mathbf{n}$ (see Figure 2.6):

$$c_{1,x} = \begin{cases} 1, & n_x > 0, \\ 0, & n_x \leq 0, \end{cases} \qquad c_{1,y} = \begin{cases} 1, & n_y > 0, \\ 0, & n_y \leq 0, \end{cases} \qquad c_{1,z} = \begin{cases} 1, & n_z > 0, \\ 0, & n_z \leq 0; \end{cases}$$

$$c_{2,x} = 1 - c_{1,x}, \qquad c_{2,y} = 1 - c_{1,y}, \qquad c_{2,z} = 1 - c_{1,z}.$$

Note that these corners are expressed relative to $\mathbf{x}$. If and only if they lie on different sides of the triangle's plane (or one lies exactly on the plane), the plane

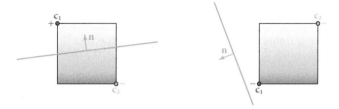

Figure 2.6. For testing whether a plane overlaps a voxel, the two opposing voxel corners c_1 and c_2 for which the vector c_1-c_2 best aligns with the plane normal $\mathbf{n}$ are determined. An overlap occurs if they are located in different half spaces of the plane (as on the left).

overlaps V. This can be easily checked by inserting the two voxel extrema $\mathbf{x} + \mathbf{c}_1$ and $\mathbf{x} + \mathbf{c}_2$ into the plane equation and comparing the results' signs:

$$\big(\mathbf{n} \cdot (\mathbf{x} + \mathbf{c}_1 - \mathbf{v}_0)\big)\big(\mathbf{n} \cdot (\mathbf{x} + \mathbf{c}_2 - \mathbf{v}_0)\big) = (\mathbf{n} \cdot \mathbf{x} + d_1)(\mathbf{n} \cdot \mathbf{x} + d_2) \leq 0, \qquad (2.1)$$

where $d_k = \mathbf{n} \cdot (\mathbf{c}_k - \mathbf{v}_0)$. If the signs differ, the product of the results is negative; it is zero if one of the corners is located on the plane.

2D triangle/box overlap. Finally, we have to test whether the triangle and the voxel overlap in all three, mutually orthogonal, 2D main projections (xy, xz, and yz). Such a 2D test can be efficiently realized with *edge functions* [Pineda 88]. An edge function is simply (the left-hand side of) a 2D line equation for one triangle edge:

$$e_i(\mathbf{p}) = \mathbf{m}_i \cdot (\mathbf{p} - \mathbf{w}_i), \qquad (2.2)$$

where $i \in \{0, 1, 2\}$ is the index of the edge going from $\mathbf{w}_i$ to $\mathbf{w}_{(i+1) \bmod 3}$, $\{\mathbf{w}_i\}$ are the 2D triangle's vertices, and $\mathbf{m}_i$ denotes the edge's normal. This normal points to the inside of the triangle and is given by

$$\mathbf{m}_i = \big[w_{(i+1) \bmod 3,y} - w_{i,y}, w_{i,x} - w_{(i+1) \bmod 3,x}\big]$$

if the triangle is oriented clockwise and by

$$\mathbf{m}_i = \big[w_{i,y} - w_{(i+1) \bmod 3,y}, w_{(i+1) \bmod 3,x} - w_{i,x}\big]$$

in the case of counterclockwise orientation. Consequently, a point $\mathbf{p}$ is inside a triangle if the edge functions for all three edges yield a nonnegative result.

Taking the xy-projection as a concrete example, the triangle's 2D projection T^{xy} is given by the vertices $\mathbf{w}_i = [v_{i,x}, v_{i,y}]$. Its orientation can easily be determined by checking the triangle's normal $\mathbf{n}$; if $n_z > 0$, it is oriented counterclockwise. The voxel's 2D footprint V^{xy} corresponds to the box with corners $\mathbf{b} = [x, y]$ and $\mathbf{b}' = [x + 1, y + 1]$.

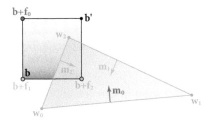

Figure 2.7. To determine whether a box (defined by corners $\mathbf{b}$ and $\mathbf{b}'$) and a triangle (with vertices $\mathbf{w}_0$, $\mathbf{w}_1$, and $\mathbf{w}_2$) overlap, for each triangle edge, we check whether the corresponding critical box corner $\mathbf{b} + \mathbf{f}_i$, implied by the edge's normal $\mathbf{m}_i$, is on the interior side of the edge line.

To test whether T^{xy} and V^{xy} overlap, we determine for each edge i that corner $\mathbf{f}_i$ of V^{xy} to which the edge's normal $\mathbf{m}_i$ points, that is,

$$f_{i,x} = \begin{cases} 1, & m_{i,x} > 0, \\ 0, & m_{i,x} \leq 0, \end{cases} \qquad f_{i,y} = \begin{cases} 1, & m_{i,y} > 0, \\ 0, & m_{i,y} \leq 0 \end{cases}$$

(see Figure 2.7), and evaluate the edge function for it. It is easy to see that only if $\mathbf{f}_i$ is on the interior side of the edge, that is, $e_i(\mathbf{b} + \mathbf{f}_i) \geq 0$, can there be any overlap of T^{xy} and V^{xy}. Hence, we have to check whether this is fulfilled for all three edges. Actually, it turns out that this is also sufficient for an overlap to occur if the bounding box of T^{xy} and V^{xy} overlap, which is always the case in our setup.

Single-triangle, many-voxel testing. Since, in general, a triangle is tested against multiple voxels for overlap, it is reasonable to compute all quantities that depend only on the triangle in the beginning and then to reuse them for the individual voxel overlap tests. Employing the reformulation

$$e_i(\mathbf{b} + \mathbf{f}_i) = \mathbf{m}_i \cdot (\mathbf{b} + \mathbf{f}_i - \mathbf{w}_i) = \mathbf{m}_i \cdot \mathbf{b} + g_i,$$

with $g_i = \mathbf{m}_i \cdot (\mathbf{f}_i - \mathbf{w}_i)$, this means that in a setup phase, the triangle normal $\mathbf{n}$, the distances d_1 and d_2, as well as the quantities $\mathbf{m}_i$ and g_i (for $i = 0, 1, 2$ and each of the three projections xy, xz, and yz) are determined. The actual per-voxel overlap test then merely requires checking whether the expression in Equation (2.1) holds and if $\mathbf{m}_i \cdot \mathbf{b} + g_i \geq 0$ for all edges and 2D projections.

Simplifications. In several situations, it is possible to simplify the described triangle/voxel overlap test and thus reduce its cost. For instance, if the bounding box of the triangle (before clipping to the voxel grid) covers just a one-voxel-thick line of voxels, all voxels are overlapped by the triangle and no further per-voxel test is necessary. Similarly, if the bounding box corresponds to a one-voxel-thick voxel grid slice, only the corresponding 2D triangle/box overlap subtest needs to be performed for each voxel.

Candidate voxel selection. But even in the general case, a noticeable simplification is possible by integrating the overlap test with the selection of potentially overlapped voxels. Key is the observation that a triangle's voxelization is basically two-dimensional and that, hence, visiting all voxels in its bounding box, a 3D volume, is wasteful. This leads to the following strategy: First, determine the grid side that best aligns with the triangle's plane. Then look at the corresponding 2D projection, and loop over the voxel columns covered by the triangle's bounding box, applying the according 2D triangle/box overlap subtest to each. If a column passes the test, determine the range of voxels overlapped by the triangle's plane; their number is at most three per column. If the range comprises just a single voxel, it is guaranteed to be overlapped. Otherwise, the voxels are subjected to the two remaining 2D triangle/box overlap subtests to derive their final overlap status. More details are given in our original publication [Schwarz and Seidel 10].

2.4.3 Discussion

In conservative surface voxelization, generally, significantly more voxels are set than in rasterization-based surface voxelization. In Figure 2.3, for instance, increases of 132% and 305% for the torus knot and the Italian maple, respectively, occur (with respect to rasterization from one direction). Moreover, unlike in ordinary rasterization, all voxels overlapped by an edge shared by multiple triangles are set by each of these triangles, further increasing the number of voxel updates. Together with the fact that the overlap test is much more expensive, this causes conservative voxelization to be slower than surface voxelization using the rasterization-based overlap criterion.

Concerning performance, it is important to understand the implications of pursuing a triangle-parallel approach. First, the scene has to feature a large enough number of triangles to provide enough data parallelism. Moreover, the triangles should produce roughly the same amount of work. For instance, if the scene has a ground plane consisting of only two triangles, the two threads dedicated to their voxelization have to process an excessive number of voxels, easily causing all other threads to finish early, leaving many shader cores idle. In the case of such unfavorable configurations, a simple remedy is to tessellate the scene accordingly. Another option is to distribute the voxelization of a single triangle over multiple threads. This can be achieved by a blocking approach, where each triangle is assigned to those macro grid cells it overlaps, or a tiling approach, where each of the three grid front sides is split into coarse tiles, and each triangle is assigned to those tiles it overlaps from that side to which it aligns best. Each macrocell and tile, respectively, is then processed by a thread group, looping over all assigned triangles. An according implementation is left as an exercise for the interested reader.

As DirectCompute offers less opportunities for fine-tuning than CUDA, reaching performance comparable to optimized CUDA-based implementations is often hard to achieve and is partially at the mercy of the runtime and the driver. Hence, the accompanying source code does not focus on utmost performance but on legibility and structural cleanness, hopefully facilitating both adaptations and retargeting to other compute languages or platforms.

2.5   Solid Voxelization with DirectCompute

Obviously, realizing a software voxelizer using DirectCompute is not restricted to surface voxelization. In this section, we demonstrate an according approach for solid voxelization, which combines ideas from our previous solid and hierarchical, sparse solid voxelization algorithms [Schwarz and Seidel 10].

Similar to the rasterization-based algorithm from Section 2.3, we perform a 2D rasterization of the scene from one side of the voxel cube (xz this time, assuming the data layout from Figure 2.4). For each pixel whose center is covered, we determine the first voxel in the corresponding voxel column whose center is below the processed triangle and flip the state of this voxel with an atomic XOR operation. The other voxels in the column that are below this voxel are not flipped; instead, their update is deferred to a separate propagation pass that is executed once all triangles have been rendered (see Figure 2.8). This means that, after the rasterization, a set voxel indicates that all voxels below should be flipped. To obtain the final solid voxelization, these flips are carried out by the subsequent propagation pass. For each voxel column, it visits all voxels from top to bottom, flipping a voxel's state if the preceding voxel is set. This

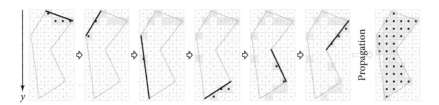

Figure 2.8. During the solid voxelization's initial rasterization pass, in each voxel column covered by a triangle, the state of the first voxel whose center is below the triangle is flipped. The state of the other voxels below is only updated in a subsequent propagation pass, which progresses from top to bottom, flipping a voxel's state if its neighbor directly above is set.

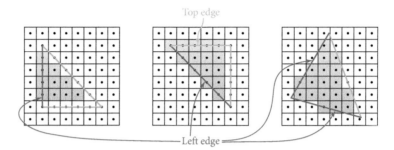

Figure 2.9. In standard rasterization, a pixel is covered by a triangle if its center is located within the triangle. In case the pixel center lies exactly on a triangle edge, it is not considered inside unless the edge is a left or a top edge.

distribution of voxel flips over two passes saves memory bandwidth and reduces the number of atomic update operations and random memory accesses compared to a single-pass approach that directly flips all voxels below, which helps performance.

For the rasterization, we again pursue a triangle-parallel approach, dedicating one thread per triangle. In the compute shader, the triangle's vertices are fetched and transformed, and their bounding box is computed and clipped against the voxel grid. If the bounding box is nonempty, we subsequently loop over all voxel columns (extending in the y-direction) within the xz-extent of the bounding box. For each column, we test in the 2D xz-projection whether the center is overlapped by the triangle. If that is the case, we compute the first voxel in this column whose center is below the triangle and flip the voxel's state.

The 2D overlap test can be efficiently realized by employing the edge functions e_i from Equation (2.2) and evaluating them at the column's 2D center position $\mathbf{q} = [x + \frac{1}{2}, z + \frac{1}{2}]$; if all three results $e_i(\mathbf{q})$ are nonnegative, $\mathbf{q}$ is inside. There is a caveat, though: if $\mathbf{q}$ lies exactly on a triangle's edge, $\mathbf{q}$ is not only inside this triangle but also inside the adjacent triangle with which this edge is shared.[3] Hence, two surface intersections are reported, with the according voxel flips canceling out each other. Except for the case of a silhouette edge, this obviously leads to wrong results because actually only one intersection with the multitriangle surface occurs. A robust remedy is to adopt a consistent fill-rule as employed in hardware rasterization, which assigns an on-edge point to exactly one side of the edge. Using Direct3D's top-left convention, an on-edge point only belongs to a triangle if the edge is a left edge or a horizontal top edge (see Figure 2.9). This can be checked by looking at the edge's normal $\mathbf{m}_i$, leading to the following

---

[3]Since we are assuming closed, watertight geometry, this is always the case.

overlap criterion:

$$\bigwedge_{i=0}^{2}\left(\underbrace{e_i(\mathbf{q}) > 0}_{\text{interior}} \vee \left(\underbrace{e_i(\mathbf{q}) = 0}_{\text{on edge}} \wedge \left(\underbrace{m_{i,x} > 0}_{\text{left edge}} \vee \underbrace{(m_{i,x} = 0 \wedge m_{i,y} < 0)}_{\text{top edge}}\right)\right)\right).$$

Since the edge-classification terms solely depend on the edge's normal, they need only be evaluated once. However, for all this to work, it is necessary that when processing the triangles sharing an edge, consistent numerical results are obtained for the common edge. One way to achieve this is to enforce a consistent ordering of an edge's two vertices.

The subsequent propagation pass proceeds slice-wise in the y-direction, operating on all voxel columns in parallel. A single thread simultaneously processes 32 columns that are consecutive in the z-direction. By design, for each y-slice, the voxels of these columns are represented by different bits of the same 32-bit buffer value; this also provides the motivation for selecting to perform rasterization from the xz-side. The employed compute shader loops over all slices from top to bottom. At each slice, it fetches the buffer value encoding the according voxel states for the 32 columns. This value is then XORed with the value for the previous slice, thus propagating state flips, and written back to the buffer.

2.6 Conclusion

This chapter has shown that (and how) GPU-accelerated binary surface and solid voxelization can be realized with Direct3D 11. On the one hand, we explored how the existing rasterization hardware can be harnessed for this task and how to cope with the absence of bitwise blending. The presented solution is characterized by random atomic buffer writes from within a pixel shader to update the voxelization. While accurate results are obtained for solid voxelization, the quality of surface voxelizations suffers from the inappropriate overlap test performed by ordinary rasterization, which is inherent to all such approaches.

Partially motivated by this shortcoming, we also, on the other hand, looked into how the whole voxelization process can be implemented in software using DirectCompute. Pursuing a simple triangle-parallel approach, for each triangle, all potentially affected voxels or voxel columns, respectively, are considered, applying an overlap test for each to determine their state. For surface voxelization, we detailed a triangle/voxel overlap test that yields a conservative surface voxelization, which obviates the deficiencies of its rasterization-based cousin. By contrast, solid voxelization relies on consistent rasterization, and we described an according approach that defers voxel state flips to a separate pass to improve performance. Overall, the covered techniques demonstrate that resorting to a compute-based software implementation for executing the voxelization offers a large degree of flexibility, and it is up to the reader to explore new overlap criteria, load balancing schemes, and voxel grid representations.

Bibliography

[Dong et al. 04] Zhao Dong, Wei Chen, Hujun Bao, Hongxin Zhang, and Qunsheng Peng. "Real-time Voxelization for Complex Polygonal Models." In *Proceedings of Pacific Graphics 2004*, pp. 43–50. Washington, DC: IEEE Computer Society, 2004.

[Eisemann and Décoret 06] Elmar Eisemann and Xavier Décoret. "Fast Scene Voxelization and Applications." In *Proceedings of ACM SIGGRAPH Symposium on Interactive 3D Graphics and Games 2006*, pp. 71–78. New York: ACM Press, 2006.

[Eisemann and Décoret 08] Elmar Eisemann and Xavier Décoret. "Single-Pass GPU Solid Voxelization for Real-Time Applications." In *Proceedings of Graphics Interface 2008*, pp. 73–80. Toronto: Canadian Information Processing Society, 2008.

[Fang and Chen 00] Shiaofen Fang and Hongsheng Chen. "Hardware Accelerated Voxelization." *Computers & Graphics* 24:3 (2000), 433–442.

[Forest et al. 10] Vincent Forest, Loic Barthe, and Mathias Paulin. "Real-Time Hierarchical Binary-Scene Voxelization." *Journal of Graphics, GPU, and Game Tools* 14:3 (2010), 21–34.

[Hasselgren et al. 05] Jon Hasselgren, Tomas Akenine-Möller, and Lennart Ohlsson. "Conservative Rasterization." In *GPU Gems 2*, edited by Matt Pharr, Chapter 42, pp. 677–690. Reading, MA: Addison-Wesley, 2005.

[Nichols et al. 10] Greg Nichols, Rajeev Penmatsa, and Chris Wyman. "Interactive, Multiresolution Image-Space Rendering for Dynamic Area Lighting." *Computer Graphics Forum* 29:4 (2010), 1279–1288.

[Pineda 88] Juan Pineda. "A Parallel Algorithm for Polygon Rasterization." *Proc. SIGGRAPH '88 (Computer Graphics)* 22:4 (1988), 17–20.

[Reinbothe et al. 09] Christoph K. Reinbothe, Tamy Boubekeur, and Marc Alexa. "Hybrid Ambient Occlusion." In *Eurographics 2009 Annex (Areas Papers)*, pp. 51–57, 2009.

[Schwarz and Seidel 10] Michael Schwarz and Hans-Peter Seidel. "Fast Parallel Surface and Solid Voxelization on GPUs." *ACM Transactions on Graphics* 29:6 (2010), 179:1–179:9.

[Wyman 11] Chris Wyman. "Voxelized Shadow Volumes." In *Proceedings of High Performance Graphics 2011*, 2011.

[Zhang et al. 07] Long Zhang, Wei Chen, David S. Ebert, and Qunsheng Peng. "Conservative Voxelization." *The Visual Computer* 23:9–11 (2007), 783–792.

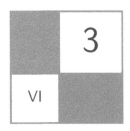

Interactive Ray Tracing Using the Compute Shader in DirectX 11

Arturo García, Francisco Ávila,
Sergio Murguía, and Leo Reyes

3.1 Introduction

Currently, the most widely used technique for real-time 3D rendering is rasterization, mainly because of its low computational cost and the availability of efficient hardware implementations. DirectX and OpenGL are the most common rasterization-based APIs used for high-end video game graphics programming. Rasterization is well suited for handling animated scenes, and no auxiliary data structures are needed to display geometrical changes. On the other hand, ray tracing is traditionally associated with high computational costs, although it could eventually become the video game rendering algorithm of the future as hardware becomes more powerful and ray-tracing techniques grow more sophisticated. Recent advances in ray-tracing engines, acceleration structures, and GPU programmability are making interactive frame rates possible for ray-tracing applications.

This chapter presents an original GPU ray-tracing application running solely on the compute shader and Shader Model 5.0 in DirectX 11. (DirectX 11.1 was released shortly after this writing. The demo uses only DX11.0 features, and a few implementation details may change in DX11.1) The implementation includes gloss mapping, normal mapping, texturing, shadowing, reflections, and a bounding volume hierarchy (BVH) for fast ray-intersection discovery. We analyze the advantages and disadvantages of using multipass ray tracing for handling a number of infinite concurrent textures versus a strategy that handles a limited number of textures in one pass. The ray tracer achieves interactive frame rates on high-end video cards and can be used as a starting point to implement more advanced rendering techniques. (See Figure 3.1.)

Figure 3.1. Sample picture generated by the ray tracer explained in this chapter.

3.2 Ray Tracing

Ray tracing is an advanced illumination technique that simulates the effects of light by tracing rays through the screen on an image plane. The degree of visual realism of the images generated via this technique is considerably higher than that obtained through other rendering methods such as rasterization. However, the computational cost is so high that ray tracing has mostly been used for offline rendering. Nevertheless, real-time ray-tracing applications are available today thanks to constant hardware improvements and algorithmic advances, which ultimately yield more efficient algorithms.

Ray tracing is traditionally known to be a trivially parallel-implementation problem given that the color computation for each pixel is independent of its neighbors. Both CPUs and GPUs are becoming more powerful year after year; however, they have intrinsically different architectures, so it is necessary to have a proper understanding of the interaction between algorithms and hardware in order to achieve optimal performance. In any case, memory handling remains a constant bottleneck, and it is one of the key points that needs to be addressed in order to attain high frame rates.

Efficient data structures are therefore required in order to solve the memory bottleneck. These structures should allow fast memory access and fast ray-geometry intersection discovery. Currently, acceleration structures are frequently used to avoid unnecessary calculations during ray traversal, the most common of which are kd-trees, BVHs, grids, and their variants.

Kd-trees are more efficient for actual rendering but tend to be slower for construction. Grids are their counterpart, having fast construction with an inefficient traversal. The BVH is a trade-off between grid construction velocity and kd-tree performance. It can be built faster than a kd-tree and can still manage to maintain competitive rendering performance.

In the real world, light travels from light sources, bounces between objects, and then reaches our eyes. This is called *forward ray tracing*, since it follows the natural path of the light rays. However, in a ray-tracing implementation, forward ray tracing leads to unnecessary computation. Imagine that you are inside your bedroom and the sun rays enter through your window; such a scene, from your point of view, would be composed of everything your eyes could see inside your room and maybe near your window. What about the rays that are thrown to the roof of your house or to your neighbor's yard? From a computational standpoint, ray-tracing calculations performed for places outside of the rendered scene are obviously a waste of resources. So, to save resources, rays are cast from the eye into the scene and then bounced back to the light sources, following an inverse path. Fittingly, the process can be labeled as *backward ray tracing*; however, current state-of-the-art implementations simply refer to it as *ray tracing*.

The algorithm begins by throwing rays (called *primary rays*) from the point representing the eye into each pixel of the image. The acceleration structure tests each ray on the scene looking for the nearest intersection to the eye—which is the most computationally intensive part of the ray-tracing algorithm. Finally, the algorithm computes the color of the pixel.

Color calculation can be as complex as required by the application. For the computation of shadows, each pixel throws a new ray to each light source to check if an object is blocking the light ray's path. The computation of reflections and refractions requires new calls to the ray-tracing function using the intersected point as the new ray origin. The new direction is the reflected or the refracted direction of the original ray. The pixel color is calculated after all ray bounces (which are called *secondary rays*) have been traversed. If the ray never intersected

```
for each pixel {
   throw ray from the camera position to the pixel;
   if( ray intersects an object ) {
      if( the object is nearer than last one found) {
         nearestObject = object;
      }
   }

   if ( ray hits a primitive ) {
      foreach light {
         throw ray from intersection to light;
         calculate shadow;
      }

      recursively calculate reflections and refractions;
      calculate other desired effects;
      calculate color of the pixel;
   } else {
      pixelColor = backgroundColor;
   }
}
```

Listing 3.1. Whitted-style ray-tracing algorithm.

```
// Primary Rays Stage
generate primary rays;
for each pass {
   for each pixel {
      // Intersection Stage
      if( ray intersects an object ) {
         if( the object is nearer than last one found) {
            nearestObject = object;
         }
      }

      //Color Stage
      if ( ray hits a primitive ) {
         for each light {
            throw ray from intersection to light;
            calculate shade;
         }
         calculate normal mapping;
         calculate gloss mapping;
         calculate reflection;
         accumulate into result;
      }
      else {
         accumulate background color;
         kill pixel;
      }
   }
}
```

Listing 3.2. Our ray-tracing algorithm.

an object, the color of that pixel would be the background color (or whatever the programmer decides).

The ray-tracing algorithm described in this section is shown as pseudocode in Listing 3.1. However, the algorithm was initially proposed for CPU architectures and some adjustments are required in order to make it fit into a GPU-based architecture implementation. Listing 3.2 shows the pseudocode for our ray-tracing algorithm. The main difference between CPU and GPU implementations is that the latter requires various rendering passes to simulate recursion.

3.3 Our Implementation

This chapter describes the implementation of a real-time demo using DirectX 11.0 and Shader Model 5.0 (see also Figure 3.2):

1. The demo builds an acceleration structure (a BVH) on the CPU and sends it through a buffer to the GPU.

2. The ray-tracing algorithm writes the output on an unordered-access-view (UAV) texture as a render target directly from the compute shader.

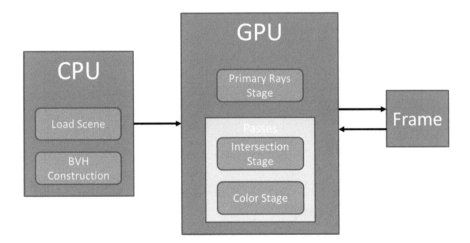

Figure 3.2. The current pipeline of our implementation is divided into three main sections: the CPU preprocess, the GPU rendering, and the final frame. The CPU preprocess consists of loading a scene and building an acceleration structure. The GPU rendering consists of three stages that perform the ray tracing algorithm. Finally, the frame is the output of this pipeline.

3.3.1   The Compute Shader

Current 3D pipelines (Figure 3.3) operate by moving data in a predetermined order through different stages called *shaders*. One of the main characteristics of the compute shader is that it "is not a part" of the pipeline. The compute shader is capable of performing calculations and rendering simultaneously, via the use of general structures similar to C++. Therefore, it is not necessary to render geometry or to ingeniously cast information into textures in order to use the compute shader.

Prior understanding of four of the concepts of the DirectX API is necessary before proceeding: the shader resource view (SRV), the unordered access view (UAV), the render target view (RTV), and the constant buffer.

- An SRV is a read-only resource that can be used as input into any shader. Textures are usually SRVs. The data that will not change during the application execution can be set as SRVs. For example, since our current application is not rebuilding the acceleration structure on each frame, it is sent as SRV to the GPU. In other words, an SRV is the knowledge base of the application.

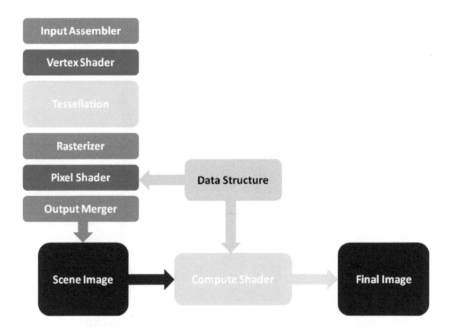

Figure 3.3. Microsoft introduced this pipeline on DirectX 10.1, and it was further improved on DirectX 11.0. Although the compute shader is physically a part of the DirectX pipeline, from the programmer's perspective, the compute shader is, for practical purposes, an independent stage.

- A UAV is a resource that can be read and written on both pixel and compute shaders (textures are usually read-only elements and the only output is set at the end of shader execution). The UAV structures are dynamic; they change throughout the application execution. This feature was introduced with DirectX 11, and it is the key for future GPGPU applications such as the ray-tracer implementation described in this chapter.

- An RTV is a resource that will be presented onscreen as a rendered frame. Optionally, the texture bound as an RTV can also be an SRV or a UAV. In the problem presented in this chapter, the RTV is a UAV since the texture is dynamically filled using the compute shader.

- A constant buffer (or cbuffer) is optimized for storing information that remains constant during the execution of shaders in the GPU, but that can be updated frequently by the CPU between calls to the GPU. It is a read-only resource with a low latency access from the GPU, which is commonly used to store the camera data—which usually changes at every frame—and other small-sized constants.

The current application cannot work on older versions of DirectX because they do not support UAVs, which are extensively used in this application. A workaround for this issue is to use the pixel shader instead. However, this is the technique that has been used to implement (non-CUDA) GPU ray tracers so far. The compute shader is a stage specifically designed for GPGPU programming, and it is ideal for applications like ray tracing. This is because the compute shader is capable of using structures similar to C++, performing reading and writing of different objects defined as UAVs or SRVs and storing the result as either a texture or a structure.

As of this writing, *GPU Pro 3* will be the first publication that includes a compute shader–based ray-tracing application. Independent researchers can use this ray tracer as a starting point to implement more advanced techniques and acceleration structures. Currently, widely available GPU ray tracers force the user to use vendor-specific APIs (like CUDA). Since this ray tracer is not linked to any video card in particular, the user may use whatever platform he or she wishes.

3.3.2 Bounding Volume Hierarchies (BVHs)

BVHs are tree-based acceleration structures that are grounded in a geometric dissection; primitives are stored on leaf nodes, and each internal node stores a bounding box of the primitives contained within it. While traversing the tree, subdivisional tests continue until an intersection with the scene geometry is found, or the test is skipped if the node box is not hit by the ray. BVHs tend to be efficiently built and deliver good performance since they can adapt to irregular primitive distributions across scene geometry.

When used in dynamic scenes, BVHs perform better than kd-trees [Gunther et al. 07], which is why interest in BVHs has grown recently. It is true that grids can be rebuilt from scratch due to their extraordinarily fast construction [Wald et al. 09], but their traversal time is neither comparable with BVH nor with kd-trees [Havran 00, Zlatuska and Havran 10]. Therefore, the BVH offers a fast traversal time in comparison with the performance of kd-trees, but with significantly faster construction time. The BVH is also a compact structure that fits GPU requirements for good performance [Zlatuska and Havran 10].

Construction. After loading the model, the acceleration structure construction is the next task to be performed. Construction is done using one core of the CPU before GPU initialization. When construction is complete, the BVH is sent as SRVs, through two structured buffers, to the GPU. The SRVs contain an ordered array of primitives, as well as an array of nodes. The first structure stores an ordered list of triangle indices used by the BVH during traversal. The second structure is a list of binary tree nodes representing a BVH.

The scope of this chapter does not cover CPU-based construction of a BVH. Our implementation is based on the BVH of the PBRT framework [Pharr and Humphreys 04], which can be consulted for further details. Briefly, the BVH construction consists of the following steps:

1. Select a primitive partition scheme—surface area heuristic (SAH) is highly recommended.

2. Create a bounding box for each primitive.

3. Recursively partition the primitives either left or right depending on the partition scheme selected until all primitives have been allocated.

3.3.3 GPU Initialization

DirectX requires certain initialization of context and resources for an application to be executed. However, it is beyond the scope of this chapter to explain this in detail. The interested reader should consult the latest DirectX documentation from Microsoft for more details. Additionally, the code provided should be self-explanatory.

The SRVs store eight data structures used in the stages of the ray-tracing algorithm. They are divided into three major categories: model information, acceleration structure data, and textures:

- *Vertices SRV.* Stores the vertex data of the model.

- *Indexes SRV.* Every three indices (referencing three vertices) represent a triangle.

- *Materials SRV.* Stores the material ID for each primitive.

- *BVH nodes SRV.* Stores the BVH node data.

- *BVH primitives information SRV.* Store the primitive information of the BVH structure.

- *Textures SRV.* Stores the textures of the scene materials.

- *Normal maps SRV.* Stores the normal maps of the textures loaded.

- *Specular maps SRV.* Stores the specular maps of the textures loaded.

The UAVs store four dynamic data structures. Each frame rendered overwrites the values of each buffer:

- *Rays buffer UAV.* Stores the rays generated in the primary rays stage and their bounces.

- *Intersections buffer UAV.* Stores the nearest intersection found by the intersection stage.

- *Accumulation texture UAV.* DirectX disallows accumulations of colors on textures that are simultaneously bound as RTV and UAV, so instead, this texture is used as a workaround.

- *Result texture UAV.* Stores final frame color and is present onscreen after each iteration.

3.4 Primary Rays Stage

The first step of the ray-tracing algorithm is the primary rays generation. This stage is fairly simple since it creates a ray per pixel with the origin located at the camera position and the direction given by the pixel position. Besides position and direction, the ray structure has one `float` indicating the maximum distance t where the ray has hit, a `float3` representing the light intensity of the current ray, and an `int` storing the `id` of the last triangle hit to prevent errors due to floating point rounding. Also, both the accumulation buffer and the result buffer are initialized during this stage.

The pinhole camera model is used to generate the primary rays. The square with coordinates $(-1, -1, 2)$ and $(1, 1, 2)$ is divided into cells that represent the pixels; the ray that starts at the point $(0, 0, 0)$ and passes through the center of that cell is used as the primary ray. In order to allow rotations and translations, the origin and cell coordinates are first transformed using the world matrix.

On this stage, the `maxT` component of the ray is initialized to a large number. This value is used on the intersection stages to only consider hits that occur at a distance in the range [origin,maxT]. An example of its use is when there is a light source and one needs to find out if that light source is visible from a hit point.

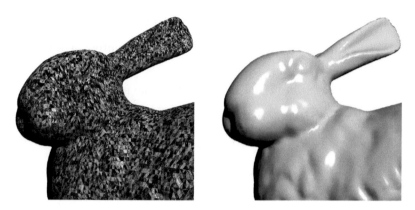

Figure 3.4. Effect of a floating-point precision error when intersecting secondary rays with primitives (left), and the image rendered after fixing this error (right). (See Listing 3.7 for details.)

In such a case, the intersection should only consider triangles that are between the hit point and the light source.

Also during this stage the `TriangleId` component is initialized to −1. This variable is used to store an identifier of the last triangle hit by the ray to prevent a secondary ray hitting the same triangle used to generate it. For instance, when projecting a ray at a mirror, the reflected ray may hit the same mirror sometimes due to numerical errors. In order to prevent such errors (see Figure 3.4), the intersection stage will only check triangles with an `id` different to `TriangleId`. Another component initialized on this stage is the reflective factor; this variable stores a `float3` that is used on the color stage before accumulating the color to the accumulation buffer. It is used to simulate how much light a surface can reflect or refract. (See Listing 3.3.)

```
//generate pixel coordinates
float inverse = 1.0f/(float(N));
float y = -float(2.f * DTiId.y + 1.f - N) * inverse;
float x = float(2.f * DTiId.x + 1.f - N) * inverse;
float z = 2.0f;

// Create new ray from the camera position to the pixel position
Ray ray;
float4 aux = (mul(float4(0,0,0,1.f),g_mfWorld));
ray.vfOrigin = aux.xyz/aux.w;
float3 vfPixelPosition = mul(float4(x,y,z,1.f),
    g_mfWorld).xyz;
ray.vfDirection = normalize(vfPixelPosition-ray.vfOrigin);
ray.fMaxT = 10000000000000000.f;
ray.vfReflectiveFactor = float3(1.f,1.f,1.f);
ray.iTriangleId = -1;
ray.iPadding = 0;
```

```
unsigned int index = DTiId.y * N + DTiId.x;
// Copy ray to global UAV
g_uRays[index] = ray;
g_uAccumulation[index] = 0.0f;
```

Listing 3.3. Primary rays stage.

3.5 Intersection Stage

Whenever a new ray (either primary or secondary) is generated, it must search through the scene to find the closest intersection with the camera space. This stage calls the function that computes the intersection between a single ray and the current geometry using an acceleration structure. A buffer stores the ID of the nearest triangle hit since this information is used by the next stage: the color computation stage.

The intersection stage code is shown in Listing 3.4. It calls the traversal function and assigns the intersection information to the corresponding buffer for each pixel. It is important to remember that the UAV buffers store the information for each pixel. Then, each pixel knows its color, its best intersection, and its primary ray.

Certainly, the acceleration structure function could be called directly instead of using an intermediary function to start traversal; however, this scheme allows for a more flexible approach where different acceleration structures or traversal algorithms can easily be added to the framework.

```
if ( g_uRays[index].iTriangleId > (-2) )
    g_uIntersections[index] = BVH_IntersectP(g_uRays[index]);
else
    g_uIntersections[index].iTriangleId = -2;
```

Listing 3.4. Intersection stage. When **iTriangleId** is equal to -2, the ray on the current pixel is no longer active.

3.5.1 Simple Traversal

The simple traversal is the naïve approach for searching the nearest intersection. Each ray tests each primitive in the scene. In other words, this function does not use an acceleration structure and might be used for debugging purposes. Bear in mind, however, that this debugging approach is only practical for scenes with only a few primitives.

```
Intersection cIntersection;
Intersection bIntersection;
bIntersection.iTriangleId = -1;
bIntersection.fT = 10000.f;
bIntersection.fU = -1;
bIntersection.fV = -1;

const int iNumPrimitives = 10;

for(int i = 0; i < iNumPrimitives; ++i)
{
    unsigned int offset = i*3;
    float3 A = g_sVertices[g_sIndices[offset]].vfPosition;
    float3 B = g_sVertices[g_sIndices[offset+1]].vfPosition;
    float3 C = g_sVertices[g_sIndices[offset+2]].vfPosition;

    cIntersection = getIntersection(ray,A,B,C);
    if(ray.iTriangleId != i &&
       RayTriangleTest(cIntersection) &&
       cIntersection.fT < bIntersection.fT)
    {
        bIntersection = cIntersection;
        bIntersection.iTriangleId = i;
    }
}
```

Listing 3.5. Simple traversal.

The traversal algorithm in Listing 3.5 returns the best intersection (the nearest intersection). The traversal iterates on each primitive of the scene (for each pixel) and tests the primitives looking for an intersection. If the ray intersects the primitive, the current intersection compares itself against the best intersection until that moment to check whether the newest intersection is better than all others previously found. This is repeated until all the primitives have been analyzed. That is the reason why this method is only for debug purposes. It does not make real-time applications possible since the traversal is the most time-consuming part of any ray-tracing algorithm.

3.5.2   BVH Traversal

The BVH traversal is what makes real-time performance possible. In this case, we chose to have one primitive per leaf node (at most) since overall performance revealed better results this way. Just like a classic BVH, the ray traverses down the structure testing against node boxes to check whether or not a ray intersects the box. The function shown in Listing 3.6 returns two distance t values, representing the nearest and farthest intersection points. It is important to note that if/else-based implementations do not perform optimally on the GPU. In-

```
float2 BVH_IntersectBox(float3 vfStart,float3 vfInvDir,
    unsigned int uiNodeNum)
{
    float2 T;

    float3 vfDiffMax = g_sNodes[uiNodeNum].vfMax-vfStart;
    vfDiffMax *= vfInvDir;
    float3 vfDiffMin = g_sNodes[uiNodeNum].vfMin-vfStart;
    vfDiffMin *= vfInvDir;

    T[0] = min(vfDiffMin.x,vfDiffMax.x);
    T[1] = max(vfDiffMin.x,vfDiffMax.x);

    T[0] = max(T[0],min(vfDiffMin.y,vfDiffMax.y));
    T[1] = min(T[1],max(vfDiffMin.y,vfDiffMax.y));

    T[0] = max(T[0],min(vfDiffMin.z,vfDiffMax.z));
    T[1] = min(T[1],max(vfDiffMin.z,vfDiffMax.z));

    //empty interval
    if (T[0] > T[1])
    {
        T[0] = T[1] = -1.0f;
    }

    return T;
}
```

Listing 3.6. Bounding box intersection function.

stead, a min/max-based implementation must be used and a manual unroll is recommended since ray tracing is commonly performed on a three-dimensional space.

The traversal algorithm consists of the following steps:

1. Initialize variables.

2. Pop a node from the stack.

3. Perform a ray-box intersection with the current node box.

4. If an intersection is found, check if the node is either a leaf or an internal node. If it is a leaf, test the primitives inside the node. If it is an internal node, push its children into the stack.

5. Repeat Steps 2–4 until the stack is empty (no more nodes left).

The BVH implementation shown in Listing 3.7 is stack based. An array, called **stack**, stores the nodes-to-visit and simulates the behavior of a stack. If the ray does not intersect the node box, the stack pops a node for the next iteration. On the other hand, if the ray does intersect the node, two actions may be performed depending on whether the node is a leaf or an internal node.

- If the node is a leaf, the ray tests the primitive, looking for an intersection. If the leaf node contains more than one primitive, then an extra ray-box intersection test is recommended before testing the primitives themselves. That operation would also add more execution branches and increase the number of comparisons, which is the main reason why the authors suggest just one primitive per leaf node.

- If the node is an internal node, its children are added to the stack for future tests. The push order of the left and right children depends on the ray direction. If the direction of the ray on the current axis is negative, then the right child is pushed first and vice versa. This process repeats itself until the stack is empty. In other words, the loop ends when the array offset becomes zero.

```
[allow_uav_condition]while(true)
{
    // Perform ray-box intersection test
    float2 T = BVH_IntersectBox(ray.vfOrigin,vfInvDir,iNodeNum);

    // If the ray does not intersect the box
    if ((T[0] > bIntersection.fT) || (T[1] < 0.0f))
    {
        // If the stack is empty, the traversal ends
        if(iStackOffset == 0) break;
        // Pop a new node from the stack
        iNodeNum = stack[--iStackOffset];
    }
    // If the intersected box is a Leaf Node
    else if(g_sNodes[nodeNum].nPrimitives > 0)
    {
        // Get the triangle iId contained by the node
        iTrId = g_sNodes[iNodeNum].primitivesOffset;
        iTrId = g_sPrimitives[iTrId];

        // Get the triangle data
        int offset = iTrId*3;

        float3 A=g_sVertices[g_sIndices[offset]].vfPosition;
        float3 B=g_sVertices[g_sIndices[offset+1]].vfPosition;
        float3 C=g_sVertices[g_sIndices[offset+2]].vfPosition;

        cIntersection = getIntersection(ray,A,B,C);
        // Search for an intersection:
        // 1. Avoid float-precision errors.
        // 2. Perform ray-triangle intersection test.
        // 3. Check if the new intersection is nearer to
        // the camera than the current best intersection.
        if((ray.iTriangleId != iTrId)
            && (RayTriangleTest(cIntersection)  )
            && (cIntersection.fT < bIntersection.fT))
        {
            bIntersection = cIntersection;
```

```
            bIntersection.iTriangleId = iTrId;
            bIntersection.iRoot = iNodeNum;
        }

        // If the stack is empty, the traversal ends
        if(iStackOffset == 0) break;
        // Pop a new node from the stack
        iNodeNum = stack[--iStackOffset];
    }
    // If the intersected box is an Inner Node
    else
    {
        // Depending on the ray direction and the split-axis,
        // the order of the children changes on the stack.
        int dirIsNeg[3] = { vfInvDir < 0 };
        const int iAxis = -g_sNodes[iNodeNum].nPrimitives;
        const int aux = dirIsNeg[iAxis];
        stack[iStackOffset++] = (iNodeNum+1)*aux + (1-aux)*
            g_sNodes[iNodeNum].primitivesOffset;
            aux + (1-aux)*(iNodeNum+1);
    }
}
```

Listing 3.7. BVH traversal.

Due to floating-point precision errors, secondary rays might hit the primitive where the secondary rays were generated. In order to prevent such errors, the secondary ray checks if the primitive intersected in the previous pass is different from the current primitive analyzed. If both primitives are the same, the primitive being tested is skipped. Figure 3.4 shows the effects of this glitch, which produces a noisy image.

Some specific tags must be added to the code to allow the correct compilation of the shader. The [allow_uav_condition] tag indicates that the loop termination depends on a UAV buffer that changes dynamically during execution. This will not change the application's behavior; in fact, it should be thought of as a warning tag of something that must be carefully coded.

3.6 Color Stage

The color stage computes the color for each pixel. It uses different effects to add realism to the final frame. Those effects require secondary rays and more than one pass to accomplish a better visual impact. The ray tracer described in this chapter includes phong or flat shading, texturing, normal mapping, gloss mapping, environment mapping, and reflections.

3.6.1 Common Rasterization Techniques

The ray tracer implements several techniques that are common in rasterization engines, such as flat and phong shading, texturing, normal mapping, gloss mapping, and environment mapping. When implementing these techniques in a common rasterizer, the 3D rasterization pipeline takes care of interpolating values between adjacent vertices (using the GPU), so that the information needed to compute these effects is already present at each pixel to be rendered. The ray tracer, however, runs on the compute shader, so this vertex information is not interpolated by the pipeline. Instead, the triangle-ray intersection function returns the barycentric coordinates of the intersection, and these coordinates are then used to interpolate the information needed at each pixel.

An interesting side effect of the ray-tracing engine is that it already behaves as a rasterizer that uses "deferred shading." In deferred shading, the rasterizer prerenders the scene to know which pixels are ultimately visible, so as not to waste resources computing effects for pixels that will be obscured by other geometry. With the ray-tracing engine, this comes free since the closest intersection to the camera is always computed.

Another point that must be noted is that the implementation of environment mapping is also slightly different. This is detailed next.

3.6.2 Environment Mapping

Environment mapping is a technique that provides a texture-based representation of a scene's surrounding environment. It is often used to simulate reflections on a closed surface or to represent the horizon and the sky of an open scene. Two techniques can be used to do environment mapping: spherical mapping and cube mapping. We used the latter in the ray tracer, since it is more accurate. The

Figure 3.5. Images rendered by the ray tracer using environment mapping with three reflections. The Stanford Bunny (left) is running at 47 frames per second and the Stanford Dragon (right) at 22 frames per second.

```
const float4 tx_Environment = g_sEnvironmentTx.SampleLevel(
    g_ssSampler, g_uRays[index].vfDirection.xyz,0);
//Environment mapping
vfFinalColor.xyz = vfFactor.xyz * tx_Environment.xyz;
// This indicates that the Environment Mapping has
// been applied to the current pixel.
g_uRays[index].iTriangleId = -2;
```

Listing 3.8. Environment mapping.

impact on the performance is negligible and it adds an interesting effect, as shown in Figure 3.5.

In order to implement environment mapping, rays must be cast from the scene into the environment. Then, the direction of the ray is used to sample the environment map and get a color. However, the ray tracer already casts rays, so implementing this technique in the framework is rather straight-forward: whenever a ray misses the geometry (i.e., when the ray-triangle intersection is void), the environment map is sampled once. If the ray is primary, then the color will end up in the "background"; if the ray comes from a reflection or a refraction, then the color sampled from the environment map will be mixed with the color of the surface and will be back-propagated through all the previous bounces. In any case, the environment map must be sampled exactly once, and this is indicated in the code by setting a flag in the **iTriangleID** field of the current ray. The code in Listing 3.8 is self-explanatory. Basically, environment mapping enables a predetermined background texture and allows the background to be reflected into the scene.

3.6.3 Ray Bounces

A ray bounce might be understood as a reflection or a refraction. However, the current ray tracer only includes reflections due to performance issues when using both effects at the same time. It is an interesting challenge to add material support for both refractive and reflective objects while maintaining a real-time frame rate.

The naïve implementation for both reflections and refractions is based on throwing a new ray for each effect. In other words, an extra rendering pass for each ray bounce is required. This leads to computing n images to create one frame (where n is the number of ray bounces), which translates into a high computational cost. Performance can be traded for realism; however, in the ray tracer provided, the number of ray reflections is controlled by the user via a global parameter.

Implementing reflections in code is quite simple, as shown in Listing 3.9. The CPU function controlling the rendering must add an extra pass to compute a

```
g_uRays[index].vfReflectiveFactor *= tx_SpecularColor;
g_uRays[index].vfOrigin = vfHitPoint;
g_uRays[index].vfDirection = vfNewDirection;
g_uRays[index].iTriangleId = iTriangleId;
```

Listing 3.9. Ray bounces.

frame. If three reflections are simulated, then three extra passes are added. It is important to notice that the primary-rays shader must not be executed since a reflection is a secondary ray. Both the intersection stage and the color stage are executed for each pass. However, at the end of the color stage execution, the ray's buffer must be modified. The new origin is the intersection found by the last ray stored in that pixel. The new direction is given by the reflection of the last ray stored in that pixel. The reflective factor is diminished a little bit after each bounce according to the specular map. This is done to account for the fact that, in nature, only a portion of the incident light is reflected.

Computing pixel color. The color at each pixel is computed using the well-known Phong illumination equation. Then, two more rays are cast from the current point: one ray is sent to the light source in order to figure out if the current point is shadowed and another ray is reflected according to the current normal (an example of this simple illumination scheme is shown in Figure 3.6). This

Figure 3.6. Happy Buddha (1,087,716 triangles) and Welsh Dragon (2,210,673 triangles) ray-traced with phong shading and shadows.

```
// Apply color to texture
g_uAccumulation[index] += vfFinalColor;
g_uResultTexture[DTid.xy] = g_uAccumulation[index];
```

Listing 3.10. Compute color.

reflected ray is recursively traced and accumulated with the current color as shown in Listing 3.10.

3.7 Multipass Approach

A multipass approach is not about having multiple ray bounces. Currently, a single pass is enough to compute all pixel colors no matter what material is attached to the intersected primitive thanks to texture arrays. A multipass approach renders one material per pass, which is useful when limited resources are available such as number of textures or texture memory.

Older versions of DirectX were limited to allocating eight textures simultaneously, and the last version released in June 2010 is capable of allocating up to 128 textures. However, it is possible to have an infinite number of textures using a multipass approach by changing the material-to-render on each pass. Obviously, performance is impacted by this approach and some code reordering will be needed.

The shader needs to know what the current rendered material is in advance. The constant buffer is the best choice since it is optimized for constant variables and for changing its values constantly on the CPU (which the multipass approach will perform). The shader computes the pixel color just as if the current intersected primitive had the current-material-to-render attached to itself. Otherwise, the shader is skipped. On each pass, the SRVs, or any buffer that stores the texture information, should be updated with the current-material-to-render information.

Another feasible approach that balances resource availability and performance would be to load 128 materials after each pass. This way, 256 materials could be rendering by performing two passes—but the code becomes even more complicated.

3.8 Results and Discussion

The tests were executed on an Nvidia GTX 480. The Stanford Dragon, the Happy Buddha, and the Welsh Dragon are used to directly measure the frames per second (FPS) of our framework so that it may be compared against other

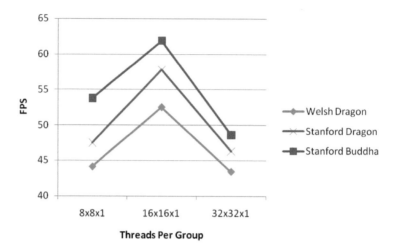

Figure 3.7. Performance of different compute shader threads per group configurations. The tests were executed with shadows, phong shading, and gloss mapping but without environment mapping, reflections, or normal mapping. The x-axis shows the number of threads per group and the y-axis the number of frames per second.

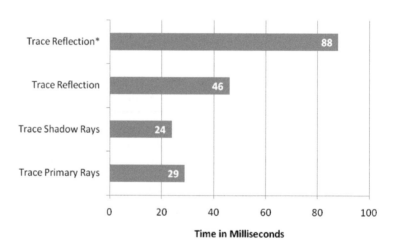

Figure 3.8. Time needed to execute each render step for a single frame. The x-axis shows the time in milliseconds, and the individual rendering steps are plotted in the y-axis. The results are averaged using six different cameras on the Crytek Sponza model. The tracing algorithm includes both ray generation and ray-triangle intersection. Each step is computed independently, and two different measures were computed for tracing one reflection: with and without normal mapping and shadows.

ray tracers. The Crytek Sponza was used to measure the performance on a more realistic context with an averaged FPS given different camera positions and directions. The grid size is $64 \times 64 \times 1$, and the group size is $16 \times 16 \times 1$ to launch a total of 1,048,576 threads in the compute shader. The resolution is set to $1{,}024^2$, where each thread computes the color of one pixel.

The best configuration for evenly distributed threads is a grid size of $64 \times 64 \times 1$ groups and a group size of $16 \times 16 \times 1$ threads. This is shown in Figure 3.7, where this tendency remains regardless of the model used.

The full capabilities of the ray-tracing framework are exploited by scenes such as Crytek Sponza. Figure 3.8 shows the time needed by each render step to produce a single frame. Ray-box and ray-triangle intersections are the most time-consuming operations and rely heavily on the effectiveness of the acceleration structure employed. Based on recent publications (such as [Pantaleoni and Luebke 10, Kalojanov et al. 11, Garanzha et al. 11]), these render times still allow a full BVH/grid reconstruction on the GPU at every frame while still maintaining real-time frame rates.

3.9 Optimization

In order to reduce branches, the color stage skips if the ray does not intersect any primitive. Since each group computes the color of a 16×16 pixel patch, the primary rays on the same warp test against similar objects reducing the number of branches. However, secondary rays are not coherent, which impacts significantly the final execution time when shading, reflections, or both are active. The ray stage could be decomposed in different kernels for reordering, which would improve ray coherence [Garanzha and Loop 10].

Although current hardware supports double-precision floating-point variables, it is preferable to use single-precision floating-point variables in order to speed up the ray tracer. A ray-tracing algorithm does not require high-precision calculations, and the differences in the images produced using either method are not noticeable.

In a GPU application, it is very important to properly set up the grid/group/thread configuration. The GPU computation tasks are commonly addressed as grids. A grid is conformed by one or more thread groups. A thread group is conformed by one or more threads. Since GPUs were created for massive parallel execution, the hardware must have a large workload divided into small tasks. Three rules should be met to take full advantage of the power of the GPU [Fung 10]:

1. The ratio of the number of thread groups per multiprocessor should be greater than 2. The number of thread groups in the ray tracer is 4,096 and the number of multiprocessors is 16. The ratio is 256, which is clearly greater than 2.

2. The number of thread groups should be greater than 100 in order to scale well to future devices and greater than 1,000 to scale across multiple generations. The number of thread groups in the ray tracer is 4,096, which is more than four times the number of thread groups suggested to scale to multiple generations.

3. The number of threads per thread group should be a multiple of the warp size. The number of threads per group in the ray tracer is 256, which is a multiple of 32 (the warp size) since $256/32 = 8$.

3.10 Conclusion

This chapter described a step-by-step ray-tracing implementation in the compute shader using Shader Model 5.0 in DirectX 11.0. The application includes the most-used effects in ray tracing and allows programmers to add their own code or to modify the existing code in order to improve the visual effects and their performance.

The compute shader capabilities will improve video game quality and other real-time DirectX-based applications. The techniques described in this chapter can be easily attached to different stages of current commercial applications. Furthermore, similar research fields such as radiosity, ambient occlusion, or global illumination can take advantage of the framework described here.

3.11 Further Work

We are currently interested in developing dynamic scenes, refractions, and global illumination effects on the ray tracer. The BVH might be rebuilt on each frame [Pantaleoni and Luebke 10] in order to accomplish dynamic scenes and enable interactive applications, such as video games, with a ray tracing–based renderer. It would be desirable to build a CPU–GPU hybrid to take advantage of the CPU power as well, given that the current ray tracer does not use the CPU during the frame calculation.

A Monte Carlo approach has been implemented on the current ray tracer, pursuing global illumination effects like those shown in Figure 3.9 (the implementation of global illumination is not included in the demo). However, rendering a single frame takes several minutes. Currently, decreasing the rendering time of global illumination effects in order to produce photorealistic images is an open challenge in computer graphics. Due to the GPU architecture and the capabilities of the compute shader, this DirectCompute stage seems like a desirable target with which to try out global illumination approaches.

Figure 3.9. Global illumination.

3.12 Acknowledgments

The authors would like to thank the Stanford Computer Graphics Laboratory for the Happy Buddha, the Stanford Dragon, and the Stanford Bunny models; Bangor University for the Welsh Dragon model (released for Eurographics 2011); Crytek for its modified version of the Sponza model; and Matt Pharr and Greg Humphreys for their permission to base the BVH implementation on the PBRT framework [Pharr and Humphreys 04].

Bibliography

[Fung 10] James Fung. "DirectCompute Lecture Series 210: GPU Optimizations and Performance." http://channel9.msdn.com/Blogs/gclassy/DirectCompute-Lecture-Series-210-GPU-Optimizations-and-Performance, 2010.

[Garanzha and Loop 10] Kirill Garanzha and Charles Loop. "Fast Ray Sorting and Breadth-First Packet Traversal for GPU Ray Tracing." *Computer Graphics Forum* 29:2 (2010), 289–298.

[Garanzha et al. 11] Kirill Garanzha, Simon Premož, Alexander Bely, and Vladimir Galaktionov. "Grid-based SAH BVH Construction on a GPU." *The Visual Computer* 27 (2011), 697–706. Available online (http://dx.doi.org/10.1007/s00371-011-0593-8).

[Gunther et al. 07] Johannes Gunther, Stefan Popov, Hans-Peter Seidel, and Philipp Slusallek. "Realtime Ray Tracing on GPU with BVH-based Packet Traversal." In *Proceedings of the 2007 IEEE Symposium on Interactive Ray Tracing*, pp. 113–118. Washington, DC: IEEE Computer Society, 2007.

[Havran 00] Vlastimil Havran. "Heuristic Ray Shooting Algorithms." Ph.d. thesis, Czech Technical University in Prague, 2000.

[Kalojanov et al. 11] Javor Kalojanov, Markus Billeter, and Philipp Slusallek. "Two-Level Grids for Ray Tracing on GPUs." In *EG 2011: Full Papers*, edited by Oliver Deussen Min Chen, pp. 307–314. Llandudno, UK: Eurographics Association, 2011.

[Pantaleoni and Luebke 10] J. Pantaleoni and D. Luebke. "HLBVH: Hierarchical LBVH Construction for Real-Time Ray Tracing of Dynamic Geometry." In *Proceedings of the Conference on High Performance Graphics, HPG '10*, pp. 87–95. Aire-la-Ville, Switzerland: Eurographics Association, 2010.

[Pharr and Humphreys 04] Matt Pharr and Greg Humphreys. *Physically Based Rendering: From Theory to Implementation*. San Francisco: Morgan Kaufmann Publishers, 2004.

[Wald et al. 09] Ingo Wald, William R Mark, Johannes Günther, Solomon Boulos, Thiago Ize, Warren Hunt, Steven G Parker, and Peter Shirley. "State of the Art in Ray Tracing Animated Scenes." *Computer Graphics Forum* 28:6 (2009), 1691–1722.

[Zlatuska and Havran 10] M. Zlatuska and V. Havran. "Ray Tracing on a GPU with CUDA: Comparative Study of Three Algorithms." http://dcgi.felk.cvut.cz/home/havran/ARTICLES/ZlatuskaHavran2010wscg.pdf, 2010. Proceedings of WSCG '10, Communication Papers.

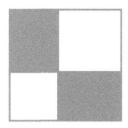

About the Editors

Wessam Bahnassi is a software engineer with a background in building architecture. This combination is believed to be the reason behind Wessam's passion for 3D engine design. He has written and dealt with a variety of engines throughout a decade of game development. Currently, he is a lead rendering engineer at Electronic Arts Inc., and a supervisor of the Arabic Game Developer Network. Although a bit out of context here, his heart beats for the Syrian revolution, as well as the other Arabic revolutions in general, to which he dedicates this work.

Wolfgang Engel is the CTO/CEO and cofounder of Confetti Special Effects Inc. (www.conffx.com), a think tank for advanced real-time graphics research for the video game and movie industry. Previously he worked for more than four years in Rockstar's core technology group as the lead graphics programmer. His game credits can be found at http://www.mobygames.com/developer/sheet/view/developerId,158706/. He is the editor of the *ShaderX* and *GPU Pro* book series, the author of several other books, and speaks on graphics programming at conferences worldwide. He has been a DirectX MVP since July 2006 and is active in several advisory boards in the industry. He also teaches "GPU Programming" at UCSD. You can find him on twitter at @wolfgangengel.

Carsten Dachsbacher is a full professor at the Karlsruhe Institute of Technology. Prior to joining KIT, he was an assistant professor at the Visualization Research Center (VISUS) of the University of Stuttgart, Germany, and post-doctoral fellow at REVES/INRIA Sophia-Antipolis, France. He received a MS in computer science from the University of Erlangen-Nuremberg, Germany, in 2002 and a PhD in computer science in 2006. His research focuses on real-time computer graphics, interactive global illumination, and perceptual rendering, on which he has published several articles at various conferences, including SIGGRAPH, I3D, EG, and EGSR. He has been a tutorial speaker at Eurographics, SIGGRAPH, and the Game Developers Conference and a reviewer for various conferences and journals.

Christopher Oat is Lead Graphics Programmer at Rockstar New England where he works on real-time rendering techniques used in Rockstar's latest games. Previously, he was the Demo Team Lead for AMD's Game Computing Applications Group. Christopher has published his work in various books and journals and has presented at graphics and game developer conferences worldwide. Many of the projects that he has worked on can be found on his website: www.chrisoat.com.

Sebastien St-Laurent holds a degree in computer engineering from Sherbrooke University in Quebec (Canada) where he graduated at the top of his class in 1999. Since then, he has worked at many video game companies, including Z-Axis, Microsoft, and Neversoft. His interest, focus, and passion has always been computer graphics. Sebastien St-Laurent is also a published author who has written *Shaders for Game Programmers and Artists* and *The COMPLETE Effect and HLSL Guide*.

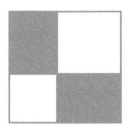

About the Contributors

Francisco Ávila received his BSc from ITESM, Mexico, in December 2011. He has been a research intern in the Visual and Parallel Computing group at Intel since April 2010. He is pursuing a PhD degree, and his research interests include GPGPU and parallel algorithms.

Florian Bagar is a Rendering Software Engineer at Havok Inc., in Southern Germany. He previously worked as a Senior Programmer at Sproing Interactive Media GmbH. He studied computer graphics and digital image processing at the Vienna University of Technology, where he received an MSc degree in 2010. His current interests include real-time rendering, game development, multi-platform development, optimization, and engine design.

Pál Barta is pursuing a MS degree at the Technical University in Budapest, Hungary. Over the last two years, his main focus has been on computer graphics. His 2010 BSc thesis topic was order independent transparency, which later evolved into the volumetric transparency method described in this book.

Jiri Bittner is an assistant professor of electrical engineering of the Czech Technical University in Prague. He received his PhD in 2003 at the same institute. His research interests include visibility computations, real-time rendering, spatial data structures, and global illumination. He has also participated in creating commercial projects that deal with real-time rendering of complex scenes.

Alan Chambers obtained an MSc with Distinction in computer science from the University of Wales, Swansea in 2002. Since then he has worked at Sony Computer Entertainment Europe on games such as *Formula 1* and *WipEout*. He is now the Lead Graphics Engineer at New Zealand's largest game development studio, Sidhe, and has a specific interest in engine programming and optimizations. Alan is also a keen pilot and can often be found cruising around the skies of New Zealand in his spare time.

Elmar Eisemann is an associate professor at Telecom ParisTech (ENST). Previously, he was a senior scientist heading a research group in the Cluster of Excellence (Saarland University / MPI Informatik). He has also worked at MIT, UIUC, and Adobe and as local organizer of the Eurographics Symposium on Rendering (2010). His interests include real-time and perceptual rendering, alternative representations, shadow algorithms, global illumination, and GPU acceleration techniques. He has published several articles at various conferences, book chapters, and journal papers and coauthored the book *Real-Time Shadows*. He obtained an MS degree in 2004 and a PhD degree in 2008 in mathematics/computer science from Grenoble University. In 2011, he received the Eurographics Young Researcher Award.

Arturo García holds a BS degree in computer sciences from the University of Guadalajara. He received an MS degree in computer science from CINVESTAV and an MBA degree from ITESO. He is currently Engineering Manager at Intel.

Pascal Gautron received his PhD from the University of Rennes, France, for his work on interactive global illumination. He is now a senior scientist at Technicolor Research & Innovation. His major fields of interest are global illumination, rendering of participating media, and interactive navigation in large environments. He also contributes to high-quality rendering and real-time previsualization of post-production assets for the Moving Picture Company.

Mark Gjøl is a systems developer at Zylinc, with a focus on mobipe platforms. This interest has initially been realized as the spare-time project *Floating Image* for Android, which has achieved a rating of 4.3/5.0 with more than 950,000 downloads. He received an MS degree in computer graphics from the Danish Technical University in 2007.

Mikkel Gjøl is a graphics programmer at Splash Damage, a UK-based company that recently released the game *Brink* on the Xbox360, Playstation3, and PC. He received an MS degree in computer graphics from the Danish Technical University in 2005.

Thorsten Grosch is an associater professor of computational visualistics at the University of Magdeburg, Germany. Prior to this appointment he worked as a post-doctoral fellow at MPI Informatik in Saarbruecken. Thorsten received his PhD at the University of Koblenz-Landau; his main research interest is in both the area of real-time and physically accurate global illumination.

Holger Gruen ventured into 3D real-time graphics right after his university graduation, writing fast software rasterizers in 1993. Since then he has held research and also development positions in the middleware, games, and the simulation industries. He addressed himself to doing developer relations in 2005 and now works for AMD's product group. Holger, his wife, and his four kids live in Germany close to Munich and near the Alps.

Niklas Henrich works as a researcher at rmh new media GmbH in Cologne, Germany. He studied computational visualistics at the University of Koblenz-Landau, where he received his PhD in 2011. His main research interests are global illumination algorithms and the colorimetrically correct output of the rendering results.

Matthew Johnson is a software engineer at Advanced Micro Devices, Inc., with over 13 years of experience in the computer industry. He wrote his first game as a hobby in Z80 assembly language for the TI-86 graphic calculator. Today, he is a member of the DirectX 11 driver team and actively involved in developing software for future GPUs. Matthew currently lives in Orlando, Florida, with his lovely wife.

Nickolay Kasyan is a Senior Rendering Engineer at Crytek, where he has been working on graphics technology and engine design for the past seven years. He received an MS in computer science from the Kharkov National University of Radio Electronics. Soon after, his passion for computer graphics led him to the development of 3D engines and later to Crytek. Nickolay has worked on titles such as *Crysis, Crysis Warhead,* and recently *Crysis 2*. He is currently focused on the development of graphics technology for the next generation of Crytek products.

Oliver Klehm is a PhD student in the computer graphics group at the Max Planck Institute (MPI) for Informatics. In 2011 he received an MSc from the Hasso-Plattner-Institut, Potsdam, Germany. His research interests include interactive global illumination and visibility algorithms, as well as general-purpose GPU programming. In addition to an algorithmic focus, he is also interested in designing complex software that incorporates sets of different algorithms.

Balázs Kovács is a BSc student at the Technical University in Budapest, Hungary. His research interests include interactive global illumination rendering techniques and tomographic reconstruction algorithms in CUDA.

Dzmitry Malyshau is a game engine developer at JVL Labs Inc. He was born and grew up in Belarus, graduated in applied math and computer science, and later migrated to Canada to work on interactive touch-screen games. Aside from experimenting with different rendering pipelines, he is actively researching compression techniques, networking security, and artificial intelligence problems.

Jean-Eudes Marvie is a Senior Scientist at Technicolor Research & Innovation. He received an MSc degree from the University of Rennes 1 and a MEng degree from the National Institute of Applied Sciences in 2001. He was awarded a PhD in computer graphics by INRIA in 2004. His research interests are real-time rendering, large models visualization and generation, procedural modeling and rendering, distributed applications dedicated to interactive visualization, rendering on large displays, and virtual reality. He is currently leading a team of 10 researchers, applying these techniques to the field of interactive previsualization for cinema production at Moving Picture Company and also to interactive applications on set-top boxes at Technicolor Digital Delivery Group. He previously applied some of these techniques for real-time visual effects on live broadcast systems for Grass Valley.

Oliver Mattausch is currently working as a post-doctoral researcher at the University of Tokyo. Previously, he was a researcher at the Institute of Computer Graphics and Algorithms of the Vienna University of Technology, where he also received an MSc in 2004 and a PhD in 2010. He has coauthored several papers and articles in the fields of real-time rendering and scientific visualization. His research interests are real-time rendering, visibility computations, shadow algorithms, and real-time global illumination.

Pavlos Mavridis is a software engineer at the Foundation of the Hellenic World, where he is working on the design and implementation of real-time rendering techniques for virtual reality installations. He received his BSc and MSc degrees in computer science from the University of Athens, Greece. He is currently pursuing his PhD in real-time computer graphics at the Department of Informatics of the Athens University of Economics and Business. His current research interests include real-time photorealistic rendering, global illumination algorithms, texture compression, and texture filtering techniques.

Stefan Müller is director of the IWM / Institute for Computer Visualization at the University of Koblenz-Landau and professor of computer graphics. His research focus includes interactive computer graphics, in particular virtual and augmented reality.

Sergio Murguía received a BSc from the University of Guanajuato in 2005 and an MSc from the Center of Research in Mathematics (CIMAT) in Mexico. In 2009, he joined Intel to work on software validation of DirectX and OpenGL drivers. He is currently working as a software validation engineer for high performance products. His areas of interest include computer graphics and photorealistic rendering.

Georgios Papaioannou is currently an assistant professor of computer graphics at the Department of Informatics of the Athens University of Economics and Business. He received a BSc in computer science and a PhD degree in computer graphics and pattern recognition, both from the University of Athens, Greece. In the past, he has worked as a research fellow in many research and development projects, and as a virtual reality software engineer at the Foundation of the Hellenic World. His research is focused on real-time computer graphics algorithms, photorealistic rendering, virtual reality systems and three-dimensional pattern recognition. He has contributed many scientific papers in the above fields and has coauthored one international and two Greek computer graphics textbooks. He is also a member of IEEE, ACM, SIGGRAPH, and Eurographics Association and has been a member of the program committees of many computer graphics conferences.

Emil Persson is developing rendering technologies at Avalanche Studios. He was deeply involved in creating the visual technology for *Just Cause 2* (as covered in *GPU Pro*) and continues to develop the engine for future titles. Previously, Emil was an ISV Engineer at ATI / AMD where he assisted the world's top game developers with optimizations, implementing rendering techniques, and taking full advantage of the latest hardware, as well as writing technical papers and developing SDK samples. Emil has a website (http://www.humus.name) where he blogs about graphics technology and posts demo applications.

Leo Reyes studied computer engineering at the University of Guadalajara, Mexico. He received his MS and PhD degrees in computer vision from the Center of Research and Advanced Studies (CINVESTAV). His research interests include computer vision, computer graphics, image processing, and artificial intelligence. He is currently working at Intel Labs in Guadalajara.

Donald Revie graduated from the University of Abertay with a BSc (Hons) in computer games technology before joining Cohort Studios in late 2006. He worked on Cohort's Praetorian Tech platform from its inception, designing and implementing much of its renderer and core scene representation. He also worked individually and with others to develop shaders and graphics techniques across many of the company's projects. Since leaving Cohort Studios in early 2011 he has been continuing to refine his ideas on engine architecture and pursuing his wider interests in game design and writing.

Tobias Ritschel is a postdoctoral researcher at the CG Group, Télécom ParisTech (CNRS). He received his PhD in computer science at the Max-Planck-Institut Informatik, in Saarbrücken, Germany, in 2009 and was awarded the Eurographics Dissertation Prize at Eurographics 2011. His research interests include interactive global illumination rendering, GPU programming, perception, and GPU geometry processing.

Daniel Scherzer is currently a post-doctoral research fellow at the Max-Planck Institute for Informatics, Saarbrücken. He also gives lectures at the Vienna University of Technology and the FH Hagenberg. He previously worked at the Ludwig Boltzmann Institute for Archaeological Prospection and Virtual Archaeology and as an assistant professor at the Institute of Computer Graphics and Algorithms of the Vienna University of Technology, where he received an MSc in 2005, an MSocEcSc in 2008, and a PhD in 2009. His current research interests include temporal coherence methods, shadow algorithms, modeling and level-of-detail approaches for real-time rendering. He has authored and co-authored several papers in these fields.

Christian Schüler has been in the games industry since 2001 in various roles as engine programmer, technical lead, and consultant, contributing to a total of seven shipped games. He has an interest in 3D and shading algorithms as well as in sound synthesis. He is currently self-employed, doing serious games and simulation for naval training at the time of this writing.

Nicolas Schulz is a Graphics Engineer at Crytek, where he works as part of the R&D Core Team. He is currently working on visual quality and performance improvements to the CryENGINE 3 across all platforms and was responsible for the Stereo-3D implementation in *Crysis 2*. Before joining Crytek, Nicolas worked on various academic research projects, including augmented reality applications, crowd simulation, and high-quality rendering of virtual characters. During that time, he also wrote several advanced rendering engines with a strong focus on software design.

Hans-Peter Seidel is the scientific director and chair of the computer graphics group at the Max Planck Institute (MPI) for Informatics and a professor of computer science at Saarland University, Saarbrücken, Germany. He is cochair of the Max Planck Center for Visual Computing and Communication (MPC-VCC) (since 2003), and he is the scientific coordinator of the Cluster of Excellence on Multimodal Computing and Interaction (M2CI) that was established by the German Research Foundation (DFG) within the framework of the German Excellence Initiative in 2007. In addition, Seidel is a member of the Governance Board of the newly established Intel Visual Computing Institue (IVCI) (since 2009).

Ari Silvennoinen is Principal Programmer and Research Lead at Umbra Software, where he is focusing on next generation rendering technology research and development. His primary areas of interest include visibility algorithms, real-time shadow techniques, global illumination, and rendering optimization in general. Ari holds a MS degree in computer science from the University of Helsinki and has previously worked with the 3D graphics research group at Helsinki University of Technology (now Aalto University School of Science and Technology).

Gaël Sourimant is a researcher at Technicolor Research & Innovation. He received his PhD in computer vision from the French University of Rennes 1 in 2007. After working on 3D reconstruction and rendering for 3DTV at the INRIA lab, his research interests now focus on real-time rendering, image processing, and procedural geometry modeling.

Tiago Sousa is Crytek's Principal R&D Graphics Engineer. He has worked at Crytek for the past eight years on all of Crytek's numerous demos and engines, and has shipped game titles, including *Far Cry* and *Crysis*. More recently he completed work on *Crysis 2*, Crytek's first multiplatform game, and he continues to work on multiplatform projects. He spends most of his time thinking outside the box, inventing his own general solutions for any fun computer-graphics related problem.

Michael Schwarz is currently a postdoc at Cornell University and holds an MS and a PhD, both in computer science, from the University of Erlangen-Nuremberg, Germany. His graphics-related research interests include real-time computer graphics, GPU techniques, global illumination, scalable approaches, procedural modeling, and perception-aware graphics.

László Szécsi is an associate professor at the Technical University in Budapest, Hungary. He gives lectures in programming, computer graphics, and computer game development. His research revolves around global illumination, real-time rendering techniques, and the combination of the two. László has published numerous scientific papers and has been a regular contributor to the *ShaderX* book series.

Sinje Thiedemann is working as a software developer for the real-time visualization company PI-VR GmbH in Darmstadt, Germany. In 2010, she received her diploma degree in computational visualistics from the University of Koblenz-Landau. Her research interests include approximate, as well as physically based, global illumination.

John White was, until recently, a Senior Rendering Engineer at Electronic Arts Black Box working on *Need For Speed: The Run*. He works in all areas of rendering development and specializes in both low-level GPU optimizations and high-level rendering architecture. Having previously presented at GDC, his current focus is on post-processing techniques, local and global lighting, shadowing, and level-of-detail techniques. Prior to working at EA, John worked at Deep Red Games in the UK, where he architected and developed the in-house rendering run-time and tool-chain that powered their PC-based strategy games. Before this, John worked in the R&D department at Gremlin Interactive, where he developed their in-house low-level rasterization, math, and Win32 libraries. Published games include *Need For Speed: Hot Pursuit, Skate 2, Skate 1, NBA Live 07, NBA Live 06, Vegas Tycoon, Monopoly Tycoon, Risk II, Actua Soccer 3,* and *Actua Tennis*.

Michael Wimmer is an associate professor at the Institute of Computer Graphics and Algorithms of the Vienna University of Technology, where he received an MSc in 1997 and a PhD in 2001. His current research interests are real-time rendering, computer games, real-time visualization of urban environments, point-based rendering, and procedural modeling. He has coauthored many papers in these fields, was papers cochair of EGSR 2008, and is papers cochair of Pacific Graphics 2012.

Egor Yusov has been employed as a graphics software engineer by Intel Corporation for the last five years, where he has been working on a wide variety of 3D technologies. He received a PhD in computer science from Nizhny Novgorod State Technical University, Russia, in 2011. His research interests include real-time visualization and rendering, data compression, GPU-based algorithms, and shader programming.

Index